Armenia

THE BRADT TRAVEL GUIDE

Nicholas Holding

Bradt Travel Guides Ltd, UK
The Globe Pequot Press Inc, USA

First published 2003

Bradt Travel Guides Ltd
19 High Street, Chalfont St Peter, Bucks SL9 9QE, England
www.bradt-travelguides.com
Published in the USA by The Globe Pequot Press Inc, 246 Goose Lane,
PO Box 480, Guilford, Connecticut 06475-0480

ISBN 1 84162 081 5

British Library Cataloguing in Publication Data
A catalogue record for this book is available from the British Library

Photographs
Front cover Nicholas Holding (Tatev Monastery)
Text Nicholas Holding, with one photograph by Marat Shahbekyan (MS)
Illustrations Carole Vincer
Maps Steve Munns. Regional maps based on ITM *Armenia*.

Typeset from the author's disc by Wakewing
Printed and bound in Italy by Legoprint SpA, Trento

Contents

THE BRADT STORY

The first Bradt travel guide was written in 1974 by George and Hilary Bradt on a river barge floating down a tributary of the Amazon. In the 1980s and '90s the focus shifted away from hiking to broader-based guides covering new destinations – usually the first to be published on those places. In the 21st century Bradt continues to publish these ground-breaking guides, along with others to established holiday destinations, incorporating in-depth information on culture and natural history alongside the nuts and bolts of where to stay and what to see.

Bradt authors support responsible travel, with advice not only on minimum impact but also on how to give something back through local charities. Thus a true synergy is achieved between the traveller and local communities.

*

When I read this manuscript I thought it was extraordinary that we were about to publish the first full guide to a country that seems to have everything: a fascinating history, vibrant culture and rewarding natural history. We feel privileged to have found an author, Nicholas Holding, whose breadth of knowledge does justice to such an interesting new destination and whose enthusiasm for Armenia shines out on every page. I am proud to be publishing him.

Hilary Bradt

Hilary Bradt

19 High Street, Chalfont St Peter, Bucks SL9 9QE, England
Tel: 01753 893444; fax: 01753 892333
Email: info@bradt-travelguides.com
Web: www.bradt-travelguides.com

Author/Acknowledgements

AUTHOR

Born in Wigan (then in Lancashire, but now part of Greater Manchester), Nicholas Holding moved to Scotland in 1965 and graduated from the University of St Andrews with a degree in electrical engineering. He and his wife Deirdre – whom he married in 1970 – have always been interested in the communist world, and made their first visit to the Soviet Union in 1973. The downfall of communism enabled them to travel more freely around the former Soviet bloc, and sparked their interest in Armenia. After a career in the Scottish electricity supply industry, Nicholas took early retirement in 2000; he and Deirdre still live in Scotland.

ACKNOWLEDGEMENTS

This book would not have been possible without the help of two people in particular. Especial thanks are due to Anahit Shahverdyan, tourism manager at Armenia Travel + M in Yerevan, who has acted as my interpreter and guide when in her country, answered innumerable queries about all things Armenian, corrected my mistakes and translated material from books and articles. Secondly, thanks are due to my wife Deirdre for reading and commenting on the draft text and for tolerating a house so full of Armenian articles and books that they have usurped several rooms.

Thanks are also due to Marat Shahbekyan whose 4WD has got me to some fairly inaccessible places, to Vasil Ananian of Yerevan for help with natural history and to Neil Taylor of Regent Holidays, Bristol who, as author of the Bradt travel guides to Estonia and Baltic capitals, provided encouragement and advice.

Introduction

This is a guidebook to the present-day Republic of Armenia together with the territory of Nagorno Karabagh. In the English-speaking world, an individual's knowledge of Armenia generally falls into one of two categories. Most people know nothing about it at all. The others, a small minority, not only speak the Armenian language, although neither they nor their parents were born in Armenia, but also have some knowledge of the culture and often tragic history. When it comes to who actually visits Armenia nowadays the numbers in the two categories are more evenly balanced. Armenia has one of the most successful and supportive diasporas in the world and present-day Armenia is very dependent on them. So far as Nagorno Karabagh is concerned, the contrast is even more stark with the diaspora being wholly familiar with its recent past while few others would claim even to have heard of it, apart from those who are well informed politically and might recall its name as the scene of some half-remembered conflict around the time that the Soviet Union disintegrated.

This book is aimed primarily at the general tourist who is interested in seeing the country and understanding something of its long and complex history. I am not a member of the diaspora and do not speak Armenian. Nevertheless even fairly knowledgeable members of the diaspora should find it useful as they, like virtually all other visitors to Armenia, unfortunately confine themselves at present to only half a dozen places. It appears that few visitors know anything about many of the other sights in Armenia which warrant a visit. As a consequence, only a handful of visitors to Armenia spend more than a week in the country and the average visit lasts a mere four or five days. This book seeks to rectify that regrettable situation and demonstrate that Armenia has a huge potential for visitors. Not just for general sightseeing, although its spectacular gorges and medieval buildings certainly provide plenty of excellent opportunities for that, but also for activities such as hiking, birdwatching, architectural tours, historical visits, botanical trips, angling, horse riding and caving. Although many visitors will probably continue to combine a visit to Armenia with one to neighbouring Georgia or Iran, there is quite enough in Armenia alone to occupy several holidays. Indeed, the most commonly heard complaint from visitors is that they had insufficient time. Sometimes the visitors are in a tourist coach lamenting that they are faced with long journeys and few stops as the tour operator decided that they must see the prescribed sights with the minimum possible number of nights in the country. At other times, fitter people gaze longingly out of the bus window at the fantastic potential for hiking which they have no opportunity to explore.

Armenia is actually a very easy country to visit for three reasons. Firstly, its people are overwhelmingly friendly, helpful and welcoming: I have only ever once encountered an unhelpful and unwelcoming attitude on my travels around the country. Secondly, Armenia is unique in that any tourist from any country can get a 21-day visa over the internet and pay for it by credit card. (At the moment this only applies to tourists arriving by air but the arrangement will be extended in due course to land borders as well.) Thirdly, there is very little crime and the risk of theft or being short-changed is much lower than in most other European countries. Is Armenia in Europe? It certainly feels far more like a southern European country than an Asian one and it is a member of the Council of Europe and the Organisation for Security and Cooperation in Europe. In addition, the Armenian people have been Christian for 1,700 years and from 1828 to 1991 they were ruled by another country whose culture, the Bolshevik Revolution notwithstanding, was fundamentally Christian. On a more practical level, Armenia has an international telephone dialling code (374) in the European sequence and the British post office charges the European rate for letters sent to Armenia from Britain.

The potential difficulties are the language barrier, the lack of good maps (though there is now at least a fairly adequate road map) and the sometimes poor infrastructure. Fortunately the latter two are improving but very, very few people outside the large hotels and travel agents in Yerevan speak English or any other western European language. The main second language is, and is likely to remain, Russian so visitors travelling on their own may well find it convenient to consider employing an English-speaking guide or else arranging accommodation in advance. Either can be done through one of the Yerevan travel agents or an overseas agent who specialises in the country. When hiring a car, it is generally cheaper to hire one with a driver than to drive oneself although the car is then likely to be older. Depending on the expected destinations a 4WD vehicle can be requested, essential for getting to some places and quite helpful for many others.

Things are changing fast in Armenia. Indeed, the pace of road building and repair seems to be accelerating and new hotels are appearing or old ones are being renovated throughout the country. Cafés and restaurants are proliferating, especially but not exclusively in Yerevan which can surely not support any more. Restoration work is enhancing the most frequently visited historic sights although I rather like the atmosphere at some of the more remote, unrestored ones. There is no doubt that many comments made in this book will quickly be superseded. Armenia has so much to offer visitors. It will never become a mainstream tourist destination like Mallorca or Florida but few visitors to Armenia leave disappointed. I very much hope that this guide will encourage others to go to such off-the-beaten-track places as Makaravank, Dashtadem and Selim caravanserai. They will be rewarded by seeing enthralling sights in a country in transition. After centuries of foreign domination Armenia is now once again an independent nation preserving for future generations its unique heritage.

Note on transliteration

There is no standard transliteration from the Armenian alphabet into English. For example the principal city of northwest Armenia can appear in English as Gyumri, Gyumry, Giumri or G'umri while the province of which it is the capital is Shirak in English, Schirak in German or Chirak in French. Some transliteration schemes even resort to letters borrowed from Czech and Slovak such as č, š and ž which few English speakers know how to pronounce anyway. For place names I have usually followed those used by Brady Kiesling and Raffi Kojian in *Rediscovering Armenia*. Occasionally this does result in combinations of consonants appearing such as those in Smbataberd, Aghjkaghala and Ptghni but these are actually quite close to the Armenian pronunciation. So far as surnames are concerned, the ending '…ian' has been preferred to '…yan' for the many which end this way (eg: Abovian rather than Abovyan) except where this would result in the ending '…aian' or something similar and there '…ayan' has been used (eg: Babayan rather than Babaian).

Part One

General Information

ARMENIA FACTS

Location A landlocked country in the southern Caucasus between the Black Sea and the Caspian Sea bordered by Georgia, Azerbaijan, Iran and Turkey. The border with Nagorno Karabagh is not recognised internationally. Yerevan, the capital, is on the same latitude as Naples, Madrid and New York. It is on the same longitude as Volgograd in Russia, Baghdad and Sana'a, Yemen. It is 5 hours' flying time from London.

Area 29,800km² – similar to Belgium and Maryland. Note, however, that following the 1994 ceasefire the territory administered is 31,200km².

Population 3 million resident in the country at the date of census (October 2001) but the population was considered to be 3.5 million because of persons temporarily abroad. Around 96% are ethnic Armenians, 2% Russian and the remainder mostly Yezidis and Kurds.

Government Presidential parliamentary republic with universal adult suffrage.

Major cities Yerevan (population – 1998 estimate – 1.24 million); Vanadzor (163,000), Gyumri (121,000).

Administrative Divisions The country is divided into the capital (Yerevan) and ten provinces (*marz*): Shirak, Lori, Tavush, Aragatsotn, Gegharkunik, Kotayk, Armavir, Ararat, Vayots Dzor, Syunik.

Currency Dram (abbreviated to AMD) divided theoretically into 100 luma. The current exchange rate is about UK£1 = AMD850; US$1 = AMD585.

Language Armenian, an Indo-European language. Russian is also widely understood but western European languages are not.

Alphabet The unique Armenian alphabet, currently with 39 letters, was devised around AD400.

Religion Very predominantly the Armenian Apostolic Church. There are a few Roman Catholics, mostly in Shirak province, and there are several sects seeking converts. The Yezidis are Zoroastrian fire worshippers and the Kurds are Muslims.

Weights and Measures Metric system.

Electricity 220V AC; European 2-pin plug.

National flag Three horizontal stripes: red, blue, orange.

National anthem Land of our fathers, Free, Independent (*Mer Hayreniq, azat, ankakh*); words adapted from a poem by Mikhail Nalbandian (1829–66); music by Barsegh Kanachian (1885–1967).

Symbols of Armenia The classical symbol is the khachkar ('cross stone'). The grape and pomegranate are also used as symbols as is the eagle which appears on the coat of arms.

Public holidays See page 45.

Background Information

HISTORY

Visitors to Armenia are confronted by the country's history everywhere they look and not just in the prehistoric sites or splendid medieval monasteries which are a major attraction of Armenia for most visitors. Other aspects of Armenia's history are reflected in the legacy of Soviet-era apartment blocks identical to those in Kaliningrad or Omsk, and in the huge investment in modern Armenia funded by the country's large, important and successful diaspora. Further observations soon strike the visitor: that the oldest surviving building in the country, at Garni, looks Greek rather than Armenian and quite different from any other; that there are no Roman remains; that the old churches and monasteries were built within certain very restricted time periods interspersed with long periods from which nothing seems to have survived; that different foreign influences seem to have been significant at different epochs. Visitors will also see everywhere signs written in a distinctive and unique alphabet, the use of which is a large factor in determining what it means to be Armenian. Beginning to make sense of all this jumble of impressions necessitates gaining some understanding of Armenia's long and varied history.

During this history there were periods of independence as an Armenian nation, though often with the nation divided into separate kingdoms because of internal struggles for supremacy by individual families. These periods were separated by much longer spells of foreign rule, by a whole host of different peoples at different times. The 20th century regaining of independence after centuries of foreign rule, briefly at first from 1918 to 1920 but then lastingly since 1991, owes little to the nations, notably Britain, which repeatedly let down the Armenian people between 1878 and 1923. However, perhaps the West can take some of the responsibility for the Soviet Union's bankruptcy and collapse.

The legendary origins of the Armenian people

Although all foreigners call the country Armenia, Armenians themselves call it Hayastan: literally the Land of Haik. Chapter 8 of the biblical book of Genesis states that Noah's ark grounded on Mount Ararat. Chapter 10 records that Togarmah was a son of Gomer who was a son of Japheth who had accompanied his father Noah on the ark. According to Armenian legend the Armenian people are the descendents of Haik who was the son of Togarmah and therefore the great-great-grandson of Noah. Their name for their country records this.

According to the legend, of the three sons of Noah, Japheth and Ham settled with their families in the Ararat region while Shem subsequently moved away to the northwest. Ham's and Japheth's sons gradually spread out to the various regions of the Armenian plateau. When Japheth's great-grandson Haik was 130 years old, he travelled south to the city of Shinar (probably present-day Babylon in Iraq) and worked on the building of the Tower of Babel (Genesis chapter 11). After the Tower eventually collapsed, Haik, a handsome man with curly hair, good eyesight, and a strong warrior (despite his age), was able to defy even Nimrod (or Bel as he is known in the legend), the tyrannical ruler of Assyria. Nimrod had ordered that he should be worshipped by his people but Haik refused and moved back north with his family (including his 300 sons) to the lands around Ararat. Nimrod resented Haik's departure, and ordered him back, even seeking to lure him by reminding him that Armenia had a less favourable climate than Assyria. When Haik refused, Nimrod marched north with his army which outnumbered Haik's and battle was joined on the shores of Lake Van. Nimrod, according to the legend, wore iron armour but Haik drew his bow, and shot him with a three-feathered arrow which pierced the armour, killing the king. Seeing this happen, the Assyrian army turned and fled. Haik returned to Ararat and died at the age of 400. The discovery of boundary stones and of Babylonian writings dating from Nimrod's reign confirm the battle and the manner of Nimrod's death as described in the legend. The traditional Armenian calendar begins with the year that the battle is said to have taken place.

The name Armenia by which everybody else knows the country was first used by Greek historians about 3,000 years ago although in legend the name commemorates the great leader of the country Aram who was sixth in line of descent from Haik.

Ancient history

Crudely worked stone tools found on the slopes of Mount Aragats have been dated to around 600,000 to 800,000 years ago and more sophisticted ones such as spear points and knives to the period between 40,000 and 100,000 years ago. The transition from hunting and gathering to a more settled way of life sustained by agriculture began in Armenia in the Arax valley about 10,000BC. However, the first people to leave significant traces on the Armenian landscape did so in the form of petroglyphs, or images carved on rock, which can be found in various regions of Armenia. Those in the Gueghamian mountains west of Lake Sevan have been studied in detail but the carvings in other regions are similar. They are believed to date from around the period 5000BC to 3000BC. The oldest show both wild animals such as deer, boar, wolves, foxes, snakes, rabbits, storks and game birds as well as the earliest domestic animals such as dogs and goats. Pictures of hunters using bows, clubs or slings are common and the hunters are often accompanied by their dogs. However, the carvings also show many animals tethered or bound indicating that some of the game may have been kept alive either for future consumption or even for breeding.

In the later carvings the portrayal of human figures had developed considerably from the original vertical line with a circle for the head. As well as outstretched or raised arms some figures began to have waving arms, one of the first representations of movement. There are also many carvings of celestial bodies: the sun, moon, stars, and also lightning. Some of the later carvings show a multitude of carts and chariots drawn by oxen or bulls with stellar symbols on their fronts and these are likely to be connected with a cult of the sun.

Little is known about these hunters but during the period when the later carvings were created a series of villages and fortified settlements developed in the Arax valley based on metalworking. Local high-quality supplies of ore led to the forging of copper and bronze and then the smelting of iron by around 3000BC. Artefacts found in these settlements include black-varnished red and grey pottery in geometric patterns, similar to those of contemporary Minoan culture. Burial goods suggest a religious belief centred on the sun and planets. Armenia has two monuments from this period believed to be astral observatories.

At Metsamor (Armavir province) there is a series of stone platforms dated to 2800BC oriented towards Sirius, the brightest star visible, and there are also numerous carvings showing the position of stars in the night sky together with a compass pointing east. At Karahunj (near Sisian in Syunik province) there is an elaborate arrangement of stones in which holes are bored strongly suggesting an astronomical purpose and possibly enabling the tracking of solar and lunar phases. It has even been suggested that it was in Armenia at this period that the signs of the zodiac were named: certainly the animal signs are all of creatures which would have been familar in Armenia with no obvious omissions apart possibly from the leopard.

Urartu

These early peoples spoke a variety of languages but, probably around 1165BC, another people migrated into Armenia and they spoke the language from which present-day Armenian is descended. Their close affinity to the Phrygians (who lived in the north of present-day Turkey) is attested by classical writers such as Herodotus and Eudoxus and this suggests that they came into Armenia from the west.

During the 9th century BC the empire of Urartu developed to incorporate eventually much of Anatolia and most of present-day Armenia. Why the local rulers should have decided to co-operate under central leadership is not clear but it may have been the result of increasing Assyrian aggression. By the reign of the Urartian king Sarduri I (reigned c840–c825BC) the capital had been established at Tushpa, present-day Van in Turkey. Expansion was achieved through a series of military campaigns with Argrishti I (reigned c785–c763BC) extending Urartian territory as far as present-day Gyumri and his successors taking the land west and south of Lake Sevan. Urartian expansion provoked Assyrian concern and in 735BC the Assyrian king Tiglath Pileser III invaded as far as Van. It was not however until 715BC that Urartu began to suffer a series of catastrophic defeats, not just against the Assyrians but also against other neighbours, and in 714BC King Rusa I committed suicide on hearing news of the sack of the temple at Musasir. The 7th century BC was to become a period of irreversible decline with Urartu finally disappearing around 590BC: it did however outlive Assyria which had fallen to Babylon in 612BC and its name survives to this day in the form of Mount Ararat.

This first state on Armenian territory, Urartu was briefly an important regional power able to rival powerful neighbours. An inscription reveals that it had 79 gods of whom 16 were female. Clearly the most important was Tushpa, god of war: he had over three times the volume of sacrifices offered to his nearest rival. Seventeen bulls and 34 sheep were specified, presumably on some regular basis. The accumulation of animal remains in temples must have been a problem: a room at one site yielded to archaeologists 4,000 headless sheep and calves sacrificed over a 35-year period. Armenia's metalworking skills were important in sustaining Urartu and irrigation works supplied water to vineyards, orchards and crops. The empire was more or less self-sufficient in most goods with the exception of tin (needed to make bronze) which was probably imported from Afghanistan. However, fragments of Chinese silk have been found, providing evidence of foreign trade.

Urartu's cities, linked by a network of good roads, were well developed with high walls, moats, and towers at their entrance gates. One Assyrian opponent claimed that the walls reached to 240 cubits – around 120m – but this looks suspiciously like exaggeration to prove his own valour. Van probably had a population of around 50,000 while Armavir had around 30,000. Numerous forts were built throughout the country for defence and as bases for future attacks. They were built in defensible sites and surrounded by walls whose height may have reached 20m and whose thickness was from 2m to 3m. They were constructed of massive stone blocks up to a height of 2m. Above this level construction was in mud brick.

Foreign rule after Urartu

The Medes dealt the final blow to Urartu in 590BC. What happened to the Armenians subsequently is not clear but during the 6th century BC the Persian Achaemenids under Darius extended their empire to include the country. Political autonomy vanished, a situation that prevailed until the Persians were defeated by Alexander the Great in 331BC. However the Persians did not seek to impose their culture or religion on their subject peoples though there was in practice probably some influence on Armenian religion: it is thought that the Persians followed an early form of Zoroastrianism which involved belief in a supreme creator God opposed by an uncreated evil spirit. The Armenians did not follow Zoroastrianism absolutely: whereas Zoroastrianism disapproved of animal sacrifice the Armenians continued to practise it, notably by sacrificing horses to the sun god. The defeat of the Persians in 331BC did not lead to Greek rule over Armenia. Armenia in fact achieved a greater degree of independence. Alexander's policy in the captured Persian empire was to continue the existing administrative system under Iranian satraps. For Armenia he appointed Mithrenes who was probably the son of the deposed Persian king, Orontes. Mithrenes took the title of King of Armenia. The Greek empire did not long outlive Alexander's death in 323BC as there was a period of rivalry and war between his potential successors. By 301BC Seleucus had become satrap of Armenia but his dynasty was to control Armenia only nominally and sporadically with real power in the hands of the Orontid kings, the successors of Mithrenes. The impact of Greek civilisation was, however, increasingly felt and there was a partial revival of urban life which had largely disappeared under the Persians. In around 200BC the satrap Antiochus III was probably involved in the removal of the last Orontid king, Orontes IV, but ten years later he provoked the wrath of Rome through his invasion of Greece. Defeated at the battle of Magnesia, his own generals then switched sides to Rome and for this they were awarded by Rome in 189BC with the title of kings of independent Armenia.

Empire

The settlement with Rome compromised the territorial integrity of Orontid Armenia but also marked the start of a period of territorial expansion which saw the reacquisition, for the first time since defeat by the Medes in 590BC, of much of present-day Armenia. In particular the area south of Lake Sevan as far as the present-day Iranian border was taken back from the Medes. The acquisition of empire reached its apogee under Tigranes the Great who came to power in c95BC but Tigranes' success clearly created a hindrance to further Roman expansion in the east. Tigranes' father-in-law was Mithridates VI, king of Pontus, and Tigranes unwillingly got dragged into the (third) war between Rome and Pontus when he refused to surrender his father-in-law to the brusque and offensive Roman envoy. Tigranes' new capital Tigranocerta, which he had modestly named after himself, consequently fell to a Roman siege in 69BC and, although Tigranes subsequently made good some of the losses, his son deserted him for Rome and formed an alliance with Pompey. Tigranes was forced to make peace and Pompey rearranged the political geography. Armenia suffered considerable territorial losses and Antiochus I, a distant descendent of Darius the Great, became king. For the next 80 years Armenia, although independent, had kings appointed by Rome and it became increasingly dependent on Rome for keeping them in power. In due course Roman authority weakened and by the AD50s Rome was unable to prevent the Parthians imposing their choice of king, Trdat I, on Armenia. After a period of instability reflected in further fighting it was agreed by Parthians and Romans in AD63 that Trdat would be king of Armenia but crowned by the Roman emperor, Nero.

There then began a fairly stable period for the Armenian kingdom with the kings holding the throne with Roman approval. This was punctuated by the Roman Emperor Trajan's policy of expansion which saw Armenia conquered in AD114 only for the Romans to suffer defeat and withdraw after a rebellion in AD116. In AD253 Armenia was captured by the Persian Sassanians and it remained under Persian rule until a Roman victory over Persia in AD298. There were Christians elsewhere in the region from around AD100 and by AD300 there were Christians in Armenia, albeit in small numbers and with few in the elite. Zoroastrianism remained the main religion and animal sacrifice continued to be practised.

Conversion to Christianity

The adoption of Christianity as the state religion of Armenia, the first country in which this happened, is perhaps the single most important event in Armenian history. Although traditionally said to have happened in 301 there is debate over the precise date but it certainly happened by 314. King Trdat IV held power, like his predecessors, with the support of Rome against the continuing threat from Persia. The precise date of Armenia's conversion is interesting as it reflects differently on Trdat's motives depending on when it was. AD301 was before the persecution of Christians by the Roman Emperor Diocletian in 303 and it was also before the Roman edict of toleration of Christianity in 311 and the conversion of the Emperor Constantine in 312. A later date for Armenia's conversion suggests a much closer alignment with imperial thinking as adopting Christianity in 314 would have been more than likely to please an emperor who had himself just become a Christian. There is an account of Armenia's conversion which claims to have been written by a contemporary but in reality it was written in c460, a century and a half after the events. In this account, well known and much quoted in Armenia, Trdat had Gregory the Illuminator, who was in his service, tortured to persuade him to give up Christianity. Gregory refused and Trdat additionally realised that Gregory's father had murdered his, Trdat's, father. As a consequence Trdat then had Gregory imprisoned in a snake-infested pit for 12 years at a place now occupied by the monastery of Khor Virap, and he also persecuted other Christians (including the nuns Hripsime and Gayane whose names become very familiar when visiting Armenian churches). Trdat is said to have behaved like a wild boar (though in what respect he imitated these rather engaging animals is not clear), while torments fell on his household and demons possessed the people of the city. Eventually Trdat's sister had a vision, Trdat proclaimed Christianity the state religion, and Gregory was released to become Bishop of Caesarea.

Conversion required much change in social customs and this change did not happen quickly. In particular Zoroastrianism permitted polygamy and it promoted consanguineous marriages between the closest of relatives as being particularly virtuous. A church council in 444 needed to condemn the apparently continuing practice of consanguineous marriage while as late as 768 another needed to emphasise that a *third* marriage is detestable adultery and an inexpiable sin. The church also found it difficult to suppress mourning customs including wailing, pulling of hair, rending of garments, slashing of arms and faces, dancing and the playing of trumpets.

Partitioned Armenia

By c387 Rome and Persia had decided to abolish Armenia as an independent state and to divide the country between them, a move which was finally accomplished with the removal of the last Armenian king in 428. The intervening 40 years were ones of weakness, decline and foreign domination though with a strengthening Christian presence. Present-day Armenia lies in the part which came under Persian rule after 428. A major hindrance to the acceptance of Christianity was removed through the creation in c400 of the Armenian alphabet by Mesrop Mashtots. This permitted the Scriptures to be made available in Armenian for the first time and for other religious works to be published. Although this important education programme was centred in Persian-controlled Armenia, permission was obtained from the Roman empire (whose capital had by this time been moved to Constantinople) to set up schools there as well. However, the Persian monarchy's increasing dependence on the Zoroastrian religious establishment led to pressure on Armenian Christians under Persian rule to convert to Zoroastrianism. The first crisis occurred in 450 when taxes were imposed on the church and the nobility was ordered to convert. The Armenians made an alliance with some Huns and the combined force defeated the Persians in 451 although with heavy casualties. Subsequently the taxes were removed and freedom of religion granted although the patriarch and some clergy were executed and many nobles were imprisoned. Persia continued to discriminate in favour of Zoroastrians in making important appointments, a situation which prevailed until the death of the Persian king in 484.

Roman expansion finally restarted in the 6th century but it was to make little headway despite several campaigns against Persia until 591 after which the frontier was redrawn to place some of the western parts of present-day Armenia under Roman rule: the new border ran just west of Garni. However, neither Rome nor Persia was prepared for a new wave of invaders, Arabs who, from the 630s, invaded fighting in the name of Islam. The Persians were soon defeated and the Romans lost major provinces. By 661 Armenia was under Arab rule though there were promises of religious freedom. Armenian revolts in the early 8th century gave rise to some temporary Arab repression but it was only from the rule of Caliph Umar I (717–720) onwards that Armenian Christianity was seriously threatened. Orders were given that Christian images should be torn down, financial levies were increased and pressure was applied to convert to Islam. This stimulated the creation of a cycle of rebellion, harsher treatment, another rebellion and even harsher treatment until by c800 annual taxation on Armenia amounted to 13 million dirhams, 20,000 pounds of fish, 20 carpets, 200 mules, 30 falcons and 580 pieces of cloth. Under these conditions many Armenians chose to leave the country for Roman areas.

Restoration of monarchy

Conditions eased in the 9th century to the extent that the caliph agreed in 884 to the restoration of Armenian monarchy for the first time in 456 years and Ashot I was crowned king of Armenia, the first ruler of the Bagratid dynasty. For the next 40 years however Armenia went through a period of continued unrest as different leaders struggled with each other for power and territory. In addition a prolonged rebellion against the caliph led by his governor in Azerbaijan, who was responsible for collecting Armenian taxes, led to both caliph and governor presenting their own separate tax bills. Armenia was not a united nation but this time was one of great flourishing for Armenian scholarship, literature and church building. This was particularly the case during the reign of King Abas (928–952) who succeeded in establishing a degree of security but during the 960s and 970s after his death the renewed struggle for succession led to increasing fragmentation of the country and by the end of the 10th century there were five separate Armenian kingdoms – three Bagratid (based at Kars, Ani and Lori), one Artsruni based in Vaspurakan east of Lake Van, and one Syunian in the south of present-day Armenia. Armenia's political fragmentation, however, inevitably left it unable to cope with renewed expansion by the Roman empire's successors in Byzantium during the 11th century though Byzantine rule was to be benign in comparison with the new invaders from the south, the Seljuk Turks, who ravaged cities and brought political and economic disruption even to the Byzantium-controlled areas after 1045. The victory of the Seljuk Turks over the Romans in 1071 led to the latter's demise as a significant power and to the establishment of Seljuk rule over Armenia. The immediate consequence of the Seljuk conquest was another period of migration, this time to areas such as Georgia, Ukraine and Syria. A new separate Armenian kingdom arose in Cilicia (on the Aegean coast of Turkey) which was to last until it was overrun in 1375 by the Mamluks, the Turkish military dynasty which then ruled Egypt. Although important in Armenian history, Cilicia lies wholly outside present-day Armenia and is therefore not relevant to this guidebook.

Seljuk power in turn waned and in a series of campaigns culminating in 1204 a Georgian army which included many Armenians defeated the sultan's forces. Georgian influence increased, reflected in the style of a number of Armenia's finest churches in present-day Lori province, only for Armenia to be conquered yet again, this time by the Mongols in a series of campaigns culminating in 1244. High taxation created the usual resentment and rebellion. In 1304 matters worsened for Armenians when Islam became the official religion of the Mongol empire and religious persecution became a matter of policy. In turn Mongol power declined and between 1357 and 1403, following a series of invasions by the Mamluks, tens of thousands of Armenians were transported as slaves. By 1400 most of Armenia had passed to a Turkmen dynasty called the Black Sheep. A second Turkmen dynasty called the White Sheep became established further west.

Russia versus Turkey

The end of the Byzantine empire came in 1453 when the Ottomans took Constantinople (Istanbul). Further Ottoman aggression saw Armenia itself conquered from the White Sheep, who were now ruling it, by the 1530s. Yet again Armenia became a battleground as hostility grew between the Ottomans and Persia, until in 1639 the two powers agreed that western Armenia would be controlled by Turkey and eastern Armenia by Persia. A further wave of emigration from the Persian territories began around 1700 because of taxation and persecution; this time many went to India. A local rebellion in southern Armenia led by David Bek, together with invasion in 1722 by Russian forces under Peter the Great, saw Persian rule largely end and in 1724 most Persian territory was divided between the Ottomans and Russia although Persia retained Nagorno Karabagh. David Bek died in 1728 and in 1730 his successor Mkhitar Sparapet was betrayed by Armenian villagers as a result of Turkish threats. That same year David Bek's territory, centred at Tatev, fell to Turkey. Russian expansionism in the area restarted under Catherine the Great. In the conquered lands, largely Muslim, Russian policy was to encourage Christians to settle and Muslims to leave. Starting in 1796 the Russians began a further series of campaigns conquering the west Caucasian khanates. These khanates were effectively autonomous Turkish principalities (although nominally vassals of the Persians under the 1724 treaty) and they occupied an area roughly equivalent to present-day Armenia and Azerbaijan.

At that time Armenians, having been subject to so many varieties of foreign rule and persecution for so long, were scattered throughout the Caucasus and eastern Anatolia rather than concentrated in the Armenian heartland. However, in 1826 Russia began a forced exchange of population which resulted ultimately in the creation of an Armenian-dominated state in the khanate of Yerevan. Russia gained dominance in the south Caucasus by defeating Persia in the war of 1826–28 and the Ottomans in the war of 1828–29 and these victories further encouraged Armenians to migrate into Russian-controlled areas of Armenia while they simultaneously encouraged Turks to leave. Conditions in Ottoman-controlled regions were certainly difficult for Christians. Muslim courts did not even allow testimony from them until 1854 and even after that it was usually discounted. Christians paid higher taxes than Muslims, and they were not allowed to bear arms to defend themselves whereas Muslims were. Reports on the conditions within Ottoman-controlled Armenia became known in the West through exiles, travellers' publications, and official reports and started to cause wide concern.

Britain and Armenia

Britain and Turkey were on the opposite side to Russia in the Crimean War. The treaty which ended the war in 1856 required Russia to evacuate some Armenian areas which it had occupied during the war. Although this was put into effect, British officers on the spot, especially in the 1870s, were still stressing the risk to the trade routes across the Ottoman empire which they believed were threatened by Russia's renewed interest in southerly expansion. In 1877 the British ambassador in Constantinople went so far as to write (exaggerating considerably) that in the event of a Russian conquest of Armenia 'The consequence would be the greatest blow ever struck at the British Empire'. Britain therefore supported Turkey against Russia though there was a simultaneous British realisation that Turkey's chance of retaining Armenia would be greater if it treated the native Armenian population better. The British government's concern, however, was with who controlled Armenia and hence the trade routes. It was not concerned with the Armenian people except insofar as their support for Russia would weaken Turkey's hold on the region.

Russia again defeated the Ottomans in 1877–78, thereby gaining control of eastern Anatolia. The three treaties of 1878 are crucial to understanding subsequent British concern over Armenia. The first was signed between Russia and Turkey in March. In it Turkey ceded large areas to Russia and this of course increased British concern about the threat to trade routes. In the second, signed in June, Britain promised to defend Turkey against further Russian agression in exchange for two commitments by Turkey: one was to hand Cyprus over to Britain; and the other was to agree to British reforms which would improve the lot of Christians in the Ottoman territories – principally Armenia. The third treaty, (Treaty of Berlin) was signed by all the major European powers including Turkey, Russia, Britain and Germany. Signed in July, this treaty restored to Turkey large areas which had been ceded in March. In it Turkey also promised to introduce reforms to improve the lot of the Armenians. Crucially those reforms no longer had to be agreed with Britain, and Russia was to evacuate the specified areas even before the reforms had been introduced. What had been Britain's responsibility to enforce in June 1878 became in July nobody's. Moreover the sultan in July lost any real threat of action being taken if he did not comply as the power best able to make him do so, Russia, was the last which Britain wished to see involved. It was this crucial abandonment of British influence on the plight of the Armenians together with the increasingly harsh and cruel treatment of the Christian Armenians by the

Muslim Turks and Kurds which led the devoutly Christian and humane Gladstone to make the Armenians' plight the subject of the last major speech of his career in 1896. His speech to an audience of 6,000 in his home city of Liverpool led to the resignation of the leader of his party, Lord Rosebery, a fortnight later. There is no doubt that the removal of pressure on the sultan by Britain between June and July 1878 led to the disastrous consequences culminating in the genocide of 1915.

The Muslim Ottoman government saw Christian Armenians as likely supporters of the Christian Russian conquerors: other Christian parts of the Ottoman empire such as Greece and Bulgaria had already experienced revolution with foreign support. The Armenians meanwhile saw the Ottomans as oppressors of their increasingly nationalistic feelings just as the Greeks and Bulgarians already had. Consequently the migration of both Christian Armenians and Muslim Turks increased after the Russian victory in 1878. Demonstrations by Armenians for greater autonomy were violently suppressed (over 1,000 demonstrators were massacred on one occasion) and a refusal to pay the tribute demanded by the Kurds in addition to government taxes led to weeks of slaughter. Western ambassadors protested about the excessive violence used against the demonstrators but took no other action, not even when 300,000 Armenians died in the pogroms of 1894–96. Conditions grew even worse when the Young Turk movement, which had previously promulgated a programme of reform and courted the Armenian population, changed tack and adopted in 1909 a policy of 'Turkization' of all Ottoman subjects. Twenty thousand were massacred among the Armenian community in Cilicia that year, ostensibly to prevent an Armenian uprising.

Meanwhile in the Russian-controlled areas the climate of liberalism was in recession. The Russian government was no more enthusiastic about Armenian nationalism than the Ottoman and a policy of Russification, similar to that adopted at the time in other parts of the Russian empire such as Finland, came into being. Armenian schools, societies and libraries were closed. References in print to the Armenian nation or people were banned and Armenian church property was taken over by the Tsar. Not surprisingly many Armenians emigrated, principally to the USA.

World War I and genocide

The Ottoman empire entered World War I on the German side but it was already in a state of rapid decline: between 1908 and 1912 it had lost 33% of its territory and the Armenians were the only significant Christian people to remain under Ottoman rule. In 1915 Russia, which had joined the Allied side, inflicted a disastrous defeat on the Ottomans. The Ottomans saw Russian and diaspora Armenians fighting against them and this inflamed their existing suspicions concerning the loyalty of their Armenian subjects: their knowledge of how they had already treated the Armenians would in any case hardly have reassured them concerning their likely loyalty. The 60,000 Armenians serving in the Ottoman forces were quickly demobilized and organised into labour groups in February 1915 only to be massacred by April. It was also ordered that Armenians living in regions near the war front should be moved to the Syrian desert and the Mesopotamian valley with the clear expectation that, even if they survived the forced marches under difficult conditions, they would not survive the inhospitable terrain and hostile tribesmen of these regions for long. In reality not only those Armenians in the frontier regions but also those living nowhere near the frontier regions were deported and then either massacred or left to starve in the desert. Large-scale massacres of Armenians developed, including the Armenian intelligentsia in Constantinople and other cities who were arrested on April 24 and then murdered. There is some dispute as to the authenticity of evidence which suggests that it was the central Ottoman government which ordered the massacres, though they were evidently carefully planned as they were carried out simultaneously in all regions of the Ottoman empire. But there is no doubt at all that around one and a half million Armenians died in the first genocide of the 20th century. It was recognised as such by the United Nations in 1985 and 1986, and by the European Parliament in 1987. However, no Turkish government has ever accepted that these very well attested events happened. The message of the genocide was not lost on Adolf Hitler, a keen student of history who, on the eve of his invasion of Poland in 1939, rallied his generals with the words 'Who still talks nowadays of the extermination of the Armenians?'

The first Armenian republic

Following the Russian Revolution in November 1917, Russian forces began withdrawing from the areas of Ottoman Armenia which they had occupied: Lenin was well aware that disillusion with the war was rampant in the Russian army and that withdrawal was necessary to ensure the soldiers' loyalty. Consequently in Anatolia Armenians were fighting the Ottomans virtually alone. There was a short respite from fighting following the formation in Moscow of a Caucasian federation on April 24 1918 uniting Armenia, Georgia and Azerbaijan but ethnic and religious differences quickly led to its demise. Turkey then started a new offensive attacking Armenia from the west while Russian Menshevik and Turkish forces based in Azerbaijan attacked from the north and east. The Turks advancing from the west were initially successful, retaking the territory west of the Arax river and capturing Alexandropol (Gyumri) on May 15. They invaded the Arax valley occupying the village and railway station of Sardarapat on May 21 from which they launched an offensive towards Yerevan the following day. It was to be a decisive defeat for Turkey. For three days the Turks attacked the Armenian forces under Daniel-Bek Pirumian but were repelled and on May 24 the Armenians went on the offensive and routed the Turks. The victory at Sardarapat followed by others at Bash-Aparan and Gharakilisa between May 24 and 28 led to a declaration of independence on May 28 1918 when the first Republic of Armenia was established under the Dashnak Party. The territories of Nakhichevan and Nagorno Karabagh were incorporated into the Armenian republic but were excluded from Armenia only a week later when Armenia and Turkey signed a peace treaty at Batum on June 4. However, Turkey's involvement in World War I ended with its capitulation on October 30 and the question of Nakhichevan and Nagorno Karabagh was automatically reopened.

The Armenians hoped that the victorious allies would keep their promises and enlarge the borders of the new Armenian state after the armistice in November. Eventually the Treaty of Sèvres in August 1920 granted Armenia borders which were adjudicated by President Woodrow Wilson of the USA in November of that year. However, Turkey had meanwhile invaded Armenia in September and seized part of the country. The Bolsheviks had also invaded Armenia, in April 1920, and the combined pressure of Turks and Bolsheviks caused the collapse of the Armenian government notwithstanding the deliberations about its borders taking place far away in France. In reality acceptance of Bolshevik rule was for the Armenians the only real defence against the Turks. Armenia was formally incorporated into the Transcaucasian Soviet Federated Socialist Republic on November 29 1920.

The Bolsheviks made large territorial concessions to Turkey, notably by handing over areas which had been under Russian rule even prior to 1914 including the historic Bagratid capital of Ani and the city of Kars. Soviet historians have claimed that the Bolsheviks wanted a quick agreement with Turkey because they believed that a Turkish delegation was in London where David Lloyd George, much more in favour of newly-secularised Turkey under Ataturk than Bolshevik Russia under Lenin, was offering Turkey rule over the Caucasus as a protectorate. This protectorate, the Bolsheviks believed, would include Armenia but, much more important from both Russian and Western perspectives, the Baku oilfields in Azerbaijan. It is, however, more likely that Lenin's real motive behind the concessions was to encourage Ataturk whom he (mistakenly) believed would be an ardent supporter of the communist cause. He probably also believed that Turkey was militarily too strong for Russia to be able to win a campaign in Armenia and these two factors led to Russia's concurrence with Turkey's proposals for the border. Had any Armenians been involved in the Moscow discussions between Russia and Turkey it is inconceivable that Ani would have been relinquished. The Treaty of Sèvres was formally replaced in 1923 by the Treaty of Lausanne, effectively abandoning any pretence of Western support for an independent Armenia and reconfirming the message of 1878 that the Western powers, whatever their feelings about the sufferings of the Armenian people, would relegate action to the 'too difficult' pile.

Soviet Armenia

From 1921 Lenin made overtures to the new Turkish government, led by Ataturk, which was under attack by Greek forces, Turkey having reneged on its promise to return historic Greek lands in Asia Minor in return for Greek support during the war. By 1921 Greek troops were approaching Ankara. Soviet Russia initially helped Turkey, Lenin still believing that Ataturk was intent on building a socialist state on the Soviet model. Lenin also agreed with Turkey that Nagorno Karabagh, Nakhichevan, Syunik and Zangezur would be incorporated into Azerbaijan. However, Lenin eventually came to realise that Ataturk had no intention of building a socialist state and withdrew support. Meanwhile, led by Garegin Nzhdeh, an Armenian who had fought successful guerrilla campaigns against the Turks during Bulgaria's struggle for independence, Armenian forces fought a successful campaign in Syunik and Zangezur (southern Armenia) against the Red Army and the Turks simultaneously. Stalemate developed and Nzhdeh forced Lenin to compromise and accept his terms that Syunik and Zangezur would be incorporated into the Republic of Armenia rather than into Azerbaijan. He can thus be seen as the person who saved the south of Armenia for the country. Subsequently he went into exile and, after Hitler's coming to power, pursued fruitless negotiations with Nazi Germany in an attempt to regain for Armenia the lands occupied by Turkey. He died in a Soviet prison in 1955 but his remains were secretly returned to Armenia in 1983. He is buried at the beautiful (but little-visited) Spitakavor monastery in Vayots Dzor province.

Between 1921 and 1924 Armenia witnessed a resurgence of intellectual and cultural life and Armenian intellectuals, believing that they at last had a homeland, came from abroad, notably the architect Alexander Tamanian who had drawn up ambitious plans for the creation of a fine capital for the First Republic and who returned to complete his plans. These resulted in the creation of the buildings around Republic Square, possibly the finest of all Soviet architectural ensembles – admittedly not a field in which the competiton is stiff. He also planned green belts, gardens and residential areas for a city capable of housing a then unimaginable population of 150,000. Yerevan State University was also constructed and professors were recruited from the West. This was also the era of Lenin's New Economic Policy, forced on him by the failure of communist orthodoxy to deliver material benefit, and limited private enterprise was consequently tolerated.

In 1923 Stalin, who was then Commissar for Nationalities, adopted a divide and rule policy which led to Nagorno Karabagh (whose population was largely Armenian) and Nakhichevan (which also had a substantial Armenian majority) being placed in Azerbaijan. Additionally the new Soviet republics were created in such a way that they did not have continuous boundaries: for example isolated villages deep inside Armenia were designated part of Azerbaijan. This was a deliberate, conscious attempt by Stalin to encourage ethnic tensions between Armenians and Azeris so as to discourage them from uniting together against Soviet rule. The Transcaucasian Federation was abolished in 1936 and Armenia became a Soviet republic in its own right though still with the artificial 1923 boundaries.

Economic growth was impressive but the abolition of the New Economic Policy caused considerable resentment, especially among farmers. Although Armenia did not suffer deliberate mass starvation during the forced collectivisation of agriculture in the same way as Ukraine did in 1932–33, it did suffer along with other parts of the Soviet Union during Stalin's purges between 1934 and 1939. At least 100,000 Armenians were victims. Persecution of Christians also reached a height in the mid to late 1930s and all churches except Ejmiatsin were closed by 1935. The head of the church was murdered in 1938 and the entire Armenian political leadership along with most intellectuals was condemned to death for the crime of bourgeois nationalism (ie: being perceived by Stalin as a threat to himself).

Stalin's pact with Hitler in August 1939 did not save the Soviet Union from attack for long and Germany invaded on June 22 1941. German troops never reached Armenia: they approached no closer than the north Caucasus where the oilfields around Grozny were a principal objective as Hitler simultaneously wanted to secure their output for Germany and to deprive the Soviet Union. About 630,000 Armenians out of a population of two million fought during World War II (or the Great Patriotic War as it is called throughout the former Soviet Union) of whom about half died.

Armenia experienced rapid growth after 1945 with Yerevan's population increasing from 50,000 to 1,300,000. Huge chemical plants were established in Yerevan, Leninakan (Gyumri) and Kirovakan (Vanadzor) and Armenia became one of the most highly educated and most industrialised of the Soviet republics. By contrast, a new wave of repression began in 1947 with the deportees being exiled to the infamous gulag camps of Siberia. After Stalin's death, probably by poisoning at the instigation of the secret police chief Lavrentii Beria, conditions relaxed and during the Brezhnev era (1964–82) dissenters were merely certified insane and kept among the genuinely mentally ill in mental hospitals.

The coming to power of Gorbachev in 1985 saw an upsurge in Armenian nationalism, especially over the question of the enclave of Nagorno Karabagh. Gorbachev refused to allow its transfer from Azerbaijan to Armenia. There were demonstrations in both republics and, especially following Soviet government inaction after the killing of 30 Armenians by Azeris at Sumgait, an industrial city north of Baku, in February 1988 many Armenians fled from Azerbaijan to Armenia while at the same time many Azeris fled in the opposite direction. In July 1988 Nagorno Karabagh declared its secession from Azerbaijan and in December the pressure group known as the Karabagh Committee, which had meanwhile broadened its objectives to include democratic change within Armenia itself, was arrested and held in Moscow without trial for six months. In early 1989 Moscow imposed direct rule on Nagorno Karabagh and rebellion broke out. In November that year Armenia declared that Nagorno Karabagh was a part of Armenia as a result of which Turkey and Azerbaijan closed their borders with Armenia and imposed an economic blockade: the problems this caused were greatly exacerbated because of the closure, as a precautionary measure, of Metsamor nuclear power station following a major earthquake in December 1988.

The third republic

In July 1990 elections were won by the Armenian National Movement which had developed from the Karabagh Committee. Its leader, Levon Ter-Petrossian, became president of the Armenian Supreme Soviet which declared independence from the Soviet Union in August. (This was quite legal as, under the Soviet constitution, all republics were nominally free to secede.) The new government took a moderate line over the Nagorno Karabagh dispute and tried to distance itself from the fighting. The collapse of the Soviet Union in August 1991, following the failed putsch against Gorbachev, was followed by a referendum on September 21 in which the population of Armenia overwhelmingly voted in favour of independence. Meanwhile Azerbaijan likewise declared itself independent. However, after Armenia signed a mutual assistance treaty with Russia and certain other members of the Confederation of Independent States (CIS) in May 1992, Russia started supplying arms to Armenia which was able to drive Azerbaijan out of most of Nagorno Karabagh, the area between Armenia and Nagorno Karabagh, as well as border areas with Iran. After the death of around 25,000 combatants a ceasefire was declared in 1994 and largely holds firm at the time of writing. During the conflict the closure of the Turkish and Azerbaijan borders together with frequent sabotage of the gas pipelines in southern Georgia (used to supply gas to Armenia) resulted in Armenia becoming heavily dependent on Iran for supplies. It might now be possible to resolve the dispute if Armenia were willing to give up the southernmost part of its territory bordering Iran in exchange for Nagorno Karabagh but the Armenian government's understandable wish to retain this direct link with Iran makes any short-term settlement of the dispute unlikely. Meanwhile Azerbaijan apparently hopes that Russia will lose interest in the area and cease supporting Armenia.

Armenia adopted a new presidential constitution in 1995 and in September 1996 Ter-Petrossian was re-elected president. He appointed Robert Kocharian, a former leader of Nagorno Karabagh, as prime minister and he was elected president in turn when Ter-Petrossian resigned in 1998. Parliamentary elections in May 1999 brought the opposition Unity Alliance to power with Vagen Sarkisian of the nationalist Republican Party (HHK) as prime minister and Karen Demirchian (loser of the presidential election) as speaker but on October 27 1999 both of them, along with six others, were assassinated when gunmen stormed into parliament. The trial of the killers in late 2001 has not clarified the motives behind the attack. On March 22 2000 Arkady Gukasian, the president of Nagorno Karabagh, narrowly escaped an assassination attempt for which the former defence minister Samuel Babayan was jailed for 14 years.

A bitter struggle for power within the Armenian government led to some senior ministers being ousted and by mid-2001 the People's Party of Armenia (HZhK, led by Stepan Demirchian, son of the assassinated speaker) was becoming unhappy with its role as junior partner in the ruling coalition. Some of its members joined communists and the Hanrapetutian (Republic) party of former prime minister Aram Sarkisian (the assassinated prime minister's brother) in blocking an important bill on civil service reform. In August 2001 Kocharian proposed controversial changes to the constitution while the opposition predictably called on him to resign. In September 2001 HZhK left the coalition and joined the opposition in calling for Kocharian's impeachment on charges of violating the

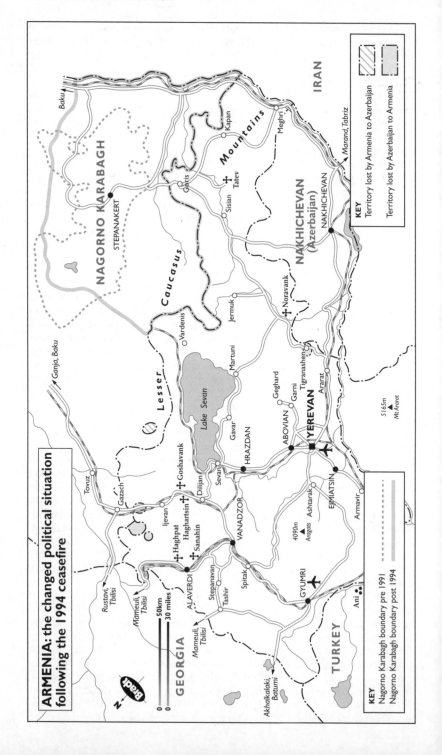

ARMENIA: the changed political situation following the 1994 ceasefire

constitution, condoning terrorism, and causing a political and economic crisis. A further scandal blew up that month when an Armenian resident of Georgia, a member of the pro-Kocharian Dashnak party, was beaten to death in the gentlemen's toilet of Yerevan's Aragast jazz club by members of Kocharian's bodyguard. The president had just left the club and the bodyguard apparently objected to anti-Kocharian remarks which they had heard him making. The following month around 25,000 joined anti-Kocharian demonstrations and 400,000 signed a petition demanding his resignation. A conspicuous feature of the subsequent trial of one of the bodyguards on the fairly minor charge of involuntary manslaughter was the unwillingness of any of the several dozen people who had witnessed the events to come forward and testify, apparently because of fear of what might happen to them at the hands of the police.

The present

In the first round of the presidential election held on February 19 2003, there were nine candidates, all male, including the incumbent Robert Kocharian. The official result was that Kocharian had received 49.48% compared to 28.22% for Stepan Demirchian and 17% for Artashes Geghamian in third place. Since a candidate must achieve 51% of the vote for an outright victory a second round of voting was required. The entire campaign had been conducted with a great deal of mudslinging, little discussion of important issues such as education, taxation and welfare, and little in the way of specific proposals for constitutional or legislative change. Neither Demirchian, son of the former parliamentary speaker assassinated in 1999, nor Geghamian even mentioned Nagorno Karabagh with all its implications for the country. Both, however, advocated closer ties with Russia and, though Demirchian was non-specific, Geghamian advocated joining the rouble zone and changing Armenia's legislation in the fields of customs and taxation to match Russia's. One of Demirchian's few concrete proposals was to abandon the 1996 local government reforms and revert to the Soviet era divisions.

Two invited teams of international observers spent six weeks in the country prior to the election. The reports of those from the Organisation for Security and Co-operation in Europe (OSCE) differ markedly from those of the CIS observers. Among the shortcomings, the OSCE observers noted that there had been pre-election intimidation and incidents of disruption of campaign events, including one instance of violence, pre-election manipulations including schemes to impersonate voters, and the heavy use of public resources in support of the incumbent. The international observers on polling day assessed the voting process positively in 90% of polling stations but noted that there were unauthorised people including government officials in 23% of polling stations who often acted in an intimidatory manner. Irregularities noted at some stations included cases of ballot-box stuffing, individuals voting more than once, a policeman carrying a box of at least 50 passports (used in the election as evidence of identity) out of a polling station and intimidation of candidates' proxies, two of whom were seen being assaulted. (In Armenian elections a proxy is the appointed representative of a candidate in a polling station, who acts as an observer on the candidate's behalf; if he notices any irregularity his report must be attached to the result of the count submitted by the returning officer.) The count itself was negatively assessed by the international observers in 20% of polling stations some of whose results showed a striking disparity both in voter turnout and outcome from the otherwise consistent pattern of results.

The second round with two candidates was held on March 5 and resulted in a win for Kocharian with 67.44% of the vote as opposed to 32.56% for Demirchian.

The OSCE observers were even more condemnatory of the process. Indeed, this time some polling stations recorded more votes than there were registered voters. Between the rounds the police arrested 142 of Demirchian's supporters on charges of hooliganism of whom 77 were given short jail sentences and the others fined. Publicly funded TV and radio made no attempt to fulfil its legal obligation to report even-handedly and the state-funded newspaper *Hayastani Hanrapetutian* also gave overwhelming support to the incumbent. The extent of all this election fraud led the observers to conclude that the election 'fell short of international standards for democratic elections'. All this was in complete contrast to the CIS observers who considered the elections to be 'democratic and legitimate' with 'no mass violations of the Electoral Code'. As one local newspaper commented it was rather a 'dialogue of civilisations' with the (mostly western) European observers having different expectations from those of former Soviet republics.

The parliamentary election held on May 25 2003 resulted in a similar clash of views although, as on previous occasions, there was less actual malpractice than in the presidential election. The Western observers referred to 'serious incidents and shortcomings' and hoped that 'there will be no return to the sense of impunity evident in the recent presidential election'. The CIS observers thought the election 'transparent and democratic' and praised the Armenian authorities for 'ensuring fair elections'. Turnout in the poll was 52% with six of the 21 parties and blocs breaking the 5% threshold required to gain seats in the new parliament. The largest share of the vote, 24.5% of the votes cast, went to the Republican Party which is supportive of the president. The next largest share of the vote, 14.2%, went to the Justice bloc led by Stepan Demirchian who had been runner up in the presidential election in March. The Communist Party gained a mere 1.6% of the votes and bottom of the poll with 0.3% was The Fist of Armenian Braves Party.

ECONOMY

Between 1960 and 1988 Soviet Armenia achieved growth of 30% in GNP. (During the same period, growth of GNP in the USA was 135%.) But the following years were catastrophic for the economy. Firstly the devastating earthquake in northwest Armenia in December 1988 resulted in 25,000 deaths, 20,000 injured and 500,000 made homeless and caused huge damage to infrastructure. This was to be followed by the breakup of the Soviet Union and war with Azerbaijan so that between 1989 and 1994 GNP fell from US$4,500m to US$652m. By 1994, however, the Armenian government had launched an ambitious IMF-sponsored economic programme which has resulted in positive growth rates of about 6% or more since then. This is partly because the well-educated Armenian population has a much stronger work ethic than in some other states of the region, partly because the country has enjoyed relative political stability and partly because the support of the diaspora has been considerable. Even so, in 1998 average monthly income was as low as US$16 and about 60–70% of the population was estimated to be living below the poverty level. By 2001 GNP growth was estimated at 9.6%. Inflation too has been brought under control, falling from a horrific 4,964% in 1994 to as low as 2% in 2002 although there have recently been some signs of a rise from that figure.

Prior to the Soviet collapse in 1991, Armenia had developed a large industrial sector, supplying machine tools, textiles and other manufactured goods to the other Soviet republics in exchange for raw materials and energy. By 1994 most of this had closed. Given the state of the plants, the privatisation of industry has inevitably been slow but there has been renewed emphasis by the Kocharian administration and a few plants have partially reopened. In agriculture there has been a reversion to small-scale agriculture away from the large agro-industrial complexes of the Soviet era. The sector has considerable need for investment and updated technology. Armenia remains a net food importer, and its mineral deposits are small.

In 2000 agriculture accounted for 29% of GNP although it employed 44% of the working population according to official figures, industry accounted for 32% of GNP though employing 42% of the population and services for 39% of GNP while employing 14%. The official unemployment rate was 10.9% although most independent observers consider that the true figure is double this. However, these figures can be misleading since the many subsistence farmers, tradesmen and owners of small businesses are considered to be employed even though they receive no salary as such – the other way of looking at these numbers is to bear in mind that only 20–30% of the population is actually paid wages.

The main exports are cut diamonds (which are imported uncut – Armenia has no sources of diamonds), scrap metal from closed industry, brandy, and copper ore. By value the main export trading partner in 2000 was Belgium at 23% (to which the diamonds go), Russia with 15% of exports, USA with 13% and Iran with 10%. The principal imports in 2000 were natural gas, petroleum, tobacco products, foodstuffs and diamonds, and the sources of imports were Russia at 15%, USA at 12%, Belgium at 10% and Iran at 9%.

GEOLOGY AND GEOGRAPHY
Visitors to Armenia can hardly fail to be aware of two key geological features of the country: the lesser Caucasus mountain range which projects into the country, with the dormant volcano of Mount Aragats being the highest peak at 4,090m; and the frequency of earthquakes. The two are both accounted for by the theory of plate tectonics. Under this theory, which has been generally accepted internationally since the 1960s, the outermost shell of the earth or lithosphere is formed of a dozen or so large rigid slabs of rock together with many smaller ones. These slabs, called tectonic plates, are around 75km thick and comprise the thin outer crust plus the solid part of the mantle. The plates float on the liquid part of the mantle or asthenosphere which is several hundred kilometres thick and the slow movement of the plates is due to convection currents in the asthenosphere caused by heat escaping from the earth's core. As the enormous plates move, they grind against each other and stress builds up until there is a sudden movement of one plate against another resulting in an earthquake when rocks break along fault lines. Armenia is on the line where the Arabian plate, moving at about 2.5cm per annum, is colliding with the larger Eurasian plate and it is consequently very prone to earthquakes. About 25 million years ago the Caucasus mountains themselves were formed as a consequence of this collision. Quite young as mountain ranges go, they are largely volcanic rocks such as basalt, andesite and tuff, all three of which have been used as building materials in Armenia. Basalt and andesite are magma (liquid material from the asthenosphere) which escaped to the surface during the collision of the plates and then solidified. The difference between the two is in the relative proportions of silica, iron and magnesium. Tuff by contrast is formed when small rock fragments (less than 2mm across) which have spewed out from a volcano become fused together on the ground. Tuff has long been the building material of choice in Armenia when it is available and it is highly characteristic of the country. Today the biggest working tuff quarry is close to the town of Artik in Shirak province. Another consequence of the volcanic past is that the semi-precious stone obsidian can be found here. Obsidian, which occurs in a range of colours and is used to make jewellery, is a glassy rock formed through the very rapid solidification of lava. In Armenia it occurs most commonly in the Hrazdan

region. Apart from these volcanic rocks, Armenia also has substantial deposits of the sedimentary rock limestone and in some of these are extensive though little-known cave systems. The most important mineral deposits are of copper and molybdenum.

Prior to the war with Azerbaijan, landlocked Armenia was bordered to the north by Georgia, to the east by Azerbaijan, to the south by Iran and to the west by Turkey and by the detached part of Azerbaijan known as Nakhichevan. The borders totalled 1,254km: 164km with Georgia; 566km with Azerbaijan; 35km with Iran; 268km with Turkey; and 221km with Nakhichevan. The area of the country was 29,800km², slightly smaller than Belgium and slightly larger than the American state of Maryland. An additional complication was that five small detached enclaves within Armenia were actually part of Azerbaijan while Azerbaijan had a small Armenian enclave within its borders. The ceasefire in 1994 has led to a considerable change. Firstly, all these small enclaves have now been occupied by the surrounding power. Secondly, Nagorno Karabagh, which had been an autonomous region within Azerbaijan, declared itself an independent republic; the present-day republic of Nagorno Karabagh does not incorporate all the territory of the former autonomous region since Azerbaijan holds the northern part. Thirdly, Armenia was left in control of a considerable area of the former territory of Azerbaijan and much of this is now administered by Nagorno Karabagh. In total some 20% of former Azeri territory is now either occupied by Armenia or else forms part of Nagorno Karabagh. A noticeable change in 2002 was that for the first time maps were starting to show the occupied territories as a part of Armenia and Nagorno Karabagh. Relatively few people live in them since the Azeri population has fled and Armenian refugees have not chosen these territories in which to settle. The international community still recognises the pre-1991 boundaries with the apparent exception that foreign diplomats driving from Yerevan to southern Armenia do not seem to bother to avoid the former Azeri enclave through which the main road passes. Only Armenia recognises the independence of Nagorno Karabagh.

Armenia is a very high country. The lowest part, the Debed valley at the Georgian border in the northeast, lies at 400m while the average altitude is 1,370m and only 10% of the land is under 1,000m. Although mountainous in parts, much of Armenia is more a high plateau fissured by deep gorges. The volcanic soil in the valleys means that the ground is highly fertile but irrigation is essential because of the low rainfall and about 10% of the entire land is irrigated. Even so, Armenia is a net importer of food. The growing of food crops is obviously unfeasible in the mountainous areas but is equally unfeasible on much of the plateau because of the lack of water although some of the alpine meadows are used for the production of hay. The mountains do support a surprisingly large population of cattle as well as sheep and goats and livestock can often be encountered at unexpected elevations in fairly inaccessible places. About 20% of the land is arable, while 24% is pasture and about 15% is forest. Fruit growing is important. Fruits as diverse as pomegranates, grapes, strawberries, peaches, persimmons and apples are grown but two fruits native to Armenia and which were consequently first eaten here remain important although they have now spread to the rest of the world. One is the apricot – its scientific name, *Armeniaca vulgaris*, reflects this – and Armenians claim with some justification that their apricots are the best in the world. Apricot stones 6,000 years old have been found at archaeological sites and today there are about 50 varieties in the country. The other is the sweet cherry or mazzard, *Prunus avium*, from which all the world's 900 varieties of sweet cherry have been cultivated. It spread to the West very early and was known in Greece by 300BC. Walnuts, pistachios, almonds and hazelnuts grow wild in Armenia and they too are now extensively cultivated.

Also of great importance is that Armenia is possibly the country where wheat was first cultivated, perhaps about 10,000 years ago. Two native species of wheat, *Triticum urartu* and *T. araraticum*, still grow in protected fields in the Arax valley.

A major feature of the country is Lake Sevan whose surface area was formerly 1,416km² but this has been reduced by abstracting water for hydro-electric and irrigation purposes. It is one of the world's largest high-altitude lakes with its surface originally 1,915m above sea level. There is commercial exploitation of fish stocks although the introduction of alien species has led to the virtual extinction of the endemic trout.

Armenia has a number of significant rivers which all flow east into the Caspian Sea. Hydro-electric schemes on these rivers are important as the only indigenous energy resource within the country which has been developed and they provide around one third of electricity requirements. Another third of electricity is generated using nuclear power and the balance is thermal generation mostly using imported gas. Electricity is exported to Georgia and there are seasonal exchanges with Iran. Gas is mostly imported from Russia by pipeline through Georgia although the Armenian and Iranian gas networks are to be linked in future. Armenia has no known reserves of coal, oil or gas.

CLIMATE

Armenia has a generally dry, continental climate: less dry than Iran to the south but much drier than Georgia to the north. With cold winters and hot summers, Armenia becomes increasingly warm as one heads south but the effect of altitude is more pronounced than that of latitude. The warmest part of the country is the area along the Iranian border, while the Arax valley including Yerevan is also very warm, with summer temperatures rising to 44°C at times while it can drop to around –15°C on January nights. Most other places in Armenia are colder than this with the average temperature in Gyumri, for example, being 3°C cooler, while on the country's higher peaks snow can linger throughout the year. There is no spring in the western European sense and the transition from winter to summer is abrupt: in 2003 for example it was quite late, happening suddenly on May 1. In some years there is an autumn but summer generally lingers on until the end of October.

CONSERVATION

Armenia has a network of national parks and reserves which were created in Soviet times and have been retained. Unfortunately the country's economic plight means that staffing has been reduced and little can be done to enhance these areas. More generally the energy blockade during the war with Azerbaijan saw trees cut down for fuel, particularly in the vicinity of major cities such as Vanadzor. Efforts are being made to replant such areas, partly with diaspora funding, but much remains to be done. The reversion to subsistence farming, as a result of the closure of much of the country's economic base when the Soviet Union collapsed, has led to increased overgrazing in many upland areas with a consequent degradation of habitat.

NATURAL HISTORY

The number of species of animals and plants in Armenia is very high for a country of its size which lies wholly outside the tropics. This is largely accounted for by the great altitudinal variation and the diversity of vegetation zones. Armenia is normally described as having six distinct zones: semi-deserts, dry steppes, steppes, forest, subalpine and alpine. Semi-deserts account for about 10% of the country and occur in the Arax valley and adjacent mountain slopes up to an altitudes of

1,200-1,300m, as well as in the Arpa valley around Vaik, and in the Meghri region. The land has generally been cultivated for millennia except for a few patches where sand has accumulated and a semi-desert landscape has resulted. Cultivation has required extensive irrigation and these irrigated areas now account for most of the fruit, vegetable and wine production. Dry mountainous steppes are found at higher altitudes than semi-deserts (above 1,500m) in the Arax valley and some other areas, but are also found at lower altitudes (above 800m) in the northeast in areas which were originally forested. A range of soils is found and in the Arax valley these are mostly stony. Irrigation of dry steppes has allowed some cultivation of crops and fruit. Mountain steppes are the dominant landscape for most of the country, particularly at altitudes above 1,500m. In the northeast of the country and also in the south, ridges among these highland meadow steppes often contain patches of forest. Elsewhere forests are usually found on the mid-zone of mountains though in some regions the forests have been much affected by the cutting of trees for fuel during the energy shortage years in the early 1990s. The most extensive forested areas are now in the northeast. Subalpine meadows occur at higher altitudes than steppes and forests, including highland mountain ranges. Alpine meadows occur higher still and are important pasture lands even though climatic conditions are severe with long cold winters and snow cover lasting up to nine months. So-called azonal landscapes (meaning that the soil type is determined by factors other than the local climate and vegetation) cover the remaining 10% of the territory of the country and include wetlands, as well as saline and alkaline areas in the Ararat valley where the underground waters are close to the earth surface, resulting in water vaporisation and salt precipitation.

Mammals

Armenia's mammal list was recently increased from 76 to 83 when seven additional species of bat were identified. However, one of the mammals on the list, striped hyena, is probably extinct in the country and the status of the Caucasian birch mouse (*Sicista caucasica*) is unknown. Another six are officially classified as endangered: the distinctive Armenian subspecies of mouflon (*Ovis orientalis gmelini*), Persian ibex or wild goat (*Capra aegagrus*), marbled polecat, otter, Pallas's cat (or manul) and brown bear (or grizzly bear as the same species is known in North America). Despite bears being classified as endangered, their droppings can often be encountered while walking in the mountains, sometimes surprisingly close to habitation. Other interesting mammals include leopard, said to be quite common (although very rarely encountered) in the Khosrov preserve where it preys mainly on the Persian ibex and also occasionally seen in parts of the south, as well as lynx, wild cat, wolf, ibex, porcupine, roe deer and wild boar. However, no mammals in Armenia can be descibed as easy to see and, apart from a wolf disturbed from its daytime retreat and a few unidentified bats, I have only ever observed red fox, brown hare, European souslik (*Citellus citellus*), and Vinogradov's jird (*Meriones vinogradovi*), the jird being one of five species of gerbil found in Armenia.

Birds

The standard field guide lists 346 species of bird as having been recorded in Armenia up to 1997. However, as there are only a few observers many vagrants and casuals must go unrecorded. Armenia is at the boundary of two faunal zones and the north sees northern species at the southern limit of their range while the south sees southern species and those from the eastern Mediterranean at their northern limit. Raptors are surprisingly common and easy to see. Five species of eagle breed in Armenia: lesser spotted, golden, booted, steppe, and short-toed snake-eagle.

This is in addition to osprey, four vultures, two harriers and a good selection of buzzards and falcons. Other large and conspicuous birds include white and black storks, the former mainly in the Arax valley where their nests are conspicuous in some places on top of electricity poles. The Dalmatian pelican breeds in the country and great white pelicans are year-round visitors. Specialities of the Caucasus include Caucasian grouse and Caspian snowcock, both of which are endangered and difficult to see without a knowledgeable local guide in their subalpine and alpine meadows. Smaller birds of note include both eastern and western rock nuthatches, white-tailed lapwing, Persian wheatear, Armenian gull, white-throated robin and Finsch's wheatear. Raptor migration in autumn is very rewarding as Armenia is on a major flightway between the Black and Caspian seas with the most numerous species being steppe buzzard, steppe and lesser spotted eagles, and Monatgu's and pallid harriers, honey buzzard, Levant sparrowhawk, lesser kestrel and black kite. September sees migrating demoiselle cranes at Lake Sevan with daily totals of up to 4,500 being recorded.

Anyone interested in Armenia's birds is strongly recommended to join the Ornithological Society of the Middle East, c/o 6 Mansion Drive, Tring, Hertfordshire HP23 5BD, UK (fax: +44 1442 822623; email: webmaster@osme.org) who can assist with birdwatching trips to the country as well as funding small projects such as the survey of Armash fish ponds currently under way. A local expert on the country's birds (and also its 53 species of dragonfly) who has led many birdwatching groups is Vasil Ananian (email: vananian72@yahoo.com). He can be relied upon to track down Armenia's most interesting specialities.

Amphibians and reptiles

Armenia's dry climate is reflected in the paucity of amphibian species and lack of specialities. All eight species in the country have a wide distribution even though only one is also native to the UK. Widespread European species are marsh frog (*Rana ridibunda*), green toad (*Bufo viridis*), eastern spadefoot toad (*Pelobates syriacus*), European tree frog (*Hyla arborea*) and smooth newt (*Triturus vulgaris*). The others, not included in most field guides, are banded frog (*Rana camerani*), lemon-yellow tree frog (*Hyla savignyi*) and banded newt (*Triturus vittatus*).

By contrast, Armenia is very rich in reptile species with a total of 50 although some are now threatened by denudation of the habitat as a result of overgrazing. The Mediterranean tortoise, *Testudo graeca*, may occasionally be encountered as one crosses a track. Ponds may contain one of two species of terrapin, European pond terrapin (*Emys orbicularis*) and stripe-necked terrapin (*Mauremys caspica*).

The geckos which can frequently be seen on the outside walls of buildings in the countryside are Caspian rock geckos, *Tenuidactylus caspius*. The Caucasian agama (*Laudakia caucasia*) is a lizard with a decidedly prehistoric, dragon-like appearance. Like all agamas, it has a plump short body with a long thin tail, a triangular head and long legs. Agamas are capable of some colour change to match their background. Two legless lizards which might be mistaken for snakes (though being lizards rather than snakes they have eyelids and they can shed their tails to escape a predator, a practice known as autotony) are the slow worm (*Anguis fragilis*) and the European glass lizard (*Ophisaurus apodus*). Skinks are lizards which, while not usually completely legless, generally in Europe have vestigial legs only of little or no apparent value for locomotion. The Armenian fauna includes several skinks: two-streaked lidless skink, *Ablepharus bivittatus;* Chernov's lidless skink, *Ablepharus chernovi*; golden grass skink, *Mabuya aurata*; and the Berber skink, *Eumeces schneideri*. The other lizard species are typical lizards belonging to the large family Lacertidae. Ones of particular interest are those with a limited range outside Armenia such as stepperunner (*Eremias arguta*), Balkan green lizard (*Lacerta trilineata*) and Caucasian green lizard (*Lacerta strigata*). Even more unusual is the Armenian lizard (*Lacerta armeniaca*) in which a proportion of the females practise parthenogenesis – in other words without fertilisation by a male they lay eggs which hatch and produce a daughter that is an exact genetic copy of the mother.

Snakes are very well represented with 23 species and they are more commonly seen than in many countries. Interesting snakes include the sand boa, *Eryx jaculus*, one of Europe's few snakes which kill their prey by constriction, mostly small lizards and rodents in this case. Largely nocturnal, it rests by day in rodent burrows or under large stones. Unusually the snake is viviparous, the female giving birth to about 20 live young which feed on small lizards. The Montpellier snake, *Malpolon monspessulanus*, belongs to the family Colubridae, snakes whose fangs are at the back of the mouth. Such snakes find it difficult to inject their venom into large objects. Unusually for a snake this diurnal species possesses good vision and, when hunting, it sometimes rises up and looks around, thus rather resembling a cobra. The Montpellier snake reaches 2m in length. A much smaller colubrid is the Asia Minor dwarf snake, *Eirenis modestus*, which only grows to 15cm and feeds on insects. Dahl's whip snake, *Coluber najadum*, is another diurnal snake. Very slender, it is extremely fast moving but rarely exceeds a metre in length. Another whip snake is the secretive and weakly venomed mountain racer, *C. ravergieri*. Caucasian rat snake, *Elaphe hohenackeri*, is one of Europe's smaller snakes, only growing up to about 80cm. Very unusually for a snake it is often found in the vicinity of human habitations where it frequents piles of stones and holes in old stone walls.

Vipers are among the snakes which, unlike the colubrids, have fangs at the front of their mouth. They are consequently much more dangerous because they do not need to get their mouth round the victim in order to inject poison. There are several interesting species in Armenia which have a very limited distribution. Armenian viper (*Vipera raddei*) is now seriously threatened in the country through pasturing and overgrazing while Darevsky's viper, *V. darevskii*, described as recently as 1986, also has a very limited range and is similarly threatened. Bites from these species can be fatal as can those from Armenia's more widely distributed vipers. Perhaps the most dangerous of all is the blunt-nosed viper, *V. lebetina*, at 2.5m one of the largest of its genus. An able climber of trees, the danger from this snake lies mainly in the extreme speed of its attack and the method of biting: rather than bite and withdraw, it keeps its teeth lodged in its target and works its jaws to pump more venom in. It is not a snake to be approached lightly, although it generally makes a loud hissing before attacking, thus giving some warning.

Fish

Of the 31 species of fish found in Armenia, six have been introduced. Common whitefish, *Coregonus lavaretus*, was introduced into Lake Sevan from Lake Ladoga in Russia with a view to increasing commercial fish production and this was followed by goldfish, *Carassius auratus*, from eastern Asia. Fish farms are responsible for introducing silver carp (*Hypophthalmichthys molitrix*) from China and Pacific salmon (*Salmo gairdneri*). Presumably Pacific salmon was preferred to the native Caspian salmon, *S. caspius*, because of the ease of obtaining stock. Grass carp (*Ctenopharyngodon idella*) was brought from China with the hope of improving water quality in irrigation systems and marshy lakes as it is herbivorous and so helps to control aquatic vegetation. By contrast mosquito fish, *Gambusia affinis*, was brought from the southeast part of the USA because, as its name implies, it eats mosquito larvae and hence assists in the control of malaria.

Apart from these exotics there has been some stocking of waters with common carp, *Cyprinus carpio*, which has been introduced to lakes in Lori province as well as Dilijan and Ijevan reservoirs. On the other hand overfishing of rivers has led to a decline in the abundance of trout, *Salmo trutta*, and European catfish or wels, *Silurus glanis*. However, chub, *Leusciscus cephalus*, remains common in lakes. Drastic reduction in the water level of Lake Sevan has led to the virtual extinction in Armenia of the endemic Sevan trout, *Salmo ischchan* (see page 126). Paradoxically its successful translocation into Lake Issyk-kul in Kyrgyzstan, although having negative consequences for the indigenous Issyk-kul fish fauna, has probably saved this fish from extinction. Stocks in Lake Sevan of Sevan khramulya, *Varicorhinus capoeta*, have also seriously declined but it survives in some of the lake's tributaries.

Other fauna

About 17,000 species of invertebrate have been identified in Armenia but this must only represent a small fraction of the total. Two groups may be of particular interest to visitors but for very different reasons. Armenia has three species of scorpion which fortunately are rarely encountered. However, they occur on the rocky and stony ground such as that which surrounds many monasteries and form an additional reason to wear robust footwear as well as taking care when scrambling up slopes. Far more conspicuous is the abundance of butterflies. About 570 of lepidoptera (moths and butterflies) have been identified in Armenia but that is clearly only a small percentage of the total since it compares with a figure of 2,600 for the UK which, although larger, has a much less suitable climate. A well-illustrated guide to the butterflies of the whole of the former Soviet Union including Armenia is available – it was published in Sofia, Bulgaria and is obtainable from specialist booksellers worldwide – but unfortunately its two enormous heavy volumes make it difficult even to take *to* Armenia let alone carry around.

Flora

Identified so far in Armenia have been 388 species of algae, 4,166 fungi, 2,600 lichens and 430 mosses in addition to the very large total of 3,555 species of vascular plants. Since Armenia's flora is very extensive it is perhaps surprising that gymnosperms (basically conifers) should be poorly represented by a mere nine species: five junipers, one pine and two shrubby members of the family Ephedraceae whose American relatives include Nevada joint fir and desert tea.

One third of the forests are oak forests and they are widely distributed across the country. Of the four oak species found in Armenia, two (Caucasian oak, *Quercus macranthera*, and Georgian oak, *Q. iberica*) are typical of these forests. Caucasian oak is the more frost- tolerant species and is found throughout the country at altitudes as high as 2,600m. By contrast, Georgian oak is typically restricted to altitudes between 500 and 1,400m and is mostly found in the north and the extreme south. Other species found in oak forests are ash (*Fraxinus excelsior*), hornbeam (*Carpinus betulus*), Georgian maple (*Acer ibericum*), cork elm (*Ulmus suberosus*) and field maple (*Acer campestre*). A third oak species, Arax oak (*Quercus araxina*) is now declining, probably because of agricultural development.

Another third of the forest is the beech forests of northern Armenia. They are dominated by Oriental beech (*Fagus orientalis*). They are mostly on north-facing slopes at an altitude of 1,000–2,000m. Other species in beech forests include small-leaved lime (*Tilia cordata*), Litvinov beech (*Betula litwinow*) and spindle-tree (*Euonymus europaeus*). Hornbeam forests occur at altitudes of 800–1,800m. Other trees found in these forests include the various oaks, field maple, ash, Caucasian pear (*Pyrus caucasicum*) and Oriental apple (*Malus orientalis*). Scrub forests are found in both north and south of the country occurring at altitudes of 900–1,000m in the north, but at much higher altitude in the south (1,800–2,000m). These forests support around 80 species of xeric trees and shrubs, all of which are adapted to growing in an arid environment, and are drought tolerant and light-loving. As well as thorn forest dominated by juniper, broad-leaved forests also occur characterised by species such as Georgian maple, various cherries, pistachio (*Pistacia mutica*), almond (*Prunus dulcis*), buckthorn (*Rhamnus catharticus*) and wild jasmine (*Jasminum fruticans*).

THE PEOPLE

The long periods of foreign rule, often accompanied by religious persecution, have led to the Armenian people becoming widely scattered and not comprising a majority in any territory. What distinguished them as Armenians was their church and their language. During the 19th century this changed as a result of the Russian conquest of eastern Armenia. There was a deliberate Russian policy of encouraging Christian immigration and Muslim emigration. Although the Tsarist regime was initially tolerant of Christians who were not Orthodox believers this changed as a consequence of increasing Armenian nationalism as well as more general concerns about national feelings and socialism in the Russian empire. By the end of the century a policy of deliberate Russification of its subject people was being applied. The movement of population resulted, at the start of the Bolshevik regime, in the new Armenian Soviet Socialist Republic having an Armenian majority but with a significant Azeri minority. Similarly Azerbaijan had many Armenians within its boundaries, a number increased through the boundaries being deliberately gerrymandered. There was little Russian immigration to Armenia in either Tsarist or Soviet periods but the large population movements during the conflict with Azerbaijan between 1988 and 1994 resulted in massive emigration of Azeris and immigration of ethnic Armenians from Azerbaijan.

The population at the 1979 census was 3.8 million of whom 91% were ethnic Armenians. The census in February 1989 gave a population of 3.3 million but is regarded as unreliable since it took place only two months after the devastating earthquake in northwest Armenia which made obtaining data within the region almost impossible. The most recent census in October 2001 gave two figures for population: the number of people resident in Armenia at the time was 3 million but inclusion of family members who were temporarily resident abroad but had been in Armenia within the preceding 12 months boosted the population to 3.5 million. According to the head of the census bureau, the 3 million figure is comparable to the 3.8 million and suggests that a net 800,000 people have left the country since independence. At present about 96% of the population is ethnically Armenian, 2% Russian and the remainder mostly Yezidis and Kurds.

Life in Armenia

Life for ordinary Armenians is far from easy. Many, perhaps even most, people in what was in Soviet times a fairly heavily industrialised country have either reverted to subsistence agriculture if they live in rural areas or else have sought to become small-scale vendors of some kind of goods or other if they live in towns. For parents it is their hope that education will help their children to escape the widespread poverty. The population has fallen by around 25% since the 1980s as a result of emigration in search of work and the low birth rate. Yet it cannot really be said that Armenians look either despairing or unhappy. They cope with the problems and family members help each other out.

Perhaps the most conspicuous problem is that of water supply. Leaking mains mean that water supply in most towns and cities has to be restricted to a few hours a day to prevent large quantities running away to waste. Sometimes it can even be cut off for days. In rural areas water has either to be obtained from the village spring and carried in buckets, or else there might be a well in the garden (or even in the kitchen). In both urban and rural areas water has to be stored in quantity for use when needed.

Virtually every family except for those living in flats grows as much food as it can with all the family members, children included, working hard planting potatoes and other vegetables by hand and subsequently harvesting them, again by hand. In late summer women can be encountered in the villages winnowing grain, preserving fruit for the winter by drying it in the sun, and making fruit juices and home-made vodkas to last through the winter. Throughout the year they also join their neighbours in the baking of *lavash*, Armenia's classic flatbread. Keeping the home clean is difficult for women as few have domestic appliances. The level of dirt is increased by the wood-burning stoves which are very common and the seas of mud which almost engulf villages particularly in late winter at the time of snow-melt and which are aggravated by the numbers of livestock kept in the villages.

Very many families keep their own livestock and even in towns cattle and sheep can often be seen being tended by a family member. (Unlike western Europe even sheep have to be taken back to the house at night because of the danger from wolves.) In some areas free-range pigs wander freely through the village foraging for food. Armenians are very hard working, even more important now when so much work has to be done by hand because machinery, fertilisers, weedkillers and pesticides are all unaffordable. (This has the incidental benefit of making much Armenian food unofficially organic.) Even so, lack of suitable land results in Armenia being a net importer of food which results in a permanently adverse trade balance. For well-educated Armenians, life is not necessarily much easier. Salaries are low, there is serious underfunding of education and health, and career prospects are limited. Many such people seek work abroad, mostly in Russia.

The Christian faith is important to very many Armenians, their church binding them together as a community as it has for 1,700 years while simultaneously uniting them internationally with Christians elsewhere. It is the Armenian Christians of the diaspora who pay for most of the very necessary infrastructure investment in Armenia. Few countries are so heavily dependent on help from abroad. Yet despite all these difficulties, Armenians are generous to a fault. Desperately poor people welcome you into their homes and provide refreshments, often unintentionally embarrassing Western visitors who feel awkward about accepting from those who obviously have so much less. Especially in rural areas, people are fascinated by the few Westerners who appear and are genuinely touched that people from so far away could even have heard of Armenia let alone be interested enough to come. Having said that, pride in the country's history and language is intense with Armenians well aware of the artistic and spiritual achievement of their great monasteries and of the contributions made by many distinguished Armenians in history.

EDUCATION

The Soviet education system was successful in producing a well-educated population and a literacy rate of 100% was reported as early as 1960. In the Soviet period, Armenian education followed the standard Soviet programme with control from Moscow of curricula and teaching methods. After independence Armenia made changes to the Soviet system. Curricula were changed to emphasise

Armenian history and culture and Armenian became the dominant language of instruction. Russian was still widely taught, however, as a second language but throughout the system the formerly compulsory clutter – such as History of the Communist Party of the Soviet Union, Political Economy, Dialectical Materialism, Historical Materialism, Foundations of Marxist-Leninist Aesthetics and Foundations of Scientific Communism – was all dumped.

Children normally start school at the age of seven years but this was changed to six after independence. Following concern that six is too young, parents now have the option of sending their children to school at either six or seven. Schooling is normally for ten years. University courses last between five and seven years. Education has suffered severely from lack of funding since the end of the Soviet period, with the low salaries paid to teachers being a particular disincentive from entering this profession. A principal difficulty has been the developing gap between what is taught at school and the standard required in the entrance examination for Yerevan's universities which requires parents to fork out for private tuition to remedy the schools' deficiencies. Yet incredibly, so highly is education regarded, that since independence and despite the falling population, Yerevan's 12 state universities have been augmented by 25 private ones. Armenians who do not seek a university education are very much in a minority despite the cost to their parents. After paying the cost of private tuition prior to their children sitting the entrance examinations parents must then find between $250 and $900 annually in course fees as well as paying for their children's everyday needs. Even after graduation many graduates face considerable problems finding work relevant to their qualifications. The most highly regarded diplomas are issued by the State institutions – particularly those presented to students who scored high enough marks in the entrance examinations to receive free tuition. Competition for the free places is inevitably fierce and they only go to students with excellent marks – though corruption within the system means it is not unknown for less-talented students to buy free entry from unscrupulous academics.

RELIGION

Ethnic Armenians are overwhelmingly members of the Armenian Apostolic Church, whose head, the *Katholikos*, has his seat at Ejmiatsin. It is called Apostolic because Christianity is believed to have been brought to Armenia by Jesus's disciples Bartholomew and Thaddeus (or Lebbaeus as he is called in St Matthew's gospel). It is also sometimes called the Gregorian Church because it was founded in Armenia by St Gregory the Illuminator. All visitors to Armenia will visit several of the churches in which the layout and form of worship are quite different from that in the West. It is more similar to the Orthodox Church but even here there are some major differences in that Armenian churches do not have an iconostasis with its royal doors and, doctrinally, the Armenian Church has not adopted the views of the Council of Chalcedon in 451 about the duality of Christ's nature. (The Council of Chalcedon affirmed that Christ was both fully human and fully divine, having two natures in one being. The Armenian Church did not participate in the Council nor accept its formulation. It holds the view that the nature of Christ is beyond human understanding.) At one end of the church will be a raised altar dais called a *bema*. In active churches a curtain can be drawn across it during parts of the service (see below). A legacy of the Soviet period is that there is a shortage of priests and the economic plight of many people means that there is a shortage of money to pay priests anyway. Accordingly, many churches do not have regular worship and an individual priest might have to look after six churches.

When visiting any Armenian church it is normal on entry to buy candles and then light them (matches are provided), placing them upright in the trays of sand. The only exceptions to this rule are the new cathedral in Yerevan where candles are forbidden (there is a special place for them underneath the building) and members of large tour groups who do not always need to do so. Women do not need to wear headscarves unless taking communion. It is correct to leave a church walking backwards so as not to turn one's back on God. It is still common for an animal (and, more particularly, the salt with which the animal will be seasoned), always male and usually a ram or a cock, to be presented by a family for sacrifice. Sacrifice is usually carried out by the priest outside the church after the Sunday service. Firstly the priest blesses the animal and salt at a special stone called the *orhnakar* ('blessing stone') and then he sacrifices the animal at the *mataghatun* ('sacrifice house'). The animal will have been given in thanksgiving for some event such as recovery from a serious illness. It is partly a form of charity since some of the meat from the slaughtered animal will be given to the poor although the donor's family and friends will eat the rest, always boiled and never roasted or barbecued. The animals destined for slaughter are beautifully groomed before being offered to God in this way. Another frequent sight outside churches is a tree or shrub to which numerous scraps of cloth are tied. Each scrap is attached by a person making a private prayer.

Worship

Worship usually lasts for about two and a half hours, the service having been extended by additional prayers at various times over the centuries. Despite its length there are no seats except in some modern churches built using diaspora money. Worship is quite different from that in Western churches. Visitors need not attend the whole service except that at some churches (notably Sevan) the building is so crowded that it is difficult either to enter or to leave. (Geghard is a good option on a Sunday morning for those staying in Yerevan with access to transport.) Even for those with no knowledge of the Armenian language the beauty of the singing is deeply impressive.

The devout fast on Sunday morning before going to church. For the celebrant priest the liturgy begins in the vestry. He acknowledges his sinfulness and how privileged he is to be able to lead the people in worship. The deacon then hands him in turn the various items of the vestments and he puts them each on with a brief prayer. The priest and deacon now enter the nave but do not go immediately up to the *bema*. At first they remain among the congregation where the priest symbolically washes his hands and then asks the congregation to pray for his forgiveness. Once they are up on the *bema*, the curtain is drawn across it to avoid distracting the congregation with the preparations. After the elements have been prepared the curtain opens and the deacons lead the priest in a procession round the altar and down into the nave, walking round the whole church offering incense and inviting the faithful to kiss the cross which the priest carries.

After two hymns, one of which is sung every Sunday and the other of which varies, the deacon symbolically holds the gospel book over the priest's head and there is a further procession around the altar accompanied by another hymn. This is followed by readings from the Bible and more prayers. The main part of the service, the Liturgy of the Eucharist, starts with the priest removing his crown and slippers in obedience to God's command to Moses at the burning bush. The deacon processes around the altar holding the veiled chalice above his head. At the end of the procession the deacon hands the elements to the celebrant. The so-called kiss of peace which follows is a ritualised greeting everyone makes to their neighbours. A long sequence of prayers and hymns concludes with the curtain being again closed, this time for the priest to receive communion while hidden from view – it is traditional in all Eastern churches for the celebrant to receive communion out of sight of the congregation. Communion is now distributed: as communicants stand before the priest they make the sign of the cross and say 'I have sinned against God'. Thereupon the priest places a small part of the bread which has been dipped into the wine directly into the mouth of the communicant who again makes the sign of the cross. (The sign is made in the same way as in the Orthodox Church – right breast before left – but the opposite way from the Roman Catholic practice which is left breast before right.) This is followed by more prayers and hymns during part of which the curtain is closed while the priest and deacons reorganise the altar. The service ends with the congregation kissing the gospel book.

Church names
The great majority of Armenian churches are dedicated to a small number of people or events. Although this guidebook uses English names throughout visitors will often see an English transliteration of the Armenian name used on the spot. Apart from a few dedicated to Armenian saints, the common ones are:

Sourb Amenaprkich	Holy Redeemer
Sourb Astvatsatsin	Holy Mother of God
Sourb Asvatsnkal	Holy Wisdom of God
Sourb Arakelots	Holy Apostles
Sourb Grigor	St Gregory the Enlightener
Sourb Hakob	St Jacob
Sourb Haratyun	Holy Resurrection
Sourb Karapet	Holy Forerunner (ie: St John the Baptist)
Sourb Nshan	Holy Sign (of the Cross)

Marriage in Armenia
Traditional marriage in Armenia differs somewhat from that in many other European countries and in North America. Tourists are almost bound to see weddings, particularly on Saturdays, and might be interested to know more about what is happening.

The first point to note is that fewer young people than formerly are getting married, but not because they are simply living together as in many Western countries. In general Armenian couples do not do this. Young Armenian couples marry and then expect to have their first child a year or so after the wedding and the wife will stay at home to look after it. A young Armenian man will often not make a proposal of marriage unless he feels confident that he will be able to support his wife and child. In today's uncertain economic climate (after decades of Soviet predictability) many young men feel unsure that they will be able to support a family and hence stay single. Of course not every young man takes so thoughtful a line, believing perhaps that his family will help him (as they undoubtedly will), but a considerable number of potential bridegrooms understandably consider this aspect. The problem of housing also arises. Economic uncertainty means that young people are reluctant to borrow money to buy a house or flat and the alternative of living with the husband's parents may or may not be feasible. Armenia's marriage rate has fallen by 50% since Soviet days (there were 28,023 marriages registered in 1991 but only 12,459 in 1999) but the divorce rate by even more. Armenia now has the lowest fertility rate among member states of the Council of Europe.

A second point to note is that Armenians tend to have quite small families. A couple will generally only have further children if they believe that they can support them. This is similar to the view of many Western couples but economic uncertainty, or at least the perception of it, is greater in Armenia than in the West and this impacts on family size.

As traditionally happened in the West, if a man wishes to marry a woman he will go to her father to ask for her hand in marriage. A difference in Armenia is that he will usually be accompanied by his parents and possibly by other very close relatives such as his brother or sister. Unlike the West wedding ceremonies are not planned long in advance: rarely more than a month ahead and sometimes only a few days. On the wedding day the bride will be helped to get ready by her maid of honour (the equivalent of chief bridesmaid): this is always one of her unmarried sisters if she has any and a close friend only if she has no unmarried sister. It is never a married woman: the concept of a matron of honour doesn't exist in Armenia. The bridegroom's family provides and pays for the bride's dress: the bridegroom and the brother of the cross (the equivalent of best man) bringing it to her family's house on the day of the wedding. The bridegroom will normally also be accompanied by members of his family and friends (though not by his mother) and they, together with the bride's relatives and friends, eat and drink at the house while the bride is putting on her dress and being helped to get ready. Traditionally the bride would have worn a gown of red silk with a headpiece, often made of cardboard, shaped into wings and decorated with feathers. Nowadays she usually wears a long white dress similar in style to those worn throughout the West. The bridegroom often wears a suit, though in a rather more interesting colour than one bought for sober office wear. Relatives and friends including the bridesmaid tend to dress much as in the West although pale suits for all the prominent younger men are common.

Eventually the bride and bridegroom set off for the church together (no bridegroom waiting for the bride at the altar here!) accompanied by their relatives and friends except the bride's mother who stays at home and does not attend her daughter's wedding: for her to do so is considered to bring bad luck upon the couple. The bridegroom's mother does, however, attend the wedding. The couple may have either a church service or a civil ceremony or both. If they opt to have a church service but no civil ceremony their marriage is valid in the eyes of God although it is not recognised in Armenian law and the couple are in theory at least both free to remarry. Nevertheless many couples do in fact have only a church service: the subsequent rate of separation is in practice low. The wedding party enters the church with a large decorated basket containing wedding favours to be distributed to the guests: in the past these might have been small ceramic containers with almonds in them but many modern brides choose something much less traditional and there is a demand for such exotica as glass containers decorated with sea shells. During the service the officiating priest puts a ring on the finger of the bridegroom and then of the bride before joining their hands. The bridegroom then makes his vows followed in turn by the bride.

After the ceremony all present, though still without the bride's mother, traditionally go to the bridegroom's family house for the reception although nowadays a room in a hotel or restaurant is sometimes hired for the occasion. En route there is likely to be a motorcade with blaring horns and in Yerevan driving three times round Republic Square is an essential and audible part of the proceedings. On arrival at the reception the groomsmen and bridesmaids, holding their flowers aloft, form arches through which the young couple walk and two white doves are traditionally released to symbolise their love and happiness. There is more eating and drinking, this time at the expense of the bridegroom's family, accompanied by dancing in an amalgam of traditional Armenian and more modern styles. The food will almost certainly be the menu invariably eaten on all Armenian celebratory occasions: barbecued meat, most commonly pork but sometimes lamb or chicken, accompanied by salads and vegetables together with *lavash* (see page 68). There will be the inevitable toasts. Friends, neighbours, and indeed almost anyone passing drop in to wish the newly-weds well. The party goes on until everyone has had enough.

That isn't quite the end of marriage customs. On Trndaz or fire-jumping day, February 13, the priest blesses fire and then couples who have been married or become engaged within the previous year jump over it to get rid of the small devils hanging from the edge of their clothes. In some years Trndaz coincides with St Sargis' Day whose date is variable and fixed by the Church calendar. If a footprint appears in the bowl of flour left outside the house overnight then the young man of the house will marry in the coming year. Traditionally a cake called *gata*, rather like a large flat hot cross bun with an almond filling, is eaten and older people bake salt loaves for the young to eat and to make them dream of the person they will marry.

ARCHITECTURE
Church building
For some members of the diaspora, to experience Armenia's culture and language on its home territory will be their overriding memory of a visit to the country, but for the majority of visitors it is the historic buildings which will make the greatest impression, above all the monasteries but also to a lesser degree the secular medieval buildings such as fortresses and caravanserais. Only a very few buildings survive from the pre-Christian era: little more than the foundations can be observed of the cities of the kingdom of Urartu such as Erebuni. By far the best known pre-Christian building is the sole surviving example of Graeco-Roman architecture in Armenia, built at Garni some time in the first two centuries AD at a time when the country was an ally of Rome (see page 136). The Greek style was widely employed in contemporary Roman buildings throughout the empire and the survival of no other buildings in Armenia from this era is largely the consequence of Christians destroying pagan temples after the conversion of the country. Almost certainly others would have been constructed.

The early churches were often built on the site of pagan shrines employing the same foundations and hence they had the same dimensions as the temple which they replaced; moreover the Christian altar was usually placed directly over the previous pagan one as can be seen at Ejmiatsin. From the earliest times the churches were built in stone, most commonly the volcanic tuff which is easily carved and tends gradually to harden when exposed to the atmosphere. The need to build in stone was dictated by the unavailability of suitable timber, even for roofing, and the weight of the heavy vaulted stone roof in turn dictated the need for thick walls to support it with few windows. Where tuff was unavailable, most commonly in border areas, other volcanic rocks such as basalt or andesite were used.

From fairly early days almost all churches were built with a cupola supported by a cylindrical structure called a tambour. Tambours are usually circular in cross-section when viewed from the interior of the church but are often polygonal on the outside. The preference for churches to have a cupola supported by a tambour is one of Armenian architecture's most abiding features and makes its churches very distinctive. The style rapidly developed after the conversion to Christianity and continued until the Arab invasion and conquest in the mid-7th century. Thereafter no churches were built for over 200 years until the establishment of the Bagratid dynasty in the late 9th century. Under this regime new churches began to be built, initially copying the old style but gradually starting to develop this style to provide greater height and space. Once again church building ceased after foreign invasion, this time by the Seljuk Turks after the middle of the 11th century.

The establishment of Georgian independence together with the Armenian Zakarid dynasty in the late 12th century led to a renewal of church building and, in particular, to the development of the large monastic complexes with their multiple churches and ancillary buildings which are probably nowadays the most visited tourist sights in the country. Again the traditional style was used but the quest for greater space was now satisfied by building several churches on the same site rather than by increasing the size of each structure. Inevitably, construction ceased at the end of the 13th century after the Mongol invasions and the Armenian kingdom of Cilicia also ceased to exist in 1375 following the Mamluk invasions. No more churches were built until the 17th century when construction, still in the traditional style, restarted at a time when Armenia was ruled by the Safavid shahs of Iran. Church building increased in the 19th century as Armenian national consciousness grew, inevitably to come to a complete stop with the genocide of 1915 in western Armenia and the Bolshevik Revolution in the east. Independence has inevitably led to a resurgence in church building, largely with funds provided by the diaspora, with the traditional style generally retained but with extensive use of modern materials.

Church construction

Two overriding practical constraints influenced early church architects: the need to use stone for roofs because of the lack of suitable timber, and the need to withstand fairly frequent earthquakes. The necessary strength was provided by the use of an early type of concrete in a method probably copied from Roman architects. The earliest churches were built of massive stone blocks, with mortar separating them, forming the outer and inner surfaces of the walls; between them was a thin layer of concrete. This concrete was compounded of broken tuff and other stones, lime mortar, and eggs. During the 5th and 6th centuries the technique evolved, the slabs of the stone shell becoming thinner and cement core thicker. The method of construction was then to erect finely cut slabs of tuff or other stone a few rows at a time and without mortar to form the surfaces of the outer and inner walls after which concrete was poured into the cavity between them. This concrete adhered to the facing slabs and formed a solid strong core and it is this core, rather than the thin slabs of tuff which forms the building's major support. The slabs were varied in size and height to break up the vertical and horizontal rows and thus provide protection against parts of the concrete core falling out during earthquakes. Great thought was given to enhancing the artistic appearance of churches and different churches had the tuff slabs erected in different ways. In some churches the slabs were carved and either different colours of slab might be employed to provide a contrast or else a uniform colour might be used, sometimes with mortar applied between the slabs to give a completely uniform appearance. As the technique evolved the largest stone blocks gradually came to be reserved for the lowest courses of stonework as well as for corners and smaller ones were used elsewhere. Although windows were, from structural considerations, never a significant feature of Armenian church architecture, their size and number did tend to increase over time.

Styles of church

All the earliest known churches were either of basilica construction (ie: rectangular with an apse at the east end and with three aisles) or else a simpler version of this with a single aisle. Variations included having a covered porch, one or more rooms adjoining the apse, or corner rooms at both ends. A single roof covered all three aisles. Cupolas started to make their appearance in the 5th or 6th century and both single- and three-aisle churches were then built incorporating them. In single-aisle churches the cupola rested on massive piers which jutted out from the north and south walls but in three-aisle basilica churches four free-standing pillars were usual.

The incorporation of a cupola as a central feature caused changes to church layout and the basilica style gave way to a more centrally planned church built around the cupola, sometimes with four apses or else with four arms of equal length, or sometimes with three apses and one extended arm. This resulted in what was essentially a cross-shaped church but the addition of corner rooms between the arms of the cross resulted in many church buildings being more or less rectangular in plan when seen from the outside but with the church itself cross-shaped in plan when viewed from the inside. Churches with a cupola and four arms are often referred to as cross-dome churches although cross-cupola would perhaps be less misleading as most English speakers think of domes as being hemispherical. The ultimate exemplar of this centrally planned style, the church of St Hripsime at Ejmiatsin, is still further developed. Four semicircular apses are separated from each other by four circular niches each of which leads to a square corner room, all this being incorporated within the basic rectangular shape. Another variant of the centrally planned church was to make the entire building circular although relatively few of this type were constructed and the best known, the ruined 7th-century church at Zvartnots, isn't strictly circular but has 32 sides.

The basic style of Armenian church architecture has remained to this day the centrally planned church, built around its cupola and with two or more corner rooms. However, two later developments were the additions of a narthex or *gavit* as it is usually referred to in Armenia, and the building of a belltower. Both gavit and belltower came into being during the great upsurge in monastery building from the 10th century onwards. A gavit is a square room usually attached to the west end of the church and serving as a vestibule, a room for meetings, and a burial place for notables. Apart from the relatively few freestanding ones, gavits could also house the overflow when the congregation was too large for the main church. They were sometimes very large with massive walls and, like the other parts of the church, were frequently elaborately carved. Belltowers appeared at monastery complexes from the 13th century onwards and were often detached from the church building itself. The walls of later churches, both the exterior and the interior ones, sometimes incorporate *khachkars* (see page 35). There are also occasionally carvings of the donors, often holding a model of the church.

Inside Armenian churches there may or may not be carving but the most conspicuous feature is the altar dais or *bema* at the eastern end with steps leading up to it. The entire dais forms the altar and in an active church it can be shut off by a curtain though the curtain is never closed except during parts of services. Unlike the Orthodox Church there is never an iconostasis.

Secular medieval architecture

Two types of secular medieval building will attract the attention of visitors: castles and caravanserais. Unlike the churches, neither are distinctively Armenian. Essentially Armenia's castles were situated and built according to the general thinking in castle design of the day and followed the same principles as applied throughout Europe. Caravanserais were built along the main east–west trade routes to provide secure lodging for merchants and their pack animals. They are generally rectangular and sometimes surprisingly large, reflecting just how important this trade was. Only a single, fairly small, door was provided so that the caravanserai would be easily defensible against robbers. Inside there were rows of stalls with feeding troughs for animals and booths for the merchants.

THE ARTS
Khachkars

Khachkars, carved memorial stones, are an important, conspicuous and beautiful feature of Armenian decorative art. The word khachkar literally means cross-stone. In quiet streets in central Yerevan it is possible to see even today the stonecarvers at work, using traditional methods to create these endlessly varied monuments in a revival of this ancient tradition. The earliest khachkars date from the 9th and 10th centuries, a period when Armenia had gained effective independence from the Arab caliphate and separate Armenian kings each ruled their individual states. This flowering of Armenian craftsmanship under independence was paralleled in architecture: some of Armenia's finest monasteries date from this period.

The earliest datable khachkar is one erected at Garni by Queen Katranide, wife of King Ashot Bagratuni I, in 879 in mediation for her person. Securing the salvation of the soul was the most common reason for erecting khachkars but some were put up to commemorate military victories or the completion of churches, bridges, fountains and other constructions. Even unrequited love might be commemorated this way. The dominant feature of the design is generally a cross, occasionally a crucifix, resting on a rosette or sun disc design. The remainder is covered with complex patterns of leaves, bunches of grapes or abstract geometrical patterns. Occasionally the whole was surmounted by a cornice showing biblical characters or saints. The absolute peak of khachkar design was probably between the 12th and 14th centuries. Amazingly elaborate and delicate patterns were created using the same elements of design. Depiction of the crucifixion and resurrection become more common and at this time some khachkars came to be erected as a spiritual protection against natural disasters. The supreme masterpieces are probably that by Timot and Mkhitar in the porch of Geghard monastery which dates from 1213, the Holy Redeemer khachkar at Haghpat monastery which was created by Vahram in 1273, and that at Goshavank created by Poghos in 1291. Some good examples have been transported to the Historical Museum in Yerevan and the cathedral at Ejmiatsin. There can, however, be no substitute for seeing them where they were originally erected.

The Mongol invasion at the end of the 14th century led to a decline of the tradition and although there was a revival in the 16th and 17th centuries, the artistic heights of the 14th were never regained

Some khachkars, often recording donations, are embedded in the walls of monasteries but the majority are free-standing. Armenia has over 40,000 surviving khachkars. An amazing sight is the so-called field of khachkars at Noratus, the largest of several groupings of khachkars in Armenia. This is an old graveyard with 900 khachkars marking graves and the endless variations of design make a visit there particularly rewarding. Noratus is especially interesting because examples there span the whole period from the 10th to the 17th century.

Illuminated manuscripts

If khachkars are the symbol of Armenia, the painting of illuminated manuscripts is undoubtedly Armenia's other great contribution to the world of art. The beauty and skill represented in the many surviving examples is rarely equalled and never surpassed in other cultures. Extensive sets of pictures were used to illustrate manuscripts of the books of the Bible and obviously books such as Genesis or Exodus, where there is plenty of physical action, lent themselves particularly to this art form with some manuscripts having up to 750 illustrations. The most elaborate manuscripts tended to be those of the four gospels which were frequently bound with sumptuous covers of ivory or metalwork. A characteristic feature of these copies of the gospels is the set of canon tables which were designed to show which passages of the individual gospels were in agreement with any of the other three. They were arranged with columns of figures under decorative arches, often highly elaborated and usually accompanied by the scenes or symbols of the evangelists. Before the gospel itself there is a picture of the evangelists, again within an architectural structure and also with a writing desk, lectern and writing implements.

The purpose of these books was as an aid to worship. They were made to be displayed on the altar as well as to be used by the priest reading to the congregation. A very few examples survive which pre-date the Arab conquest in 640. The subsequent repression of Christianity by the Muslims led to the suspension of artistic activity until after the end of Arab occupation in the 9th century. From then the art flourished. The importance of manuscripts to the Armenian Church is comparable to that afforded to icons by the Orthodox Church. The large number which have survived testifies to how valuable they were considered to be and how closely they were guarded in times of war. Manuscripts, particularly those believed to be endowed with miraculous powers, were given special names such as *Saviour of All* or *Resurrector of the Dead*. The manuscripts were also thought of as pledges for the salvation of the donors, as treasures in heaven, and they are therefore rarely anonymous productions. The names of the sponsor and the creators are carefully recorded so that they might be recalled by those who used the manuscripts. Given the importance of manuscripts and their beauty it is unfortunate that the only place in Armenia where manuscripts can readily be seen is the Matenadaran (Manuscript library) in Yerevan where a handful are on display in the small exhibition room.

Music

Both traditional folk music and classical music have fallen on hard times since 1991 with the reductions in state funding. Folk music can now most often be heard on national holidays but a more convenient possibility is to go to one of the Yerevan restaurants where a folk ensemble plays each evening. At the time of writing the ensemble at Our Village comprises a singer together with players of the *oud, kemenche, duduk* and *dhol* while Caucasus has a singer together with players of the *oud, tarr, shvi, duduk* and *dhol*. The *oud* is a 12-stringed (two strings for each note) ancestor of the lute and guitar with a distinctive bent neck. The *tarr* is another lute-like instrument but smaller than the *oud*. The *kemenche* is a three-stringed violin played with the instrument held vertically resting on the lap. The *duduk* makes the sound most often associated with Armenian music. It is a low-pitched woodwind instrument, with a large double reed, made from apricot wood. The *shvi* ('whistle') by contrast is a high-pitched woodwind instrument without a reed and with eight holes, seven for playing and a thumb hole. The *dhol* is a cylindrical drum with one membrane being thicker to give a low pitch and the other thinner to give a higher pitch. Other distinctive instruments which may be encountered include: the *zurna*, a higher-pitched wind instrument than the *duduk* but also with a double reed and made from apricot wood; the *kanun*, a plucked box zither, trapeziform in shape, which is played resting on the player's knee or on a table, the strings being plucked by plectra attached to the fingers; and the *dumbeg* which is an hourglass-shaped drum with a membrane made of lambskin at only one end, the other end being open.

It was the Russian conquest in the 19th century which brought Western classical music to Armenia and the fusion of the folk-inspired Russian nationalistic composers such as Rimski-Korsakov and Borodin with the existing Armenian traditional music was to result in a distinctively Armenian style. Full of bright colours and rhythms it is vigorous rather than cerebral, music of the heart rather than the head. The best-known Armenian composer outside the country is undoubtedly Aram Khachaturian (1903–78), though broadcasters frequently and incorrectly refer to him as Russian. In particular his violin and piano concertos are regularly encountered in concert and the ballets *Spartacus* and *Gayaneh* have often been staged outside Armenia. Most people would probably recognise the 'Sabre Dance' from *Gayaneh*. Armenian opera has made little impact abroad but there have been recent American stagings of *Arshak II* by Tigran Chukhadjian, first heard (incomplete) in Italian at Constantinople in 1868, and *Anoush* by Armen Tigranian which was first performed at Alexandropol (present-day Gyumri) in 1912. To make these acceptable to Stalinist censors both had to have their plots changed during Soviet times: the alterations required to *Arshak II* in 1945 at the end of the Great Patriotic War included changing the character of Arshak from that of a tyrannical leader to that of a virtuous and unselfish one, and changing the composer's tragic ending into a hymn of rejoicing, presumably in the hope that the audience would identify Stalin with the now virtuous, unselfish and victorious Arshak. *Arshak II* is considerably influenced by Verdi but *Anoush* aims at a fusion of classical Western music with distinctive Armenian melody and harmony. In Yerevan the Armenian Philharmonic Orchestra gives regular concerts and opera and ballet are staged throughout the winter in the Opera and Ballet Theatre.

Another distinctive Armenian form is that of liturgical music. It is sung without instrumental accompaniment and is based on a so-called Phrygian scale rather than the major and minor scales familiar in Western music. The number of surviving compositions is considerable: more than 1,000 from the Middle Ages survive on parchment and the range is diverse, sometimes quick and sprightly, sometimes solemn, sometimes dramatic. Only later did composers start to write polyphonically. The best-known composer of more recent times is Komitas (1869–1935) who wrote many wonderful chants as well as other compositions in traditional Armenian style. To listen to this beautiful music in any of Armenia's churches on a Sunday morning is an experience which every visitor should seek out.

Dance

Dance in Armenia can broadly be divided into traditional dance and classical ballet, the latter considerably influenced by the Russian school. The traditional dances which are encountered in Armenia today are those of eastern Armenia and as such differ in some respects from the dances of Armenian groups abroad which usually represent the western Armenian tradition. The energetic men's dance *Jo Jon* (also called *Zhora Bar*) comes from Spitak province. *Mom Bar*, meaning *Candle Dance*, was originally from the Lake Sevan region and is now traditionally the last dance at wedding parties. The candles are blown out at the end of the dance signalling that it is time for guests to leave. Women's solo dances called *Naz Bar*, meaning *Grace Dance*, are improvisatory with intricate hand gestures used to tell stories of love, betrayal, conflict and triumph. In Yerevan, in particular, choreographic schools and song and dance ensembles preserve the tradition in a form suitable for stage presentation, although funding is more difficult than in the Soviet era.

The musical accompaniment can be played on traditional instruments or sung (or both). Costumes for women are invariably sumptuous, whether based on medieval court dress or on simpler peasant dress. Brightly coloured shimmering dresses are decorated with gold embroidery and pearls. A light lace veil surmounts the embroidered hat. For men costume is simpler. Full trousers and embroidered tunics or else the *cherkessa*, traditional Caucasian dress similar to Cossack style, with red, white or black silk trousers, leather boots, woollen or fur hat, and a dagger in the belt. Men's dances are martial and vigorous; women's are graceful with elaborate gestures.

Funding is also more difficult for classical ballet, performed at the Spendiarian Opera and Ballet Theatre. The standard of dance remains high but numbers of Armenian dancers are making successful careers in western Europe and North America and the pool of talent remaining in Yerevan is diminished.

Drama

Greek drama was popular in Armenia and several amphitheatres were built during the Hellenistic age including one at Tigranakert, the new capital which Tigran II built. When Romans sacked the city in 69BC the actors were killed during the celebration games which followed. After the conversion of Armenia to Christianity in the 4th century drama was suppressed by the church and there is no record of any Armenian theatre until the 18th century when plays were put on by the Armenian community in Venice. The first recorded performance of a play in Armenia proper since the 4th century is often said to have been of Alexander Griboyedov's *Woe from Wit* in 1827 at the palace of the Yerevan Fortress with members of the Imperial Russian Army as the cast. That seems highly unlikely as this scathing satire on corruption, ignorance and bribery in Tsarist society was banned during the author's lifetime and not staged until 1831.

The first regular theatre in Yerevan opened in 1865 and in that year Gabriel Sundukian (1825–1912) published *Khatabala* which may be said to represent the foundation of a realistic Armenian drama. Theatres were established in several Armenian communities both in Armenia and among the diaspora in cities such as Teheran and Tbilisi but those in Ottoman-controlled areas were repressed after anti-Armenian action started in earnest in 1894. During the Soviet period drama blossomed with a healthy diet of Armenian and Russian works as well as Armenian translations of foreign classics, particularly Shakespeare who translates very well into Armenian. Since 1991, as with all the arts, the curtailment of government subsidies has led to considerable retrenchment although several theatres survive at Yerevan and Gyumri.

Literature

Written Armenian literature could clearly not develop until the creation of the alphabet by Mesrop Mashtots in the early 5th century and any early pagan oral tradition would almost certainly have been suppressed after the conversion to Christianity. Apart from the Bible, other theological works were soon translated from both Greek and Syriac after the creation of the alphabet. Some of Mesrop Mashtots' pupils also wrote original works: Eznik wrote a treatise on the origins of evil and the subject of free will called *Refutation of the Sects* while Koriun wrote a biography of Mashtots in about 443. The *Epic Histories* were written in the 470s by an anonymous cleric and give an account of Armenian history between about 330 and 387 bringing together traditional stories about kings from Khosrov III to Arsaces II and patriarchs. The author sought to draw parallels between historic and contemporary events and, when he wrote about a dying ruler urging his son to die bravely for their Christian country since by doing so he would be dying in the service of God and the church, it was undoubtedly meant to apply to his readers.

This tradition of martial resistance and martyrdom was continued in the *History* written by Lazarus of Parp, abbot of the monastery of Vagharshapat (now Ejmiatsin), which continues the story after 387, when the *Epic Histories* break off, as far as 485. In describing the events of 451, the author describes the Armenians finding the Persians unprepared at Avarayr and then holding off since they wanted martyrdom more than victory. He wrote that the face of one martyr was illuminated before his death as a sign of his imminent transformation into an angel. Widows of martyrs and women whose husbands were imprisoned by the enemy are considered to be living martyrs.

From the late 5th century onwards, translations from the Greek were made of secular works including the writings of philosophers such as Aristotle and Plato and of the medical writers Hippocrates and Galen. Meanwhile the writers of histories continued to stress martyrdom. In the *History* by Yeghishe, probably written in the late 6th century, the account of the revolt in 451 goes even further than had Lazarus of Parp in emphasising martyrdom and justifying armed resistance as well as giving the clergy a leading role. The Armenians are depicted as treating Persian promises of religious freedom as deceitful.

The period after the Arab conquest was a low point for Armenia generally and it was the 10th century before a literary revival took place. Competition between monasteries for endowments led to an interesting forgery. The *History of Taron* (Taron is the area north of Lake Van) was written some time between 966 and 988 but claims to have been started in the 4th century by Zenob of Glak, the first bishop of Taron, and then continued by John Mamikonian, the 35th bishop of Taron, in the 7th century. The book states that Glak was Gregory the Enlightener's first foundation, earlier even than Ejmiatsin, while the truth was that Glak was a new foundation in the 10th century. The supposed history includes a completely bogus story of Glak's possession of miracle-working relics of John the Baptist which had produced divine intervention in war. The purpose of all this monastic skulduggery was twofold. Firstly it was an attempt to show that Glak, being Armenia's oldest monastery, was worthiest of endowment, more so even than Ejmiatsin and Dvin. Secondly, and even more explicitly, in the book some ascetics pray that anyone who makes generous gifts to the monastery from their 'sinful' wealth should be delivered from tribulation; they are answered by a voice from heaven which assents. Rather more prosaic is the description of the cutting off of enemy noses: 24,000 on one occasion.

The 10th century produced several rather more reliable histories while the *Book of Lamentations* by Gregory of Narek (c950–1010), a long poem comprising prayers about the wretchedness of the soul, the sinfulness of mankind, and the certainty of salvation remains a classic of Armenian literature. It is the earliest written work still widely read and was completed in 1002. Its author is usually considered to be Armenia's greatest poet and has been translated into 30 languages. Armenia's national epic, *David of Sassoun*, also dates from the 10th century although it was not committed to print until 1873. It recounts the story of David's family over four generations with Sassoun, its setting, symbolising Armenia. David in particular embodied a symbol of the Armenians who fought foreign oppression in the 7th and 8th centuries.

Nerses Shnorhali ('Nerses the Gracious', 1100–73) was a great lyrical poet, musician, theologian and philosopher who became Katholikos Nerses IV in 1166. His greatest poem *Lament on the Fall of Edessa* (present-day Urfa in Turkey) records the capture of that city in 1144 by the Turks who slaughtered most of its inhabitants together with the archbishop. Nerses is also the author of several hymns still used in the Armenian communion service.

By the late 13th century poems on love and other secular themes began to appear and grow as an important force in Armenian literature. The greatest of these poets, Constantine of Erznka, wrote poetry on springtime, love, beauty and light, allegorically exalting the Christian mysteries. Constantine broadened the scope of Armenian poetry, moving away from religious terminology towards the imagery of the natural world. This was taken even further until in the 15th and 16th centuries pure love poetry came to Armenia. Its first great exponent was Nahapet Kuchak, who is thought to have lived near Lake Van in the 16th century but may have lived earlier and elsewhere. His poems have deep, often erotic, emotional passion, stunning imagery and wit and are as vividly alive today as when they were written. Sayat Nova (1712–95) was perhaps the culmination of this tradition. Poet and composer in Georgian and Persian as well as Armenian he wrote of courtly love and the beauty of his unattainable beloved.

The development of the novel throughout the Western world in the late 18th century inevitably impacted upon Armenia. The first great Armenian novelist was Khatchatur Abovian (1805–48). He was the first author to abandon the classical Armenian language and use modern spoken Armenian for his works. His most famous novel is *Armenia's Wounds*, set during the Russian conquest of Armenia from Persia in 1826–28 and dealing with Armenian people's suffering under foreign domination. Abovian was also a noted translator of Homer and Schiller. Further impetus to the quest for Armenian identity was given in the novels of the other great 19th-century Armenian novelist, Raffi (pen name of Hakop Melik-Hakopian, 1835–88). The grandeur of Armenia's historic past was recalled in novels such as *The Madman* (1881), *Samvel* (1886) and *The Spark* (1887).

The writings of Hovhannes Tumanian (1869–1923) encompass fables and epic poetry. An admirer of Shakespeare and translator of Byron, Goethe and Pushkin it is regrettable that his work is not better known outside Armenia. He wrote patriotic verse with titles such as *In the Armenian Mountains*, *Armenian Grief* and *With My Fatherland* but also legends such as *A Drop of Honey* in which the eponymous drop is the cause of a war. The work, based on a medieval legend, concludes with the few terrified survivors asking themselves what caused the worldwide conflagration. Tumanian moralised without preaching, notably in works such as *My Friend Nesso*, a story about how the most handsome boy in the village turns into an evil, dishonest man and ends up living out a deprived life at the bottom of society. Similarly, *The Capture of Fort Temuk* traces the criminal path which leads from simple ambition to treason. Most Armenians consider that Tumanian's masterpiece is *Anoush*, a tragic story of village life in which Anoush's brother kills her lover for breaking a village taboo. The work is much more than a simple story, the author expressing his philosophy of life, his ideas about the existence of man and the world of human passions. His ardently expressed love for Armenia led to his being tried in 1908 for anti-Tsarist activities and he was later very active in seeking to help victims of the genocide.

Tumanian appears on the AMD5,000 banknote while the figure on the AMD1,000 note is the poet Eghishe Charents (1897–1937). Born in Van, then under Turkish rule, he was involved in anti-Turkish activity as part of the Armenian self-defence corps as early as 1912. His early work reflects this in pieces such as *Three Songs to a Pale Girl* (1914) and *Blue-Eyed Homeland* (1915). In 1915 he moved to Moscow to continue his education at the university thereby witnessing the Bolshevik Revolution and becoming greatly influenced by its ideology. In 1918 he joined the Red Army. Returning to Yerevan an enthusiastic

Previous page Priests, Ejmiatsin Cathedral precinct (MS)

Above St Hripsime Church, Ejmiatsin

Below left Parish priest, Bjni

Below right Khachkar, Tatev Monastery

supporter of communism in 1919, at this stage of his life his writings covered topics such as civil war in Russia and Armenia, world communism, famine, poverty, World War I and the Bolshevik Revolution. From the mid-1920s there is a gradual change in his work as he became disillusioned with communist rule and increasingly nationalistic. His satirical novel *Land of Nairi* (1925) starts to reflect this but his last published collection of poems, *Book of the Road*, published in 1933 was to make him notorious. One poem called *The Message*, ostensibly in fulsome praise of the genius of Stalin, contains a second message hidden in the second letter of each line: *Oh! Armenian people, your salvation lies only in your collective power*. Inevitably deemed nationalistic by the Soviet authorities he was arrested shortly afterwards by the NKVD (forerunner of the KGB). He died in prison, an early victim among the tens of millions killed at Stalin's behest although it was claimed by the Soviet authorities that he had committed suicide while on hunger strike. All his works were banned until his rehabilitation in 1954, the year after Stalin's death.

Later Armenian writers could inevitably have no personal experience of a pre-Soviet world or even of the genocide. Hovhannes Garabedian (1915–84) however came much closer than most since his mother was widowed by the genocide shortly before his birth. Growing up in considerable poverty, he attracted attention when his first work *Beginning of Spring* was published in 1935. He acquired the name Hovhannes Shiraz because one writer commented that his 'poems have the fragrance of roses, fresh and covered with dew, like the roses of Shiraz' (Shiraz is a town in Iran). His many works include parables and translations as well as a great deal of poetry and is immortalised for Armenians by such lines as: 'Let all nations reach the moon, but Armenians reach Ararat'. A critic of Armenia's corrupt Soviet government, his protests included publically urinating one evening on the statue of Lenin in Yerevan.

Gevorg Emin was born in 1919, slightly later than Shiraz. Qualifying as a hydraulic engineer in 1940, his knowledge of the technological world of dams, pipelines and power stations is reflected in the concrete images and complex relationships between people and technology which he employs metaphorically. Subtle and witty, his work was translated into Russian by Boris Pasternak. A more establishment figure than Shiraz, his book *Land, Love, Era* was awarded the Soviet State Prize for Literature in 1976.

Paruyr Sevak (1924–71) was another staunch critic of the corrupt Soviet government to the extent that most Armenians believed that his death was murder at the hands of the KGB rather than the result of a road accident – and certainly the spot where the alleged accident took place is a straight, unobstructed section of road with little traffic. The tenor of his writings is conveyed in titles such as *The Unsilenceable Belfy* (1959) and *Let there be Light* (1971).

Not all Armenian writers spoke Armenian as their native language. The novelist Gosdan Zarian (1885–1969) was the son of a staunchly Armenian father who was a general in the Tsarist army and he was brought up speaking Russian and French but not Armenian. His youth was spent in various Western countries where he frequently ate with Lenin in Geneva and knew Picasso in Paris. He only started to learn Armenian in 1910, studying with the Mekhitarists on the island of San Lazarro in Venice. He moved to Constantinople in 1913 and two years later was one of the few Armenian intellectuals who managed to escape the genocide, in his case by fleeing via Bulgaria to Rome. He returned to Istanbul in 1920 and in 1922 moved to Yerevan. Thoroughly disappointed with the Soviet regime, he left in 1925 and spent a nomadic existence including spells in the USA and Lebanon before returning to Armenia in 1961. His poem *The Bride of Tetrachoma*, first published in Boston in 1930, was republished in Yerevan in 1965 while a bowdlerized edition of his novel *The Ship on the Mountain*, first published in Boston in 1943, appeared in Yerevan in 1963.

Probably the best-known Armenian writer outside Armenia is William Saroyan (1908–81). Born to Armenian parents at Fresno, California, he sprang to fame in 1934 with his first book *The Daring Young Man on the Flying Trapeze*. His first successful Broadway play *My Heart's in the Highlands* was first performed in 1939. He was awarded both the Drama Critic's Circle Award and the Pulitzer Prize for *The Time of Your Life* (1939) but he refused to accept the latter since he believed that 'Commerce should not patronize art'. A prolific writer, Saroyan acknowledged Armenian culture as an important source of his literary inspiration and his work gave international recognition to Armenia. A year after his death, half of his cremated remains were interred in the Pantheon of Greats in Yerevan, Armenia, while the other half remained in Fresno, California.

Painting

Russian expansionism into Armenia and its subsequent greater contact with western European painting greatly influenced the development of Armenian realistic painting in the 19th century. The first notable painter to break away from the medieval manuscript tradition was Hakop Hovnatanian (1806–81) whose family had been painters for nearly 200 years. (His grandfather's grandfather had contributed to the decoration of Echmiatsin cathedral in the late 17th century.) He painted portraits of his contemporaries in an original manner which fused elements of the painting of illuminated manuscripts with European traditions of portaiture: everything in these portraits is expressed through the face, above all the eyes, and the hands of the conventionally posed sitter.

By contrast Hovhannes Aivazovsky (1817–1900), often referred to as Ivan Aivazovsky – its Russian equivalent – shows little Armenian influence. He was born to an Armenian father at Feodosia in the Crimea and painted wonderful seascapes, either calm seas with beautiful lighting effects, violent storms sometimes with men struggling to survive (over half his seascapes), or surprisingly vivid pictures of the historic sea battles of the Russian navy. Though with few equals in his ability to capture the many moods and colours of the sea, his non-marine pictures are decidedly more pedestrian. His achievements were probably more recognised internationally than is the case with any other 19th-century Armenian painter and he was even awarded the Légion d'Honneur in 1857.

Another recipient of the Légion d'Honneur was Zakar Zakarian (1849–1923) who left his home in Constantinople to train as a doctor in Paris but who later turned to painting. His still lifes with their careful composition and interplay of light and dark frequently incorporate a glass of water, interpreted by his contemporaries as expressing his feeling from his Paris home of the tragic events in his homeland. Gevork Bashinjaghian (1857–1920) developed the painting of landscapes with his calm, serene views, mostly of Armenia although he also travelled. Vardghez Sureniants (1860–1921) was a much more versatile artist. Like Bashinjaghian a painter of landscapes, he also painted many Armenian subjects and his 1895 painting *Desecrated Shrine* was a response to the massacres of Armenians by Turks. He additionally painted historical subjects; he was a gifted book illustrator and in 1899 was chosen to illustrate Pushkin's *Fountain of Bakhchisarai* as part of the centenary celebrations; and as a stage designer he was chosen by Konstantin Stanislavsky in 1904 to design his Moscow production of Maurice Maeterlinck's symbolist drama *Les Aveugles* (*The Blind*).

The landscapes of Eghishe Tatevosian (1870–1936) reflect the strong influence of French painters as well as of his teachers in Moscow and the French influence is even stronger in the works of Edgar Shaheen (1874–1947) who studied in Paris. Vano Khodjabekian (1875–1922) was a complete contrast: a primitivist who on his arrival in Yerevan in 1919 created some moving scenes of the plight of the refugees who had escaped the Turkish massacres. Hovsep Pooshman (1877–1966) was another painter of still lifes, mostly incorporating oriental statuettes and with titles such as *The Golden Decline of Life* and *The Murmur of Leaves*.

Probably the most brilliant and certainly the most influential Armenian artist of the early 20th century was Martiros Sarian (1880–1972) whose works mirror the creative intellectual ferment in the artistic world of the day and show an amazing feel for colour and form. He was born near Rostov-on-Don, Russia and studied in Moscow. His first visit to Armenia in 1901 resulted in the cycle *Stories and Dreams* which shows much symbolist influence. From 1909 he turned towards a more representational style using large areas of single colour with great attention to shapes and contrasts and the qualities of light. Another artist working through the revolutionary period was Hakop Kojoyan (1883–1959). He produced haunting landscapes as well as works which take a stylised medieval approach and book illustrations for authors such as Gorki. His *Execution of Communists at Tatev*, however, seems likely to have been painted for political reasons.

The Soviet period saw those Armenian painters who remained in the country and were approved by the regime supported while others were harassed regardless of their talent. Gyorgy Yakulov (1884–1928) worked as a stage designer in Tiflis and Yerevan before being invited to Paris by Diaghilev where his work had immense success. He travelled in both China and Italy and his paintings reflect an attempt to combine traditional orientalism with the Italian High Renaissance. Sedrak Arakelian (1884–1942) was a follower of Sarian whose own lyrical landscapes successfully capture ephemeral moments in the Armenian countryside. Another follower, Arutiun Galents (1908–67), was one of the children who escaped the genocide of 1915. His parents both died and he was brought up in an orphanage in Beirut. Not surprisingly his work reflects the tragic circumstances of his childhood. Minas Avetissian (1928–75) is regarded particularly highly in Armenia. Again a follower of Sarian, much of his work was destroyed either in a fire at his studio in 1972 or in the 1988 earthquake which destroyed both his frescos at Leninakan (present-day Giumri) and the museum dedicated to his work at Dzhadzur, his native village. He himself was tragically killed when he was knocked down by a car which had mounted the pavement. A complete contrast to these followers of Sarian is Alexander Bazhbeuk-Melikian (1891–1966) who can be regarded more as a follower of Degas. He painted women. In warm clear colours, whether exercising on a swing or combing their hair, they are elegant and at ease.

Ervand Kochar (1899–1979) was a sculptor and designer as much as a painter and his best-known work in Armenia is perhaps the striking statue of David of Sassoun on horseback which stands outside Yerevan railway station while the work most noticed by visitors may be the statue of Haik Bzhshkian, also on horseback, which stands by the road to Garni (see page 102). The three-dimensional quality of his paintings tends to express his interest in sculpture. Petros Konturajian (1905–56) was another child who was orphaned by the genocide of 1915. He went to Paris and became a successful painter of the city under the influence of Cézanne and the Cubists. In 1947 he returned to Armenia but he failed to come to terms with Soviet conditions and committed suicide. Hakop Hakopian (1928–75) also moved to live in Armenia at a similar age to Konturajian but was able to adapt, perhaps because life under Brezhnev was less intolerable than under Stalin. His still lifes and landscapes have a dramatic quality expressing deep anxiety. Girair Orakian (1901–63), is another painter who was driven from his home city of Constantinople He spent most of the rest of his life in Rome. His paintings expressing the struggles between life and death of the poor can again be understood against his childhood background.

If Ivan Aivazovsky is Armenia's best-known 19th-century painter outside the country, the best-known 20th-century one is probably Garnik Zulumian, also known as Carzou (1907–2000) He worked as a stage designer as well as a painter and engraver and his paintings often reflect a decorative and theatrical quality. Claiming that Picasso was no painter at all, he claimed the only truly great painters were Claude Lorrain, Watteau and Dali. Carzou's response to the Armenian earthquake of 1988 was the painting *Armenia: Earthquake. Hope*, in which a naked woman is shown standing over ruins against a background of Armenian buildings and mountains.

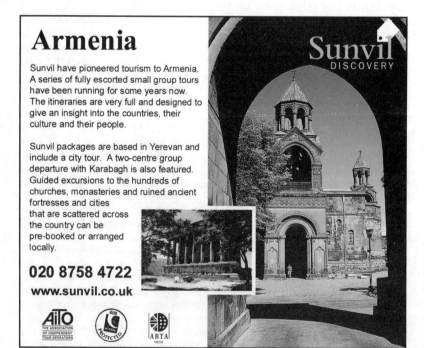

Practical Information

WHEN TO VISIT

Winter in Armenia can be bitterly cold and should be avoided by visitors if at all possible. Also, many of the sights are inaccessible because of snow. That apart, the timing of any visit has to be a compromise because of the altitudinal variation in the weather. The best times to go are generally late May and June or else late September and October. The former sees the flowers at their very considerable best and is the nesting season for birds. The latter is drier but of course there are few flowers and much of the country is parched and brown. These periods of late spring and late summer are also when visibility is better with frequent views of Mount Ararat. It is usually invisible in summer because of heat haze.

PUBLIC HOLIDAYS

New Year's Day	January 1
Christmas Day	January 6
Army Day	January 28
International Women's Day	March 8
Good Friday	
Day of Motherhood and Beauty	April 7
Genocide Memorial Day	April 24
Victory and Peace Day	May 9
First Republic Day	May 28
Constitution Day	July 5
Independence Day	September 21
Earthquake Memorial Day	December 7
New Year's Eve	December 31

Vardevar

Although not a public holiday, the Vardevar festival, held on a Saturday in July, is a date for which visitors should be well prepared. The precise date is fixed according to the lunar calendar and varies from year to year. As well as church services, the festival involves children collecting water, stalking passers-by, and then throwing it over them. That the more water-affluent children will have managed to stockpile many buckets worth means that nobody that day should wear smart clothes or indeed any clothes which might be damaged by water. Inevitably Vardevar is therefore a risky day to get married. It is also most unwise, despite the temperature in July, to drive around with car windows open unless certain that no children are lurking out of sight behind a tree or wall. Adults can and do retaliate against the water throwers, for example by using their own stockpiled supplies to effect revenge on the miscreants below by aiming at them from the safety of the balconies of their apartments. Armenia is not the only country to have such a festival – Thailand and Myanmar (Burma) for example both have similar festivals to celebrate the Buddhist new year. It is likely that their common origin lies in some pagan worship of water spirits, probably involving a cleansing ritual not dissimilar to that involved symbolically in Christian baptism.

OPENING TIMES

In town centres most shops open around 09.30 and remain open until around 19.00. Some shops, especially food shops and markets, are open daily but specialist shops such as bookshops may be closed on Sunday. Small shops and kiosks in residential areas are open for very long hours – often until after midnight – while some roadside stalls remain open for 24 hours.

HIGHLIGHTS

I am particularly fond of medieval buildings such as monasteries or fortresses in spectacular scenic settings and having a pleasant walk to get there adds to the enjoyment. Despite its accessibility by a good road and despite the number of tourists who go there, Noravank with its splendid setting and wonderful carvings is a must-see. Khor Virap is worthwhile if the visibility is good for giving the best views of Ararat. Other fine sites accessible to tourist buses are the monasteries of Haghpat, Haghartsin, Amberd (together with its adjacent castle) and Tatev and the prehistoric stones at Karahunj. The monastery of Marmashen is also worth seeing for those with a car.

However, my favourites are the wonderful carvings at Makaravank (which is accessible by car), the fortress of Smbataberd on its ridge (which makes a fine walk combining it with Tsakhats Kar monastery), the field of khachkars at Noratus (accessible by car), Selim caravanserai (4WD required), Khuchap and Khorakert monasteries (4WD), Spitakavor monastery (best to walk up the gorge), Kobayr monastery (short uphill walk), Hnevank (short walk), the petroglyphs on Mount Mets Ishkhanasar (4WD or horse) and the monastery of Gndevank approached along the old road from the north (walk or 4WD if there haven't been recent rockfalls).

Churches

The great majority of churches and monasteries are either open all the time or else open all day with the caretaker selling candles to visitors. In only five cases have I found a church locked during the daytime. In two of these cases I failed to gain entry (St John the Baptist near Lanjar and the Mother of God church at Garni). At the other three (Akhtala, Ddmashen and Odzun) it was possible to get in by asking a passer-by who the keyholder was.

Of course there is a risk that the keyholder might be away working in the fields, visiting the dentist or at a wedding and on two visits to Odzun it has only been possible to get in once.

SUGGESTED ITINERARIES

Detailed itineraries are inevitably going to depend on the interests of the visitor, the time of year, and on whether or not Armenia is being combined with a trip to neighbouring Georgia or Iran. A reasonably fit first-time visitor in summer should try to stay two or three days in Vayots Dzor province to see the main monasteries as well as Selim Caravanserai and the fortress of Smbataberd. It is worth continuing south as far as Sisian in Syunik province to see Karahunj, Tatev and the petroglyphs on Mount Mets Ishkhanasar if visiting after the snow melt. The cave village of Khndzoresk is also worthwhile. In the northeast everyone goes to the

monasteries in the Debed valley but Makaravank in T[...]
worthwhile. The adventurous should try to go to Khuch[...]
wanting to go to the northwest to see the aftermath of [...]
more years on could call at numerous places en route,
Mastara are perhaps my favourites. Once in the northv[...]
visited as well as Harichavank.

INFORMATION

Some information is available from Armenia Information, a service provided by the Armenian Tourism Development Agency with funds from the United States Agency for International Development. They have a useful library of books which can be consulted, maintain registers of all types of accommodation and will try to help put people in touch with appropriate contacts in Armenia. They are a useful first point of contact for anyone arriving without accommodation booked as their register of accommodation in Yerevan includes homestays. The office is open daily from 09.00 to 19.00 at 3 Nalbandian Street (tel: +374 1 542303/542304; email: help@armeniainfo.am; web: www.armeniainfo.am).

The best internet source of information is www.cilicia.com which is reasonably comprehensive on sites but it is patchy on practical information and some of the descriptions of buildings which are used have not been well translated from the Russian original. This website also covers Nagorno Karabagh. There is some useful practical information on www.tacentral.com but much of the country is not covered.

The most useful map of the country is the pocket atlas *The Roads of Armenia* published in Yerevan by Collage Ltd. Costing AMD4,000, it covers the country together with Nagorno Karabagh at a scale of 1:600,000 but is not always accurate. As well as roads, rivers, railways and mountain summits are shown. Unfortunately the atlas does not appear to be available outside Armenia. The other road atlas, *Armenia Atlas of Roads*, is at a larger scale of 1:200,000 but its failure to mark rivers and mountain summits is perverse and it excludes Nagorno Karabagh. The best maps available outside the country are that covering Armenia and Azerbaijan at a scale of 1:650,000 published by International Travel Maps of Vancouver BC (tel: +1 604 687 3320), and that covering the whole of the Caucasus at a scale of 1:1,000,000 published by Gita Shenassi in Iran. Both are available through Stanfords, 12 Long Acre, London, WC2E 9LP, UK (tel: 020 7836 1321; fax: 020 7836 0189; email: customer.services@stanfords.co.uk; website: www.stanfords.co.uk).

TOUR OPERATORS
UK

The war in Iraq led to many group tours from the UK being cancelled (unnecessarily) in 2003 and the following is therefore rather an amalgam of what operated in 2002 and what was intended for 2003. It should be regarded only as an indication of what might be available during the currency of this guidebook. Prices quoted are from London and assume two people sharing a room. They may not be strictly comparable to each other because some operators include all meals while others do not and the standard of accommodation differs.

Birdquest Two Jays, Kemple End, Clitheroe, BB7 9QY; tel: 01254 826317; fax: 01254 826780; email: birders@birdquest.co.uk; web: www.birdquest.co.uk. Will be starting a 16-day tour to Armenia and Georgia in 2004.
Regent Holidays 15 John St, Bristol BS1 2HR; tel: 0117 921 1711; fax: 0117 925 4866; email: regent@regent-holidays.co.uk; web: www.regent-holidays.co.uk. Can organise any

y in Armenia and Nagorno Karabagh (combined with Georgia and Azerbaijan if
.red) for individuals or groups. They also offer a 14-day group tour to Armenia and
.orgia with an optional 7-day extension to Azerbaijan. The tour goes as far south as Tatev
.nd spends 6 nights in Armenia including a night at Sisian. The cost is £1,590 plus £669 for
the Azerbaijan extension.

Silk Road Tours 371 Kensington High St, London W14 8QZ; tel: 020 7371 3131; fax: 020
7602 9715; email: sales@silkroadtours.co.uk; web: www.silkroadtours.co.uk. Can organise
any itinerary for individuals but also offers a 15-day tour to Armenia, Georgia and
Azerbaijan which spends 3 days in Yerevan with local excursions.

Steppes East The Travel House, 51 Castle St, Cirencester, Glos GL7 1QD; tel: 01285
651010; fax: 01285 885888; email: sales@steppeseast.co.uk; web: www.steppeseast.co.uk.
Offers mainly tailor-made itineraries but also runs a group tour to Armenia and
Georgia.

Sunvil Holidays Sunvil House, Upper Square, Isleworth, Middx TW7 7BJ; tel: 020 8758
4722; fax: 020 8568 8330; email: europe@sunvil.co.uk; web: www.sunvil.co.uk. Offers an
8-day trip wholly within Armenia, travelling as far south as Noravank, for £1,577. All
nights are spent in Yerevan. A 3-day extension to Stepanakert, Nagorno Karabagh is
available for a supplement of £350. Sunvil can also offer tailor-made itineraries though the
only hotels outside Yerevan which they recommend to clients are those at Tsapatagh, on
the north side of Lake Sevan, and at Gyumri.

Explore Worldwide, 1 Frederick St, Aldershot, Hants GU11 1LQ; tel: 01252 760 000;
fax: 01252 760 001; email: res@exploreworldwide.com; web: www.exporeworldwide.com.
Offers a 'Land of the Golden Fleece' trip. (The fleece was kept at Colchis, near present-day
Batumi on the Black Sea coast of Georgia.) The 16-day trip spends 6 nights in Armenia, 2
of them away from Yerevan but it does not go south of the capital. The cost is £1,095–1,145
and a 4-day Azerbaijan extension is available for an extra £300. Explore has local agents in a
number of countries. These include: Australia (Adventure World, 3rd Floor, 73 Walker St,
North Sydney, NSW 2060; tel: 02 8913 0755; fax: 02 9956 7707; email:
info@adventureworld.com.au); Canada (Trek Holidays, Edmonton; tel: 1 888 456 3522;
fax 780 433 1283; email: adventures@trekholidays.com; web: www.trekholidays.com);
Ireland (Maxwells Travel, D'Olier Chambers, 1 Hawkins St, Dublin 2; tel: 01 677 9479;
fax: 01 679 3948); New Zealand (Adventure World, 101 Great South Rd, PO Box 74008,
Remeura, Auckland; tel: 9 524 5118; fax: 9 520 6629; email:
discover@adventureworld.co.nz); USA (Adventure Center, 1311 63rd St, Suite 200,
Emeryville, CA 94608; tel: 800 227 8747; fax: 510 654 4200; email:
ex@adventurecenter.com).

Traveller 92/93 Great Russell St, London WC1B 3PS; tel: 07906 696926; email:
info@thetraveller2004.com; web: www.thetraveller2004.com. Offers specifically cultural
tour to Armenia for £1,695. Of the 9 nights, one is spent away from Yerevan at Sevan. The
tour does not go south of the capital.

ACE Study Tours Babraham, Cambridge CB2 4AP; tel: 01223 835055; fax: 01223
837394; email: ace@study-tours.org; web: www.study-tours.org. Offers a cultural tour
combining Armenia with Georgia at a cost of £2,490 for 14 days, 7 of which are spent in
Armenia at Yerevan. The tour goes as far south as Noravank.

Ornithological Society of the Middle East OSME, c/o 6 Mansion Dr, Tring, Herts
HP23 5BD, UK; fax: 01442 822623; email: sales@osme.org. Provides the most
comprehensive tour of Armenia – it even reaches the Iranian border. This is the 12-day trip
run for members only. Groups stay in Yerevan, Dilijan, Vaik and Kapan.

USA

In the USA two companies which offer arrangements to Armenia are both based
at Glendale California and both also have offices in Yerevan.

Levon Travel 1132 North Brand Bd, Glendale, CA 91202; tel: 818 552 7700 and 800 445 3866; fax: 818 552 7701; web: www.levontravel.com. It also has offices at 10 Sayat Nova Boulevard, Yerevan (tel: 01 525 210; fax: 01 561 483), in the foyer of the Armenia Hotel, Yerevan, and in Nagorno Karabagh at 16a Yerevanian St, Stepanakert.

Menua Tours 3467 Ocean View, Glendale, CA 91208; tel: 818 248 9771; fax: 818 249 9990; email: info@menuatours.com; web: www.menuatours.com. Also has offices in Yerevan in the foyer of the Ani Plaza Hotel (tel: 01 527 372; fax: 01 583 901).

Austria
Biblische Reisen Stifsplatz 8, 3400 Klosterneuburg; tel: +43 2243 353770; fax: +43 2243 3537715; email: info@biblische-reisen.at; web: www.biblische-reisen.at. Runs group tours concentrating on churches and monasteries.

Georgia
Georgica Travel 22 Shanidze St, Tbilisi, Georgia; tel: +99532 25 21 99; fax: +99532 98 56 07; email: georgica@caucasus.net; web: www.georgica.caucasus.net

Germany
Biblische Reisen Silberburststrasse 121, D-70176 Stuttgart; tel: +49 7116 19250; fax: +49 7116 192544; email: info@biblische-reisen.de; web: www.biblische-reisen.de. Runs group tours concentrating on churches and monasteries.

Ventus Reisen Krefelder Strasse 8, D-10155 Berlin; tel: +49 3039 100332/00333; fax: +49 3039 95587; email: office@ventus.com; website: www.ventus.com. Group tours and individual arrangements.

Israel
Geographical Tours 37 Sheerit Israel St, Jaffa; tel: +972 3 5159018; fax: +972 3 5188014; mobile: +972 55 390595; email: geotours@geotours.com; web: www.geotours.com. Runs group tours including both Armenia and Nagorno Karabagh. Can also make individual arrangements.

Eco-Field Trips 11 Nes Ziona St, Tel-Aviv (tel: +972 3 5160754; fax: +972 3 5100456; email: mail@eco.co.il; website: www.eco.co.il) Runs group tours and can make individual arrangements.

Italy
Metamondo via Ca' Rosso 21A, 30174 Mestre (VE);tel: +39 41 5357 211; email: info@metamondo.it; web: www.metamondo.it) Group tours.

Netherlands
Koning Aap Reizen Meidoomweg 2, 1031 GG Amsterdam; tel: +31 20 7887700; fax: +31 20 7887701; email: info@koningaap.nl; web: www. koningaap.nl. Group tours and individual arrangements.

Yerevan
Apart from the American agents, there are around 35 more travel agents in Yerevan, an excessive number given the actual number of tourists who visit the country. Visitors who do not speak Armenian are strongly recommended to deal with those who have experience in making ground arrangements for tour operators from the UK since they will have staff who speak reasonable English: those dealing mainly with the diaspora may not speak as good English since the members of the diaspora usually speak Armenian. Possible agents include:

Armenia Travel + M 9 Pushkin St, Yerevan; tel/fax: 01 563 667, 01 562 104, 01 543 379; email: consulting@armeniatravel.am; web: www.armeniatravel.am. I have had arrangements made throughout Armenia and Nagorno Karabagh by this company and can vouch for their efficiency and flexibility.

Tatev – TTT 19 Nalbandian St, Yerevan; tel: 01 524 401, 01 543 360, 01 543 361; fax: 01 524 402; email: info@tatev.com; web: www.tatev.com

Tatian's Travel 29 Sayat-Nova Av, Yerevan; tel: 01 540 692; fax: 01 561 776; email: tatiantr@arminco.com; web: www.discoverarmenia.am

Saberatours – Sevan 10 Vardanants St, Yerevan; tel: 01 525 448; fax: 01 564 030; email: sabera@arminco.com; web: www.saberatours.com

Special interest visits

Armenia lends itself to special interest visits. A local birdwatching (and dragonfly) expert who has conducted many visitors round the country is Vasil Ananian (email: vananian72@yahoo.com) and he can organise suitable tours to find the desired specialities. The diversity of accessible vegetation zones means that botanical tours are also very rewarding and these are likely to become more common in the future. Horse riding is also available at a number of locations such as the southern slopes of Mount Aragats and at Sisian. Most of the country away from the Ararat valley has huge hiking potential and visitors are free to wander where they like, the only problems being absence of maps and the difficulty of avoiding hospitality at every cottage. Armenia has superb caving with more than 10,000 caves in most regions of the country often concentrated along the river gorges. Most of the caves are little known although there is an active Armenian Speleological Society. Reportedly some of the best caving, though only for the experienced, is in Vayots Dzor province. Magili Cavern is in the gorge which leads to Noravank and is 1.7km deep. Stone tools and artefacts have been discovered in the cave, as well as more recent ceramic fragments from the 9th century onwards. The cave is home to thousands of insectivorous bats. The passageway is horizontal and varies from just enough for a person to crawl through to a spacious 10–15m in width. This very warm cave is open and the very steep entrance has a hand line to assist visitors. Other caves are strictly for the expert. At 3.3km Archeri ('Bear') cave near Yeghegnadzor is Armenia's longest with some of the most spectacular stalactites and stalagmite formations in Europe. Unlike Magili it is far from horizontal with a vertical range of 145m. The cave gets its name from the remains of bears found here. Mozrovi, about 7.6km west of Arpi, has fine speleothems (mineral deposits of calcium carbonate precipitated from solution).

RED TAPE

All visitors require visas except passport holders of Azerbaijan, Belarus, Georgia, Kazakhstan, Kyrgystan, Moldova, Russian Federation, Tajikistan, Turkmenistan, Ukraine, Uzbekistan, Bulgaria, Cuba, Hungary, Romania, and Yugoslavia Federal Republic. Tourist visas are easy to obtain and are valid for 21 days. It is impossible to obtain one for longer although they can, in theory at least, be extended once in Yerevan. There are three quite different methods of obtaining a tourist visa. If travelling by air to Zvartnots airport in Yerevan then it is possible to obtain an electronic visa over the internet. Simply go to the web page of the Armenia foreign ministry (www.armeniaforeignministry.com), complete the application page and pay the US$60 fee by credit card. (Many Yerevan hotels and some travel agencies also have links to the relevant page on their websites.) The visa is normally issued within two working days and confirmation that it has been issued is sent electronically. It can then be collected on arrival at Zvartnots. It is intended that this quick and easy system will be extended to land borders in the future and presumably to other airports handling international flights such as Shirak airport at Gyumri. However this has not yet happened and anyone who is arriving at any other point of entry must have a conventional visa. Anyone who does not have a credit card will also need a conventional visa.

The application form for a conventional visa can also be downloaded from the foreign ministry website and application should be made to the appropriate embassy although note that applications from residents of the US states of Alaska, Arizona, California, Colorado, Hawaii, Idaho, Missouri, Nevada, New Mexico, Oregon, Texas, Utah, Washington and Wisconsin should apply to the consulate general in Los Angeles and not to the embassy in Washington DC. The fee for the visa must be paid by certified cheque or money order. Cash, credit cards and personal cheques are not accepted. Visas are normally issued in seven working days but there is a rush service costing US$83 in three working days: this is of course slower than the electronic system. Visas for children under 16 are issued free of charge.

For any other type of visa an invitation is required. In the case of business trips it must be certified by the Consular Department of the Ministry of Foreign Affairs or for private trips by the Passport and Visa Department of the Ministry of Internal Affairs.

Tourist visas can also be obtained at all the main borders (though not at the extremely minor crossing from Georgia near Khuchap monastery on the road over the Wolf's Gates Pass), and at present at a lower fee of US$30 payable in cash. It seems unbelievable that the new electronic visas cost twice the price of a visa issued at the airport but that is, for the time being, the case. However, the procedure at the border can be quite slow, particularly for those who are last off the plane or bus, and it seems likely that the new electronic visa system will ultimately supersede this arrangement. It is not even mentioned on the foreign ministry website.

Visas can be extended, in theory at least, on application to OVIR whose office is behind 15 Mashtots Avenue but the advice usually given is to pay the fine for overstaying on departure. It amounts to US$3 per day overstayed.

Armenian embassies abroad

Argentina Av Pte Roque Saenz Pena 570, Piso 3, Buenos Aires 1035; tel: +54 114 3452051, 3452037, 3451882; fax: +54 114 3432467

Austria Neubaugasse 12–14/1/16, 1070 Vienna; tel: +43 1 5227479; fax: +43 1 5227481; email: armenia@ycom.or.at

Belarus 17 Kirov St, Minsk; tel/fax: +375 172 275153, 231321; fax: +375 172 272339

Belgium Rue Franz Merjay 157, 1050 Brussels; tel/fax: +32 2 346-5667; fax: +32 2 344-9701; email: armembel@wanadoo.be

Brazil (Consulate General) Av São Luiz, 192 – Conj 1301 – CEP 01046 – 913, São Paulo; tel: +55 11 255 7707; fax: +55 11 159 4151

Bulgaria 11 fl April 20 St 11, 1606 Sofia; tel: +359 2 526046, 547970; fax: +359 2 526046; email: armembsof@sof.omega.bg

Canada 7 Delaware Av, Ottawa, Ontario K2P OZ2; tel: +1 613 2343710, 2342860; fax: +1 613 2343444, 2342790; email: erac@ican.net

China 4-1-61, Tayuan Diplomatic Apartments, Beijing, 100600, PR China; tel: +86 10 653 25677; fax: +86 10 653 25654; email: hajk@a-1.net.cn

Egypt Mohamed Mozhar 20, Cairo; tel: +20 2 7374157, 7374159; fax: +20 2 7374158; email: armenemb@idsc.gov.eg

France 9 Rue Viète, 75017 Paris; tel: +33 1 4212800; fax: +33 1 42129802, 42129801; email: ambarmen@wanadoo.fr

Georgia 4 Tetelashvili St, Tbilisi; tel: +995 32 951723, 964286; fax: +995 32 990126; email: aspet@access.sanet.ge

Germany Hillman St, 5, D 13-467 Berlin; tel.: +49 30 405 09110/12/13/15; fax: +49 30 40509125; email: armemb@t-online.com

Greece 159 Syngrou Av, 17121 Nea Smyrni, Attiki; tel: +30 10 934 5727, 931 8077; fax: +30 10 931 8100; email: armemb@hol.gr

India E-1/20, Vasant Vihar, New Delhi – 110057; tel: +91 11 615 3031, 614 7328; fax: +91 11 614-7329; email: armemb@vsnl.com

Iran 1 Ostad Shahriar St Corner of Razi, Jomhouri Eslami Av, Teheran, Iran; tel: +98 21 670 4833/38; fax: +98 21 670 0657

Iraq Baghdad; tel/fax: +964 1 718 8866

Italy Via dei Colli della, Farnesina 174, 00194 Roma; tel: +39 06 329 6638, 329 7764; fax: +39 06 329 7763; email: gaghikb@tin.it

Kazakhstan 579 Seyfulin St, Almaty 480075; tel: +7 3272 692 932; fax: +7 3272 692 908; email: acod100@hotmail.com; web: www.geocities.com/armkazembassy

Lebanon Rabieh, Mtaileb, Jasmin St, Beirut; tel: +961 4 402 952; fax: +961 4 418 860; email: armenia@dm.net.lb

Poland 02-908 Warszawa, ulica Woziwody 15; tel: +48 22 832 1030; tel/fax: +48 22 642 0643; email: main@embarmenia.it.pl

Romania Bucuresti, Str Colotesti 1, apt. 2; tel.: +40 1 321 5930; fax: +40 1 321 5679; email: armembro@starnets.ro

Russia Armiansky per 2, Moscow 101000; tel: +7 095 924 1269; tel/fax: +7 095 924 4535; fax: +7 095 924 5030; email: armembru@df.ru

Syria Malki, Ibrahim Hanano St, PO Box 33241, Damascus; tel: +963 11 373 2992; fax: +963 11 3711757; email: am309@net.sy

Turkmenistan Kioroghli St 14, Ashgabad; tel: +993 12 295 542, 354 418; fax: +993 395 538/49; email: eat@online.tm

Ukraine 35 Volodimirska St, Kiev; tel: +380 44 224 9005; fax: +380 44 216 4996, 224 0500; email: armenia@desp.kiev.ua

United Arab Emirates PO Box 6358, Abu Dhabi: tel: +971 2 676 9222; fax: +971 2 676 4888; email: aremir@emirates.net.ae

UK 25A Cheniston Gardens, London W8 6TG; tel: +44 207 938 5435; fax: +44 207 938 2595; email: armembuk@onetel.net.uk

USA 2225 R St NW, Washington, DC 20008; tel: +1 202 319 1976; fax: +1 202 319 2982. Consular section: tel: +1 202 319 2983; fax: +1 202 319 8330; email: amembusadm@msn.com; web: www.armeniaemb.org. Consulate General also at 50 North La Cienega Boulevard, Suite 210, Beverly Hills, Los Angeles, CA 90211; tel: +1 310 657 6102, 657 7320; fax: +1 310 657 7419.

GETTING THERE AND AWAY
By air

Yerevan has two airports, at Zvartnots 10km west of the city and Erebuni closer to the centre on the south side. Since the breakup of the Soviet Union, all flights have used Zvartnots (EVN) except for the thrice-weekly helicopter to Stepanakert in Nagorno Karabagh which used Erebuni until it was discontinued in 2002. Zvartnots is now operated under a 30-year lease by an Argentinian company which introduced the novelty of baggage trolleys but they proved short-lived and have now vanished. The new management has also considerably increased the range of catering facilities and shops and it is now easy to buy a cup of coffee. Meanwhile the new airport authorities attracted considerable criticism for being unable to cope with the bad weather of January 2003. The airport can be reached by bus 107 from Mashtots Avenue but this is of no use to passengers arriving on the British Airways or Austrian Airlines flights since it does not operate at night.

Some general points should be borne in mind so far as air travel is concerned. Firstly, for journeys within the CIS fares for citizens of non-CIS countries are considerably higher than the fares charged to citizens of those states: in general think of anything up to twice as much as the locals pay. Secondly, anyone transiting via Russia, Ukraine or Georgia will require a transit visa. In theory passengers changing at Moscow Sheremetevo can go to a special transit desk and be escorted between Sheremetevo I (from which Yerevan flights operate) and Sheremetevo II (from which flights to the West operate) without the need for a Russian transit visa. This sometimes works despite the glum unhelpful staff – it's easier for Russian speakers – but at times some travellers have found the transit desk unstaffed. Also the facility cannot be used when flying to Armenia with an electronic visa because the Armenian visa is only technically issued on arrival in Yerevan and is not valid for transit purposes in Russia. Thirdly, many of the airlines serving Yerevan have no office in the city nor at the airport and, while tickets can readily be booked through a travel agent, it is not possible easily to contact many of these airlines which are based in various Russian or Ukrainian provincial cities. Fourthly, as the text shows, many of these services operate only weekly so don't miss the plane; should you do so you won't get a refund. Lastly, all flights to Soviet destinations are on Russian-built aircraft. These aircraft are now banned from western European airports on environmental grounds (too noisy) but are used almost exclusively by the plethora (around 350–400) of airlines operating within the CIS.

At the time of writing only two western European airlines fly into Armenia: British Airways from London Heathrow and Austrian Airlines from Vienna. However, Czech Airlines has now announced that it will begin twice-weekly flights from Prague in June 2003. British Airways currently operates on Sundays, Wednesdays and Fridays leaving Heathrow mid-afternoon and arriving at Yerevan five hours later shortly after midnight local time. From March 2003 the flights started operating non-stop rather than calling at Tbilisi, Georgia and instead they now continue to Tashkent, Uzbekistan. The return flights leave Yerevan in the late morning on Mondays, Thursdays and Saturdays arriving at Heathrow at about 13.00 local time. Although the A320 airbuses on the route carry British Airways livery and the staff wear British Airways uniforms they are actually operated by British Mediterranean Airways (Cirrus House, Bedfont Road, London Heathrow Airport, Staines TW1 7NL; tel: 01784 266300; reservations/enquiries: 0870 850 9850; fax: 01784 266354; email: info@britishmediterranean.com; web: www.britishmediterranean.com), an independent franchise of British Airways. The inflight service is usually good and the reclining seats in business class are exceptionally comfortable. Although the 00.35 arrival at Yerevan may not seem ideal, for passengers from western Europe it is a very civilised time to arrive since it corresponds to 20.35 in Britain or 21.35 in France. Do not, however, expect to be able to change money at Yerevan airport at that time of night. Nor does public transport operate. If at all possible arrange to be met although taxis are available. During the day there is an airport bus although this has been banished by the airport management to a stop 300m away and, in the absence of baggage trolleys, passengers have to carry their luggage. However, with a fare of only AMD200 it's much cheaper than a taxi. Obviously connections are available at London to destinations worldwide. British Airways' office is at 19 Sayat-Nova Avenue in Yerevan (tel: 521383 and 528220) but it is unnecessary to reconfirm flights.

The Austrian Airlines flight is less conveniently timed. Clearly scheduled to suit insomniacs, it leaves Vienna at 22.20 on Mondays, Wednesdays and Fridays arriving in Yerevan at 04.45 local time (which is a scarcely more civilised 01.45 in Vienna). The return flights on Tuesdays, Thursdays and Saturdays leave Yerevan at 05.30 (requiring check-in by 04.30) and arrive in Vienna at 06.25 local time. Again worldwide flight connections are available from Vienna, though on a reduced scale in comparison to London Heathrow. Airbus A320s are used on the service. The Austrian Airlines office is on the 1st floor, AUA Business Centre, 9 Alek Manukian Street (tel: 512201/02/03; fax: 512206).

The future of Armenian Airlines is uncertain following its takeover by Siberian Airways in April 2003. Following the sale of (the insolvent) Armenian Airlines to Siberian Airlines the position regarding flights is extremely confusing. The information given in this guide book is subject to considerable change. It had a number of international flights to western Europe using an airbus A320 until January 21 2002 when the plane suffered a serious engine failure and the company had insufficient funds to replace the failed engine. A new private company, Armenia International Airways, was formed using diaspora money and took over the routes formerly operated by this plane using another airbus. Flights serve Paris on Mondays and Thursdays, Frankfurt on Saturdays, Amsterdam on Wednesdays and Sundays, Athens on Fridays, and Dubai on Tuesdays and Fridays. The remaining Armenian Airlines flights are still operated by the original company using a mixture of Russian-built planes which do not meet the western European environmental standards and hence cannot serve destinations in these countries. Prior to the takeover the company had been heavily in debt and was threatened in December 2002 with having all its flights to Russia stopped because of non-payment of bills for air traffic control. The scale of future operations is speculative but the current schedule offers the following destinations: Aleppo, Syria is served on Mondays; Anapa, Russia on Saturdays; Ashkhabad, Turkmenistan on Sundays; Beirut, Lebanon on Fridays; Ekaterinburg, Russia on Thursdays; Istanbul, Turkey on Tuesdays and Fridays; Kharkov, Ukraine on Sundays; Kiev, Ukraine on Mondays; Krasnodar, Russia on Mondays, Wednesdays, Fridays and Sundays; Mineralnye Vody, Russia on Mondays, Thursdays and Sundays; Moscow Vnukovo, Russia daily; Nizhny Novgorod, Russia on Wednesdays; Novosibirsk, Russia on Fridays; Odessa, Ukraine on Thursdays; Rostov-on-Don, Russia on Tuesdays and Saturdays; St Petersburg, Russia on Saturdays; Samara, Russia on Wednesdays; Simferopol, Ukraine on Thursdays; Sochi, Russia on Tuesdays, Fridays and Sundays; Stavropol, Russia on Wednesdays and Saturdays; Tashkent, Uzbekistan on Thursdays; Tebriz, Iran on Thursdays; Teheran, Iran on Mondays; and Volgograd, Russia on Sundays. There are clearly some interesting possibilities in this list for combining other destinations with Armenia!

Destinations served by other airlines are: Anapa, Russia on Sundays by Aviaexpress Cruise; Astrakhan, Russia on Wednesdays by Astrakhan Airlines; Chelyabinsk, Russia on Mondays by Chelyabinsk Air and by Ankor Airlines also on Mondays; Donetsk, Ukraine on Saturdays by Donbass Eastern Ukrainian Airlines; Istanbul, Turkey on Thursdays and Fridays by Armavia; Kiev, Ukraine on Fridays by Air Ukraine; Krasnodar, Russia on Tuesdays and Saturdays by Krasnodar Airlines; Lviv, Ukraine on Saturdays by Aeroalliance Airlines; Maikop, Russia on Sundays by Aviation Lines of Adygeya; Mineralnye Vody, Russia on Tuesdays, Wednesdays and Saturdays by Aviaexpress Cruise and on Fridays by Caucasian Mineralnye Vody State Airlines; Moscow Sheremetevo daily except Tuesdays and Thursdays by Aeroflot; Moscow Vnukovo daily by Siberian Airlines and also by Armavia; Nizhny Novgorod, Russia on Saturdays by Nizhnygorodsk Airlines; Novosibirsk, Russia on Mondays by Siberian Airways; Odessa, Ukraine on Saturdays by Odessa Air Enterprise; Rostov-on-Don, Russia on Wednesdays and Sundays by Aeroflot-Don; Samara, Russia on Saturdays by Samara Airlines; Saratov, Russia by Saratov Air on Fridays; Sochi, Russia on Wednesdays by

Chernomor Avia and on Mondays by Aviaexpress Cruise; Stavropol, Russia on Thursdays by Aviaexpress Cruise; Teheran, Iran on Thursdays by Caspian Air; Ufa, Russia on Tuesdays by Bashkirian Airlines; Ulyanovsk, Russia on Tuesdays by Perm Airlines; Volgograd, Russia on Fridays by Volgaviaexpress; Voronezh, Russia on Fridays by Voronezhavia; Zaporozhe, Russia on Fridays by Konstanta.

Yerevan's Zvartnots is not actually the only Armenian airport with international services. Shirak airport at Gyumri has three each week which serve Krasnodar, Russia on Thursdays, Rostov-on-Don, Russia on Fridays and Moscow on Saturdays. Anyone arriving at this little-used airport should note that there are no taxis and no telephones to summon one.

By train

It is quite possible to arrive in Armenia by train. An overnight service operates from Tbilisi on even dates departing at 16.05 and arriving in Yerevan at 06.40 the next morning. The northbound service leaves Yerevan at 19.00 on odd dates (though not on both the 31st and the 1st as these are consecutive dates) and arrives in Tbilisi at 07.15. En route the train calls at 12 intermediate stations including Vanadzor and Gyumri but mostly at inconvenient hours of the night. Trains have four classes: *obshi* (open seating on wooden benches), *plas* (reserved seats, possibly on wooden seats, more often on padded seats) and two types of compartments: *coupé* (compartments with sleeping berths for 4), and *CB* (SV in English) or Luxe, a compartment for two. Toilets on the train are not noted for their cleanliness and food is not available so bring some food rather than rely entirely on your fellow passengers to share their usually ample provisions. The ride is highly scenic but the best bits are covered in the dark except to some extent in midsummer. The fares for the full journey are very low: obshi – AMD2,100; plas – AMD2,900; coupé – AMD 4,350; CB – AMD8,250.

By bus

It is easy to travel by bus from either Georgia or Iran and there are also services from Russia and Turkey both of which operate via Georgia. In theory a Georgian transit visa should not be required for holders of Armenian visas spending less than 72 hours in Georgia but don't bet on this being honoured and, to avoid potential problems, obtain a Georgian visa in advance of travel. Tickets should be bought in

TAKING SOUVENIRS HOME

By law exporting any work of art from Armenia other than something mass produced in a factory requires approval from the government's Department of Cultural Heritage Preservation at 5 Tumanian Street (tel: 551920) which issues a permit for an item to leave the country. This is rigorously enforced in the case of paintings (sometimes even those painted last week by an unknown artist and bought at Vernissage) and handmade carpets but often less so in the case of other items such as carvings or embroideries. Anyone wishing to go through the procedure needs to take the item along with two photographs of it and pay a fee of AMD500 per item up to a maximum of AMD5,500 for 11 items or more. There are, however, frequent reports of customs officers at the airport citing rules written and unwritten and refusing to allow the export of paintings in particular despite the purchaser having the correct paperwork. Bribery is reported to work in these cases.

advance if at all possible. A small supplement of AMD100 is charged when doing so but it is well worth paying. The baggage allowance on buses is 20kg with excess being charged at AMD250 per kg.

From Georgia direct buses leave Tbilisi at 08.00 and 10.00 daily, taking 7 hours for the journey to Yerevan via Stepanavan and Ashtarak at a cost of US$6.50. The return service also operates at 08.00 and 10.00 and takes 7 hours. There is a bus from Batumi on Georgia's Black Sea coast leaving at 07.00 on Mondays and Fridays and taking 12 hours for the journey via Gyumri at a cost of US$18. The return service leaves Yerevan also on Mondays and Fridays at 07.00 and takes 12 hours.

From Iran the bus leaves Teheran on Tuesdays, Wednesdays, Fridays and Sundays at 09.00 and is scheduled to arrive in Yerevan 31 hours later. The fare is US$50. The southbound service leaves Yerevan at 09.00 on Tuesdays, Wednesdays, Fridays and Sundays and is slightly slower; allow 34 hours for the journey to Teheran.

The bus from Moscow takes a gruelling 72 hours for a fare of US$65. The departure times from Moscow should be checked locally but the northbound service leaves Yerevan at 04.00 on Wednesdays and Sundays. The fare is US$65.

From Istanbul the bus leaves on Wednesdays and Saturdays at 17.00 and from Yerevan on Wednesdays and Sundays at the same time 'or when it is full'. The eastbound journey is scheduled to take 32 hours but westbound is much slower at 48 hours because of the delays at the Turkish border. The fare is US$45. This service does not operate from Yerevan's bus station but from outside the sports stadium.

TRAVEL WITHIN ARMENIA

Public transport is of limited use in Armenia because most of the main sights are in isolated places. Details of the very few train services and information about long-distance buses from Yerevan are given opposite. It should be noted that almost all services are radial from Yerevan, exceptions being the services from Vanadzor west to Gyumri and east to Dilijan. Villages tend to be served by a bus from the local provincial capital, or other major town in a few cases, but typically only once daily with a morning service from the village to the provincial capital and an afternoon return. This of course makes it impossible to reach many villages by bus without an overnight stay.

The towns in the immediate vicinity of Yerevan are mostly served fairly frequently from the capital but even these buses are of limited use because such important and popular sites as Khor Virap and Geghard are at some distance from the nearest village and have no public transport. Geghard is most often combined with Garni as a half-day trip by car or tourist coach and it's very frustrating to catch the bus to Garni only to find oneself unable to continue to Geghard (which is actually more worth seeing). Similarly Khor Virap is regularly combined with Noravank but in that case neither can be reached by public transport.

Major towns have local internal bus services but few of these serve places of any tourist interest, with the exception of Sanahin, which has a bus service from Alaverdi (although most visitors opt for the cable car).

An economical way of visiting the country is to catch a bus to a major city and then hire a local car with driver to see the places in the neighbourhood. The advantage of this approach is that one does not need to pay for the driver's accommodation, which one does if visiting more distant regions using a car and driver hired in Yerevan. Long-distance bus routes usually face competition from minibuses, which operate the same route with a shorter journey time. They charge higher fares but the vehicles are rarely well maintained and the shorter journey times are achieved by driving at breakneck speed, however tortuous and potholed the road. The buses are equally ancient but at least the speeds are lower.

Train

There are only a handful of internal train services within the country but a couple of them may be of use to visitors. A train leaves the main railway station in Yerevan for Gyumri at 08.00 arriving at Gyumri at 12.30. The fare is AMD480. The return train leaves Gyumri at 17.15, arriving at Yerevan at 21.48. To reach the main railway station take the metro to Sasuntsi Davit which adjoins the railway station. The other useful route is that from Yerevan to Hrazdan, Sevan and Shorzha. This train does not, however, leave from the main railway station but from Arabkir station. Arabkir station is reached from the top of the Cascade by following the railway tracks to the left (standing with one's back to the Cascade) for 400m. The station's appearance is that of a minor wayside halt rather than a city terminus. Arabkir station can also be reached by minibus 43 or 45 from the Zoravar Andranik metro station. Trains depart for Hrazdan at 08.20 and 19.00 with the former being extended to Sevan and Shorzha in summer arriving in Sevan at 11.30 and Shorzha at 12.30. The fares are AMD250 and AMD320 respectively. Trains return from Hrazdan at 06.20 (arriving Arabkir at 08.10) and 17.00 (arriving Arabkir at 18.50) with the latter train starting back from Shorzha in summer at 15.40 calling en route at Sevan at 16.40.

The only other passenger trains are two local commuter trains into Yerevan in the morning from Arax (just west of Ararat on the Gyumri line) and Yeraskh (the last station on the line to the south before the closed border with Nakhichevan). These arrive at Yerevan at 09.38 and 08.53 with the return workings leaving Yerevan at 17.00 and 16.30 respectively.

Bus

All main towns are linked by bus services although when travelling between the north and south of the country it is invariably necessary to change at Yerevan. Apart from buses to Ijevan and Dilijan buses depart from the New Cilicia bus station which is about 800m from Victory Bridge in the Zvartnots direction. It can be reached by many minibus routes including 13, 15, 23, 27, 54, 67, 68, 75, 77, 90, 94 and 99. The bus station is a large A-frame building and, although working 24 hours, the café is open only from 06.00 until 17.00. The left luggage office is always open. The principal departures are: Alaverdi (10.00); Artik (13.00, 14.30, 16.00); Berd (10.15); Goris (08.30); Gyumri (hourly from 09.30 to 17.30); Jermuk (11.30); Kapan (08.00); Martuni (10.30); Meghri (09.00); Noyemberian (11.30); Sisian (08.40); Stepanakert (08.00, 09.00); Stepanavan (13.00, 16.30); Talin (07.45, 12.45, 13.45, 15.00, 16.00); Tashir (08.45); Vaik (13.30); Vanadzor (09.30, 11.00, 14.00, 15.30, 16.30); Vardenis (09.00, 11.00, 14.30, 16.00); Yeghegnadzor (12.30, 15.00). Buses to Ijevan and Dilijan leave from the northern bus station which is on the Sevan highway close to the city boundary. It can be reached by buses 2 and 27.

There are also frequent minibus services to the main towns which are more expensive, more frequent, quicker, and leave when full. Many depart from the New Cilicia bus station but those to Sevan mostly go from Isahakian, just north of Yeridasarakan metro station and others nearby go to Dilijan and Vanadzor. Minibuses to Gyumri and Vanadzor operate from Zoravar Andranik metro station.

Driving

With a very few exceptions, roads are full of deep pot-holes and, except in the very centre of major towns, assorted livestock. Drivers seek to avoid the worst of the pot-holes and the livestock by weaving to and fro and frequently going off the road altogether. Keeping to the right is only practised when passing another vehicle. Additionally, many rural routes linking villages are unmetalled and can become seas of mud after rain. This applies even more to the roads within villages where the daily passage of animals from their accommodation within the village to the fields and back ensures that village streets end up like farmyards. Drivers are adept at avoiding the livestock and so manage on the whole to avoid the human population as well. Do not assume that because a car is coming straight towards you that this represents danger as the driver is probably merely dodging the pot-holes and regards you as just another obstacle to avoid by swerving.

The only speed limits ever observed are those dictated by the state of the road surface which means that on the few good roads traffic is very fast. Seat belts are never worn. Petrol is available in two categories: normal (93 octane) and super (95 octane). Unleaded fuel is unavailable but diesel is widely sold. Although ordinary petrol stations exist, some even with talking (Armenian speaking) petrol pumps imported from Germany, much fuel is dispensed in cans from parked roadside tankers. The quality of the petrol supplied in this way seems identical with that from the talking pumps.

HEALTH

All travellers to Armenia should ensure that they are up to date with immunisation against **hepatitis A**, **tetanus** and **diphtheria**. It is also sensible to be immunised against **typhoid**. In addition some visitors, depending on what they are likely to be doing, and their duration and location of stay, may be advised to have protection against **polio**, tick-borne encephalitis, malaria, hepatitis B and rabies.

Tick-borne encephalitis (caused by a virus in the same family as yellow fever) is spread through the bites of infected ticks which are usually picked up in forested areas with long grass. Anyone liable to go walking in late spring or summer when the ticks are most active should seek protection. Although the vaccine is not licensed in the UK, it can be obtained by GPs or clinics on a named-patient basis. It is unavailable in the USA. The schedule consists of three doses that can be administered over a four-week period. Alternatively, you can have two doses in quick succession, and a third the following year. Whether you receive pre-exposure vaccine or not, after walking through long grass you should check for ticks. It is easier if you can get someone else to look for you. Remember, too, to check through the hair, where ticks may drop from overhanging branches – this is especially important for children.

After being eliminated in the 1960s **malaria** reappeared in 1994 following the reduction in control measures. It is largely confined to a small area in the Ararat plain roughly from Khor Virap in the north as far south as Yeraskh although among the 329 reported cases in 1999 were ones in the outer southern suburbs of Yerevan. The main road to the south passes through the malarial area but as mosquitoes are mostly active after sunset it may be unnecessary to take precautions if simply passing through. Birdwatchers visiting the much-favoured Armash fish ponds are, however, recommended to do so. Malaria in Armenia is exclusively of the benign *Plasmodium vivax* form and the risk exists only between June and October. The currently recommended prophylaxis is either chloroquine or proguanil. Remember, though, that no anti-malaria tablets are 100% effective and the best protection against mosquitoes is to use an insect repellent containing DEET. It is also wise to see a doctor immediately if you experience a fever over 38°C anything from seven days into an infected area up to one year afterwards.

Vaccination against **hepatitis B** is recommended for those working in hospitals or other medical settings or for anyone working closely with children. Three doses of vaccine are recommended for adequate protection. There are three vaccine schedules available that can be given over a period of four weeks to six months. The one selected will depend on the time available before travel. Whether or not you receive the vaccine it is advisable to carry a medical kit containing sterile needles, sutures, etc.

Rabies vaccination is essential for anyone likely to be in close contact with animals although at the time of writing there had been no reported cases since 1997. For maximum protection, three doses of vaccine are needed and can be taken over a four-week period.

Travel clinics and health information

A full list of current travel clinic websites worldwide is available on www.istm.org/. For other journey preparation information, consult ftp://ftp.shoreland.com/pub/ shorecg.rtf or www.tripprep.com. Information about various medications may be found on www.emedicine.com/wild/topiclist.htm.

UK

Berkeley Travel Clinic 32 Berkeley St, London W1J 8EL (near Green Park tube station); tel: 020 7629 6233

British Airways Travel Clinic and Immunisation Service There are two BA clinics in London, both on tel: 0845 600 2236; web: www.britishairways.com/travelclinics. Appointments only at 111 Cheapside; or walk-in service Mon–Sat at 156 Regent St.

Fleet Street Travel Clinic 29 Fleet St, London EC4Y 1AA; tel: 020 7353 5678; web: www.fleetstreet.com. Injections, travel products and latest advice.

Hospital for Tropical Diseases Travel Clinic Mortimer Market Centre, 2nd Floor, Capper St (off Tottenham Ct Rd), London WC1E 6AU; tel: 020 7388 9600; web: www.thhtd.org. Offers consultations and advice, and is able to provide all necessary drugs and vaccines for travellers. Runs a healthline (09061 337733) for country-specific information and health hazards.

MASTA (Medical Advisory Service for Travellers Abroad), at the London School of Hygiene and Tropical Medicine, Keppel St, London WC1 7HT; tel: 09068 224100. This is a premium-line number, charged at 60p per minute. For a fee, they will provide an individually tailored health brief, with up-to-date information on how to stay healthy, inoculations and what to bring.

MASTA pre-travel clinics Tel: 01276 685040. Call for the nearest; there are currently 30 in Britain.

Mediserve 27 Wimpole St, London W1M 7AD; tel: 020 7436 8978; fax: 020 7636 3834; email: mediserve@virgin.net

NHS travel website www.fitfortravel.scot.nhs.uk, provides country-by-country advice on

---

QUICK TICK REMOVAL

Asian ticks are not the prolific disease transmitters they are in the Americas, but they may spread Lyme disease, tick-bite fever and a few rarities. Tick-bite fever is a non-serious, flu-like illness, but still worth avoiding. If you get the tick off whole and promptly, the chances of disease transmission are reduced to a minimum. Manoeuvre your finger and thumb so that you can pinch the tick's mouthparts, as close to your skin as possible, and slowly and steadily pull away at right angles to your skin. This often hurts. Jerking or twisting will increase the chances of damaging the tick, which in turn increases the chances of disease transmission, as well as leaving the mouthparts behind. Once the tick is off, dowse the little wound with alcohol (local spirit, whisky or similar are excellent) or iodine. An area of spreading redness around the bite site, or a rash or fever coming on a few days or more after the bite, should stimulate a trip to a doctor.

immunisation and malaria, plus details of recent developments, and a list of relevant health organisations.

Nomad Travellers' Store and Medical Centre 3–4 Wellington Terrace, Turnpike Lane, London N8 0PX; tel: 020 8889 7014; fax: 020 8889 9529; email: sales@nomadtravel.co.uk; web: www.nomadtravel.co.uk. Also at 40 Bernard St, London WC1N 1LJ; tel: 020 7833 4114; fax: 020 7833 4470 and 43 Queens Rd, Bristol BS8 1QH; tel: 0117 922 6567; fax: 0117 922 7789.

STA Travel 40 Bernard St, London; tel: 020 7837 9666; web: www.statravel.co.uk

Thames Medical 157 Waterloo Rd, London SE1 8US; tel: 020 7902 9000. Competitively priced, one-stop travel health service. All profits go to their affiliated company, InterHealth, which provides health care for overseas workers on Christian projects.

Trailfinders Immunisation Centre 194 Kensington High St, London W8 7RG; tel: 020 7938 3999.

Travel Deals 70 North End Rd, London; tel: 020 7371 6570; web: www.traveldeals.uk.com

Travelpharm The Travelpharm website, www.travelpharm.com, offers up-to-date guidance on travel-related health and has a range of medications available through their online mini-pharmacy.

The Vaccination Clinic 131–135 Earls Court Rd, London; tel: 020 7259 2180; web: www.vaccination-clinic.cwc.net

Irish Republic

Tropical Medical Bureau Grafton Street Medical Centre, Grafton Buildings, 34 Grafton St, Dublin 2; tel: 1 671 9200.

USA

Centers for Disease Control 1600 Clifton Rd, Atlanta, GA 30333; tel: 877 FYI TRIP; 800 311 3435; web: www.cdc.gov/travel. A comprehensive range of advice is available on the internet.

Connaught Laboratories PO Box 187, Swiftwater, PA 18370; tel: 800 822 2463.

IAMAT (International Association for Medical Assistance to Travelers) 417 Center St, Lewiston, NY 14092; tel: 716 754 4883; email: info@iamat.org; web: www.iamat.org. A non-profit organisation that provides lists of English-speaking doctors abroad.

Canada

IAMAT (International Association for Medical Assistance to Travellers) Suite 1, 1287 St Clair Av W, Toronto, Ontario M6E 1B8; tel: 416 652 0137; web: www.iamat.org

TMVC (Travel Doctors Group) Sulphur Springs Rd, Ancaster, Ontario; tel: 905 648 1112; web: www.tmvc.com.au

Australia, Thailand

TMVC Tel: 1300 65 88 44; web: www.tmvc.com.au. Twenty-two clinics in Australia, New Zealand and Thailand, including:

Auckland Canterbury Arcade, 170 Queen St, Auckland City; tel: 373 3531

Brisbane Dr Deborah Mills, Qantas Domestic Building, 6th floor, 247 Adelaide St, Brisbane, QLD 4000; tel: 7 3221 9066; fax: 7 3321 7076

Melbourne Dr Sonny Lau, 393 Little Bourke St, 2nd floor, Melbourne, VIC 3000; tel: 3 9602 5788; fax: 3 9670 8394

Sydney Dr Mandy Hu, Dymocks Building, 7th Floor, 428 George St, Sydney, NSW2000; tel: 2 221 7133; fax: 2 221 8401

New Zealand

TMVC See above

IAMAT PO Box 5049, Christchurch 5; web: www.iamat.org

South Africa
SAA-Netcare Travel Clinics PO Box 786692, Sandton 2146; fax: 011 883 6152; web: www.travelclinic.co.za or www.malaria.co.za. Clinics throughout South Africa.
TMVC 113 DF Malan Dr, Roosevelt Pk, Johannesburg; tel: 011 888 7488; web: www.tmvc.com.au. Consult the website for details of clinics in South Africa.

Switzerland
IAMAT 57 Voirets, 1212 Grand Lancy, Geneva; web: www.iamat.org

In Armenia
Visitors will probably do a fair amount of passive smoking. Cigarettes are consumed in large quantities with around 40% of women smoking (the better-educated ones more likely to do so than those who did not receive higher education) – and around 60% of men. Only 15% of the adult population has never smoked. Surveys show that 35% of Armenian smokers believe that smoking will do them no harm while 45% believe that passive smoking is harmless. Even 39% of Armenian doctors smoke in front of their patients. Nevertheless life expectancy remains among the highest in the CIS at 70.5 years for men and 74.5 for women, according to official statistics, but 62 and 71 respectively according to the American CIA.

Armenia's economic problems have had a serious impact on health care. The fertility rate of women has plummeted to less than half its 1990 rate and is now the lowest in all 35 member states of the Council of Europe. Towns and villages are consequently often experiencing falling population although the country's abortion rate officially remains below the European average. Aid workers, however, claim that women are choosing to terminate pregnancy in unprecedented numbers and one worker even identified a woman who had had almost 40 abortions. Preliminary indicators from a UNICEF-conducted nutrition survey in Armenia suggest that malnutrition has tripled to 12% of children up to the age of five and the infant mortality rate is more than three times the average of EU member states. Armenia's government can now fund less than 30% of the nation's health budget and UNICEF reports that one hospital director freely admits that patients are illegally charged for drugs, 'since that is the only way that we can afford to keep our doors open'. The steep increase in maternal mortality is directly attributed to reduced health expenditure. Health workers, like teachers, report intermittent payment of salaries. The United Nations says that one third of Armenia's population is living in 'extreme poverty', surviving on less than US$1 per day, and it classifies more than two-thirds of the population as 'poor'.

A reciprocal health agreement exists for British citizens, which means that health treatment including dental treatment is free on production of a UK passport. However, drugs still need to be paid for. Many US health insurance policies do not include Armenia so special cover needs to be purchased. It is prudent for all visitors to ensure that their insurance will cover repatriation, or at least evacuation, in the event of serious illness or accident.

SAFETY
Most visits to the country are trouble free. There is little crime and, despite reports of the occasional pickpocket around the markets in Yerevan, visitors who take sensible precautions are unlikely to experience any problems. There aren't any 'no go' areas of poor housing or of struggle for supremacy between rival gangs; nor do

areas become dangerous after dark. Armenia just isn't that kind of country. The biggest problem in towns is the risk after dark of either tripping up on pavements in need of repair or else falling into holes dug during the pavement's reconstruction. Watch out too for missing manhole covers. This can also be a major hazard in ill-lit subways.

The military situation does mean that some areas along the 1994 ceasefire line should definitely be avoided because of the risk from occasional snipers on the Azerbaijan side and, particularly in Nagorno Karabagh, from minefields. To the best of my knowledge all places mentioned in this guide are perfectly safe to go and sights where the unresolved conflict means that safety is problematic have been excluded. Visitors to Nagorno Karabagh should, however, note that consular services are unavailable there if they do encounter any problems.

Armenia's rate of deaths in road traffic accidents has historically been proportionately much higher than that in the UK despite considerably lower traffic levels. The Armenian figure is likely to deteriorate even further as the improved roads tempt drivers to higher speeds and increasing traffic levels mean that it is even more dangerous than it was previously to drive round blind bends on the wrong side of the road. In fact the old pot-holed tracks, where speeds were perforce low as drivers sought to avoid the deepest ruts, have undoubtedly helped to keep the accident rate down. In Armenia seat belts are never worn.

There are no particular safety problems for women as the strongly traditional family values ensure that they will not receive unwelcome attention. It is true that a woman walking alone in the late evening is an uncommon sight but it does not imply that she would be vulnerable if she did. Women drivers are virtually unknown in Armenia. If you do see a woman driving a car the chances are that she is not Armenian.

Other dangers and annoyances

Even the US Department of State warns visitors to Armenia that the traffic police often seek bribes at periodic checkpoints on main routes. All visitors other than those in tourist buses can be certain of being frequently stopped. One member of the diaspora was stopped three times in 15 minutes but that is admittedly exceptional. The diaspora claim that it is AMD1,000 each time but some local drivers say that this is untrue. It is certainly the case however that the number of traffic police is preposterously high and that they deliver little perceptible benefit to the country.

As mentioned elsewhere in this guide, there is danger from earthquakes, poisonous snakes, deep holes concealed by long grass at several monasteries and various other hazards ranging from the potential for dehydration when it's hot to the possibility of frostbite when it's cold. The vast majority of visitors suffer none of these although it is rather difficult always to take precautions against earthquakes. Possibly the only sensible advice is to avoid Soviet-era flats.

It is, however, necessary to supervise children very closely at many historic sites. Apart from the deep holes concealed by long grass and the snakes which find convenient lairs in the piles of fallen stones, much of the masonry of less-frequented buildings is precarious and Armenian castle builders were adept at locating their fortresses on the top of precipices. Even at touristy places like Noravank the cantilevered steps which give access to the second floor of the mausoleum require considerable care – especially descending. Just to reach a few of the sites requires hill-walking skills and appropriate footwear – it may not be a long walk to Baghaberd, for example, but it is extremely steep and made difficult by unstable scree.

WHAT TO TAKE

Apart from obvious items like walking boots and a compass if you're going hiking or binoculars if you're birdwatching there are a few other items which are best brought into the country. Any drugs which you may need should be brought as these may be difficult to obtain, particularly away from Yerevan. Bring a small torch and carry it around as it is needed when visiting the subterranean rooms at a few sites. Slide film is difficult to obtain in the country and high-quality processing of slide film is impossible. (Film for prints is readily obtainable and processing is usually of good quality.) Clothing is largely dependent on time of year and activities planned but do note that Armenians recognise foreign tourists by their casual clothes. Armenians regularly dress much more smartly and stylishly than most Westerners. (By contrast they recognise members of the diaspora because they always look as if they are dressed for a special occasion.) If there is any likelihood of being invited for dinner into somebody's home, or even going to an orchestral concert or the opera, it is worth taking something smarter. Note that Armenian women do not have pierced parts of their body other than their ear lobes, men do not wear earrings, and neither sex sports tattoos.

MONEY

Armenia's own economic problems coupled with the disintegration of the financial markets of the former Soviet Union reinforced the need for Armenia to have an independent monetary policy. The introduction of the dram (officially abbreviated to AMD) as a national currency on November 29 1993 made an independent monetary policy possible. Each dram, which is simply the Armenian word for money, is made up of 100 luma, the Armenian word for a small part of anything. Initially the exchange rate was US$1 = AMD14. By the end of March 1994 it had reached US$1 = AMD230 and the year ended at US$1 = AMD400. However it then stabilised but has now drifted down to US$1 = AMD585 and UK£1 = AMD900. There were originally five denominations of banknotes: AMD10, 25, 50, 100, 200. Inflation subsequently forced the addition of AMD500, 1,000 and 5,000 notes. In 1997 these were superseded by a completely different design of banknote depicting famous Armenian males. Some of the old notes remain in circulation as there are no immediate plans to demonetise them. The new notes depicted: AMD50 – the composer Aram Khachaturian (1903–78); AMD100 – the astrophysicist Viktor Hambartsumian (1908–96); AMD500 – the architect Alexander Tamanian (1878–1936); AMD1,000 – the poet Eghishe Charents (1897–1937); AMD5,000 – the writer and poet Hovhannes Tumanian (1869–1923); AMD20,000 – the painter Martiros Sarian (1880–1972). In 2003 the AMD50 and AMD100 notes started to be replaced by coins but it is likely to be some time before the changeover is complete.

Armenia is very much a cash-based society. Only a handful of hotels and luxury shops aimed at Western visitors accept credit cards while travellers' cheques can most easily be exchanged at HSBC branches in Yerevan. Travellers' cheques issued by Thomas Cook or American Express are easiest to cash and ones denominated in US dollars are preferred but those denominated in euros are also accepted. Armenia has six hole-in-the-wall cash machines, all in Yerevan and operated by HSBC. Any card which will work in an HSBC machine in the UK will work in them. They are available 24 hours per day and are located: in the foyer of the Hotel Armenia, 1 Amirian Street; close to Republic Square at 2 Khorherdarani Street; at 11 Abovian Street; at the Armenergo building, 27 Abovian Street; at the HSBC branch, 3 Komitas Avenue; and close to the opera house at the junction of Moskovian Street and Baghramian Avenue.

MAKING THE BEST OF YOUR TRAVEL PHOTOGRAPHS
Nick Garbutt and John R Jones
Subject, composition and lighting
As a general rule, if it doesn't look good through the viewfinder, it will never look good as a picture. Don't take photographs for the sake of taking them; film is far too expensive. Be patient and wait until the image looks right.

People
Armenians generally love to have their photographs taken, and will usually happily pose for a picture. There's nothing like a wonderful face to stimulate interest. Travelling to remote corners of the world provides the opportunity for exotic photographs of colourful minorities, intriguing lifestyles and special evocative shots which capture the very essence of a culture. A superb photograph should have an instant gut impact and be capable of saying more than a thousand words.

Photographing people is never easy and more often than not it requires a fair share of luck. Zooming in on that special moment which says it all requires sharp instinct, conditioned photographic eyes and the ability to handle light both aesthetically and technically.

- If you want to take a portrait shot, it is always best to ask first. Often the offer to send a copy of the photograph to the subject will break the ice – but do remember to send it!
- Focus on the eyes of your subject
- The best portraits are obtained in the early morning and late evening light. In harsh light, photograph without flash in the shadows.
- Respect people's wishes and customs. Remember that, in some countries, candid snooping can lead to serious trouble.
- Never photograph military subjects unless you have definite permission.

Wildlife
There is no mystique to good wildlife photography. The secret is getting into the right place at the right time and then knowing what to do when you are there. Look for striking poses, aspects of behaviour and distinctive features. Try not only to take pictures of the species itself, but also to illustrate it within the context of its environment. Alternatively, focus in close on a characteristic which can be emphasised.

- Photographically, the eyes are the most important part of an animal – focus on these, make sure they are sharp and try to ensure they contain a highlight.
- Look at the surroundings -- there is nothing worse than a distracting twig or highlighted leaf lurking in the background. Although a powerful flashgun adds the option of punching in extra light to pep up the subject, artificial light is no substitute for natural light, and should be used judiciously.
- At camera-to-subject distances of less than a metre, apertures between f16 and f32 are necessary to ensure adequate depth of field. This means using flash to provide enough light -- use one or two small flashguns to illuminate the subject from the side.

Landscapes
Good landscape photography is all about good light and capturing mood. Generally the first and last two hours of daylight are best, or when peculiar climatic conditions add drama or emphasise distinctive features. Never place the horizon in the centre – in your mind's eye divide the frame into thirds and either exaggerate the land or the sky.

Equipment

Keep things simple. Cameras which are light, reliable and simple will reduce hassle. High humidity in many tropical places, in particular rainforests, can play havoc with electronics.

For keen photographers, a single-lens reflex (SLR) camera should be at the heart of your outfit. Remember you are buying into a whole photographic system, so look for a model with the option of a range of different lenses and other accessories. Compact cameras are generally excellent, but because of restricted focal ranges they have severe limitations for wildlife.

Always choose the best lens you can afford – the type of lens will be dictated by the subject and the type of photograph you wish to take. For people, it should ideally should have a focal length of 90 or 105mm; for candid photographs, a 70–210 zoom lens is ideal. If you are not intimidated by getting in close, buy one with a macro facility which will allow close focusing.

For wildlife, a lens of at least 300mm is necessary to produce a reasonable image size of mammals and birds. For birds in particular, even longer lenses like 400mm or 500mm are sometimes needed. Optics of this size should always be held on a tripod, or a beanbag if shooting from a vehicle. Macro lenses of 55mm and 105mm cover most subjects and these create images up to half lifesize. To enlarge further, extension tubes are required. In low light, lenses with very fast apertures help (but unfortunately are very expensive).

For most landscapes and scenic photographs, try using a medium telephoto lens (100–300mm) to pick out the interesting aspects of the vista and compress the perspective. In tight situations, for example inside forests, wide-angle lenses (ie: 35mm or less) are ideal. These lenses are also an excellent alternative for close ups, as they offer the facility of being able to show the subject within the context of its environment.

Film

Film speed (ISO number) indicates the sensitivity of the film to light. The lower the number, the less sensitive the film, but the better quality the final image. For general print film, ISO 100 or 200 fit the bill perfectly; under weak light conditions use a faster film (ISO 200 or 400). If you are using transparencies just for lectures then again ISO 100 or 200 film is fine. However, if you want to get your work published, the superior quality of ISO 25 to 100 film is best. Try to keep your film cool - it should never be left in direct sunlight (film bought in developing countries is often outdated and badly stored). Fast film (ISO 800 and above) should not pass through X-ray machines.

Different types of film work best for different situations. For natural subjects, where greens are a feature, Fujicolour Reala (prints) and Fujichrome Velvia and Provia (transparencies) cannot be bettered. For people shots, try Kodachrome 64 for its warmth, mellowness and superb gentle gradation of contrast; reliable skin tones can also be recorded with Fuji Astia 100. If you want to jazz up your portraits, use Fuji Velvia (50 ISO) or Provia (100 ISO), although if cost is your priority, stick to process-paid Fuji films such as Sensia 11. Remember that between May and October, the days are usually bright in Armenia, so a less-sensitive film is your best bet.

Nick Garbutt is a professional photographer, writer, artist and expedition leader, specialising in natural history. In 1996, he was a winner in the 'BBC Wildlife' Photographer of the Year Competition. John R Jones is a professional travel photographer specialising in minority people.

By far and away the usual way of obtaining drams however is by changing cash at one of the innumerable exchange offices in the country. Dollars are again the preferred currency though euros and roubles are widely accepted and a few places, mostly in Yerevan, will take British pounds. It is usually possible to exchange other currencies at the centre of Yerevan's currency exchange district which is Tigran Mets Avenue, the street running south from Republic Square towards Zoravar Andranik metro station. However, as a general rule visitors to Armenia should bring most of their funds in cash US dollars, regarding other forms solely as an emergency reserve. This is even more the case outside Yerevan. The lack of crime makes doing so safer than might be imagined. There is less concern than formerly about accepting notes in less than pristine condition but it can still prove difficult to get rid of ones which are torn or marked. There is also sometimes wariness about accepting the older design of US dollar notes owing to the number of forgeries in circulation. Do not when changing money accept AMD20,000 notes as few shopkeepers can give change for so large a note.

Although all purchases in Armenia should be paid for in drams, there are a few places where dollars are welcome. Vernissage market is one: most of the stallholders even quote prices in dollars (though they will of course accept drams). Departure tax at the airport can also be paid in either currency although it's cheaper in drams.

BUDGETING

Apart from Western-style hotels, the price of which is indicated in the body of the text, most things of interest to tourists are very cheap with the notable exception of internet access. In particular, outside Western-style hotels and a few Yerevan restaurants it is difficult to spend more than AMD5,000 on a meal. Public transport fares are very low – AMD3,000 will get you by bus to anywhere in the country. Car hire is cheaper than in western European countries and cheaper with a driver than without - but don't expect a new vehicle. Car hire with driver costs around US$50 for a normal car and US$70 for 4WD. In addition the cost of fuel must be paid and the driver's expenses if he is away from home.

ACCOMMODATION

An ambitious building programme has resulted in Yerevan being over-provided with upmarket hotels. There is a wide choice of hotels within the central area although some visitors might prefer, particularly in midsummer, to stay outside the central district. Expect to pay Western prices at these hotels. There are also some less expensive hotels, mostly built in the Soviet era for tourist groups and since renovated. Budget travellers are much better seeking homestays rather than hostel accommodation with the possible exception of that run by the university. Information about Yerevan accommodation is given on page 83.

Outside Yerevan accommodation is much less readily available. Most towns have a Soviet-era hotel which was used to house refugees in the early 1990s, has never recovered, and is not recommended. On the positive side, however, there is a sparse network of motels. Also good new hotels have been constructed in Vanadzor and Gyumri, the two largest cities after Yerevan. One or two of the Soviet-era hotels have been renovated and are now pleasant if sometimes basic places to stay. Also a new chain of Tufenkian hotels aimed at Western tourists is being developed in restored buildings. The first outside Yerevan opened on Lake Sevan in 2002, one is promised for the Debed valley in 2003 and another may be added near Areni in 2004.

Another feature of the Soviet era were the guesthouses run by various bodies to provide accommodation for their members while on holiday. They are therefore usually in pleasant surroundings. Some of these have been sold off while in other cases they remain in the hands of the original owner. It is possible to stay at most of them and they are generally inexpensive. The standard varies enormously. The privatised ones are usually well managed even though they often need a lot of new investment. Those still in the hands of the original owners vary from the fascinating and pleasant to one in which it was necessary to sleep with the window open to avoid choking on the dust and where the wealth of dead insects in the bedroom provided an interesting identification challenge. (It isn't mentioned in this guide.)

Homestays are available throughout the country and provide a real insight into Armenian family life particularly as meals can be organised. All visitors should try to include one or two. For those who speak neither Armenian nor Russian they can be organised through one of the Yerevan travel agents.

It is a fact of Armenian life that many parts of the country have water available only for limited periods each day. It has to be turned off at other times to prevent it running to waste through leaky pipes. Hot water is continuously available in upmarket hotels only.

EATING AND DRINKING

Two points need to be made about eating in Armenia. Firstly, Armenian cuisine has much more in common with Turkish, Persian or Arab cooking (all of which at one time ruled Armenia), than it does with the cooking of Russia, which also ruled Armenia, or that of western Europe. Secondly, given the range and interest of dishes which can be experienced in an Armenian household, the menus of restaurants and hotels are repetitive, predictable, and after a day or two, boring. Very sadly, almost all restaurant menus, especially away from Yerevan, have been reduced to a few salads followed by grilled or barbecued meat and vegetables. Armenian thinking is quite different from that in Britain or France, for example, where one goes to a restaurant for a good meal. In Armenia one goes to a restaurant to give the wife of the family a rest and accepts that the food will be less good than at home. The only way most tourists can begin to appreciate the range of Armenian cookery is to get a travel agent to organise for them some homestays with dinner included. The hostess is likely to outshine any restaurant in the vicinity. Having said that, it is also true that the quality of restaurants has improved out of all recognition since Soviet days when surly staff glumly informed customers that everything they asked for from the menu was unavailable and meals took hours as the staff frequently vanished to enjoy a long rest. Nowadays one problem for foreigners who are not used to it is quite the reverse: meals can be served too quickly with the second course arriving before the first is half eaten. (It is the normal Armenian custom to serve everything at once. Avoid this if you wish by only ordering one course at a time.)

The quality of the ingredients is extremely high because Armenia produces a wide range of excellent fruit and vegetables as well as pork, poultry and lamb. The only exception is beef which tends to be less satisfactory because it is predominantly from Caucasian Brown cattle, a breed developed between 1930 and 1960 by crossing Swiss Brown bulls with cows of the local Lesser Caucasus breed. The resulting beef does not compare with Aberdeen Angus, beef shorthorn or Hereford. Also the Armenian practice of eating beef and lamb fresh rather than hanging it for up to three weeks after slaughter tends to make it tougher and less flavoursome than in the West.

The quality of Armenia's fruit and vegetables is so high, partly because the climate favours them, partly because they have not been bred to survive transport to a supermarket in another continent and partly because they do not have to appear absolutely identical to every other example of that fruit or vegetable which the supermarket sells. Probably apricots, native to Armenia, are the most famous produce but in season markets and the ubiquitous roadside vendors pile their stalls with peaches, cherries, apples, pears, quinces, grapes, figs, pomegranates, plums, oranges, lemons, melons, water melons, tomatoes, squashes, aubergines, peppers, asparagus, cucumbers, courgettes, onions, potatoes, carrots, peas, beans, cabbages, okra, a whole range of mushrooms, almonds, walnuts and hazelnuts.

A staple ingredient of Armenian cookery is *bulghur*. Traditionally it is made by boiling whole grains of wheat in large cauldrons until they begin to soften upon which they are removed and dried in the sun. The grains are cracked open and the kernels divided into categories depending on size. This process ensures that they will keep for years without deteriorating. Fine bulghur is preferred for *keufteh* (see below) while coarse bulghur is preferred for pilaffs and soups.

Warning to vegetarians: Armenian dishes may not be what they seem from the menu. For example, mushroom salad may contain as much chicken as mushroom and, because the ingredients will be chopped fine and mixed up together, it will be impossible to avoid the chicken. Always ask before ordering.

Breakfast
Most Armenians make do with a cup of coffee or tea together with bread, butter, jam and possibly cheese. Occasionally a tomato omelette *(loligov dzu)* will be offered, in the Armenian version of which onions are first gently fried, then chopped tomatoes are added and finally whipped eggs are poured on (sometimes with a little cream and curry powder added) for the final cooking. Yoghurt *(madzoon)* is also likely to be offered. In smaller establishments you will be asked the evening before what you will want and when. In homestays the uneaten food from the night before (of which there will be a great deal since Armenian cooks greatly overestimate visitors' appetites) will also be laid out. It is not unknown for the evening's undrunk brandy also to be proffered at breakfast. The main Yerevan hotels offer something considerably more than this (though minus the brandy) with a whole buffet breakfast available and a variety of omelettes but this is pandering to Western hotel eating habits rather than authentically Armenian. Nor can one or two Soviet-style guesthouses which offer semolina and boiled beef be regarded as remotely Armenian.

Lunch
Many restaurants start serving meals by 12.00 and service is continuous until late evening. Armenians argue that one should eat when one is hungry rather than be guided by the clock. Traditionally though, lunch is a fairly light meal with the main meal being taken after work. For visitors lunch is often an excuse to buy some fresh produce at the market. The basis for the picnic is *lavash*, Armenia's classic flatbread. Although traditionally unleavened, some present-day cooks cheat and use yeast. It is baked rapidly in an oven set into the ground called a *tonir* and comes in the form of thin sheets which can be readily stored since *lavash* is successfully freshened even after it has dried out by sprinkling a little water on it. In villages where there is no market people still bake it in their own houses, often several women saving on fuel and having a social morning by baking bread together, each making enough to last her family for a few days or longer. Tomatoes and cucumbers together with cheese and sour cream make an excellent filling. Other possibilities obtainable at any market are the spiced dried meats such as *basturma*, which is dried, salted and flattened beef surrounded by a dried mixture of paprika, garlic and cumin, or *sojuk* which is spiced and salted

minced beef (sometimes mixed with pork or lamb), all formed into a sausage and then dried. In the Sevan area smoked fish can be bought to make another variant.

An alternative lunch would be to call at one of the roadside barbecue stalls and have lunch there and, of course, the restaurants are open if it's either raining or else too hot. In towns it might be possible to find a café selling the traditional Armenian fast food *lahmadjoun*. This tasty speciality comprises a thin dough base covered, in similar style to a pizza, with tomato, herbs, spices and very small pieces of meat. It's normally rolled up and eaten like a sandwich.

Dinner

The main meal is eaten in the evening. Bread will certainly be provided, usually *lavash*, but some restaurants particularly in Yerevan have taken to giving foreigners ordinary bread and reserving the *lavash* for Armenians unless foreigners specifically ask. The meal usually begins with a selection of salads which can incorporate both raw and cooked vegetables, peas, beans, herbs, fruits, nuts, bulghur, eggs and meat. In season romaine lettuce is used but in winter cabbage is substituted. Often the salads will double up as an accompaniment to the main course. Popular salads include cucumber and tomato salad (*varounki yev loligi aghtsan*), green bean salad (*kanach lobov aghtsan*), kidney bean salad (*karmir lobov aghtsan*), aubergine salad (*simpoogi aghtsan*) and potato salad with sour cream (*titvaserov kartofili aghtsan*).

The second course would traditionally have been soup although this is not now commonly served in summer and restaurants frequently have none available. Some of the soups are actually so substantial as to be main courses while others are cold concoctions for summer. Armenian soups are excellent so take any opportunity to try one – if you can manage yet more food. A popular summer soup is *jajik*, chilled yoghurt and cucumber soup, which can either accompany the main course or precede it. Other cold soups made with apricots, cornelian cherries (*Cornus mas*), currants, mulberries, or sweetbrier (*Rosa rubiginosa*) can be served as either a first course or a dessert. More substantial soups for winter include *targhana abour* made with yoghurt, mint and onion, *shoushin bozbash* (lamb soup with apple and quince) and *missov dziranabour* (lamb soup with apricots).

The main course would usually be based on meat or fish. Fish is obviously less common than in countries which are not landlocked but whitefish from Lake Sevan is sometimes available and also trout from Armenia's rivers. Beware of some of Yerevan's restaurants which offer sea fish, smoked salmon or shellfish imported from goodness knows where. Leave such dishes to the expatriates who want to be reminded of home.

Unfortunately, restaurants rarely offer dishes which have been cooked by braising or casseroling although such dishes certainly form part of traditional Armenian cookery. Chicken is far more likely to be roasted, perhaps with a stuffing (*pilavov letzvadz hav*) based on rice or bulghur and with some vegetables or dried fruit, or else it might be barbecued (*khorovadz varyag*) or fried. A really upmarket restaurant might offer a more imaginative stuffing such as would be used in Armenia on festive occasions. Game is very rarely offered, probably because so little of it survives. Lamb is immensely popular and a huge variety of lamb stews is cooked in the country with ingredients from quinces (*missov sergevil*) and apricots (*missov dziran*) to artichokes (*missov gangar*) and leeks (*missov bras*). They are fascinating, delicious dishes, usually served with a rice pilaff (*printzi pilaff*) or bulghur pilaff (*tzavari pilaff*), but the chance of finding one on a restaurant menu is slight. You will, however, find lots of barbecues (*khorovadz*) using lamb (*gar*), pork (*khoz*), beef (*tavar*), chicken (*hav*) or, occasionally, veal (*hort*). The meat will come with vegetables, of very high quality but not prepared or cooked with the flair and imagination shown in an Armenian household.

Other dishes occasionally encountered include *dolma* of which there is a whole range. They comprise vegetables or occasionally fruits which have been stuffed with meat or with rice. Vine leaves or cabbage leaves are most commonly used depending on the season but the range of vegetables used in Armenian homes is staggering: artichokes, chard, aubergines, peppers, courgettes, onions, tomatoes, apples, melons and quinces. The stuffing could be made from some combination of minced beef or lamb, rice, bulghur, dried fruits, chopped vegetables, yoghurt, and a mixture of herbs and spices. Needless to say a visit to an Armenian home is necessary to encounter this kind of range but some restaurants do include some of the more common ones on the menu.

Keufteh is another classic style of Armenian cookery. It is bulghur which has been mixed with finely chopped vegetable and herbs and often with lamb as well. Again there are innumerable variations depending on the cook and the availability of seasonal ingredients. It can be cooked or uncooked, hot or cold, and some have two separate mixtures, one for the core and one for an outer shell. In the popular *sini keufteh* the inner stuffing is made from butter, onions, minced lamb, pine nuts and spices while the outer shell comprises bulghur, more lamb, onion and other spices. It is prepared in a baking dish before being cut into squares and then baked. It can be eaten hot or cold with vegetables or salad.

Dessert and pastries

Dessert as often as not consists of fresh fruit accompanied by cheese. In summer ice-cream is served but is always factory rather than artisan produced. Pastries are more often eaten with a cup of afternoon tea or coffee or in the late evening. Armenia's best pastries, and very good they are too, are those which exploit its fruit and nuts. *Baklava* is widely available and exists in many forms. Layers of buttered filo pastry stuffed with some combination of nuts, apples, cheese and cream is formed into rolls or diamonds and then baked. Afterwards it is covered either with honey or with a sugar and water syrup that has been flavoured with lemon. Also excellent are the dried fruits such as apricots, peaches or plums which have been stuffed with nuts. Another interesting and enjoyable novelty is fruit or sour lavash, similar to the ordinary lavash but made with fruit. Plum was the classic fruit to use but nowadays a wide range of fruits is employed.

Drinks

Armenia is justly renowned for its brandy, its coffee and its spring water. Other drinks such as some of the herbal teas – particularly the thyme tea – are well worth trying and certain of the wines are passable without quite threatening the industries of Chile or Australia just yet. Armenian alcohol consumption is at the bottom end of the European range. Although beer can be drunk freely, social etiquette has established formal rules for the drinking of wine and spirits. They may be drunk only when eating and each table has its *tamada* who is responsible for making toasts: no-one drinks without a toast. Toasts can be extremely long, with persons around the table requesting the tamada to be allowed to toast. The theory is that the tamada is able to regulate the alcohol intake of those present and stop people getting drunk. Unfortunately it doesn't always work because the tamada himself sometimes ends up inebriated forcing everyone else to keep going. For most Westerners anyway this ritual is irksome since they are both forced to swig a glass of brandy or vodka when they don't want one or else they are forbidden to enjoy a sip of wine with the food. Women will be let off drinking at every toast but it is considered unacceptable for men not to drink every time. It should be noted that Armenians themselves often prefer to drink brandy or vodka with meals rather than drink wine, quite contrary to Western habits. Indeed while one often sees Armenians drinking vodka, drinking even Armenian wine is largely the prerogative of foreigners.

Armenia's drinks industry suffered from two heavy blows in the late 1980s. Firstly Soviet President Gorbachev launched a strong anti-alcohol campaign and then during the blockade years in the early 1990s goods could not reach its main market in the rest of the CIS. As markets could not import Armenian products other, often inferior, suppliers were only too happy to step into the void. As a result of both these factors production and sales fell considerably eventually bottoming out in 1996 since when there has been some recovery.

Armenian brandy sprang to prominence at the Yalta conference in 1945 when Stalin plied Winston Churchill, the British prime minister, with it and Churchill declared that it was better than any French brandy. Many would still agree. Although called cognac in Armenia and the rest of the former Soviet Union, this is forbidden under Western trade rules which specify that cognac must be produced in the Cognac region of France. Armenian brandy comes in a variety of qualities. At the bottom of the range is three star, so called because it has been kept (in oak casks) for three years after fermentation. Up to six years the number of stars indicates age but beyond six years special names are given. The Ararat factory in Yerevan, founded in 1887 and now owned by Pernod Ricard, offers Ani (six years old), Select (seven years old), Ahtamar (ten years old), Celebratory (15 years old), Vaspurakan (18 years old) and Nairi (20 years old). Prices range from AMD1,500 for a 500ml bottle of three star to AMD4,000 for Ani and AMD25,000 for Nairi. About 70% of production is exported to Russia. Other quality producers are Great Valley and MAP and they also export a large proportion of their production. There are around a dozen smaller firms producing inferior products.

Vodka is distilled by more than 45 small and medium-sized companies in Armenia, including Avshar, Vedi-Alco, SGS (based in Nagorno Karabagh), Garib and Artashat-Vincon. Production has been increasing steadily since 1996 and in 2000 Armenia began exporting its vodka, mainly to the United States and Cyprus. As well as ordinary vodka, several traditional Armenian varieties are made in people's homes such as mulberry vodka, grape vodka and apricot vodka. Many of the vodkas are pleasant enough but they do not compare in quality to the brandy, though they are popular in Armenia.

There are more than 15 wineries in Armenia but output of wine has continued to decline. Armenia grows a range of grape varieties but the climate does not lend itself to the 'cool climate' grape growing such as is becoming more popular in the New World and the wineries have had insufficient funds to be able to invest in temperature-controlled fermentation. A considerable number of different white and red wines is available, many of the reds being sweet or semi-sweet. Although the best-known grape variety in Armenia is Areni, used for making dry red wines, the most enjoyable Armenian wines are those made by the Ijevan winery from Georgian grape varieties. Saperavi is used for the reds and Rkatsiteli for the whites. Although some very cheap wine is available, the more drinkable bottles cost about AMD1,800 to AMD2,000, slightly more in a restaurant whose mark-ups, other than in Western-style hotels, rarely exceed 25%.

Although imported beer is occasionally encountered, usually from Heineken or Russia's Baltika brewery, two indigenous brands are ubiquitous throughout the country. Both Kilikia (brewed in Yerevan) and Kotayk (brewed in Abovian) brands are produced in the same two styles: a light Pilsner lager and a Münchner dunkel ('Munich dark') lager. Local connoisseurs tend to prefer the Kilikia brand but many visitors opt for Kotayk. Beer costs around AMD250 for a 500ml bottle bought from a stall but this rises to AMD300 in a provincial café and AMD350 in central Yerevan.

Haikakan surch, Armenian coffee, (also called *sev surch*, black coffee) is excellent and the perfect end to a meal, ideally accompanied by a glass of brandy. It is brewed in small long-handled copper pots using very finely ground beans and served in small cups in a similar way to Turkish coffee. It is usually served slightly sweetened (called *normal* with the stress on the second syllable) and even visitors who drink coffee without sugar at home may prefer it this way. If coffee is desired without any sugar then ask for it *surch arants shakari*. In a café coffee costs around AMD100. Instant coffee is also available and tastes just like it does everywhere else. Tea (*tay*) in Armenia can be either a standard brand of tea bag dunked in a cup or, in households in rural areas, herbal. Some wonderful teas, especially thyme tea, may be encountered made from a whole gamut of different herbs collected from Armenia's hillsides during the summer and then dried. Unfortunately they are rarely available in hotels or restaurants.

Water is another joy in Armenia. The water from Armenia's springs is delicious and always safe to drink. Many of these springs are located by the sides of roads or tracks or at monastic sights and, quite often, picnic tables are provided. It may seem bizarre to recommend spring water but all visitors should make an effort to try it. Bottled water is also available. Jermuk is the most common source but Dilijan and Bjni may also be encountered. It is almost invariably carbonated on the grounds that people would not pay money to buy anything else.

Pasteurised fruit juices are widely available, normally in cartons, as is the usual international range of bottled soft drinks together with some local competitors. A particular joy which might be encountered during a homestay is fruit juice made from the family's own fruit trees. Cornelian cherry juice is especially recommended. Occasionally one of the more traditional restaurants will have a novel juice on offer: sea buckthorn juice is one possibility. Despite its name sea buckthorn, *Hippophae rhamnoides*, a small tree of the oleaster family, grows in Armenia.

MEDIA AND COMMUNICATIONS
Telephone
The government has been considerably criticised for granting Armentel, 90% Greek owned with the remaining shares held by the European Bank for Reconstruction and Development, a monopoly on telephone services for 15 years in return for a commitment to invest US$300 million by 2006. The monopoly on mobile-phone services has since been reduced to five years. There is widespread dissatisfaction with Armentel which is generally perceived to have increased charges to above the regional average with no perceptible improvement in service.

Mobile-phone service is available only in the vicinity of Yerevan, Armavir, the Ararat towns, Ejmiatsin, Sevan and Gyumri; Armentel also provides internet access at these places though at prices higher than in the West. Local internet service providers serve Vanadzor, Sisian, Goris and Kapan. In Yerevan, Ejmiatsin, Sevan and Gyumri, international dialling is available from any phone. Otherwise it is best to go to the main post office in any town to make international calls.

Dialling Armenia from abroad the country code is 374 followed by the local city code without the initial 0. The city code for Yerevan is 1. Those for other cities include Alaverdi (53), Armavir (37), Ashtarak (32), Dilijan (680), Ejmiatsin (31), Gyumri (41), Ijevan (63), Jermuk (87), Kapan (85), Meghri (860), Sevan (61), Sisian (830), Stepanavan (56), Talin (490), Tsaghkadzor (23), Vanadzor (51). The code for accessing mobile phones is 9 except for those on the ITN (Iskra 2) network for which it is 96.

In Yerevan and a few other places calls can be made from public card-phones in the streets, the cards being on sale at post offices. In the many towns without card-phones it is necessary to go to the main post office to make a call. The procedure involves writing the number required on a form, handing it to the clerk, and then waiting to be connected manually. Post offices are open for this purpose well into the evening daily including Sundays.

A curious feature of Armenian use of the internet is that it cannot cope with the Armenian alphabet and, surprisingly, not even the Cyrillic alphabet with any reliability. Therefore Armenians emailing each other tend to transliterate these languages into Roman letters. This might eventually lead to a more standardised transliteration of place names into English and other Western languages. If carrying out internet searches, problems arise because of the lack of standardisation of spelling (see page viii).

Postal services

These are nothing like as unreliable as sometimes claimed although they can be quite slow. Items have taken as little as six days from Yerevan to Scotland and as little as nine days in the opposite direction. It is sometimes slower, particularly from the provinces. It is unnecessary to address the envelope in Armenian script as Roman letters seem to work quite well, at least if the postcode (zip code) is included. Other than at the main post offices in Yerevan, counter clerks never seem to know what the correct postage is but they do eventually come up with a figure and the letters do arrive. It is fairly easy to buy postcards in Yerevan but they are hard to find elsewhere as Armenians simply don't send them. They do however send Christmas cards and the post can consequently be slower then.

CULTURAL DOS AND DON'TS

As is made clear throughout this guide, Armenians are extremely hospitable and, especially in rural areas, visitors will often be invited into people's houses for coffee. Accept with good grace, however poor the family. The invitation is sincere and the family will be genuinely pleased to see you. If dining with a family, perhaps on a homestay, expect to be plied with far more food than it is humanly possible to eat. It is however polite to at least try every dish.

When visiting churches it is customary to buy candles (expect to pay AMD100) and then light them. Unless intending to take communion there is no particular need to dress more conservatively than anywhere else in Armenia.

Armenians do tend to dress more smartly than Westerners and also more formally. Going to the theatre or concert is an occasion for formality (suit or dress) rather than for dressing down. Shorts are worn in summer but are not particularly common.

It is normal to greet people any time you meet them outside a town (Just say 'Barev dzez' – 'Hello'). Expect people in rural areas to be very curious about where you come from and what you are doing - as well as wanting to know what you think about Armenia. It is very hard not to interact with local people, although the language barrier is considerable. Very few people speak English, and even those who do (such as English teachers) may have difficulty in understanding the language when spoken by a native English speaker, so unaccustomed are they to hearing it.

GIVING SOMETHING BACK

Armenia is highly dependent on charitable help from abroad, mainly but not exclusively provided by members of the diaspora. All contributions to programmes great and small are welcome. These might range in size from a new classroom for a village school to 150km of new road and they also cover green projects such as the planting of trees to replace those cut down for firewood during the electricity shortages of 1992–95. Donations can be made via the website of the Hayastan All-Armenian Fund (www.himnadram.org) or through one of the local branches. The UK address is Hayastan All-Armenian Fund Great Britain, Armenian Vicarage, Iverna Gardens, Kensington, London W8 6TP (tel and fax: 0208 993 2266; email: acarapeti@aol.com). Donors can be certain that their money will be used to fund the project specified. It will not end up in some corrupt politician's pocket: the diaspora go to see how their money has been spent and would never tolerate corruption.

Part Two

The Guide

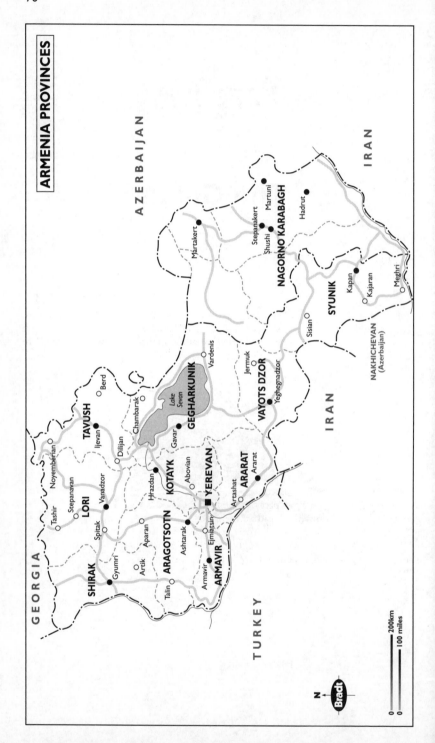

ARMENIA PROVINCES

Yerevan

Armenia's capital stands on the Hrazdan river which flows south from Lake Sevan to join the Arax south of the city. The river in its deep gorge skirts the centre of the city on its western side and consequently many visitors only ever see it as they cross Victory Bridge (so called because it was built in 1945) on the drive into the city from Zvartnots airport. Yerevan's lower parts are at an altitude of around 900m above sea level but the higher parts up on the plateau are around 1,200m. Precipitation is light at 277mm per annum with May being the wettest month (43mm) and August the driest (8mm). The average temperature (measured over 24 hours) varies from –3°C in January to 26°C in July though these averages mask considerable diurnal variation: night-time lows in January are around –15°C while daytime highs in July reach 44°C. Yerevan is a very sunny place with an average of 2,579 hours of sunshine annually (there are 8,760 hours in a year) and only 37 days classed as non-sunny.

Yerevan's centre, Republic Square, boasts some of the finest Soviet-era buildings in the whole of the former USSR and there is a surprising range of architectural styles within the whole central area owing largely to the fusion of Armenian and Russian styles. Outside the central core of the city, Soviet influence is rampant owing to the rapid expansion of the city during that epoch when its population increased 30 times. Although Yerevan's fortunes have waxed and waned considerably over time, and it was never the capital of Armenia prior to 1918, it is actually a very old city. The Urartian king Argrishti I (ruled c785–c762BC) established a garrison of 6,600 troops at Erebuni in the southeast part of the present city in 782BC, thus making Yerevan older even than Rome which is traditionally claimed to have been founded in 753BC. About a century later, the Urartian king Rusa II (ruled c685–c645BC) chose a different site, Teishebai Uru ('City of [the God] Teisheba') overlooking the Hrazdan river which he believed would be less vulnerable to attack by the Scythians. It is now known as Karmir Blur ('Red Hill') in the western part of the modern city. Erebuni had grown within 100 years to be a substantial settlement but the establishment of Teishebai Uru caused its rapid decline.

Proximity to the fertile plain ensured that Yerevan remained a significant settlement as, along with the rest of Armenia, it was caught up over the centuries of turmoil, its size fluctuating considerably as the degree of urbanisation in the country varied. Eventually it was destroyed almost totally by an earthquake in 1679. The collapsed bridge over the Hrazdan was quickly replaced by a new four-arch structure and Yerevan's importance began to rise again as it found itself close to the frontier line where the Persian, Turkish and Russian empires were jostling for supremacy. At the time of the earthquake Yerevan itself was under Persian rule, with a mixed Christian and Muslim population. In 1684, at the request of the

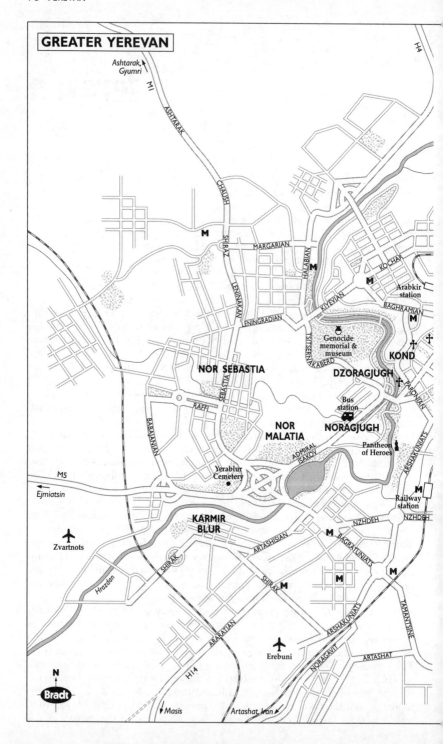

GREATER YEREVAN

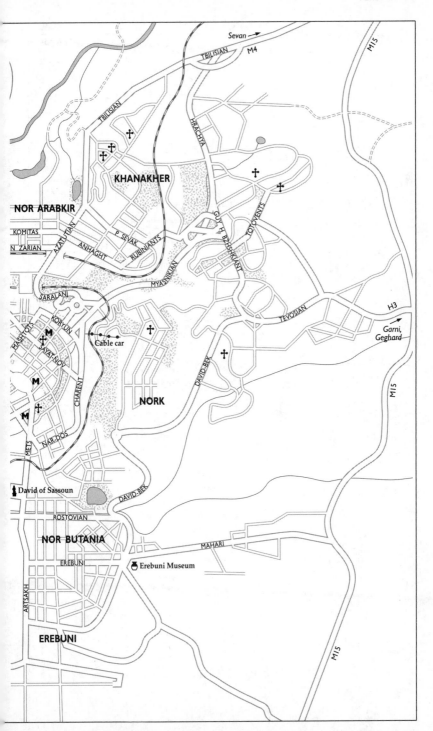

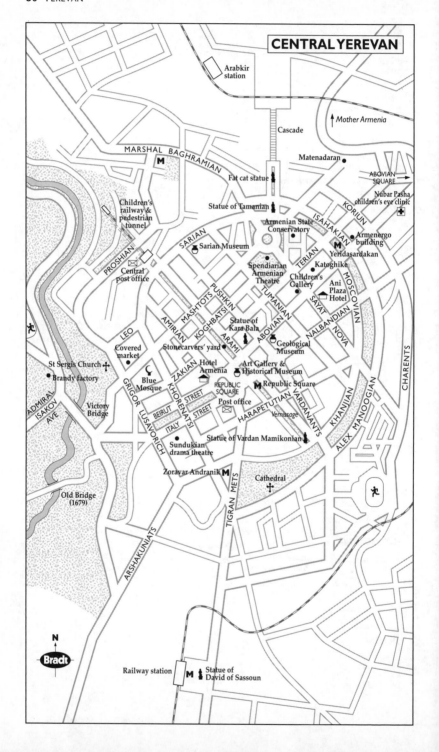

CENTRAL YEREVAN

Arabkir station

Cascade

↑ Mother Armenia

MARSHAL BAGHRAMIAN

Matenadaran

ABOVIAN SQUARE →

Fat cat statue

Statue of Tamanian

Nubar Pasha children's eye clinic

Children's railway & pedestrian tunnel

Armenian State Conservatory

ISAHAKIAN

KORIUN

MOSCOVIAN

Armenergo building

SARIAN

Sarian Museum

TERIAN

Yeridasardakan

PROSHIAN

Central post office

Spendiarian Armenian Theatre

Children's Gallery

Katoghike

TUMANIAN

SAYAT NOVA

Ani Plaza Hotel

MASHTOTS

PUSHKIN

KOGHBATSI

ABOVIAN

NALBANDIAN

CHARENTS

LEO

AMIRIAN

ARAMI

Statue of Kara Bala

Geological Museum

Covered market

Stonecarvers' yard

St Sergis Church ✝

Brandy factory

GRIGOR LUSAVORICH

ZAKIAN

Hotel Armenia

Blue Mosque

Art Gallery & Historical Museum

KHANJIAN

VARDANANTS

ALEX MANOOGIAN

Victory Bridge

ADMIRAL ISAKOV AVE

KHORENATSI STREET

BEIRUT STREET

REPUBLIC SQUARE

Post office

Republic Square

HARAPETUTIAN

Vernissage

ITALY STREET

Statue of Vardan Mamikonian

Old Bridge (1679)

Sundukian drama theatre

Zoravar Andranik

TIGRAN METS

Cathedral ✝

ARSHAKUNIATS

N

Bradt

Railway station

Statue of David of Sassoun

French king Louis XIV, Shah Suleiman II permitted French Jesuits to establish a mission there to try to persuade the Katholikos to accept the supremacy of the pope and bring the Armenian church into the Roman Catholic fold. The missionaries achieved little and greatly lamented the loss of the excellent Yerevan wine when Shah Hussein, who had succeeded his father, banned all wine throughout the Persian empire in 1694. A new main church to replace those destroyed in the earthquake was erected in 1693–94 and a new central mosque in 1765–66.

Russian expansion southwards into the Caucasus began under Peter the Great in 1722, ostensibly with the object of protecting Orthodox believers. It was a fairly gradual process. In 1801 Russia formally annexed eastern Georgia as the new Russian province of Tiflis and installed Prince Paul Tsitsianov, Georgian born but Russian educated, as governor. In 1804 Tsitsianov led a 5,000-strong Russian army south and attacked Yerevan on May 1. Despite besieging the town from July 2 until September 3 he was forced to withdraw but the following year he was asked by two Armenian notables to try again so as to save the Christian population of Yerevan from Muslim oppression. His haughty reply was to the effect that he did not care even if the Christians at Yerevan were 'dying in the hands of unbelievers' because 'unreliable Armenians with Persian souls' deserved in his view to 'die like dogs' since they had done nothing to help him when he was besieging the city. Tsitsianov was killed at Baku in 1806 and in 1808 Russia made a second attempt, this time under Field Marshal Ivan Vasilievich (1741–1820) but had no more success. Eventually General Ivan Paskevich (1782–1856), a veteran of the battle of Borodino, succeeded and led victorious Russian troops into Yerevan on October 2 1827. On this occasion the Tsar awarded him the title Count of Yerevan but he subsequently gained the additional title Prince of Warsaw as a further token of the Tsar's appreciation after he was responsible for killing 9,000 Poles during the second Polish uprising against Russian rule in 1831.

The Russian conquerors found a town which in 1828 had 1,736 low mud-brick houses, 851 shops, ten baths, eight mosques, seven churches, seven caravanserais and six public squares all set among gardens surrounded by mud walls. On the one and only visit to Yerevan by a Tsar, Nikolai I in 1837 described the city as a 'clay pot' and matters only changed slowly in what was still a garrison town: the principal Russian settlement in Armenia was Alexandropol (Gyumri) rather than Yerevan. Occasional traces of 19th-century Yerevan can still be found although Yerevan's importance was to change out of all recognition with its proclamation as capital of the First Armenian Republic on May 28 1918. The brilliant Armenian architect Alexander Tamanian (1878–1936) drew up a master plan in 1924–26 for what was now the capital of Soviet Armenia. It envisaged the creation of a large central square surrounded by imposing buildings constructed of tuff. From this square would lead broad avenues, and encircling the whole central area would be a green ring of parkland. Quite a large part of this did in fact come to pass and is described in the following section.

Tamanian did not of course foresee the 30-fold expansion of the city's population during the Soviet era to an estimated 1.2 million with its dreary urban sprawl of apartment blocks. There was in practice considerable local enthusiasm for expanding the city since any Soviet city with a population exceeding one million was considered to be of 'all Union importance' and entitled to benefits which included a metro system and a crematorium. Economic problems since independence have resulted in a fall in Armenia's population so the main focus in building, apart from the new cathedral, is on luxury houses for the new elite together with the paraphernalia of hotels, embassies and accommodation for expatriates which any capital city attracts. There is also under way considerable necessary and welcome refurbishment of infrastructure such as roads and pavements which is largely being paid for by the diaspora. By contrast the erosion of the green belt by an amazing number of cafés is rather sad.

EMBASSIES AND CONSULATES IN YEREVAN

Belarus 23 Abovian St, Apt 23; tel: 597309; fax: 567018; email: armenia@arminco.com
Bulgaria 11 Nor Aresh St, h.85; tel: 458233; fax: 454602; email: bularm@arminco.com
Canada (consulate) 25/22 Demirchian St; tel: 567903, 401238
China 12 Bagramian Av; tel: 560067, 561234; fax: 545761; email: chiemb@mbox.arminco.com
Egypt 6a Sepuh St; tel: 226755, 220117, 541352; fax: 226425; email: egyemb@arminco.com
Estonia (consulate) 43 Arabkir, h.37a; tel: 258641; fax: 251526; email: aries@arminco.com
France 8 Grigor Lusavorich St; tel: 583511; fax: 569831; email: admin@ambafran.am; web: www.ambafran.am
Georgia 42 Arami St; tel: 564357, 585511; fax: 564183; email: georgia@arminco.com
Germany 29 Charents St; tel: 523279, 524581, 586591; fax: 524781; email: germemb@arminco.com
Greece 12 Proshian St; tel: 530051, 536754; fax: 530049; email: grembarm@arminco.com
India 8th floor, Hotel Hrazdan, 72a Dzorapi St; tel: 535343, 535027; fax: 537833; email: inemyr@arminco.com
Iran 1 Budaghian St; tel: 284057, 232920, 232952; fax: 230052; email: info@iranembassy.am; web: www.iranembassy.am
Iraq 24 Sevastopolian St; tel: 261223; fax: 261322
Italy 1c Khorenatsi St; tel: 542335; fax: 542301; email: ambitaly@arminco.com
Lebanon 7 Vardanants St; tel: 526540, 561496, 589874; fax: 526990; email: libarm@arminco.com
Norway (consulate) 50 Khanjian St, Tekeyan Centre (tel: 551582, 571798; fax: 574639; email: admin@nrc.am
Poland 44a Hanrapetutian St; tel: 542493, 542495; fax: 542498, 542496; email: polemb@arminco.com
Romania 3 Sepuh St; tel: 274701, 275860, 265207; fax: 544144
Russia 13a Grigor Lusavorich St; tel: 567427, 589843; fax: 567197, 582463; email: rossia@arminco.com; web: www.armenia.mid.ru
Syria 14 Bagramian Av; tel: 524028, 524036, 529023; fax: 524058; email: syria.em.arm@netsys.am
Thailand (consulate) 8 Amirian St; tel: 560410; fax: 544425; email: info@thaiconsulate.am
Ukraine 58 Yerznkian St; tel: 586856, 228296; fax: 227402; email: ukremb@internet.am; web: www.erevan.am/ukrembassy
UK 34 Baghramian Av; tel: 264301; fax: 264318; email: britemb@arminco.com; web: www.britemb.am
Uruguay 26/9 Ghazar Parpetsu St; tel: 534910; fax: 534930; email: uruguay@freenet.am
US The new US embassy on Admiral Isakov Avenue is due to open in 2004, although there are suggestions that it might slip into 2005. It doesn't yet have a telephone number.

GETTING AROUND YEREVAN
Metro

The metro consists of one line together with a short branch in the southern suburbs. The main line runs from the north side of the city across the central district and out to the south. The first section from Baregamatyun ('Friendship') in the north to Sassountsi David ('David of Sassoun') adjacent to the main railway station was opened on March 7 1981. The system was then extended south to Gortsaranayin ('Factory') in 1983, Shengavit in 1985 and Gareguin Njdehi

Hraparak in 1987. The branch to Charbakh was opened after independence in 1996 to make a total of 13.4km of route with ten stations. An extension into the northwestern suburbs is under construction which will cross the Hrazdan river on a bridge. Most of the existing route is underground with only two stations, Sassountsi David and Gortsaranayin, being built above ground. Trains are usually formed of two coaches – although the platforms were built to accommodate five coach trains – and run every five minutes. A flat fare of AMD40 is charged and entry to the platforms is by plastic tokens which can be purchased from the ticket office at any station. The maps of the route can be confusing since they show not only the operating part of the system in red but also some projected extensions in blue. When on a train it is impossible to read the names of stations since the signs are carefully positioned so as to be invisible from the trains. It is therefore necessary to listen to the announcements or else count the number of stops. The entrances to stations are marked on the surface by the blue letter 'Ս' which is capital 'M' (for Metro) in the Armenian alphabet.

Trams

Yerevan had trams as far back as Tsarist days but the present network started to be developed in 1930. It is uncertain for how much longer it will remain because the equipment is ageing and unreliable and the losses made are heavy. The scale of losses is a consequence of only half the passengers actually paying, either because they are pensioners or war veterans who are entitled to free travel or else because they simply have no money. The network has already been truncated but remains useful to visitors as the easiest means of reaching Erebuni which is accessible by tram number 7 from Zoravar Andranik metro station. It is indeed ironic that the closure of Yerevan's tram system is being contemplated at a time when other cities worldwide are reintroducing or extending tram systems as an answer to traffic congestion and air pollution. The flat fare is AMD40.

Buses

Trolleybuses were introduced to the city in 1949 to supplement the trams and they also charge a flat fare of AMD40. More recently conventional diesel buses have been added for which the fare is also AMD40 within the city. No further vehicles were purchased after independence until 2003 when some buses were bought second-hand from Marseille. Most of them still sport the legend *Ville de Marseille*. The most conspicuous means of transport is minibuses (*marshrutny*). A network of routes covers the city with the vehicles operating at frequent intervals until the small hours. To board one simply wave it down in the street and then indicate to the driver when you wish to alight. It is normal to pay when getting off. Most routes charge a flat AMD100 (more than twice the price of public transport) but a few charge less, indicated by a second number in the windscreen.

The routes most likely to be of interest to tourists are those which serve the bus station and hence pass close to the Ararat brandy factory: see page 99. Outside the city bus 107 runs to the airport at a higher fare and bus 111 travels to Ejmiatsin via Zvartnots cathedral.

ACCOMMODATION

The development of new hotels in Yerevan, particularly upmarket ones, has outstripped demand and the resulting superfluity means that it is possible in many cases for individuals making their own bookings to get a reduction on the advertised price. During the winter most hotels charge a lower rate than that quoted anyway. These establishments always quote their prices in US dollars.

Note that a few tend to quote their prices excluding Armenia's 20% VAT. Some hotels away from the central area provide free transport to and from the centre. This can be quite a pleasant option in the heat and humidity of midsummer but the inconvenience would probably outweigh the bonuses for most visitors.

At the opposite end of the scale the best option is undoubtedly a homestay, particularly as dinner can be requested and will prove to be a much more authentically Armenian experience than restaurants will provide. One snag is of course the language barrier and a second is that most parts of the city only receive water for a few hours a day so ablution may perforce be with water from a bucket at times. Also there will only be one bathroom for everyone, both you and the household. Homestays, invariably safe and usually very comfortable, can be arranged either through Armenia Information whose office is open daily from 09.00 to 19.00 at 3 Nalbandian Street (tel: +374 1 542303, 542304; email: help@armeniainfo.am; web: www.armeniainfo.am) or through Yerevan travel agents. Staying in someone's house will give you a quite different insight into Armenian life. Expect to pay a few dollars a night with a modest supplement for meals. It's best to buy a street plan beforehand and then ask the travel agent to show you where you are going as the biggest problem is often finding the right place. Take a note of the address in Armenian so that you can enquire of people and also ask which minibus goes in the right direction: or splash out on one of Yerevan's very inexpensive taxis.

Homestays are a far better option than the seedy rundown dormitories at the bus and railway stations. These are not recommended for any but the destitute and not for women under any circumstances.

Central area hotels

Ani Plaza 19 Sayat Nova Av; tel: 594500; fax: 565343; email: info@anihotel.com; web: www.anihotel.com. A 14-storey tower block with 149 rooms built in 1970 and partly renovated in 2002. Very much improved and quite pleasant. 10 minutes' walk from the centre. Singles from US$84 and twins from US$102 on the unrenovated floors and from US$138 and US$168 on the upgraded ones.

Ararat 7 Grigor Lusarovich St; tel: 510000, 541100; fax: 511101; email: info@ararathotel.am; web: www.ararathotel.am. Handy for the French, Italian and Russian embassies about 10 minutes' walk from the centre. The hotel boasts 'medical' mattresses and there is a free internet connection in each room. 52 rooms and 5 suites. From US$70 for a single room and US$80 for a double to US$900 for the presidential suite.

Armenia Marriott 1 Amirian St; tel: 599000; fax: 599001; email: info@hotelarmenia.com; web: www.hotelarmenia.com. Absolutely central with an attractive façade on Republic Square. The building dates from 1954 but has been completely modernised and the formerly small rooms have been greatly enlarged. The mattresses here are '8 inch foam king size'. All 115 rooms have separate living and sleeping areas. From US$115 plus 20% VAT. Breakfast extra.

Astafian 5/1 Abovian St; tel: 39 521111; fax: 39 564572; email: astafian@netsys.am; web: www.astafian.am. Very central. 9 rooms (all very large). From US$120 per room.

Aviatrans 4 Abovian St; tel: 567226, 567228; fax: 584442; email: hotel@aviatrans.am; web: www.aviatrans.am/aviahot.html. A small (16-room) hotel of interesting appearance built in 1999. All rooms have separate living and sleeping area but are quite small. On the main shopping street and very central. The night bar is aimed at jazz and pop music enthusiasts so be warned. Singles from US$75; doubles from US$120.

Congress Shahumian Sq; tel: 580095; fax: 522224; email: congress@arminco.com. Very central with 128 rooms. Some guests report being asked for a (refundable) US$100 deposit in case they used the phone. Singles from US$65 plus 20% VAT and doubles from US$90 plus VAT. Breakfast extra.

Erebuni 26/1 Nalbandian St; tel: 564993; fax: 564993. Huge place (220 rooms) built in 1980 for tourists and partially renovated in 2000. Very central but fairly basic and food not recommended. Singles from US$30 and twins from US$55.

Guest House of the University 52 Mashtots St; tel: 560003; email: pr-int@ysu.am. Recent refurbishment has turned this into a pleasant hotel which will accommodate tourists if there is room. Singles from US$30 and doubles from US$50.

Hy Business 8 Hanrapetutian St; tel: 567567; fax: 543131; email: hybus@arminco.com; web: www.hybusiness.com. Breakfast is served in this comfortable hotel but, unusually, no other meals and each room has at least a kitchenette to allow the preparation of food. Singles from US$90 and doubles from US$120.

Shirak 13a Khorenatsi St; tel: 529915; fax: 529915; email: shirak_hotel@infocom.am; web: www.shirak-hotel.am. Large 14-storey tower block with 110 rooms built in 1981 and renovated in 2001. 500m from centre. Hot water only available at specified times. Singles from US$42 and twins from US$72.

Yerevan 14 Abovian St; tel: 589400; fax: 564677; email: yerhot@arminco.com; web: www.hotelyerevan.com. Yerevan's oldest and most expensive hotel. It was built in 1927 and refurbished in 1998 but the 104 rooms are surprisingly small. On the main shopping street about 5 minutes from the centre. Rooftop swimming pool. Singles from US$150 and doubles from US$185 plus 20% VAT. Breakfast extra.

Hotels outside the centre

Arabkir 54 Komitas St; tel: 231990; web: www.aquarius.am/eng/harabkir.html. Close to Arabkir market, Arabkir railway station and Komitas park on the north side of the centre, a good deal more accessible now that the escalator alongside the Cascade has been repaired. A 20-room hotel, it has hot water at specified times. Singles from US$17. Doubles from US$30.

Areg 80 Bournazian St; tel: 456213; email: anazo@web.am; web: www.areg.am. Located near the main railway station and hence easily accessible by metro. Small guesthouse offering meals and free internet access 24 hours a day. Hot water available at specified times. Twin rooms from US$34.

Arma 275 Norqi Ayginer; tel: 546000; fax: 544166; email: hotel@arma.am; web: www.arma.am. Overlooking the city from the northeast, the views over Yerevan towards Ararat are stunning and the food here is way above average. It is particularly enjoyable to dine on the terrace watching the sun sink below the Turkish mountains. This 20-room hotel opened for business in 1996 and provides free transport to and from the centre – not all that far away but it's a steep climb. Singles from US$70 and doubles from US$80.

Armenian Red Cross Society Hotel 50/1 Gevork Chaush St; tel: 342349, 358341, 353297; email: archotel@freenet.am; web: arcs.nt.am. 8km north of centre. Separate buildings with studios and 1- and 2-bedroom apartments in a quiet area. Can organise hiking and riding trips. From US$18 to US$30 per person per day.

Avan Villa Nork Marash, 7/1 13th St; tel: 543122, 543422, 547888; fax: 547877; email: tufhosp@arminco.com; web: www.tufenkian.am. In Nork about 25 minutes from the centre by taxi and free transportation available. One of the new Tufenkian Heritage Hotels it has 14 rooms and is decorated in traditional Armenian style. The website also claims 'Frette Egyptian cotton sheets, Sealy crown jewel mattresses, wooden parquet floors and famous hand-made Tufenkian Armenian carpets'. (The owner of the chain is involved in carpet manufacture.) Very good Armenian cooking indeed. Doubles from US$115.

Bass 3/5 Aigedzor St; tel: 222638, 261080, 262751; fax: 230182; email: bass@lans.am; web: www.bass.am. Located on the west side of the city near the American university about 20 minutes' walk or 5 minutes by taxi from the centre. Built in 1995 it was the first new hotel to be opened after independence. Quite small (14 rooms). Very pleasant staff and very good food. Singles from US$117 and doubles from US$130.

Hrazdan 72 Dzorapi St; tel: 535332; fax: 523798; email: asimon@freenet.am; web: www.aviatrans.am/hrazdan.html. As the name implies, situated on the west side near the river. About 20 minutes' walk or 5 minutes by taxi. A 13-storey tower block built in 1976, its 51 rooms are currently being renovated. Hot water at specified times. Popular with Iranian traders. From US$45 for singles and US$55 for doubles.

Maison d'Hôte de Nork 123 Amaranotzayin St; tel: 653949. The French name simply means Nork guesthouse, Nork being the district of Yerevan to the southeast of the centre and less than 10 minutes by taxi. Attractive front garden and back courtyard with views over the city to Ararat. Singles from US$50 and doubles from US$70.

Metropol 2/2 Mashtots Av; tel: 543701; fax: 543702; email: reservation@metropol.am; web: www.metropol.am. Close to Victory Bridge about 20 minutes' walk from the centre, this 40-room hotel opened in 2001. Singles from US$110 and doubles from US$125.

Nairi 250 Amaranotsain St; tel: 650567. Also in Nork. Gradually being improved after misuse during its time as a home for refugees. It's still charging low prices although it's secure and clean. Doubles from only US$6. Breakfast not included at this price.

Olympia 56 Barbussy St; tel: 277424; fax: 271826; email: reservation@olympia.am; web: www.olympia.am. Overlooking the Hrazdan river on the northwest side about 15 minutes by taxi from the centre. Small (12 rooms) with an outdoor café. Singles from US$60 and doubles from US$80. Breakfast not included.

Sil 20 Tigran Mets Av; tel: 545000, 540708; fax: 545000; email: silhtl@arminco.com; web: www.sil.com. Close to Zoravar Andranik metro station in a noisy district about 15 minutes' walk from the centre. Opened in 1999 this 23-room hotel boasts a 24-hour restaurant. Popular with Iranians. Singles from US$90 and doubles from US$100.

Terian 5th St, Silken; tel: 390388, 399699; fax: 398699; email: info@terjanhotel.am; web: www.terjanhotel.am. About 12km to the northwest. Opened in 2002 this 8-room hotel with Italian furnishings has been built by a dentist. Very comfortable with beautiful views of Ararat but food needs to improve to match its surroundings. Swimming pool and attractive gardens. Free transport to centre. Rooms from US$65 plus 20% VAT.

Valensia 40 Miasnikian Av; tel: 524000; fax: 543571; email: valensiahotel@valensiatotel.com; web: www.valensiahotel.com. In Nork district 10 minutes from centre by taxi. Rates include free admission to adjacent waterworld which has various facilities for cooling off during the summer including a wave pool. Opened in 2001 with 58 rooms and cottages. Singles from US$80 and doubles from US$100.

EATING

Yerevan has innumerable eating places many of which, especially away from the centre, are very cheap. The following is merely a selection of interesting and popular places. Apart from these it is worth looking at Proshian Street, known locally as Barbecue Street because it is lined with places to eat in the reasonably priced range. Shaurma booths are located along many main streets (especially Tumanian, Tigran Mets and Isahakian) and sell sandwiches with *lavash* as the bread. Prices go up to AMD350 depending on the filling and location. Note that restaurants in hotels are not included in this list.

Aragast 41 Isahakian St. An imitation boat with a pleasant view over a small artificial lake with boats. Inexpensive.

Armenian Cuisine 42 Mashtots Av. Good family cooking.

Armenian Pizza 21/1 Tumanian St; tel: 580106. The best place for *lahmajoun*, Armenia's own fast food. Quick and cheap.

Bacchus 29 Tumanian St; tel: 564600. Western food with live classical music in the evenings. Those fed up with pork barbecues should head for here.

Bellagio 3 Amirian St; tel: 545900, 545200. Serves Armenian, Georgian and 'European' food. Pleasantly quiet downstairs and very reliable for quality. The waitresses are currently (2003) wearing mini-kilts in the Dress Stewart tartan. The waiters look like waiters.

Caucasus 82 Hanrapetutian St; tel: 561177, 562614. Serves traditional Armenian and Georgian food but not everything on the extensive menu is always available. Live folk music evenings in the side decorated in Armenian style: you can hear it wafting through to the Georgian side. Reservation advisable.

Chicken Coop 65 Terian St; tel: 589215. Small restaurant with good Armenian food.

Dolmana 10 Pushkin St; tel: 568931. Perhaps Yerevan's best restaurant. Very expensive indeed by Yerevan standards. Whether it's worth the money depends on who is paying.

Fiesta 21 Abovian St. Pleasant atmosphere. Varied menu. Very quiet for those wanting a peaceful meal.

Khachapuri stand Corner of Pushkin and Abovian streets. Very cheap fast food. *Khachapuri* is a Georgian bread in which the dough is baked after being filled with cheese. The stand also sells Russian fast-food specialities such as *ponchiki* (doughnuts flavoured with cinnamon) and *piroshki* (small meat pies).

Lebanese Kitchen Sargisian St opposite Shahumian statue. Lebanese *lahmajoun* isn't quite as good as Armenian but this restaurant offers a wider range of Middle Eastern food at modest prices.

Marco Polo 1/3 Abovian St; tel: 545352. Food quite good and popular with foreigners.

Old Yerevan 2 Hyusisian Av; tel: 540575. Has several separate rooms: two in the basement, one on the ground floor, one on the first floor and rooftop eating is also promised. Live Armenian folk music in evenings. Reservation advisable.

Our Village 7 Sayat Nova Av; tel: 584700. In a basement decorated with old coffee pots, radios, etc. Serves only Armenian produce and drinks. Live folk music in the evenings. Waiting staff wear traditional costume, and menus (singed at edges) have carefully placed holes burnt in them. An experience. Reservations required.

Pizza di Roma 1 Abovian St with smaller branches elsewhere. Forget the name, this place serves a wide range of food and the lunchtime salad bar for AMD1,350 is excellent quality and value. Doctors beware: the menu offers grilled surgeon.

Sherlock Holmes 25 Marshall Baghramian Av. Not sure why the name was chosen. Good salad bar plus hot dishes.

ENTERTAINMENT
Cinema
Two cinemas show films in English most evenings. **Kino Nairi**, at the corner of Mashtots and Moskovian, shows films in English at 22.00. **Kino Moscow**, on Charles Aznavour Square, shows the same film in English and dubbed into Russian in separate auditoria.

Casinos
All Yerevan's casinos have been closed and moved outside the city boundary. The Sevan highway is thickly populated while there are quite a few on the road to the airport.

Musical performance
Classical music
Opera house 54 Tumanian St; tel: 527992. Gives regular performances of opera and ballet and is due to reopen in September 2003. It is worth seeing the building for its own sake.

Aram Khachaturian Concert Hall 46 Mashtots Av; tel: 583471. Home to the Armenian Philharmonic Orchestra. Concerts throughout the season on Sundays. At present the hall is closed for renovation and performances are being held in the large auditorium of the American University of Armenia, 40 Baghramian Avenue.

Komitas Chamber Music Hall 2 Abovian St; tel: 526718. Presents regular concerts by the National Chamber Orchestra of Armenia. At present it is under renovation and performances are being held at the Hakob Paronian Theatre, 4 Khorhrdanian Street.

Jazz
There are two main jazz clubs. **Poplovak (Aragast)**, in Isahakian Park, is temporarily closed for renovation. It is well known for the murder of a Georgian Armenian by presidential bodyguards in the men's lavatories. Quite good for food, reservations are always required. **Sur Club** is on the corner of Sayat Nova and Terian.

Shopping
Craft items are best bought at Vernissage (see page 91) if in Yerevan at the weekend. Otherwise good souvenir shops are Armenian Souvenirs, 18a Tumanian Street and Salt Sack, 3/1 Abovian Street. Yerevan's biggest bookshop is Noah's Ark, Republic Square (but note that some titles available at, for example, the cathedral bookshop at Ejmiatsin, are unavailable here). Good photographic dealers include Konica, 25/14 Nalbandian Street and Jupiter Photo Express (15 Vartanants Street and 50 Terian Street).

WHAT TO SEE
A walk round Yerevan
Visitors to Yerevan are inevitably drawn to the large and imposing **Republic Square** and it is an appropriate place to start this walk: in Soviet times the square was called Lenin Square. It is certainly one of the finest central squares created anywhere in the world during the 20th century. The building on the northeast side with fountains outside is the **National History Museum** of 1926 with its white symmetrical colonnades to which the National Gallery of Art storeys in a similar colour were added in 1950. It formerly also held the Museum of the (Bolshevik) Revolution. The marriage of the 1926 original with the 1950 addition produces a curious effect looking like two quite separate buildings, one behind the other. It is sometimes claimed that Yerevan needed a large new art gallery after 1945 because many valuable works of art were brought here for safe keeping during the war years from other Soviet cities and never subsequently returned; the collection is almost certainly the finest in the former USSR apart from those of Moscow and St Petersburg. The water of the three fountains outside the museum dances in time to classical music on summer evenings while changes to the lighting are used to enhance the effect. This unusual spectacle was invented by Abraham Abrahamian, a professor in the electronics department of Yerevan university.

Underneath the square is a large bunker constructed during the Cold War to protect officials from danger in the event of a nuclear attack. Since independence, suggestions have been made that it could be handed over to the museum as an additional display area but lack of funding together with renewed tensions in the Middle East will probably ensure that it retains its original purpose for a little while longer.

To the left of the museum across Abovian Street on the northwest side of Republic Square is a government building designed by Samvel Safarian (1902–69) and built in the 1950s. It incorporates much Armenian detail but although built to harmonise with the earlier buildings it is somewhat more massive. It now houses the **ministries** of Agriculture, Energy and Fuel, and

Above Art gallery and Historical Museum, Republic Square, Yerevan

Left Statue of Kara Bala, Yerevan

Below Mount Ararat, seen over the Hrazdan River and the rooftops of Yerevan

Above Hand-made traditional rugs are sold at Vernissage, Yerevan's weekend craft market.

Right As in most Armenian villages, women at Byurakan gather together to make *lavash*, Armenia's classic unleavened flat bread.

Below The tomato vendor's car, Ijevan market

Industry. By contrast the ground floor is occupied by one of Yerevan's best bookshops. Continuing anti-clockwise, across Amirian Street is the curving façade of the **Hotel Armenia**, possibly Yerevan's best hotel after its opening in 1954 and now being extensively refurbished by the Marriott chain. Very popular with the diaspora, the Hotel Armenia offered Thai, Chinese, Mexican and Indian cuisine but no Armenian food prior to the refurbishment. However a 54-seat Armenian restaurant is promised for the future, somewhat dwarfed even so by the 148-seat Italian restaurant which is also promised. Presumably the ethnicity of the food reflects the guests' tastes. The pavement café outside is crowded by the diaspora from 08.00 when it opens until 02.00 when it closes and they are certain to meet many of their acquaintances from home if only they sit here long enough. It is worth noting that there is a cash machine inside the hotel at the foot of the grand staircase.

Still continuing anticlockwise a broad street with fountains down the middle is crossed. In the centre of the street formerly stood the statue of Lenin designed by Sergei Merkurov (1881–1952), erected in 1940 to mark the 20th anniversary of Soviet power and speedily removed, along with its huge pedestal, after independence. Standing where the statue once stood and looking at the hillside behind the museum it is possible to see the **statue of Mother Armenia** on an even larger plinth, 34m high, constructed in 1950 as the Victory Memorial in memory of the Great Patriotic War. The bronze statue of Mother Armenia, a heroic figure holding a sword, actually occupies the space formerly occupied by a 16.5m tall statue of Stalin erected in 1950; at 21m Mother Armenia is, perhaps symbolically, taller than Stalin used to be. A Soviet writer in 1952, one year before Stalin's death, claimed:

> Topping the Memorial Building is a statue of Stalin in a long great coat of which one lap is thrown open, showing the figure caught in a forward stride. In this statue wrought in Armenian bronze, the sculptor S Merkurov [the same who was responsible for Lenin], has depicted Stalin in a characteristic pose of dynamic movement, supreme composure and confidence. Stalin stands with one hand in his coat-breast and the other slightly lowered as though his arm, swung in rhythm with his step, has for one brief moment become frozen in space. Stalin's gaze rests upon the splendour of the new Armenian socialist capital, upon its new handsome buildings, its wide green avenues, upon the central square in the opposite end of the town. There, Lenin, in his ordinary workday suit, has swung abruptly around in that characteristic, impetuous, sweeping way of his, so dear and familiar to every Soviet man, woman and child. The statues are very tall and the impression is that the two great leaders exchange glances of deep understanding as they survey the prospering life around them, so much of it the handiwork of their own genius, their self-abnegating labours, their perspicacity, the wisdom that enabled them to see far into the future.

A flower bed has now replaced Lenin. His statue, with head detached, lies stored in the courtyard behind the Historical Museum.

The next building on the square, also built in 1950 and with a curving façade, houses a **post office**. Although not the main post office of Yerevan this one has a pleasing stained-glass window behind the counter depicting a woman in Armenian costume holding a telegraph tape and is useful for buying stamps, especially as the staff actually know the postal rates for letters and cards sent abroad which is not always the case in Armenia. In Soviet times it also held the Council of Trade Unions.

The final building, on the southeast side of Republic Square is a government building housing the prime minister's offices. It was partly built under Tamanian's direction in 1926 though only completed in 1941. An irregular pentagonal structure with one curved side, it is possibly Tamanian's masterpiece. An elegant colonnade above arches forms a gallery along the whole façade and is combined with Armenian detail in the capitals. The archway to the inner courtyard is surmounted by a clocktower which usually flies the red, blue and orange Armenian flag – one of the relatively few places in Yerevan where it is commonly seen. In Soviet days the flag which flew here was of course that of the Armenian Soviet Socialist Republic which actually went through four different designs. The last version, adopted in 1952, was red with a horizontal blue stripe across the middle and a yellow hammer and sickle together with a five-pointed star in the top left corner of the front.

Leave Republic Square along the street which runs between the post office and the government buildings. It is named Tigran Mets in honour of King Tigran II (the Great) who ruled Armenia from c95BC until 55BC. The street bends right after a few yards between buildings which mostly date from the 1920s and 1930s and now house the majority of Yerevan's foreign exchange merchants. It is consequently the best place in Yerevan to exchange money and there is a good chance of even being able to change such exotica as New Zealand dollars or Swedish krone.

Emerging from the avenue of exchange merchants, on the corner of Khanjian Street on the left side of Tigran Mets Street is a **statue of Alexander Griboyedov** (1795–1829), the satirical playwright whose best-known play, *Woe from Wit*, was only performed and published posthumously; in it the hero is branded a lunatic when he arrives in Moscow full of liberal and progressive ideas, a dangerous practice in both the Tsarist and the Communist eras. Griboyedov was also a diplomat instrumental in Russia's peace negotiations with Turkey following the war of 1828–29 when Russia gained control of much of Armenia. After that he was appointed Russia's ambassador to Persia but while Griboyedov was in Teheran negotiating with Persia an angry mob stormed the Russian embassy and killed him.

Just past the statue, the striking building on the right with a two-part roof is the former Russia cinema, now the **Ararat clothing bazaar**: the two parts of the roof symbolise the two peaks of Mount Ararat. Underneath it is the **metro station** originally called Hoktemberian, ('October' in honour of the October revolution of 1917), but now renamed Zoravar Andranik ('Commander Andranik') in honour of Andranik Ozanian (1865–1927). Born in western Armenia, Ozanian became head of Armenian self-defence troops in the 1890s until in 1905 he moved west to seek assistance for the Armenian cause. He subsequently participated in the liberation of Bulgaria from Ottoman rule in 1912–13 before organising Armenian units to fight alongside the Russian army against Turkey during World War I. Being more in sympathy with socialist ideals than the new Armenian government led by the Dashnak party, he left in 1918 for Bulgaria and then moved to the USA, dying in Fresno, California. His last expressed wish was to be buried in Armenia. Although he was originally interred in Fresno, after a few months his coffin was moved to Europe and he was reinterred among the renowned in the cemetery of Père Lachaise in Paris. He was finally brought to Armenia in 2000 and now rests in the Yerablur cemetery in Yerevan where the dead from the Karabagh war are buried. His statue, unveiled in 2003, can be seen at the foot of the slope leading up to the cathedral. It depicts him brandishing a sword while rather uncomfortably riding two horses at once, one of which is crushing a snake beneath its hoof.

The **cathedral**, straight ahead up the slope to the left, is dedicated to St Gregory the Illuminator (as he is always called, although St Gregory the Enlightener would be a better translation since his achievement was converting Armenia into a Christian country). It was consecrated in September 2001 to celebrate what was officially the 1,700th anniversary of Christianity becoming the state religion and to this end symbolically has seating for 1,700 people in the main church although a further 300 can be accommodated in the smaller chapels dedicated to St Trdat, the king who adopted Christianity as the state religion, and his wife St Ashken. There is also a gavit and a belltower. The cathedral may well be the first church in Armenia which visitors see but, even apart from its modernity, it is in several respects atypical. Firstly, there are seats: in Armenian churches there are normally no seats as the congregation stands. Secondly there are no candles. It is normal on entering an Armenian church to buy candles and then to light them. Here candles are forbidden and may only be lit in the vault beneath the main church which has a separate entrance on the south side. Thirdly there is an organ. Fourthly the church is well lit, having many windows as well as a large metal chandelier. Fifthly, by Armenian standards it is enormous, with a total area of 3,500m² and a height of 63m. It has been described as having more the atmosphere of a concert hall than a place of worship but it is conspicuously busy with numerous Armenians of all ages visiting and a constant succession of weddings, particularly at weekends. (See page 91 for information about Armenian wedding customs.) Rather incongruously, near the entrance is a panoply brought from the church of St Gayane at Ejmiatsin underneath which is a casket containing some of the relics of St Gregory which were brought here from the church of San Gregorio Armeno, Naples, where they had been kept for more than 500 years. They were a gift from Pope John Paul II on the occasion of the cathedral's dedication. Other relics of the saint have been built into the cathedral's foundations.

Leave the cathedral by the main door through which you entered and walk back down the slope. At the foot of the slope do a U-turn to the right into the part of the circular green belt in Tamanian's 1926 plan which was actually created. This part in summer now holds a children's funfair; beyond it are trees and cafés through which one walks until a radial road crosses the green belt. Here there is another **statue of a warrior on horseback**. It is Vardan Mamikonian, the leader of the Armenian forces killed at the battle of Avarayr in AD451 when his troops were overcome by a much larger Persian force. Made of wrought copper and unveiled in 1975, it is by Ervand Kochar (1899–1979), other examples of whose work include the fine statue of David of Sassoun outside the main railway station and several paintings in the National Gallery of Armenia.

Instead of continuing along the green belt, turn left across Khandian Street and take the left hand of the two streets. If you are here during the week you will see a broad street with some non-functioning fountains down the middle. At the weekend you will by contrast be confronted by the justly celebrated market of **Vernissage**. ('Vernissage' is a French word, literally meaning varnishing or glazing but also used in the sense of preview, or private viewing, at an art gallery.) Vernissage is unquestionably the best place in Armenia, and possibly in the Caucasus, to buy souvenirs and craft items with a huge range of items being sold, for the most part by the people who made them. The range covers carpets, embroideries, wood and stone carvings, paintings, metalwork, etc and the quality ranges from the superb to the tacky. It is generally possible to pay in either drams or dollars and, while bargaining is acceptable, you may feel that the low prices do not really reflect the work that has gone into some of the items for sale and that if a stallholder is only asking £100/US$150 in the first place for something which has clearly involved 200 hours of highly skilled work then it is unreasonable to demand any reduction in price. As well as craft items there are also stalls selling various antique items from old radios and Soviet-era medals to secondhand books.

Continue the length of Vernissage, repeatedly doubling back so as to visit each of the aisles. At the far end on the left is the side of the art gallery whose front is on Republic Square. To the right, down some steps, is **Hanrapetutian Hraparak** ('Republic Square') **underground station**. Depending on the weight or bulk of any purchases made at Vernissage, this may be a good place to break the walk.

Otherwise continue straight on along the back of the art gallery. Before turning right into Abovian Street, look first at the two buildings to the left which are at the bottom end of Abovian Street adjoining Republic Square. Abovian Street is probably Yerevan's most important shopping street and also has its best Tsarist-era buildings. It is named after Khachatur Abovian (1805–48), a teacher and writer whose best-known novel, *Armenia's Wounds*, is based around the events of the Russo–Persian war of 1826–28. Number 2 Abovian Street, on the left-hand side as one faces Republic Square, is a red and black neoclassical building constructed in 1880 as a boys' secondary school on a site where it had originally been planned to build Yerevan's cathedral. In Soviet times the building was adapted for chamber music concerts. Number 1 on the opposite side is slightly newer: built between 1900 and 1914 to house a trading business, it is also constructed of red and black tuff but is in the then fashionable art nouveau style.

Before continuing up Abovian Street walk about 300m down Arami Street, opposite to the way you have walked through Vernissage. Passing houses with balconies and the Georgian embassy on the right you will come on the left to a **stonecarvers' yard** where khachkars and other items are still created from tuff in the traditional way. To see these carvers at work is to witness the successors to over one thousand years of tradition. Return to Abovian Street and turn left up the hill: one of the buildings on the right-hand side still retains its wooden balcony with metal balustrade but it is now rather decrepit. On the left is the start of the new North Avenue linking Republic Square with the Opera and Ballet Theatre, part of Tamanian's master plan of 1926 which was not then realised but on which construction finally started amidst much controversy in 2002.

In the middle of the intended path of North Avenue is a **statue** which might have to be relocated. It is of an old man holding a bunch of roses. Created by the sculptor Levon Tokmajian and erected in 1991 it marks the exact spot where the old man it portrays used to stand in the 1930s. His real name was Karapet, but the locals gave him the name 'Kara Bala', Turkish for black boy, because of his dark complexion. He was said to have come from a well-to-do family and was married to a beautiful wife; they had a son. Kara Bala grew roses. He would take his roses to Astafian Street (as Abovian Street was then known) where he would stand and give them to girls. In particular he was said to be passionately in love with the famous actress Arus Voskanian who used to walk along Abovian Street to the theatre and he gave her one red rose every morning. However she had another admirer, a Turkish man, and this made Kara Bala so jealous that he murdered his rival for which he was subsequently tried and imprisoned.

On his eventual release he found that his wife and son had left him, that he didn't have a house and a garden any more and that his roses had been uprooted. 'I am not Kara Bala any more, I'm Dardy Bala ['dard' means sorrow in Armenian],' he kept saying, wandering sadly around the town with a bottle of wine. However he didn't stop giving flowers. Whenever he came across flowers he gave them to women and many in Yerevan still remember his going up to young couples in the 1960s to present the girl with a bunch. Eventually he died and his frozen body was found one morning sitting on a rock.

Number 8 on the right-hand side of Abovian Street was built in the 1880s, again in neoclassical style. After 1937 the building housed the Soviet Central Committee and the office of Comsomol, the Soviet youth organisation, and it was until recently still possible to detect where there was formerly a red star in the top arch of the masonry. It retains one of its original wooden doors. On the opposite side of the street at number 1/4 is the dark façade of the **Gabrielian mansion**, built in 1910 by the architect Meghrabian and combining classical and art nouveau elements.

Continue uphill across Pushkin Street. The first building on the right, with salmon-coloured stucco and red trim, dates from the 1870s and now houses the **Geological Museum**. A plaque on the wall commemorates the playwright Maxim Gorki's one-night stay in the building in 1928. Opposite it, on the left, is the red tuff **Khanzatian mansion** and just above that is the **Hovhannissian mansion**, a large building dating from 1915–16 which incorporated a hospital on the ground floor. It now houses the Armenian Society for Friendship and Cultural Relations with Foreign Countries. Note the stained-glass windows which incorporate a Star of David in the framework.

Slightly higher up the hill, still on the left, is the Russian **Stanislavski Drama Theatre** built in 1937 in constructivist style but considerably altered in 1974 when it gained a façade of yellowish tuff. Its architect Karo Alabian (1897–1959) was responsible for several interesting Soviet-era projects including Krasnopresnenskaya metro station in Moscow and the post-war reconstruction of Stalingrad.

Opposite the Stanislavski theatre is the small square called until recently Zodiac Square because its fountain incorporates each sign of the zodiac. However, in 2001 it was renamed **Charles Aznavour Square** in honour of the composer, singer and actor who was born in Paris in 1924 to Armenian parents who had fled the Turkish massacres. The square was created in the 1920s by demolishing a 17th-century Persian mosque together with the church of Sts Peter and Paul which also dated to the 17th century. The **Hotel Yerevan**, designed by Nicoghayos Buniatian (1884–1943) dates from 1926. At one time Yerevan's most elegant hotel, it once again boasts 5-star status. Its red tuff construction with wrought-iron balconies in traditional Armenian style contrasts oddly with the grey stonework of the entrance surmounted by white Ionic columns. Across the square is the **Moscow cinema** which dates from 1933. Three friezes of heroic subjects can be seen on the south wall incorporating a quotation from Lenin: 'In culture the best art is film'. Between the hotel and the cinema is the exhibition hall of the Painters' Union used for temporary shows.

Continue uphill across Tumanian Street beyond which Abovian Street widens considerably and is lined with trees. Most of the buildings here date from the 1940s. On the left is the **Children's Art Gallery**, the collection of works produced by (mostly) Armenian children. Continue across Sayat Nova Street.

In the first block on the right is the 16-storey **Hotel Ani Plaza**, while on the left behind the 1930s building of black tuff is the remaining part of the only one of Yerevan's churches to have at least partially survived the 1679 earthquake. Known as the **Katoghike** (literally cathedral, singularly inappropriate for the tiny building still standing) its current form dates from 1936 when the main church, a substantial basilica without a dome rebuilt in 1693/4, was demolished in the name of urban redevelopment. It was known that there had been a church on this site since the 13th century but until the demolition was under way it was not clear that the apse and sanctuary actually comprised this old church as was proved by inscriptions of 1229 and 1282 on the newly revealed southern façade as well as one of 1264 on the wall. Public and scientific outcry won the newly revealed church a reprieve, and since independence it has resumed a religious function It is, however, too small for services to be held and functions only as a chapel for private prayer. In front of the church is a small collection of khachkars and other sculpted fragments from the core of the destroyed basilica.

Return to Abovian Street and continue up the hill. On the right, plaques on numbers 28, 30 and 32 commemorate famous residents of these buildings which were put up in the 1930s to house artists and intellectuals. Slightly higher up, also on the right, is a 1930s art-deco building sporting the Russian word for bread. Continuing uphill Abovian Street meets the circular green belt. Steps lead down to a pedestrian underpass beneath Moscovian Street which on closer inspection proves also to house a large subterranean department store as well as a considerable part of Yerevan's secondhand book trade including a selection of often unexpected titles in English. The continuation of Abovian Street uphill is dealt with in the *Elsewhere in Yerevan section* on page 98.

The walk round Yerevan continues by ascending the steps on the left-hand side halfway along the underpass to emerge into the circular green belt with Moscovian Street on the left and Isahakian Street on the right. The first statue encountered, an old man with a walking stick, is the poet **Avedik Isahakian** (1875–1957) whose early work reflected sorrow and anguish for the fate of humankind. He left Armenia in 1911 as a result of Tsarist oppression but returned in 1936. The statue, by Sergei Bagdasarian, was unveiled in 1965. To the right just past the statue the building which looks like a large upside-down space ship is **Yeridasardakan** ('Youth') **metro station** which opened in 1981: the name reflects the number of students in this part of the city owing to the proximity of the university.

Further along is a large **pair of marble hands**, a gift from Yerevan's twin city of Carrara in Tuscany; Yerevan achieved its first twinning in 1965 when it was linked with both Carrara and Kiev. Yerevan's response to the gift was to send in return a model of a spring of water carved in tuff and decorated with Armenian motifs of which an exact copy also stands a little further on across Terian Street. Continuing along the green belt beyond Terian Street the next statue is of a pensive looking individual. This is the poet **Vahan Terian** (1885–1920) after whom the street was named. There is a small lake on which it is possible to hire battery operated boats: the restaurant on the north side is itself built in imitation of a boat. One of the cafes here may be a pleasant place to break the walk, partly because, unlike most, they do not (yet?) blast excessively loud music at customers and partly because the remaining section of Tamanian's planned circular green belt back to Republic Square was never built so that this tour must revert in the meantime to city streets. At the end of the green belt to the left is the **music school** named after Sayat Nova (1712–95), composer and poet in Armenian, Georgian and Persian languages. Outside the music school is a bust of Sayat Nova and to the left in front of the Armenian State Conservatory is a **statue of a man leaning back on a tree**; he is the composer Komitas (1869–1935) whose career is outlined on page 37. The conservatory itself has busts outside of Bach, Shostakovich, Khachaturian and Beethoven.

A visit to the Matenadaran can conveniently be made from here by turning right up Mashtots Avenue, formerly Lenin Prospekt but renamed in honour of the inventor of the Armenian alphabet; the museum faces down the street with a statue of Mesrop Mashtots outside. The walk continues straight on across Mashtots Avenue as far as the park at the foot of the Cascade. The **Cascade** was designed to be a large artificial waterfall tumbling down from the war memorial but it was left uncompleted at the demise of the Soviet Union. Plans do exist to finish the work since a fairly large part of it has been built but no date has been set. Steps lead up alongside it and there is an excellent view of the city from the top. There is also an escalator under the steps and this started to operate again in November 2002 after being out of use since 1997, thus saving the residents at the top of the hill a climb up around 500 steps. It operates from 06.30 until 23.00. The occasion of the escalator's reinstatement was the unveiling of a **statue of a fat cat**. The self-satisfied looking, well-fed cat, 2.5m high in bronze covered in black, is the work of the Colombian artist, Fernando Botero and is one of several of his cats located in capital cities. It is a gift from Gerard Cafesjian whose Family Foundation is seeking to develop in Yerevan a museum of contemporary art of which the cat is the first exhibit. It was reported in the press that while the cat was greeted with smiles by the local residents, accustomed to statuary of Soviet dimensions, the loudest cheers were for the reactivation of the much-missed escalator.

In the gardens below the Cascade is a **statue of Alexander Tamanian** much of whose work has already been seen on this walk. Carved from a single block of basalt and mounted on a marble plinth, his hands are resting on a plan of the city in this work by Artashes Ovsepian. It has been suggested that this may be the only statue of an architect in the entire world. Rather surprisingly Tamanian is facing the back of one of his finest buildings; opened in 1933 as the Yerevan State Opera house, it was renamed two years later the **Spendiarian Armenian Theatre of Opera and Ballet**. Alexander Spendiarian (1871–1928) was an Armenian composer who trained with Rimski-Korsakov. His most famous work is the opera *Almast* based on the poem *The Capture of Tmkaberd* by the poet Hovhannes Tumanian (1889–1923). Set in 18th-century Crimea, the noble and beautiful Almast is betrothed to Tatul, ruler of the Armenian fortress of Tmkaberd which is under attack by Nadir, shah of Iran. Nadir deceives Almast into betraying Tatul after which she is killed by the bored Nadir in the poem but treated very differently in the opera which has a denouement more in keeping with Soviet Armenia in the 1920s. In it the Armenian forces rise up, liberate the fortress and collectively sentence Almast to exile. Left uncompleted at Spendiarian's death, *Almast* received its premiere at Moscow in 1930 and its first Yerevan performance shortly after the new opera house opened in 1933.

At the back of the opera house (ie: on the side nearer the Cascade) is a statue of the Armenian composer who is the best known outside the country, **Aram Khachaturian** (1903–78); see page 37 for biographical details. Round the front the right-hand statue is the eponymous **Spendiarian** while to the left is **Tumanian**, a second of whose poems was the source of the most famous Armenian opera, *Anoush*. With music by Armen Tigranian it is another gloom-laden tale typical of the time when it was composed although it does contain much attractive Armenian dance music: it was first seen at Alexandropol (Gyumri) in 1912. The piece ends with Anoush leaping off a precipice after her brother has killed her lover for breaking a village taboo.

A sculpture of composer and pianist Arno Babajanian (1921–83) was erected next to the small pond (known, rather appropriately, as Swan Lake) in front of the opera house in September 2002 but had to be removed before its official unveiling because its expressionistic style met with far from universal approval. Passers-by said that the work of sculptor David Bejanian was 'an insult' and even the Armenian president, Robert Kocharian, questioned whether it was appropriate. The main objections were to the exaggerated facial features and the long fingers which, it was claimed, made Babajanian look almost like a bird. Bejanian did agree to take the work away to make the hands more realistic and to 'correct' the face, but he said that his new and unrealistic approach had made his sculpture different from other monuments of the city. He said that 'All the monuments in Yerevan are done in a similar style and if we change heads of all the monuments within one night – for example replace Tumanian's head with Spendiarian's, Sarian's with Komitas's – perhaps only the subjects will feel the change. Arno was done to be in an expressive manner so that his head couldn't be placed on the shoulders of anyone else.' There was no objection by the public to the composer's stone piano which also featured in the sculpture and that was allowed to remain. At the time of writing (May 2003) the piano was still there on its own.

The small park behind the opera house contains a statue of the painter **Martiros Sarian** (1880–1972). Rather appropriately the park is used at weekends for the sale of paintings in a similar way to Vernissage. From the back of the opera house continue down tree-lined Mashtots Avenue. It is not for the most part architecturally interesting, being lined by office blocks containing shops at street level. The first interesting building encountered is in the fifth block from the opera house. Behind elaborate doors on the left lies the **blue mosque**, built in 1765 and the only one surviving in Yerevan. During Soviet days it was the museum of the city of Yerevan but in 1999 it was renovated in Persian style at the expense of the Iranian government and is now functioning as a mosque once more. The grounds are quite pleasant with shrubs and trees and access to the interior is usually possible by asking in the office: it is the white door just to the right of the mosque doorway. The other interesting building is just past the mosque on the opposite side. It is the 1940s-built **covered market**. Designed by Grigor Aghababian (1911–77), it is immediately recognisable with its arching roof and Armenian decoration on the façade. It is a good place to buy both fresh produce and the superb Armenian dried fruits including those stuffed with nuts: those sold by vendors further from the door are in summer less susceptible to having had flies land on them. A few metres further along Mashtots Street beyond the market and mosque go straight ahead through the underpass beneath Grigor Lusavorich ('Gregory the Illuminator') Street. You quickly reach the Hrazdan gorge close to **St Sargis church**. The present church replaces one destroyed in the 1679 earthquake. It was built during the period 1691–1705 and rebuilt between 1835 and 1842. Further extensive rebuilding including a taller cupola took place from 1971 onwards and was completed in 2000. From the church there are good views over the Hrazdan to Victory Bridge, Ararat, the stadium, and the genocide memorial.

Return to Grigor Lusavorich Street and turn right in the underpass to emerge on the east side of this street facing south. After one block there is a park on the left with a **bust of Soviet war hero Nelson Stepanian** (1913–44). Keep straight on past the park as far as the next street on the left. Turn left into what was in his lifetime called Stalin Street but is now called Beirut Street. In the middle of this street is a statue of **Alexander Miasnikian** (1886–1925), a professional Bolshevik revolutionary who was appointed commissar for Armenia in 1921. He was reported to have died in an air crash although rumours arose that he had really been poisoned on the orders of Stalin because of disagreements over western Armenia. There are rose gardens and fountains in the middle of the street behind the statue. The opposite side of the street is actually called Italy Street rather than Beirut Street; the Italian embassy is on the corner.

Walk along Beirut Street. Cross over to Italy Street after a few metres to visit the **Theatre Park**, formerly named the Park of the 26 Commissars in honour of the 26 Bolsheviks who set up a short-lived government in Baku which was deposed as the Turkish army approached. They fled to Turkmenistan but were captured and executed in September 1918. The park has been renamed Theatre Park as in the park is the **Sundukian Drama Theatre**. Its company was created in 1925. The inaugural performance was of the play *Pepo* by Gabriel Sundukian (1825–1912), a story about love versus exploitation set in Tiflis (Tbilisi) and first performed in 1871. There is a statue of the eponymous Pepo in the park as well as a bust of Sundukian. The present 1,140-seat building dates from 1966 and has been closed for more than ten years although renovation is currently under way. Just beyond the entrance to the park in the central reservation is a statue of a boy holding a large jug of water. It is a reminder of the days in the 1950s when such youths used to sell water along the dusty streets of the old town.

Continuing along Beirut Street or Italy Street, depending which side you care to walk, just past the next intersection is another statue, this time of **Stepan Shahumian** and again created by the same Sergei Merkurov who was responsible for the now vanished Lenin and Stalin. Stepan Shahumian (1878–1918) was an Armenian who was instrumental in imposing Bolshevik rule in Azerbaijan and one of the 26 commissars after whom the park was named. He is further commemorated in having two towns named after him: Stepanavan in Lori province and Stepanakert in Nagorno Karabagh. Behind the statue, in the middle of the street, is a fountain with 2,750 jets, one for every year of Yerevan's existence up to the time that the fountain was installed in 1968. It extends as far as Republic Square which is where the walk started and, when the fountain is operating, the cafés lining it make it another pleasant place to rest after walking the streets of central Yerevan.

Elsewhere in Yerevan
Around the railway station
Tamanian's plan was for a new central railway terminus but this was never realised and the main station is in an industrial area south of the centre. The easiest way to get here is to catch the metro to Sassountsi David ('David of Sassoun'). The fine station building dates from 1956 and is a striking structure though it now sees much less traffic because of the closure of the border with Azerbaijan; there are now only three or four departures each day and consequently few visitors ever come here. The long façade has, uniquely for Armenia, a tall central spire that would not be out of place in St Petersburg. The finial of this spire is, equally unusually, still topped by a purely Soviet symbol being a form of the design of the coat of arms of Soviet Armenia adopted in 1937 and replaced after independence in 1992. The coat of arms was based on a design by the well-known Armenian artist Martiros Sarian (see page 43 for biographical details) and depicts the five-pointed Soviet star above Mount Ararat with a bunch of grapes and ears of wheat below. The coat of arms also bore the well-known slogan *Proletarians of all lands, unite!* but the railway station does not appear from ground level to enjoy this embellishment.

In front of the station is Ervand Kochar's very fine equestrian statue of **David of Sassoun** mounted on his horse Dzhalali. (See page 43 for further information on Ervand Kochar.) The epic stories of David of Sassoun date back to the 10th century though they were not written down until 1873. They recount the fortunes of David's family over four generations, Sassoun symbolising Armenia in its struggle against Arab domination. In the statue David brandishes a sword which is ready to fall on the invaders while water flows from a bowl over the pedestal, symbolising that when the patience of the people is at an end there will be no mercy for the oppressors. David's crest of honour was a sword of lightning, belt of gold, immortal flying horse and sacred cross.

More prosaically, on one of the tracks away from the station platform is positioned a steam engine. It is E^u class number 705 – 46, built in 1930 and one of around 11,000 E class 0-10-0s built between 1912 and 1957 as the standard design for hauling heavy freight trains. The huge number built makes them the most common of any steam locomotive design ever constructed. In the E^u variant, to which this particular example belongs, the superscript U stands for *usilennyi* – strengthened.

The far end of Abovian Street

Abovian Street has some worthwhile buildings beyond Isahakian Street where it crosses the green belt. On the left corner of Abovian and Isahakian is the **Armenergo building** housing Armenia's main electricity utility. Constructed in 1930 of black tuff, it was designed by Hovhannes Margarian (1901–63) who was also responsible for Yerevan brandy distillery.

Passing numerous vendors whose prices are among the lowest in the city and then crossing Koriun Street, the building of black tuff on the right corner is the **Yerevan medical university**. Anyone wishing to sample Yerevan's **cable car** should turn right into Koriun Street and walk along it for one block to the lower terminus. It takes travellers up to the Nork plateau and operates daily except Sundays from 08.00 until 19.00. Otherwise continuing uphill along Abovian Street on the right-hand side there is a neoclassical building of 1880 which originally housed the Guyanian Mirzorian School for Girls but now houses the university faculty of theology. After an elaborate wrought-iron fence with stone posts and flower pots enclosing a hospital courtyard is a particularly interesting building, the **Mari Nubar children's eye clinic** which includes a series of pyramids in the frieze below the cornice. This building stems from an initiative in Egypt taken on Easter Sunday (April 15) 1906. Armenians had been prospering in Egypt, and particularly so since the British occupied the country in 1882. Numbers of Armenians there were also being swelled by refugees from Ottoman oppression as well as from the Armenian–Azeri conflicts. The driving force behind the initiative was Boghos Nubar Pasha (1851–1930), an Armenian whose father, Nubar Pasha, had been prime minister of Egypt on five separate occasions between 1872 and 1895. The iniative saw the founding of the Armenian General Benevolent Fund whose mission was to establish and subsidise schools, libraries, workshops, hospitals and orphanages for the benefit of Armenian communities throughout the Middle East and adjacent regions and the Yerevan children's eye hospital was built under the auspices of this organisation. Later Boghos Nubar Pasha was to be leader of the Armenian delegation at the Paris peace conference of 1919.

On the opposite side of the street is a small park housing the original university observatory designed in the 1930s by Tamanian but superseded by the Byurakan astrophysics observatory on Mount Aragats. At the far end of the park are statues of a Greek goddess and a naked man holding a bow. The park also formerly held a statue of Gukas Gukasian (1899–1920), the founder of the Armenian Young Communist League. The plinth which supported him still bears his name.

Abovian Street opens out into Abovian Square, in the centre of which is a **statue of Abovian** himself sculpted by Suren Stepanian and unveiled in 1950. This was not the statue of Abovian originally intended for this site. That statue, made of bronze, was sculpted in Paris in 1913 by Andreas Ter-Marukian, packed up for shipment, but then, owing to some misunderstanding, it was forgotten and lay undisturbed for 20 years. When it was finally delivered in 1935 it was first erected on Abovian Street by the Moscow cinema, then moved to the children's park by the Hrazdan river, before finally in 1964 being taken to the Abovian House Museum where it remains.

The building on the right as you enter the square is a hospital of the 1930s. The **Folk Art Museum** is just beyond that.

By Victory Bridge

The high-level Victory Bridge dates from 1945, its name celebrating victory in World War II. Victory Bridge, 200m long and 34m above the river, supersedes the red tuff bridge constructed following the collapse of its predecessor in the 1679 earthquake and rebuilt in 1830 after the Russian conquest of Yerevan. The four arches of the 1679 bridge, which was 80m long and stood 11m above the river, can be seen to the south of Victory Bridge, the central two arches spanning the river itself; the smaller side ones originally crossed irrigation canals.

At each end of Victory Bridge are prominent buildings associated with Yerevan's alcohol business. At the west (airport) end is the **Yerevan brandy distillery** which stands on a plateau high above the bridge. The distillery was founded in 1887 but the present building was designed by Hovhannes Margarian, the same architect responsible for the Armenergo building in upper Abovian Street. Its façade displaying nine arches can be best appreciated when approached by the long flight of steps from the valley below. Guided tours, with sampling, can be arranged for groups. It is now owned by the French Pernod Ricard company. Unfortunately its excellent products are difficult to obtain in western Europe: presumably its owners see little point in competing with their French products.

At the other (city) end of the bridge the large, rather forbidding building constructed of basalt which faces the bridge formerly housed the **Yerevan Wine Company**: built about 1930 its shape and dimensions are exactly those of the former citadel which occupied the site and which is the reason for its appearance. Its architect Rafael Israelian (1908–73) was also responsible for the very fine memorial commemorating the battle of Sardarapat in Armavir province. It is often stated that the first performance of Griboydev's *Woe from Wit* (see page 38) was actually given in a room of the fortress by Russian army officers in 1827 but it is not clear what evidence exists for this claim. It seems unlikely that army officers would have acted in a play which was prohibited by the Tsarist authorities and which was not published until seven years later.

The children's railway

Children's railways were an exclusively Soviet phenomenon. They were not built as fairground amusements but to train children aged from 9 to 15 in the operation of real railways. The first opened at Tbilisi, Georgia in 1935. Yerevan's opened in 1937 and was extensively renovated in the late 1950s. (The second children's railway in Armenia, at Leninakan (Gyumri), never reopened after being damaged in the 1988 earthquake.) It operates during the summer when children are not at school, the first day of operation usually being Genocide Memorial Day (April 24). Children perform all the tasks under adult supervision. The line is 2.1km long along the Hrazdan gorge and starts from a gaily painted station whose architecture was clearly influenced by Yerevan's main railway station. It also incorporates stained-glass windows depicting birds. To reach it from the city walk northwest from Mashtots Avenue along the broad Karen Demirchian Street (named after the assassinated parliamentary speaker) which has defunct fountains down the middle. From the far end a long pedestrian tunnel leads to the gorge and the children's railway.

All children's railways have a track gauge of 750mm. The original steam locomotive was replaced in the late 1940s by another coal-burning steam loco, which is still on view although apparently unserviceable. It is 0-8-0 number 159-

434 of a design built in the 1930s mainly for forestry work, but subsequently made redundant in that role by more modern designs. The usual motive power is a diesel hydraulic, currently number TY² 096 dating from 1958. The route is a single track towards Victory Bridge. There are no facilities for the locomotive to run round the train at the far end and the coaches are therefore hauled out but propelled back.

The Genocide Memorial and Museum

The Genocide Memorial and Museum at Tsitsernakaberd ('Swallow Castle') are among the few points of interest on the west side of the Hrazdan river. Visiting them is strongly recommended for anyone wishing to understand Armenia and its people. In 1965 Armenians throughout the world commemorated the 50th anniversary of the 1915 genocide and the lack of any tangible symbol in Armenia itself was conspicuous to the extent that the genocide memorial was created and completed in 1967. The architects Kalashian and Mkrtchian have succeeded in creating a striking and appropriate monument. Although the ideal approach is to mount the flight of steps leading up to it, most visitors are likely to approach instead from the car park in which case the first thing they will notice is the collection of trees each of which has been planted by a distinguished visitor. Separating the museum from the monument is a 100m-long memorial wall of basalt carved with the name of villages and towns where massacres of Armenians by Turks are known to have taken place. The monument itself has two parts. There is a 44m-tall stele reaching to the sky and symbolising the survival and spiritual rebirth of the Armenian people. It is riven however by a deep cleft which symbolises the separation of the peoples of western and eastern Armenia while at the same time emphasising the unity of all Armenian people. Adjoining the stele is a ring of 12 large, inwardly leaning basalt slabs whose shape is reminiscent of traditional Armenian khachkars. The 12 slabs represent the 12 lost provinces of western Armenia and their inward leaning form suggests figures in mourning. At the centre of the circle, but 1.5m below, burns the eternal flame. The steps leading down are deliberately steep, thus requiring visitors approaching to bow their heads in reverence as they descend.

The museum was added in 1995 to commemorate the 80th anniversary of the massacres. It is a circular subterranean building and was designed by the same architects as the memorial. Much information is given on the number of victims in different parts of western Armenia and there are many photographs taken by German army photographers who were accompanying their allies the Turks during World War I. There are also examples of foreign publications about various aspects of the genocide.

Erebuni

Erebuni, on a hilltop in the southern part of the city, is the original site of Yerevan. It can be reached on tram 7 or trolley bus 2 or 4 from Zoravar Andranik metro station. Visitors can see the partially excavated remains of the site of the city together with interesting objects found there which are now housed in a worthwhile museum at the bottom of the hill. Erebuni was discovered by chance in 1950 during exploration of Arin Berd monastery which had later been built on the site. A cuneiform inscription was uncovered which can be dated to 782BC. It states: 'By the greatness of [God] Khaldi, Argrishti, son of Menua the powerful king of Biaini and ruler of Tushpa city built this splendid fortress and named it Erebuni, strength to Biaini'. (Biaini was the Urartian name for their country. Urartu was the Assyrian name.) Argrishti was the Urartian king Argrishti I (ruled c785–c762BC) who established a garrison here of 6,600 troops, the first Urartian settlement on this side of the Arax. Its heyday only lasted for about a century until the Urartian king Rusa II (ruled c685–c645BC) chose a different site, Teishebai Uru (literally City of [the God] Teisheba) overlooking the Hrazdan river which he believed would be less vulnerable to attack by the Scythians. However, Erebuni remained occupied as is testified by archaeological finds from later periods.

When visiting the site go to the museum first as the model of Erebuni there gives a good idea of the general layout. It is open 10.30 to 16.00 but closed on Mondays. An English-speaking guide is available as well as a booklet giving a brief description in five languages. Particularly interesting are three silver rythons (drinking horns in the form of animals), one of which is shaped like a horse, one like a bull's head and one like a man on horseback. The helmet of King Sarduri II (ruled c763–c734BC) is on display together with a large jug, possibly a funerary urn, with bulls' heads. There is also a good selection of jewellery, ceramics and weapons found on the site. The central courtyard of the museum is a reconstruction of the palace courtyard. Of particular interest is the stone, actually found at Tanahat monastery, Syunik (not the better-known Tanahat monastery, Vayots Dzor). It has a cuneiform inscription dedicated to the Urartian king Argrishti II (ruled 714–685BC) but the stone was made into a khachkar in the 11th century by which time no-one of course could read the inscription.

The shape of the hill on which Erebuni is built necessitated a triangular shape for the citadel. It had walls around 12m high, the lower 6m being formed of two parallel walls of large stone blocks with rubble filling the space in between the rows and large buttresses providing additional strength. Above the stone blocks clay bricks were used which were then covered with plaster. Within the citadel was the royal palace, temples and service premises, everything being connected by stairways because the slope of the hill necessitated the buildings being constructed at different levels. A good view of the walls can be had from below and it is worthwhile walking along the path which follows them right round the outside. It can be accessed from near the entrance or from some slightly rickety steps at the northwest apex of the site.

Entering the site from the access road and car park the first building on the left is the reconstructed Hall of Columns used to greet dignitaries. It has a blue wall with a frieze and the present roof is supported by six wooden columns. Continuing up the main entrance slope and steps, near the top is a copy of the Argrishti stone (original kept in museum) erected in 782BC and referred to above. Just after going through the entrance way a narrow alley goes off right to the necropolis. To the southwest of the central square was the temple of Khaldi, the chief god. It was crowned by a tower with a flat top that was probably used for sending smoke signals which would have been visible from far across the plain. Following the collapse of the Urartian kingdom and the installation of a Persian viceregent at Erebuni, the temple was converted for use as a 30-column *apadana* (reception hall). Part of this has been reconstructed and the design of frescos can be seen generally with figures of gods between horizontal bands in contrasting colours.

Northwest of the Khaldi temple was a pillared courtyard, probably used by the king for important meetings, together with a small temple devoted to Sushi, another of Urartu's 69 gods (of whom 55 were male) and used by the royal family. At its entrance is another cuneiform inscription. The palace's main reception hall was northeast of the central square. Surrounding the main buildings were living quarters for the garrison and for servants together with buildings for storing produce such as meat, fruit, wine, sesame seed oil, and milk products in *pithoi* (large urns) sunk into the ground to keep them cool. Different parts of the site are said to have had different functions but it is not obvious when walking round.

The statues on Haik Avenue

Haik Avenue in the northeast of Yerevan is the main road out towards Garni and visitors heading there frequently notice the four statues alongside the road. The first, on the left, is of a man wearing a lion skin and aiming his bow either at Turkey or at the block of flats opposite. This is Haik, great-great-grandson of Noah and legendary founder of the Armenian people. The second statue, by the well known sculptor Ervand Kochar (see page 43) is of another Haik. The figure on horseback to the right of the road brandishing a sword and looking back towards Turkey is Haik Bzhshkian (1887–1937). Born in Tabriz (Persia) he was active in revolutionary movements and also in World War I when he commanded Armenian troops. Subsequently he supported the Bolshevik cause and after service in Siberia became commissar of the military forces in Soviet Armenia. His military career continued but, inevitably, his success led him to be a victim of Stalin's purges.

The third statue, on the left and opposite a market, is of King Tigran II (the Great) who ruled from c95BC to 55BC. The last statue, also on the left, is of one of writer Hovhannes Tumanian's characters. Standing on a pile of boulders, carrying an enormous rock on his shoulders, and with a grotesque expressionistic face, it is the Strong Man of the Village.

Cemeteries

Yerevan has two cemeteries of interest. The Pantheon of Heroes, Archakuniats Avenue, is where Armenia's famous deceased are interred. The inmates most familiar to visitors are likely to be the composers Komitas and Aram Khachaturian together with the writer William Saroyan. Presumably the reason that only the upper half of Saroyan's body is sculpted as his tombstone is that only half of his ashes are here; the other half are in Fresno, California.

The cemetery of Yerablur, Sebastia Avenue, to the right off the road to Zvartnots, houses the dead from the Nagorno Karabagh war together with Andranik Ozanian, fighter against Turkey in the late 19th and early 20th centuries, and Vazgen Sarkisian, the prime minister who was assassinated in parliament in 1999. To visit this cemetery, particularly on one of the traditional Armenian days for visiting graves such as Easter Monday, is even more poignant than with most war cemeteries because the war in which they were killed is so recent (1989–94) and many of the figures tending the graves are the mothers or other close relatives of those who died. Most of the graves carry a picture of the deceased.

Museums

Warning In spring 2002 a diaspora Armenian provided funds for Yerevan's museums to refurbish themselves. Nearly all of them immediately closed and most of them remain closed at the time of writing (May 2003). The following should be taken as merely indicative of how things might be when the museums do eventually reopen. Most museums will probably charge western visitors around AMD1,000 per person after reopening although some, including the Genocide Museum and the Military Museum, are free. There was prior to closure very little labelling in English.

Historical Museum Republic Sq. Open 10.30–16.00. Closed Mon. About 5,000 exhibits on permanent display from the stone age onwards. The collection included khachkars, ceramics, maps, artefacts. There was quite a lot of information on the 19th and 20th centuries but, even prior to closure, the exhibit on the Soviet period had been replaced by displays on the First Republic and a collection of religious vestments. English-speaking guides available. In the same building as National Gallery but the entrance is on ground floor.

National Gallery Republic Sq; web: www.gallery.am. Open 10.30–16.00. Closed Mon. The third-best collection in the former Soviet Union. Previously one bought a ticket from the desk on the first floor and then took a lift to the seventh floor to start viewing. Apart from some Asian porcelain and copies of Sri Lankan cave paintings the collection largely comprises paintings from the main European schools, as well as works by the major Armenian painters. Italian artists represented include: Bicci di Lorenzo (*The Betrothal of St Catherine*); Benvenuto Garofalo (*Virgin Mary with the Christ Child*); Jacopo Tintoretto (*Apollo and Pan*); Jacopo Bassano (*Adoration of the Shepherds*); Leandro Bassano (*Good Samaritan*); Francesco Guardi (*Courtyard with Stairs*). Flemish painters include: Hans Jordaens III (*The Jews Crossing the Red Sea*); and David Teniers the younger (*Kegl Players and The Village Feast*). Dutch painters include: Jan van Goyen (*View of Dordrecht*); Pieter Claesz (*Still Life*); Jan Wijnants (*Landscape with Broken Tree*). French artists include: Louis le Nain (*The Nest Robbers*); Jean Baptiste Greuze (*Head of a Girl*); Eugène Boudin (*Sea Harbour*). Among the Russian works Ilya Repin's *Portrait of Teviashova* and Isaac Levitan's *Reaped Field* particularly stand out. The collection of Armenian works includes all the greatest Armenian painters with a good collection of Aivasovsky's seascapes and works by Martiros Sarian.

Matenadaran 53 Mashtots Av. Open 10.00–16.00. Closed Sun and Mon. Purpose-built in 1957 to house 14,000 Armenian manuscripts but the single display room shows less than 1% of them. Provides virtually the only opportunity in Armenia to see examples of this important art form. Worth paying for the English-speaking guide. Items include the oldest surviving manuscript (dating from 989), the earliest Armenian printed book (printed in Venice in 1512) and translations of many important works into Armenian.

Martiros Sarian House Museum 3 Sarian St. Open Fri–Tue 11.00–16.30, Wed 11.00–15.00. Closed Thu. The house museum of Armenia's greatest 20th-century artist (see page 43) housing around 170 of his works.

Ervand Kochar Gallery 39 / 12 Mashtots Av. Open 11.00–16.00. Closed Mon. As well as paintings from both early and late in his career (see page 43), there are also photographs of some of his sculpture.

Aram Khachaturian House Museum 3 Zarobian St. Open 11.00–16.00. Closed Mon. Contains personal memorabilia of Armenia's best-known composer (see page 37) as well as props and costumes from his ballet Spartacus. Also includes a concert hall and a collection of CDs of Khachaturian's music.

Museum of Folk Art 64 Abovian St. Open 12.00–16.00. Closed Mon and public holidays. A wide range of embroidery, lace, silver jewellery, stone carving, carpets, ornamental metalwork and ceramics. Everything in this amazing collection is the work of extremely capable amateurs.

Mother Armenia Military Museum Victory Pk, 2 Azatutian. Open 10.00–16.00. Closed Mon. Inside the structure that supports the statue of Mother Armenia and formerly supported the statue of Stalin. Originally devoted to World War II but the second floor is now devoted to the Nagorno Karabagh conflict.

Children's Art Gallery 6 Sayat Nova. Open 11.00–16.00. Closed Mon. Displays works of art by children. In 1975 Harold Wilson, the then British prime minister, donated 100 works by British children to the collection.

Geological Museum 10 Abovian St. Open 11.00–16.00. Closed Mon. Rather specialist but the skeleton of a mammoth found in a sand pit at Gyumri is interesting.

Gallery of Modern Art 7 Mashtots Av. Open 11.00–16.00. Closed Mon. Founded in 1972, it was the only such gallery in the entire USSR. With additional funds provided by the diaspora it has built up a representative collection of 20th-century Armenian painting and sculpture.

Genocide museum see page 100.

Erebuni museum see page 100.

Other Yerevan museums include

Sergei Parajanov Museum 15 Dzoragyugh. Dedicated to the film director known in Armenian as Sargis Yossifovich Paradjanian (1924–90). Sergei Parajanov was the creator of several films, which brought him worldwide praise but official Soviet condemnation: *The Shadows of Forgotten Ancestors* (1964), *The Colour of Pomegranates or Sayat-Nova* (1969), *The Legend of Suram Fortress* (1985) and *Ashik-Kerib* (1988). Parajanov's contribution is his original poetic film-language, highly valued by his contemporaries. However he also worked in other media, notably through the creation of three-dimensional collages some of which are on display together with the furnishings from his house. Many of the collages were created during the 15 years when he was barred from making films which included five years he spent in Soviet labour camps (1973–77 and 1982).

Hovhannes Tumanian Museum 40 Moscovian St. Dedicated to the writer (see page 154). The ground floor houses personal items and upstairs is a re-creation of his apartment.

Eghishe Charents Museum 1 Arami St. Dedicated to the writer (see page 40). In the writer's former house but more an archive of papers associated with many different writers than a museum devoted exclusively to Charents.

Khatchatur Abovian Museum 42nd St, Kanaker. Dedicated to the novelist and in his parents' house now in the northeast suburbs (see page 40). Exhibits cover various parts of his life such as his ascent of Mount Ararat, the Russo-Persian war of 1828–30 and his mysterious sudden disappearance, possibly at the hands of Tsarist agents.

Derenik Demirchian House Museum 29 Abovian St. Dedicated to the writer (1877–1956). Best known for his play Nazar the Brave (1923). Among the personal effects on display is Demirchian's Stradovarius violin.

Avetik Isahakian House Museum 20 Zarobian St. Dedicated to the poet (1875–1957). After his return from study at Leipzig University he was arrested by the Tsarist police and banished because of his involvement in the Armenian freedom movement. Very much an establishment figure in Soviet days, he was awarded two Lenin prizes and became a deputy to the Armenian Supreme Soviet. The museum contains personal effects and memorabilia.

Hakob Kojoyan and Ara Sargsian House Museum 62/7 Pushkin St. Dedicated to the artists (1883–1959 and 1902–69 respectively). Sargsian was a sculptor, producing works such as Hiroshima and Mother Armenia. The ground floor is dedicated to him and includes a reconstruction of his studio as well as examples of his work. Upstairs is devoted to Kojoyan with examples of his work and personal effects. He was a very talented book illustrator as well as a painter and is credited with the first Soviet Armenian painting: *The Execution of the Communists at Tatev*.

Minas Avetissian House Museum 29 Nalbandian St, 6th floor. Dedicated to the artist (see page 43) Much of the artist's work has been tragically destroyed but there are seven paintings here as well as drawings and personal effects.

Gevorg Grigorian Studio Museum 45a Mashtots Av. House museum of the artist (1898–1976) known as Giotto. The portraits and still-lives of his early period gave way later to sorrow and turmoil which form the dominant theme of his later work. Examples can be seen in the National Gallery of Art.

Alexander Spendiarian House Museum 21 Nalbandian St. Dedicated to the composer (see page 95). As well as manuscripts and personal effects, there is a display about his best-known work, the opera *Almast*.

Middle East Museum 1 Arami St. Based on the collection of the painter Marcos Grigorian, it has an excellent collection of Persian applied arts with pottery, bronzes and ritual figurines dating back five millennia as well as material from the Persian pre-Islamic Zoroastrian culture.

The Central Provinces

Any place in the five central provinces of Aragatsotn, Ararat, Armavir, Gegharkunik and Kotayk can be visited on a day trip from Yerevan except for the eastern parts of Gegharkunik. The most popular excursions are: the town of Ashtarak together with the fortress and monastery at Amberd in Aragatsotn; the monastery of Khor Virap in Ararat with its stunning views in clear weather of the mountain; the churches of Ejmiatsin and the monument and museum at Sardarapat in Armavir; Lake Sevan and the Sevan monastery in Gegharkunik; and the temple at Garni and monastery at Geghard which are close to each other in Tavush. All of these are standard places on most visitors' itineraries. The following pages make numerous other suggestions but, if the author had to choose just one, it would be the amazing field of khachkars at Noratus.

ARAGATSOTN

The province whose name means 'foot of Aragats' comprises the land around Mount Aragats, at 4,090m (13,419ft) the highest mountain in the present-day republic. The province's geography is extremely varied and it is probably best thought of as being three separate zones: the mountain itself, arid steppe to the west, and the land bordering the gorge of the Kasagh river to the east. Each of these zones has its different attractions. Ashtarak ('Tower'), the provincial capital, is in the Kasagh gorge in the southeast of the province and only 22km from Yerevan. **Accommodation** in the province is limited. The small (6-room) Zoravar motel opened in 2002 at Ujan, about 15km from Ashtarak on the Gyumri road. Contact them through the owner's mobile phone (09 427268). Doubles start at US$40. In Ashtarak the Vana Lich motel (tel: 33446) incorporates a casino and is situated close to the river in the Kasagh gorge; doubles from US$40. Otherwise the best bet is the homestays.

Ashtarak

Ashtarak is situated on the Kasagh. This river rises in the southeastern corner of Shirak province and then flows south through Aragatsotn to join the Arax south of Yerevan. Ashtarak is a pleasant town with some older buildings including some fine medieval churches. It is now rather dominated by the modern bridge carrying the Yerevan to Gyumri main road high over the gorge, bypassing the city and considerably reducing traffic over the older three-arch bridge of 1664. This older bridge has a rather unusual appearance in that the three arches are unequal in size with the southernmost arch almost twice the height of the northernmost. Prominently perched atop an outcrop on the east bank of the river between new

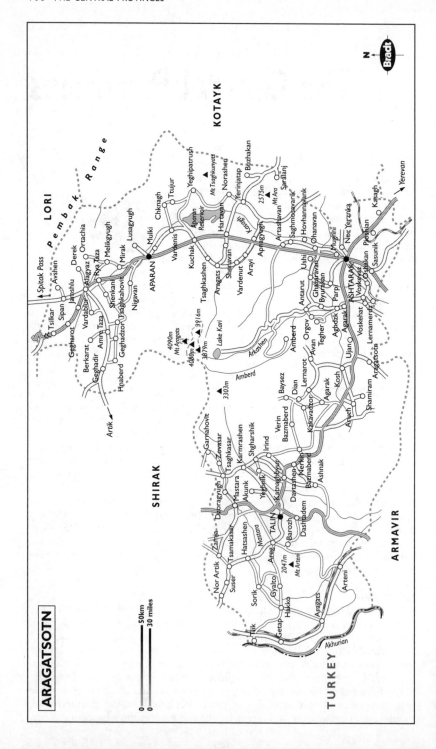

ARAGATSOTN

and old bridges is the small red tuff church of St Sargis, a modern construction on early foundations. The main part of the city however is on the west bank.

Legend states that three sisters lived here who all loved the same boy whose name was Sargis: the elder two decided to kill themselves to leave the way free for the youngest. One of the older sisters dressed in an apricot-coloured dress and the other in a red dress and then they both threw themselves into the gorge. The youngest sister learned what had happened, put on a white dress, and threw herself into the gorge after them. The prince became a hermit but three churches appeared at the edge of the gorge: one apricot-coloured, one red and one white. The problem with this legend is that the present colour of these churches doesn't correspond with it although the names do. Karmravor ('Reddish'), the church of the sister wearing the red dress is apricot coloured (though it does have a red roof); Spitakavor ('White-ish'), the church of the sister wearing the white dress is red; while Tsiranavor ('Apricot-ish'), whose sister wore the apricot-coloured dress is actually white!

By far the best preserved of the three is the small 7th-century Karmravor church dedicated to the Mother of God. It is one of the few Armenian churches of this period to have survived unaltered, even retaining a roof of tuff tiles and a tiled octagonal cupola. A single-aisle cross-dome church, it is one of Armenia's most appealing town churches. The other two churches in the legend, 14th-century Spitakavor and 5th-century Tsiranavor, are both roofless and forsaken but are only a short walk away and the views of the gorge are pleasant. These churches of the legend are on the northeast side of the city but Ashtarak's biggest church, St Marina, is in the city centre. Built in 1281, it is again a cross-dome church with octagonal tambour but the tambour and cupola here are unusually high. The tambour features attractive decoration in contrasting colours of tuff but the appearance of the whole is seriously marred by a Soviet-era addition which looks more like a large derelict shed than part of a church.

Eight kilometres southwest of Ashtarak is the village of **Oshakan** whose 5th-century church was most unattractively renovated in 1875 and then had unappealing frescos foisted on it in 1960. It is famous as the burial place of Mesrop Mashtots and the alphabet is spelled out in grass which must take an awful lot of cutting. Rather more appealing at Oshakan is the five-arch bridge of 1706 which spans the Kasagh.

Northward along the Kasagh

The main road north from Ashtarak towards Vanadzor and the Georgian border keeps for the most part to the west bank of the Kasagh. The section of road crossing directly over the Pambak range into Lori province by the Spitak Pass (2,378m) is now impassable owing to washouts, and the modern road deviates to the west over the slightly lower Pambak Pass (2,152m). The view from the road north from Ashtarak is dominated by Mount Aragats to the west; to the east the conical Mount Arai (2,575m) is prominent on the southern part of the route but further north the Pambak range rises to 3,101m at Mount Tegh. A whole succession of monasteries lie along the river many of which are interesting and attractively situated.

Mughni

The village of Mughni, nowadays within the Ashtarak city limits, lies just to the north of the main Yerevan to Gyumri road at the west end of the high viaduct over the Kasagh gorge. The 14th-century monastery of St George was completely rebuilt between 1661 and 1669 during the period when eastern Armenia saw a revival of church building thanks to the stable conditions enjoyed under the Safavid shahs of Iran. It is unquestionably one of the finest buildings of this renaissance and it is now surrounded by well-tended gardens. It is notable that the church withstood the earthquake of 1679 which flattened Yerevan and badly damaged the monastery of Hovhannavank to the north. The main cross-dome church has a distinctively striped circular tambour supporting the conical umbrella cupola and different colours of tuff are also used to decorative effect on the gable ends. The gavit, most unusually, has three arches at the west surmounted by a belfry whose cupola is supported by 12 columns. The south doorway is especially notable with elaborately carved tuff of different colours and fine carved wooden doors. Inside the church fragments of 17th-century murals survive, notably one showing the Baptism of Trdat on the north wall. The fortress wall of the monastery survives with small towers at the northwest and southwest corners. At the northeast corner the original service buildings have been restored: they originally housed the living quarters of the monks together with the refectory. St George's should be additionally commended for being the first church in Armenia to produce for visitors a well-written useful guide in English. Indeed, apart from some Soviet-era publications to museums and monuments, it is one of only two places in the country where a leaflet is available. (The other is Erebuni.) Presumably this commendable initiative is thanks to the Armenian Prelacy Ladies' Guild (New York) who funded the (well carried-out) restoration.

Hovhannavank

Situated about 5km north of Mughni, Hovhannavank ('Monastery of John') is the southernmost of two sizeable monasteries that are perched on the edge of the gorge and linked by a path which makes a pleasant, though potentially rather hot, walk: it is about 5km from Hovhannavank to Saghmosavank and there is little shade. The oldest part of Hovhannavank, perhaps the more appealing of the two monasteries, is a basilica structure of the 5th century though extensively rebuilt since then. On the south side of this early basilica stands the main church, dedicated to John the Baptist, and erected by Prince Vache Vachutian in 1216–21; the prince was governor of Ani from c1213 until 1232. The corner rooms of this church are two-storey and those at the west have cantilevered steps. As at some other churches of this period, the front of the altar dais was originally decorated with stars, pentagons and diamonds and some of this decoration survives. The gavit was built in 1250 to serve both the churches and is consequently off-centre. Four pillars divide it into separate sections each of which is differently decorated; the belfry supported by 12 columns was probably added in 1274.

The cupola of the main church collapsed following an earthquake in 1679 and then again, following another one, in 1919; the latter also damaged the south façade and still more damage resulted from the 1988 earthquake. However, the 12-sided tambour and cupola were reconstructed in 1999 and repairs are continuing. Particularly strange is the tympanum of the south door. Christ can be seen apparently blessing the five wise virgins with His right hand and rebuking the five foolish virgins with His left. Except that the virgins have beards so are they really meant to be the apostles and in that case why are there only ten? The church is surrounded by a fortified wall, originally constructed in the 13th century and rebuilt in the 17th.

Saghmosavank

Saghmosavank, like Hovhannavank church, was built by Prince Vache Vachutian. Not surprisingly the two monasteries have many similarities, not least in their situation on the rim of the gorge and in the stone used in their construction, although the architectural details are quite different. The oldest part of

Saghmosavank ('Monastery of Psalms') is the Zion church of 1215 with its round tambour and conical cupola. Inside there are frescos on the arch over the apse and carved angels over the sanctuary. The smaller Mother of God church to the south was built in 1235 and was followed by the large gavit which has an impressive entrance doorway similar to those found at the entrance to mosques. Whether this simply reflects the previous experience of the architect or had some other significance is not clear. The layout of the existing buildings required the library to be L-shaped when it was added in 1255; there is a fresco of St Gregory over the library door. As at Hovhannavank, a fortified wall surrounds the complex: the local goats enjoy standing on top of this one to keep an eye on the tourists.

North to Aparan and the Pembak Pass

With the four peaks of Mount Aragats to the west, the road continues north through fields of cabbages and past herds of cattle. Ten kilometres north from Saghmosavank at the village of Hartavan a road goes off right to **Yernjatap**: in about 4km the road starts to wind down towards the Kasagh. Turn left on to a minor dirt road which similarly winds down but slightly upstream. Standing on a knoll just before the bridge over the river are the ruins of the monastery of the Holy Wisdom of God, founded in the 5th century and renovated in 1244. It is a peaceful and isolated spot. Some restoration work was started here but it has long ceased and the damaged roof admits the elements while the gavit with its massive columns is roofless. Some decoration survives on the altar dais and the remains of a red-painted frieze are discernible.

Continuing through Yernjatap, about 5km beyond the village there is a road branching left to the village of **Buzhakan**, a resort centre in Soviet days and an excellent centre for walking. Keep straight on through the village until the main asphalt road forks left and a dirt road continues straight ahead. It is advisable to park here and walk the last 3km to Teghenyats monastery. It is a very beautiful walk. The first section is between fields as far as a half-built guesthouse, construction of which was halted when the Soviet Union collapsed. Bear left in front of the guesthouse and then continue uphill through forest. There is a small river to the right down in the gorge and the track, after winding along the hillside, drops down to ford it. It is difficult to cross when the river is in spate. The track then climbs straight up to the monastery with mud or snow revealing many bear prints. The monastery is evocatively situated with Mount Tsaghkunyats (2,844m) forming the backdrop. The ruinous 12th-century church and gavit and 13th-century refectory are complemented by a graveyard with sheep tombstones. Tombstones taking the form of animals was not in Armenia solely associated with Yezidis as the tombstones of Armenian nobility were sometimes in the form of sheep.

Returning to the main road at Hartavan and continuing north, Aparan reservoir on the Kasagh may be glimpsed over to the east: it supplies Yerevan with drinking water. Just before reaching **Aparan** town the appearance of the countryside changes with open stony grassland replacing cultivation. Aparan's church, about 100m east of the road towards the north end of the town, is one of Armenia's oldest, dating from the earliest days of Christianity in Armenia in the 4th century. Perhaps more than anywhere else in Armenia it is really possible to feel the age of this church built of dark grey tuff, and although it is now surrounded by Soviet-era buildings, the gardens in front of the church are colourful and well-tended. It is a three-nave basilica without a cupola, the naves being divided by T-shaped pillars; the roof is formed by a single barrel-vault over all three naves. At the apse a modern stained-glass window is virtually the church's only decoration. An unusual feature is the row of four large stone blocks, a little like khachkars, which form a sort of half barrier across the chancel in front of the altar dais.

Leaving Aparan a striking monument can be seen on a hill to the west. This commemorates an Armenian victory over Turkey in 1918. The remains of the Armenian General Dro were returned here from Massachusetts in June 2000. The countryside becomes greener as rainfall in this area is higher than in the lower-lying areas further south. The road passes several villages inhabited by Yezidi people. Mostly working as shepherds, they are fire-worshipping Zoroastrians and recognisable (to the Armenians) as being racially different with darker skin; the women also tend to wear more colourful clothes and a scarf over the head. As they joined the Armenians in fighting the Turks they are seen as natural allies and there is no racial discord. Modern Yezidi cemeteries are distinctive with graves that look almost like small houses. An older cemetery is by the road in the village of **Rya Taza** where there are tombstones in the form of horses for the men though much simpler ones, sometimes depicting a cradle, for women

The road climbs up through rolling hills and over the pass into Lori. Although the old road via the Spitak Pass is unusable by vehicles it would probably make an interesting walk. The whole distance from Alagyaz, where the new road branches off, to Spitak is about 25km but anyone with a driver could be taken as far as Sipan on the old road and then picked up at Lernatsk, about 5km south of Spitak, leaving about 16km to walk over the pass itself.

Mount Aragats

Mount Aragats has four separate peaks, the highest being the northernmost one at 4,090m. The four summits are situated around the rim of a volcanic crater, broken between the southern and eastern peaks by a stream which flows out. Any reasonably fit person can walk to the southern peak once the snow has melted although it is always necessary to remember that even those accustomed to walking at home will take longer here unless they are acclimatised to the altitude. It is obviously essential to take the same precautions here as are necessary when ascending any mountain. Do not consider going without walking boots, compass, waterproofs, warm clothing and water. The easiest approach is to take the road, often closed well into June, which ascends the southern slope of Aragats as far as the cosmic ray station situated by (artificial) Lake Kari at 3,190m. Visits can be arranged to the cosmic ray station which was inaugurated in 1943 to study astroparticle physics. According to the station's brochure work currently concentrates on monitoring solar activity as well as on studying the physics of extensive air showers and measuring the incident flux of galactic cosmic rays.

From the end of the road it takes about two hours to walk up to the southern peak (3,910m) by heading for the northwest corner of the summit until a rough track is encountered which leads to the top. For those wishing to reach the highest point in Armenia it takes about four hours from the end of the road and should only be attempted by those accustomed to mountain walking. Because clouds often gather round the crater from mid-morning, an early start is recommended to maximise the potential for spectacular views and to minimise the risk of becoming disorientated in cloud. Apart from the break between the southern and eastern summits the peaks are linked by high saddles and a ridge descends south from the southern peak.

South of the cosmic ray station at an altitude of 1,405m is **Byurakan astrophysical observatory** founded in 1946. The original equipment included a 45cm Cassegrainian telescope (a reflecting telescope in which incident light is reflected from a large concave mirror on to a smaller convex mirror and then back through a hole in the concave mirror to form an image) and a 52cm Schmidt telescope (a reflecting telescope incorporating a camera and consisting of a thin convex glass plate at the centre of curvature of a spherical mirror which thus corrects for spherical aberration, coma and astigmatism). Radio telescopes were added in 1950. In 1960 a larger Schmidt telescope with 102cm glass plate and 132cm mirror was installed and an important programme was started in 1965 of looking for UV-excess galaxies. It continued for 15 years and achieved considerable international renown with 1,500 such galaxies being identified. (In 1968 the observatory was awarded the Order of Lenin.) A larger 2.6m telescope was installed in 1976 and a second survey was started which was also to achieve major international recognition. The object this time was to obtain baseline data for an ongoing survey of 600 quasars, emission-line and UV-excess galaxies although the detailed work ended up providing information on about 3,000 varied objects. Since independence the 2.6m telescope has been refurbished and in 1998 the observatory was named in honour of Viktor Hambartsumian (1908–96), its founder in 1946 and familiar to all visitors because his picture appears on the AMD100 banknote.

The southern slopes of Aragats

Amberd fortress and church are beautifully situated on the southern slope of Aragats at an altitude of over 2,000m between the Amberd and Arkashen rivers but may be inaccessible because of snow as late as May. To reach them turn left off the road to the cosmic ray station. In clear weather spectacular views of the two buildings can be obtained from the approach road with Mount Ararat in the background, a view all the more impressive because the café does not obtrude when viewing from this direction, although inconsiderately parked tourist buses might. (The buses, on day trips from Yerevan, rarely arrive before 10.30 so it's quite easy to beat them.) The church, a typical cross-dome structure with an umbrella cupola, is older than the present fortress having been built in 1026 by Prince Vahram Pahlavuni, leader of the Armenian forces who fought against the incorporation of Ani into the Byzantine empire. The present fortress dates from the 12th century although there had been a stronghold here since the 7th century which changed hands several times according to the fortunes of war. The final phase of building took place after the brothers Ivane and Zakare Zakarian captured it from the Seljuk Turks in 1196. Acquired by Prince Vache Vachutian in 1215 it withstood Mongol invaders in 1236 but was finally abandoned in 1408.

Another attractive and interesting church is **Tegher**, founded by Prince Vache Vachutian's wife Mamakhatun in 1213. Constructed of basalt and commanding extensive views over the plains below, it is south of Amberd though there is no direct road link between them. The oldest part is the Mother of God church with round tambour and conical roof. The front of the altar dais shows seven arches, said to symbolise that this was the seventh church built by the family. To its right is a now-blocked secret passage down into the river gorge for water and escape. The large gavit of 1232 is particularly attractive with pleasing decoration around the base of its cupola: the pillars supporting the roof were brought from 10km away. Set into the floor is the grave of the founder and her husband and, more unusually, one grave depicting the deceased as only having one leg and another indicating that the deceased had been buried with feet pointing west rather than east. In the vicinity are the remains of other buildings including a bread oven just below the church. At the moment Tegher receives few visitors but all that may change if proposals to rebuild a nearby abandoned village as a tourist centre come to fruition.

Continuing south from Tegher the road descends through the village of **Aghdzk**. On the east side of the village street are the ruins of a 4th-century three-aisle basilica church to the south of which is a mausoleum, originally of two storeys but with only the subterranean part now intact. According to the early historians Movses Khorenatsi and Pavstos Buzand, the mausoleum was built in 364, in the period of the Armenia–Persian war, to house the bones of the kings of the Arshakuni dynasty which had been seized by the Persians but were then recaptured by the Armenian leader Vasak Mamikonian. The carvings in the chamber date from the late 4th or early 5th century and are unique in early Armenian Christian art. On the north wall is Daniel in the lions' den while on the south is a boar hunt. A torch is essential for seeing the carvings.

The western steppes of Aragatsotn
Kosh

The arid steppe which forms the western part of Aragatsotn is a complete contrast to the eastern and central parts of the province and is crossed by the main Yerevan to Gyumri road. For convenience the western slopes of Aragats are included here as they too are best accessed from that highway. Leaving Ashtarak and heading west along the main road the Arkashen river, which flows down from Mount Aragats, is crossed just before the turn for the road to Amberd and the cosmic ray station. Continuing west, 20km from Ashtarak a road leads right to the village of Kosh. At the far end of the village is a cemetery dominated by a hill on which are the remains of a small, 13th-century castle built on an earlier foundation. It is rectangular in shape with round corner towers. In the cemetery itself are the 13th-century church of St Gregory complete with sundial and the 19th-century church of St George. More interesting than either, however, is the 7th-century church of St Stephen. It is reached by taking the road out of Kosh towards Sasunik for a short distance up the hill until the church is seen in a gorge to the right. A track leads over to the church and the short walk from the road is pleasant and interesting, passing old khachkars and caves apparently formerly used by the monks. The well-preserved church itself is perched on a ledge so narrow in the side of the gorge that the shape of the roof had to be adjusted to avoid an overhanging rock. One of the church's corners is supported by a pile of rock. Inside can be discerned the remains of frescos.

Aruch and Talin

Further west and just south off the main road is the much more important but much less appealingly situated monastery of Aruchavank situated in the village of Aruch. The large cathedral church of St Gregory was built of red and grey tuff in 666 when Aruch was the seat of Grigor Mamikonian, a prince who enjoyed local autonomy during the period of Arab rule. Adjoining the church are the remains of his palace. The cupola of the church has collapsed, remaining unrestored when some work was carried out between 1946 and 1948, and the gate-like doors are padlocked although it is possible to obtain the key in the village or else look through them at the interior which is now used solely as a storeroom for material gathered from around the site. The church is unusual for one so large in having only a single nave and obtaining the key enables visitors to see the remains of the frescos in the apse. Away from the centre of the village Aruch also has a ruined caravanserai, possibly Armenia's most frequently noticed as it is just a few metres from the main Yerevan to Gyumri road on the south side. When built it was on the main route linking the then important Armenian cities of Tabriz (in present day Iran), Dvin and Kars. The caravanserai is commended as a stop for birdwatchers as it is an excellent location for the larks, wheatears and other birds of this arid plain.

The next point of interest heading west is **Talin**, also just south of the present main road. The cathedral here is more appealing than that at Aruch but the setting is dreary with ugly Soviet-era buildings and piles of rusty scrap metal lying around. The large church is surrounded by an extremely large area of tombstones. Like Aruchavank it was built in the 7th century. It has, however, three naves and is an altogether more impressive building of red and grey tuff with a 12-sided tambour decorated with arches into which windows are set. There is good 7th-century decoration around some of the windows. The remains of frescos can be seen. That in the apse probably depicts the Transfiguration while on the south wall can be seen a portion of the entry into Jerusalem. Talin lost its cupola in an earthquake in 1840 and was further damaged by another in 1931 although some restoration was carried out in 1947 and again between 1972 and 1976. The smaller church in a corner of the large site is roughly contemporaneous. An inscription records that Nerseh built it 'in the name of the Holy Mother of God for her intercession for me and my wife and Hrapat my son'. Unfortunately it isn't clear which of several Nersehs was involved.

Dashtadem

A road runs south from Talin across the Talin plateau eventually to drop down into the plains of Armavir province. Leaving Talin there is a very large ruinous caravanserai on the left: its sheer size is testament to the importance of the trade routes across Armenia. In about 6km the road reaches the fascinating village of Dashtadem. In the centre is a large fortress whose perimeter walls are entered through an arched gateway over which are interesting carvings of animals. Built according to the best theories of castle building the gateway requires anyone entering to turn through a right angle thus preventing a horseman charging the entry. A remarkable sight opens out once through the arch. Firstly there is an extraordinary keep of the 9th or 10th century to which half-round towers have been added at some later date and under which large cellars can be explored. Then there are the remains of the other buildings of the fortress. But most amazing of all is that this is not some preserved monument but home to several farmers who pile their hay up against medieval walls and also keep their livestock here. Dusk presents the extraordinary spectacle of the fortress's sheep arriving back from the fields to be followed by the fortress's cattle, a continuation of a routine seen throughout Europe in medieval days but where else now? An Arabic inscription of the month of Safar 570 (ie: September 1174) on the fortress records that it was then under the control of Sultan ibn Mahmud, one of the Shaddadid Seljuk princes who ruled in Ani. Good views of the fortress on its hill can be obtained by continuing past the village along the main road. About 2km along this main road a khachkar marks a track going off left which leads to the restored 7th-century church of St Christopher, built of rather forbidding grey stone and with a more recent detached belltower.

Mastara

Mastara is yet another village now bypassed by the main road but the church here warrants the short detour. Constructed of red tuff, most of the present structure dates from rebuilding carried out in the 7th century: it has never suffered significant earthquake damage. A surprisingly large construction, it has a massive octagonal tambour supporting a cupola invisible because of its covering of luxuriant grass. Inside the church there is a great feeling of height: the rather incongruous balcony on the west side dates from the building's use as a storehouse for the local collective farm from 1935 until 1993. Over at the edge of the village the graveyard has gravestones in the form of sheep together with what is claimed to be the largest khachkar in Armenia. The helpful church caretaker will be happy to take you and show you which it is.

ARARAT

Mount Ararat is now in Turkey but the name of this province recognises that it is the part of present-day Armenia which approaches nearest to the biblical mountain: it is only some 33km from Khor Virap monastery to the 5,165m (16,946ft) peak, separated from the lower 3,925m summit by the Anahit Pass. The whole massif looms high and spectacularly above the plain, which is only around 900m above sea level, and the views are particularly stunning during the months of early summer (late May and early June) and autumn (late September and October) when visibility is at its best. Mount Ararat is especially beautiful in early morning and late evening. Armenians liken the snow-capped peak to a bride covering her head with a veil.

Ararat province has two distinct parts. There is fertile plain along the Arax valley but most of the province is mountainous rising to 2,445m at Mount Urts. Several fairly large areas within these mountains comprise the Khosrov reservation and advance permission needs to be obtained to visit them from the Ministry of Nature Protection in Yerevan. To the south the province is bordered by the detached Azeri region of Nakhichevan: the main road and rail links are of course closed at the border. The much smaller (a mere 7km²) Azeri enclave of Karki, astride the main road linking Yerevan with the south, was the scene of fierce fighting in the early 1990s but the Azeri population has gone and the village is now inhabited by Armenians dispossessed from Azerbaijan. Karki has since been renamed Tigranashen.

The provincial capital of **Artashat**, 29km from Yerevan, is on the edge of the plain. It was established in 180BC by King Artashes I as his capital and retained that role until the reign of Khosrov III (AD330–338) when the capital was moved to Dvin. There is however little in the modern city to warrant a visit. There are no reasonable hotels in the province.

Dvin

Heading south from Yerevan along the main road, the ruins of the former capital Dvin lie about 10km to the northeast of Artashat. They have been partly excavated and the site and museum are open whenever the resident caretaker is at home (which he usually is). Simply push open the gate in the boundary fence and walk into the site. Dvin served as the capital until the Arab conquest in 640 when it became the seat of the governor. It was badly damaged by earthquakes in 863 and again in 893 but remained a significant town until the 13th century with a population, at its peak, probably of the order of 100,000. The second of these earthquakes destroyed what had been Armenia's largest church, dedicated to St Gregory and 58m long by 30m wide. Its foundations can be clearly seen and mosaics from its floor are now in the museum. Also visible behind the church are the foundations of the palace of the Katholikos and a capital from one of its columns is now Dvin's best-known exhibit. The small museum is surrounded by the caretaker's fruit trees. Its contents include finds from the site including examples of the glassware for which Dvin was renowned particularly in the 7th century. Outside are two large phalluses, one of which the caretaker uses as a stand over which to hang his jacket while the other serves as a towel rail thus combining utility with good taste. The extent of trade is evident in the finding here of coins minted in Byzantium while, conversely, coins minted at Dvin have been found in the Baltic states and Scandinavia. Behind the museum a path leads up the hill to the ruins of the citadel but it is difficult to form an idea of Dvin's historic appearance.

Khor Virap

Khor Virap ('Deep Dungeon'), prominently situated on a small hill in the Ararat plain, can be seen in the distance from the main road which passes 5km to the

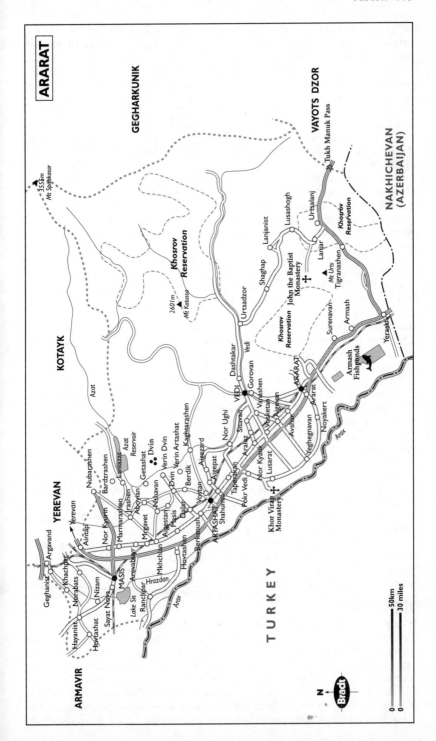

east. In contrast to Dvin, where few visitors ever go, Khor Virap receives so many that there are even souvenir stalls. Its historical significance is considerable and there are in clear weather superb views of Mount Ararat but architecturally the monastery is not particularly interesting. Khor Virap is famous above all as the place where King Trdat III imprisoned St Gregory the Illuminator for 13 years in the late 3rd and early 4th century and it is still possible to visit the subterranean cell where he was imprisoned. However, the monastery itself is a much more modern construction and dates from 1661. A large perimeter wall surrounds the rather plain church which is dedicated to the Mother of God. Access to the cell where Gregory was imprisoned is from the small St George's chapel. To the right of the altar is the entrance hole from which a long ladder leads 6m down to the surprisingly large underground chamber. It tends to be stuffy in the chamber because of a lack of air circulation combined with the number of burning candles. It should be shunned by the claustrophobic and those who do venture down should take a torch. (Do not be confused by a second hole to the right of the door of the chapel. This leads to a separate underground chamber.)

On a hillock to the left of Khor Virap as one approaches is a statue of Gevorg Chaush (1870–1907) who led Armenian *fedayi* (armed volunteers) in their struggle against the Turks in Sassoun province, the area in western Armenia around the source of the Tigris. He was killed in battle.

South from Khor Virap

The main road passes the town of Ararat, dominated by a large cement factory. To judge by the quantity of pollution usually pouring out of its tall chimney, demand for cement is high. Beyond Yeraskh the former main road and railway are both closed at the border and traffic must turn left at the roundabout to continue southwards. One passenger train each day still travels this far from Yerevan departing at 16.30. From here the present-day road turns east and starts to climb towards the Tukh Manuk Pass (1,795m) where it enters Vayots Dzor province. About 12km from Yeraskh the road crosses a former enclave of Azerbaijan: the Azeri village of Kharki, just south of the road, is now the Armenian village of Tigranashen. Nineteen kilometres from Yeraskh a road branches left for **Lanjar**. Just beyond Lanjar tracks go left off this road as it crests a hill. Take the track which keeps to the right of the mountain which in 7km reaches a monastery built in 1254 and dedicated to John the Baptist (incorrectly marked as St Stepanos on some maps). The track passes the site of a summer village used by villagers pasturing their animals. Hospitality is impossible to avoid if on foot and difficult in a vehicle. The monastery is attractively situated but unfortunately seems always to be locked. It has a circular tambour and umbrella dome with a carving of the Holy Family over the door. Above it is a second carving, presumably of God the Father.

ARMAVIR

The province is named after its capital, Armavir city, which is 46km west of Yerevan along a good dual carriageway. It is unlikely that anyone would choose to stay here as the main concentration of sights is in Ejmiatsin, or Vagharshapat as the city is now officially called, only 20km from Yerevan. The churches of Ejmiatsin together with the ruins of the one at Zvartnots were added to the UNESCO World Heritage List in 2000. The eastern part of the province merges imperceptibly with Yerevan's western sprawl where it includes Armenia's main international airport at Zvartnots. To the west the province comprises part of the flat and, in summer hot,

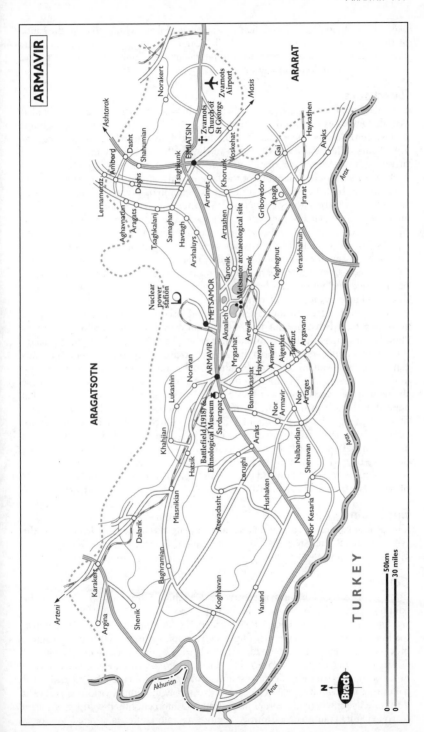

plain of the broad Arax valley. The Arax forms the border with Turkey in the south of the province while to the west the border is formed by the Akhurian river. There is little good hotel accommodation in the province but limited reason to stay here rather than in Yerevan anyway.

Zvartnots

Leaving Yerevan along a road lined by furniture shops whose wares are hauled outside each morning and then hauled back at the close of business, the first point of less commercial interest is the ruin of the huge church of **St George at Zvartnots** ('Celestial Angels'). It lies to the south of the road and the entrance driveway is marked by elaborate gates and an eagle with a ring in its beak gazing back over its shoulder, the work of the famous artist and sculptor Ervand Kochar. The church, built between 643 and 652 by Katholikos Nerses III, is believed to have been a three-storey structure but modern artists' impressions of its appearance are inevitably conjectural. Intended to surpass even Ejmiatsin cathedral by its grandeur, it is usually thought of as having been circular but in reality had 32 equal sides. Decorated with frescos, it was destroyed, probably by an earthquake in 930, to be lost under layers of dirt and debris and even the location was forgotten until its rediscovery in the early 20th century. Some limited reconstruction has been carried out but protests have caused plans to carry out a more thorough one to be held in abeyance for the time being.

At present the area on the east side is being used for laying out various stones according to which storey of the building they are thought to belong. There is some interesting sculptured decoration amongst the ruins including one capital on the southeast pillar carved with a fine representation of an eagle; beyond the ruins can be seen the remains of other buildings including Nerses' palace and a winery with vats sunk into the ground. To the west walls stand to a height of 1.5m. Inside the church the apse is now at a lower level than the main floor and there is what appears to be a baptismal font in the floor reached by going down some steps. Some Armenian sources claim that Zvarnots church is depicted upon Mount Ararat on one of the frescos in the church of Ste-Chapelle in Paris. This is fanciful as Ste-Chapelle is noted not for its frescos but rather for its stained glass which does indeed portray biblical stories including Noah's ark. However Ste-Chapelle was not built until the 1240s and it seems unlikely that the French still had a record of what Zvartnots had once looked like some 300 years after its destruction.

Ejmiatsin

The central square of the town is Komitas Square and a statue of Komitas by the same Ervand Kochar responsible for the eagle at Zvartnots was erected here in 1969.

Cathedral

Ejmiatsin became the spiritual centre for Armenia's Christians shortly after the country's conversion in the early 4th century. According to Agathangelos' *History of the Armenians*, written in about 460, St Gregory the Illuminator saw a vision in which the heavens opened and a blaze of light shone upon the earth. Through the light a procession of angels came down to the earth headed by the tall and glorious figure of Christ. Carrying a golden hammer, he came down to the ground and struck it three times with the hammer. There instantly arose a circular base of gold and a tall column of fire with a capital of cloud and cross of light. Similar visions appeared at three other sites where Hripsime and Gayane and another of their companions were martyred. The columns transformed themselves into churches covered by clouds

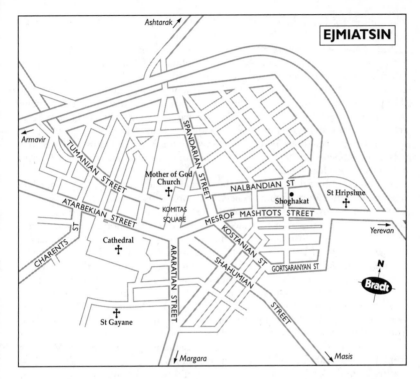

whose shape was that of a cupola. After the vision faded Gregory founded the monastery of Ejmiatsin ('Descent of the Only Begotten') on the spot where Christ had struck the hammer. In reality the monastery was founded, like many others in Armenia, on the site of a pagan temple whose altar can still be visited.

On the basis of archaeological evidence the first monastery at Ejmiatsin was of the basilica form but it was rebuilt in the 480s on a cruciform plan with four free-standing piers, four projecting apses which are circular on the interior and polygonal on the outside, and with a cupola. It was this second church, with cupola, which corresponds to Agathangelos' report of Gregory's vision, a report which fixed in Armenian culture the idea that churches should be cruciform in shape and should have cupolas. Further rebuilding was carried out in the 7th century and Ejmiatsin remained the seat of the Katholikos until 1065 when Katholikos Gregory II was forced to flee by the Turkish Seljuk invaders who were ransacking monasteries. He moved to the Armenian principality of Cilicia (roughly the region of present-day Turkey around Adana and Tarsus at the extreme northeast corner of the Mediterranean Sea) and the seat of the Katholikos remained there even after Cilicia fell to the Egyptian Mamluks in 1375. Ultimately in 1441 a Council decided that the seat of the Katholikos should return to Ejmiatsin. There are no records of any immediate reconstruction but the monastery was certainly in a very dilapidated state, with the roof in ruins and some facing stones having fallen, when in 1627 renovation eventually started. A wall was built around the precinct at this time and numerous service buildings were added. However, these were mostly destroyed in 1635–36 during the wars between Persia and Turkey for domination over Armenia and further rebuilding was required. The first of the large belltowers was built in 1654 and three others were added in 1682; that at the southern apse collapsed in 1921 to be replaced by a new structure.

Accordingly what visitors see now is the site of a pagan temple used as the site for a Christian monastery in the 4th century, rebuilt in a quite different style in the 5th century and then very extensively renovated in the 17th. The tambour and cupola, three of the belltowers, surrounding wall, service buildings and much of the exterior carving are pure 17th century. The cathedral is surrounded by gardens in which khachkars brought from different parts of greater Armenia have been erected. The museum is a more modern addition, dating from 1869 and one of the few Tsarist-era buildings here: the nearby seminary, closed during the Soviet period but reopened in 1997, is another. The carved wooden doors are also Tsarist-era and were made at Tbilisi in 1888.

The oldest wall of the cathedral is the northern which is 5th-century original. It retains two 5th-century figured reliefs with Greek inscriptions, one showing St Thecia and St Paul, the other a cross flanked by two doves. During the 17th-century rebuilding frescos were added inside the cathedral but they were removed in 1891 only to be reinstated in 1956. The cathedral treasury is reached through a door to the right of the altar dais. The museum isn't well labelled but English-speaking deacons are available who will also take visitors down to the old altar of the original pagan temple before requesting a donation. The treasury contains some curious items including what is claimed to be the lance which pierced the side of Christ, brought to Armenia by the apostle Thaddeus and long kept at Geghard; the hand of St Gregory the Illuminator; wood from Noah's ark (carbon dated to 6,000 years old); a drop of St Hripsime's blood; and similar relics as well as more ordinary ecclesiastical pieces. The museum is open daily except Mondays from 10.00 to 17.00 but on Sundays it opens only after the end of the service – usually around 13.30 but later if there is something special such as an ordination. Interested visitors can also arrange in advance for admission to the separate Treasury Museum in the Old Residence where a similar collection of historic ecclesiastical items is displayed.

The other churches at Ejmiatsin
St Hripsime
St Hripsime was one of the refugee nuns from Rome in the late 3rd century who were persecuted under the rule of King Trdat III and the king himself tried to rape her. This 7th-century church dedicated to her is unquestionably one of Armenia's architectural gems. Built by order of Katholikos Komitas in 618 it now unfortunately finds itself surrounded by undistinguished buildings between the main road in from Yerevan and the bypass. The present church is built over the mausoleum of the saint which was constructed in 395. The church has proved more resistant to earthquake damage than many more modern buildings and its appearance has remained almost unchanged apart from the addition of a small portico on the west side and a cross on the roof in the 17th century. The separate belltower was built in 1790. Standing on a raised paved area above the road and with the old fortified wall on the west side, the very pale pink tuff church is essentially a cross-dome church, with a 16-sided tambour, although it is more square than most. It has four apses with a corner room between each apse. Each corner room is, unusually for Armenia, separated from the central part of the church by a circular chamber. As so often, the cruciform shape of the church itself is not obvious from the exterior. It is also unusual in that the northeast corner room is reached by going down steps and that there is a mosaic depicting the Virgin and Child behind the altar.

St Gayane

St Gayane was the abbess of the fleeing nuns persecuted by Trdat III. Her church is slightly later, rather more pleasantly situated and of quite different style. The present church was built by order of Katholikos Ezr in 630 on the site of Gayane's martyrium. By the early 17th century it was forlorn, the roof having collapsed to leave just the walls and piers standing. Major reconstruction was therefore carried out in 1651–53 and a chapel was constructed under the east apse for the saint's relics. Unlike St Hripsime's church, St Gayane's is of the longitudinal basilica style and with an apse and corner rooms only at the east end. Free-standing pillars support the octagonal tambour. In 1683 a gallery was added at the west end: the three central arches are open while the smaller side ones built to house the remains of dignitaries of the church are blanked off and topped with six-column belfries. This gallery, prominent as one walks from the gate, gives the church a 17th-century appearance even though the main part of the building is older. On Sundays St Gayane's church is a popular place for sacrifices. The *orhnakar* is to the right of the main path leading to the front door while the *mataghatun* is in the southwest corner of the grounds.

Shoghakat

This church was built in 1694 by Prince Aghamal Shorotetsi on the site of a chapel dedicated to one of Hripsime's and Gayane's anonymous companions. Coming here after visiting Ejmiatsin's other churches gives a clear picture of both continuity and change in Armenian church architecture. In particular the continued presence of a cupola atop a tambour, octagonal in this case, follows a tradition going back to the 5th century, but a prominent six-column belfry over the porch is evidence of 17th-century ideas. Similarly the detailed ornamental carving in geometrical patterns could have been created at almost any time in the last 1,500 years. Few tourists ever go to Shoghakat, and certainly it does not compare with the main cathedral or St Hripsime, but it does provide interesting insights and locals claim that it marks the fourth place where St Gregory the Illuminator saw a vision of a column of fire.

Mother of God church

If few visitors go to Shoghakat, even fewer come here yet it has a rococo-style altar which is unique in Armenia. The original church of 1767 was wooden and the present stone building dates from the 19th century. It was built as the village church for the ordinary people of Ejmiatsin as opposed to the members of the Holy See or of the monasteries and seminaries. Even now it is near a small market and overlooked by blocks of flats. A three-aisle basilica it has paintings on the square columns depicting Christ, the Holy Family and saints. The altar, painted sky blue and white and decorated with gold leaf is made of marble and wood and in an Italianate style. Outside, the belltower was added in 1982.

Western Armavir

Metsamor

Heading west from Ejmiatsin across the fertile plain, Metsamor nuclear power station can be seen to the right (see boxed text). About 2km from the junction of the bypass with the turn-off for Ejmiatsin a conspicuous monument to the left marks the spot where a Yugoslav plane bringing relief supplies for the victims of the 1988 earthquake crashed as it approached Zvartnots airport killing all seven on board. Four kilometres beyond that, shortly after a petrol station, a road leads off left towards the village of Taronik. Take this road turning off right just before the village and then left after another 500m through an area of fish ponds (and consequently quite good for little bittern, squacco heron and other birds favouring this habitat) towards the red tuff Museum of Metsamor ('Black Swamp') which opened in 1971. The site is open 10.00 (11.00 winter) to 17.00 daily except Mondays.

The small hill on which the museum stands is the site of an important Bronze Age citadel, around 30% of which has been excavated. Although there was occupation here much earlier the important remains and finds date from around 2000BC. Excavations have revealed an important metalworking industry, an astronomical observatory, and considerable evidence of international trade. The excavation of royal tombs has shown that the deceased were buried with feet to the east, presumably to face the rising sun, and in the foetal position within a sarcophagus in the early tombs but later lying within a casket. Royalty were buried not only with their jewellery and a supply of food and wine, but also with the domestic animals and decapitated human beings, presumably their slaves who were slaughtered for the occasion.

The excavated part of the site lies just beyond the museum. The path from the museum crosses an extremely decrepit bridge and care is essential. The walls built in the second millennium BC can be seen; they were strengthened in the Urartian era. However it is the ancient observatory where various markings can be seen on the stones which is likely to be of greatest interest. Archaeologists have suggested that it was used around 2800BC to 2500BC to detect the appearance of Sirius, the brightest star in the sky, which they may have worshipped and which possibly

METSAMOR NUCLEAR POWER STATION

Metsamor nuclear power station is an early Soviet design, the first of its two 440MW units being commissioned in 1976 and the second in 1980. In the immediate aftermath of the December 1988 earthquake there was concern lest Metsamor might have been damaged. It hadn't but nevertheless it was closed in March 1989 as a safety precaution. The energy blockade by Azerbaijan, imposed as part of the war over Nagorno Karabagh, resulted in catastrophic power shortages during the winters of 1992/93, 1993/94 and 1994/95. This was not only because electricity could not be imported but the Armenian thermal power stations were dependent on imported gas supplies; those from Azerbaijan were cut off and the pipeline from Georgia was subject to repeated guerrilla attacks within Georgia. Eventually in 1994 Armenia signed an agreement with Russia providing for Metsamor to be restarted with Russian help and one of the generating units was recommissioned in November 1995.

The main technical problem with Metsamor, apart from uncertainty over the quality of Soviet materials and workmanship, is the lack of a concrete containment vessel to contain radioactive leakage in the event of an accident. A plant spokesman is quoted as saying that it could withstand an earthquake of magnitude 9.0 on the Richter scale. However, the Armenian government, under considerable pressure from abroad, has agreed to close it by 2004 provided other sources of generation can be developed. There are plans for a further three hydro-electric stations and the reliability of gas supplies is set to be increased by construction of a pipeline linking the Armenian and Iranian networks which will facilitate the import of gas not only from Iran but from Turkmenistan via Iran. The Armenian and Iranian electricity grids have also been linked. However whether this will be sufficient to allow closure of Metsamor is marked the start of their year and indicated the time to start planting crops: at that epoch Sirius was visible in summer rather than in winter as it now is.

The small museum is well worth visiting; it shows finds from the excavations at the site but there is no labelling and the staff do not speak English. Of particular interest is the basement where there is an exact reconstruction of one of the excavated royal tombs, some superb examples of gold jewellery, belt decorations in the form of lions, and a weight in the form of a frog made from agate and onyx. This weight, found around the neck of a woman, bears an inscription in Babylonian cuneiform. The ground and upper floors of the museum show examples of ceramics, jewellery, tools and other items including a very large phallus.

Sardarapat
The monument
To reach Sardarapat continue along the main road westwards as far as Armavir city. Just after what used to be a large brandy factory on the right (taken over by the French Pernod Ricard company and then closed) there is a flyover. It is necessary to turn left but to do so requires turning right and then right again over the flyover. After leaving the suburbs of Armavir the road becomes dual carriageway again as far as Sardarapat whose striking red tuff monument, in the form of two Assyrian bulls facing each other separated by a structure from which bells are hung, can be seen straight ahead. This 35m-tall structure, contrasting with the massive bulls, is built in

doubtful, particularly as Armenia's thermal generating plants are elderly and of low thermal efficiency. Metsamor was built with a 30-year design life and, since it had six years out of use, claims have been made that it could operate until 2016. Whether or not it does so may well depend on Armenia being able to fund a replacement able to supply the 40–45% of Armenia's electricity requirement which Metsamor currently satisfies.

Comparisons are sometimes made between Metsamor and the Chernobyl nuclear reactor in Ukraine which suffered a catastrophic accident with huge loss into the atmosphere of radioactive material while tests were being carried out in 1986. Such a comparison is misleading. Metsamor is a Pressurised Water Reactor (PWR) and uses light (ie: ordinary) water to cool the reactor and to generate steam. Water is also used as the moderator, the medium which slows down the neutrons to increase the chance of fission. It is therefore completely different in concept from the Graphite Moderated Water Cooled Reactor (RBMK is the Russian acronym) which failed at Chernobyl. The essential difference between the two is what happens if pockets of steam form in the coolant. In an RBMK reactor the excess steam does not lead directly to a change in the level of nuclear fission since that is controlled by the graphite moderator. Instead it leads to an increase in power generation which in turn leads to a further increase in steam and a runaway cycle develops which is exacerbated because steam is also less effective as a coolant than water. (This is essentially what happened at Chernobyl when the normal link in the control system between thermal output and the degree of moderation had been temporarily disconnected for test purposes.) In the case of a reactor like Metsamor where water is the moderator as well as the coolant, the steam pockets increase the effect of the water in its role as moderator and so the level of nuclear fission declines.

a form inspired by the funerary monuments at Odzun, Lori province and Aghudi, Syunik province.

The monument commemorates the victory by Armenian troops and irregular forces commanded by Daniel-Bel Pirumian over attacking Turkish troops who were coming down the railway from Alexandropol (Gyumri). The battle of Sardarapat lasted from May 22 to May 26 1918 and was a decisive victory resulting in the declaration of an independent Armenia on May 28 1918. The monument was unveiled in 1968 to commemorate the 50th anniversary and each year on May 28 celebrations are held here; the bells are tolled and there are performances by folk song and dance groups.

The area surrounding the monument is meticulously well kept, perhaps because it has since 1998 come under the control of the Ministry of Defence: older women sweep the paths with besoms while younger ones weed the rose beds. The monument is on a small hill and is approached from the main road up a slope with steps. This commemorative monument is probably unique among those erected anywhere in the former Soviet Union in its appropriateness, stylishness and thankful absence of banal pseudo-heroic bombast. Its designer was the evidently gifted People's Architect of the USSR Raphael Israelian (1909–73). At right angles to the approach slope, broad paths through gardens and flanked by eagles lead to a memorial wall covered with symbolic reliefs and penetrated by an arch. There is a now also a memorial garden for the dead in the conflict over Nagorno Karabagh.

The museum

Sardarapat has a second, adjacent point of interest. There is an excellent ethnographical museum which also includes some material about the battle. A path leads down to it from the memorial wall. Halfway along there is a café and to one side a restaurant. The museum is open from 10.30 to 16.00 daily except Mondays. Symbolically it has only two windows: one looking east towards Aragats and the other west towards Ararat. Apart from displays connected with the battle, it has good displays about life in the Arax valley and there is some labelling in English. There are displays of finds from various archaeological sites in the valley along with displays of crafts such as carpet weaving, embroidery and lace making. There are also displays explaining the traditional farm tasks like butter-making and other occupations such as armourer, blacksmith and goldsmith.

GEGHARKUNIK

Gegharkunik comprises the area surrounding Lake Sevan, a large, high-altitude lake whose surface level was originally 1,915m above sea level, and which formerly occupied almost 5% of the total surface area of the country. It is 78km long and 56km wide at its broadest point. Historic Armenia was a land of three large lakes but Lake Van is now in Turkey and Lake Urmia in Iran. The province also includes the beautiful and little-known valley of the Getik river which lies to the north of the lake. The Getik rises close to the Azerbaijan border and then flows northwest, roughly parallel to the lake shore but separated from it by the Areguniats range of mountains whose highest peak is Mount Karktasar (2,743m). The Getik flows into the Aghtsev river about 15km east of Dilijan.

The name Gegharkunik recalls the legends of early Armenia. Gegham was the great-great-grandson of Haik, the legendary founder of Armenia (see page 3). Gegham left Armavir and moved north to Lake Sevan where he established a city which he called Gegh. The lake he called Geghamalich ('Gegham's lake'). The name of the province translates as 'Gegham's seat' since this is where he established his capital.

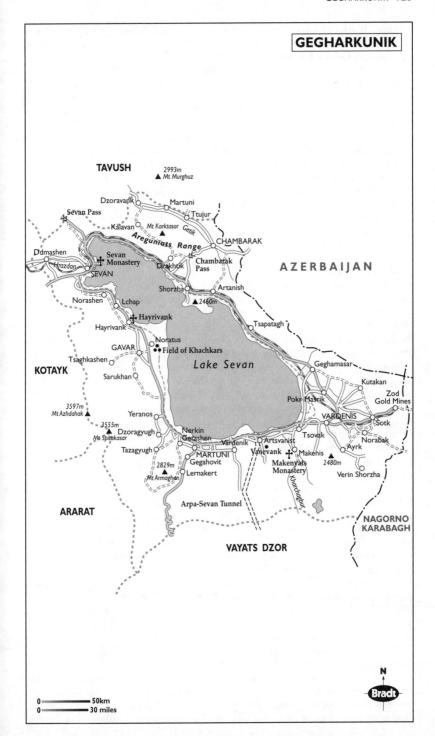

GEGHARKUNIK

TAVUSH
2993m
▲ Mt Murghuz

Dzoravank
Martuni
Ttujur

Sevan Pass
Kalavan   Mt Karktasar   Getik
▲
Aregunia<ts Range   CHAMBARAK

Ddmashen
Hrazdan   Sevan   Drakhtik   Chambarak   AZERBAIJAN
Monastery   Pass
SEVAN
Shorzha   Artanish

Norashen   Lchap
▲2460m
Hayrivank   Hayrivank
Tsapatagh

Noratus
GAVAR   ● ● Field of Khachkars
Tsaghkashen   Lake Sevan   Geghamasar

KOTAYK   Sarukhan
Kutakan
Zod
Pokr Masrik   Gold Mines
3597m
Mt Azhdahak ▲
3555m   Yeranos   VARDENIS   Sotk
▲   Dzoragyugh   Nerkin
Mt Spitakasar   Getashen   Tsovak   Norabak
Tazagyugh   Vardenik   Artsvanist   Ayrk
MARTUNI   Vanevank   Makenis
2829m   Gegahovit   Makenyats   2480m
▲   Lernakert   Monastery   Verin Shorzha
Mt Armaghan

ARARAT
Arpa-Sevan Tunnel   Kharchaghbur   NAGORNO
KARABAGH

VAYATS DZOR

N

Bradt

0 ━━━━ 50km
0 ━━━━ 30 miles

There is a lot of **accommodation** round the lake including many Soviet-era guesthouses run by various unions but at which anyone can stay. Two motels at the north end of the lake open in summer only are the Avia motel (tel: 25794 and 23539) in the town of Sevan near the railway station which has doubles from US$40 and the Sevan motel (tel: 24213; email: marat@arminco.com) which is at Lchap close to the northern tip of the lake. Doubles are available here from US$25. The predominantly youthful clientele makes it rather noisy. The only hotel at the west end of the lake open all year is the Artsnakhar (tel: 061 20450). The hotel is on the lake shore just north of Sevan town. It has very pleasant rooms: singles from US$75, doubles from US$95 and cottages also available from US$120. In December 2002 a new Tufenkian hotel, the Avan Marak Tsapatagh, opened further east at Tsapatagh (reservations via the Tufenkian office in Yerevan, tel: 543122, 543422, 547888; email: tufhosp@arminco.com). Its construction incorporates old stone barns, providing luxurious accommodation. It would even be good for beach holidays but unfortunately it isn't in a particularly interesting part of Armenia. Homestays are of course available and are the only real option for places like Martuni.

Lake Sevan

Lake Sevan, which now enjoys National Park status, is fed by 28 rivers but there is only one flowing out, the Hrazdan which flows out of the lake at the western end to become a tributary of the Arax. In 1910 the Armenian engineer Soukias Manasserian published a book entitled *The evaporating billions and the stagnation of Russian capital* in which he proposed reducing the depth of the lake from 95m to 45m, using the water for irrigation and hydro-electric generation. The reference to 'evaporating billions' is a comment on the fact that 90% of the lake's water is lost through evaporation. (Manasserian also produced a plan to reduce the level of the Aral Sea, a much better known environmental disaster.) Manasserian's scheme was developed in the Stalin era and approved by the then Armenian Soviet government though inevitably without any consultation with local people. The plan was to reduce the level of the lake by 55m which would result in a reduction in its perimeter from 260km to 80km and its volume of water from 58km^3 to 5km^3. With a breathtaking lack of realism it was planned that this drastic reduction in size would be accompanied by an equally drastic increase in the yield of fish caught in the lake of between eight and ten times to be achieved by releasing trout fry from hatcheries into the remains of the lake. A typical Stalin-era writer stated that Lake Sevan's 'scraggy, barren shores will be turned into sweet-smelling meadows, groves of nut trees and oak trees... Around it beautiful roads and promenades will be laid... There could be no objection to diminishing the size of the lake for it would would merely mean diminishing the annual evaporation of a vast quantity of moisture that rose uselessly into the air.'

Work began in 1933 to implement the scheme when the Hrazdan was deepened to increase the discharge from the lake. A tunnel was also bored 40m below the original lake level but, because of delays caused by the war, it was not inaugurated until 1949 and was then trumpeted as a major achievement of the Soviet era. The lake level started to drop by more than one metre per year.

After Khrushchev's speech criticising Stalin at the 20th congress of the Communist Party of the Soviet Union in 1956, the wisdom of the Sevan venture started to be questioned. Already problems were starting to become manifest such as the difficulty of growing the promised nut trees and oak trees on the newly-exposed shore together with a reduction in catch of the four subspecies of the endemic Sevan trout (*Salmo ischachan*). In 1958 a 'Sevan Committee' was formed and the Soviet government decreed that the lake level was to be kept as high as possible with new thermal power stations replacing two of the originally projected eight hydro-electric ones. The new power stations were to be completed by 1970 but removing water for irrigation purposes was to cease by 1965. As a result of the action then taken water level stabilised in 1962 at 18m below the original level but then eutrophic algal blooms started to occur, for the first time in 1964. A new tunnel, 49km long, was also constructed, intended to bring 200 million cubic metres of water each year north from the Arpa river into the lake. Completed in 1981 the tunnel only succeeded in raising the water level by 1.5 metres and a second tunnel 22km long was considered necessary to divert a further 165 million cubic metres each year from the Vorotan into the Arpa and thence to the lake. Only 18km of this second tunnel has ever been completed and the first tunnel is in a poor state of maintenance. Matters deteriorated after 1988 as a consequence of the economic blockade of Armenia during the war over Nagorno Karabagh and the simultaneous closure of Metsamor nuclear power station. The Hrazdan river hydro-electric stations had to be operated more to maintain at least limited electricity supplies in Armenia and the level of the lake fell 20m below its original level with a surface area of 940km^2 in comparison to the former 1,360km^2.

Quite apart from all this, the plight of the endemic trout worsened as a result of the introduction in the 1920s of common whitefish (*Coregonus lavaretus*) from Lake Ladoga and the more recent accidental introduction of goldfish (*Carassius auratus*). Catching the endemic trout has been prohibited since 1976 but the ban is poorly enforced. It is also possible that the introduced crayfish (*Astacus leptodactylus*) is another competitor and the trout is now effectively on the verge of extinction in Armenia although it survives in Lake Issyk-kul in Kyrgyzstan where it was introduced.

While there is unquestioned will within the Armenian government to raise the lake level somewhat, though not necessarily by the full 20m, funds are inevitably lacking and the World Bank considers the cost would be high because of the building and construction which has already taken place on the drained land although the benefits to tourism and fisheries have not yet been evaluated. Some environmental organisations, notably the Green Union of Armenia, claim that the cost of doing nothing will be the complete death of the lake within 20 years.

To those accustomed to the lakes of Switzerland or Scotland, Lake Sevan, with no mountains tumbling down to the water's edge, will initially seem bare and windswept. Its real attraction lies in the ever-changing colours of its surface and in the skies above it. It is also, particularly on its southern side, an area with a long history and with a great many interesting places to see. Even these historical sights bring forcibly home the problems of the lake: the best known, the monastery of Sevanavank, was formerly on an island but falling water levels have turned the island into a peninsula and visitors travel there by road rather than by boat. Other attractions of the lake, for Armenians at least, are the beaches, the only ones in Armenia. While Western visitors would be unlikely to consider landlocked Armenia as a possible destination for a beach holiday, the beaches do provide a unique experience within the country for Armenians. Privatisation has resulted in visitors having to pay to use some of those adjacent to hotels but, in compensation, they are now looked after properly and kept clean.

Sevanavank

This monastery is one of Armenia's most-visited tourist sights. The reduction in the level of the lake has both reduced the picturesqueness of the setting and boosted the number of tourist buses arriving. Although worth visiting, it is not really one of Armenia's most appealing places and owes its popularity largely to its proximity to the lake and to its accessibility from Yerevan. It is on the southwest slope of a hill overlooking the west end of Lake Sevan. The surviving buildings comprise the Mother of God church, the smaller Holy Apostles church, together with a ruined gavit. An inscription on the Holy Apostles church, the oldest of the churches and situated at the northeast of the complex, states that the monastery was founded in 874 by Princess Miriam, wife of Prince Vasak of Syunik, and daughter of the Bagratid king Ashot I. This was a time when Armenia was emerging from subjugation under the Arab caliphate and the church was one of the first to be built in Armenia after the more than 200 years of Arab Islamic domination. Not surprisingly the architects resorted to 7th-century practice in developing the design. Despite what the inscription says about Ashot being king, in 874 this was a little premature. By judicious exploitation of others' enforced absence at the caliph's court in Samarra, Ashot was able to amass great power and in 862 the caliph awarded him the title Prince of Princes. Ashot managed to remain neutral in the wars between the caliph's Arab forces and the Byzantine emperor Basil I which were being waged when Sevan monastery was built. The caliph was only to give Ashot the title king in 884, ten years after the date of the inscription; he was later followed in doing so by the Byzantine emperor.

Holy Apostles is a typical and plain cross-dome church and, in the absence of corner rooms, its interior shape can be seen from the outside. There is a large doorway between the south and west arms and a small chapel with an apse between the south and east arms. The octagonal tambour has four small windows. The larger Mother of God church is in similar style and lies to the southeast of the Apostles church: it too has an octagonal tambour. The small chapels were probably later additions. Off the Mother of God church is a ruined gavit whose roof once rested on six detached wooden columns. The finely carved wooden capitals from the gavit depicting a chalice and the tree of life flanked by two doves are now in the Historical Museum in Yerevan as are two carved walnut doors also from the gavit, one dating from 1176 and the other from 1486.

The monastery is today one of the few active seminaries in Armenia. In the past being here was not, however, necessarily a matter of choice. The French expert on the Caucasus Jean-Marie Chopin who visited the island monastery in 1830 reported that the regime was extremely strict with no meat, no wine, no youths and no women. It therefore served as a reformatory for those monks banished for their misdemeanours from Ejmiatsin. Another visitor reported that as late as 1850 manuscripts here were still being copied by hand. On the peninsula today are also the guesthouses of the President, the Government, and the Writers' Union.

Ddmashen

The village of Ddmashen, 12km west of Sevan though probably more easily reached from Hrazdan in Kotayk province, has an interesting 7th-century church of domed basilica construction. Its incongruous appearance is the result of a new 16-sided tambour being built in a different coloured stone in 1907 following earthquake damage. Very plain inside, it has a surprising number of windows, presumably added at a later date but not marring the feel of this early church.

Hayrivank

Heading southeast from Sevan along the south side of the lake it is about 22km to the monastery of Hayrivank; it can be seen on a knoll to the left of the road overlooking the lake. The monastery and surrounding rocks are all conspicuously covered with reddish-orange lichen. The monastery consists of a church from the end of the 9th century, a gavit from the 12th, and a small chapel. The topography of the rather cramped site with the ground falling away quite steeply has resulted in the south and west arms of the church being no longer discernible from the outside as the gavit and chapel had to be built forming one continuous wall with them. As with the churches at Sevan the tambour is octagonal but here the church exhibits some fine interior carving and the multicoloured interior of the dome is also striking. Every interior wall of the gavit is covered with carved crosses. There are several attractive khachkars at the monastery and just north of it can be seen the scanty remains of a fortress occupied from the Bronze Age until medieval times.

Gavar and Noratus

Not far beyond Hayrivank the main road bypasses the rather uninteresting provincial capital of Gavar which was founded as Nor Bayazit (ie: New Bayazit) in 1830 by Armenian migrants who had left Bayazit, Turkey following the Turkish defeat by Russia. In 1959 it was renamed Kamo, the *nom de guerre* of Simon Ter-Petrossian (1882–1922), one of a number of Bolshevik supporters who raised money for the party by robbing banks in particular but also post offices and railway ticket offices. He died in a road accident in Tbilisi. The city changed its name again following the Soviet collapse. Most of Gavar's industry has closed but the hosiery factory survives, exporting to the other CIS countries and seeking niche markets elsewhere.

After the Gavar turn-off the main road heads south and skirts the edge of Noratus, home to one of Armenia's most amazing sights – the field of khachkars. Turn left off the main road at one of those preposterously over-engineered Soviet-era road junctions that must originally either have had some military rationale or else have been designed by someone with a penchant for grandiosity. On the eastern edge of the town is a huge cemetery with a modern section which is quite interesting but with an array of stones from the medieval period onwards where the range and fascination of the khachkars is overwhelming. Although there are many groups of khachkars in Armenia, nowhere can rival the impression which the approximately 900 here make. It is quite impossible to do justice to the carved stones on a single visit and one can merely wander across the site gazing in amazement at a row of 15 erect ones here, an area of recumbent ones there, no two alike. Stones with single crosses, stones with multiple crosses, geometric patterns, naturalistic ones: it is quite impossible to take in the riot of carved detail. Perhaps the sheep who graze here every day eventually learn to appreciate the detail but mere tourists don't have a chance. Quite why so many khachkars were erected here is not clear: possibly not all are tombstones and some may mark events other than death. Nearby, in the centre of the village of Noratus stands the small white 9th- or 10th-century church of St Gregory with its relatively high cylindrical tambour. The narrow front of the church combines with the small rooms on the outside, which look as if they were built as later additions, the high tambour and the conical dome to give the appearance of a space rocket. There is, however, typical Armenian carving over the doorway and the altar dais inside is conspicuously large for the size of building.

Dzoragyugh and Nerkin Getashen

These two villages which lie south of the main road have interesting historic churches and also provide a picture of Armenian village life in the 21st century. Dzoragyugh ('Gorge Village') is home to two churches both of which were founded in the late 9th century shortly after Sevanavank. The larger, ruinous one, Shoghagavank, dedicated to St Peter, is situated on a hill at the western end of the village. It was built between 877 and 886 and its founder was the same Princess Miriam who founded Sevanavank. The site again has a good array of khachkars, and is where local royalty are thought to be buried, but it is no rival for Noratus. Dzoragyugh's other church still functions as the village church today and is extremely well cared for. Its interior even has carpets on the floor and the altar dais is decorated with, among other things, a carpet hanging on the wall depicting the Last Supper (and owing its composition to Leonardo da Vinci) as well as various embroideries some of which are in Western rather than Armenian style. A large, wrought-iron chandelier hangs from the ceiling. Originally built as the Masruts Anapat ('Hermitage of Masru') it was subsequently extended and now presents a plain, square appearance. The cupola and tambour are octagonal. The lower, older parts of the building are constructed of dark grey, rough-hewn basalt blocks, and contrast rather startlingly with the upper parts and tambour which are formed of red tuff, and some modern repairs effected with concrete blocks.

The next village, **Nerkin Getashen** ('Lower Getashen') was at one time the summer residence and administration centre of the Bagratid dynasty. Its large church built of dark grey basalt was founded, again in the late 9th century, but this time by Miriam's son, Gregory Supan. It is almost square in external appearance thanks to the large corner rooms which conceal the internal cross-shape. The dome and parts of the walls collapsed during the 17th century and only the east façade remains intact. Nonetheless the building still presents an impressive appearance today. However, the local Christian community has opted to build a new church, at the foot of the hill below the old one, rather than seek to repair the damage of more than three centuries.

Martuni and beyond

The main road passes through Martuni where the road over the Selim Pass (2,410m) branches off right and goes south into Vayots Dzor province, being the only road linking northern and southern Armenia which avoids the capital. Although marked on all maps as a main road it is in reality a badly pot-holed dirt track requiring, if at all possible, a 4WD vehicle and even then it is impassable in winter or after rain. Having said that, it is also true that some fairly decrepit Ladas make it over the top, at least on dry summer days. However all this might change as the diaspora may well fund an upgrade of the road although the cost of realigning the road on the southern side would be high if all the sharp hairpin bends were to be rebuilt to allow lorries and tourist coaches to come this way. It would also take away some of the pass's charm but enable more people to see the steppe eagles, black vultures and griffon vultures which are characteristic of the rolling uplands on the northern side. One of Armenia's most interesting sights, the intact 14th-century Selim caravanserai, is adjacent to the road but over the provincial border in Vayots Dzor. On the north side of the pass within Gegharkunik there is, at Geghovit, the first village south from Martuni, a ruined 5th-century church dedicated to St George, and there are petroglyphs on Mount Sev Sar to the east of the road.

Martuni acquired its present name in 1926: Martuni was the *nom de guerre* of Alexander Myasnikian, the first prime minister of Armenia in Soviet days. The renaming of towns here manages to create particular confusion as there is another Martuni, also in Gegharkunik province but in the Getik valley north of the lake. It is always necessary therefore to specify which Martuni one means: the northern one seems usually to be called Martuni Krasnoselsk region even though Krasnoselsk (Russian for red village) has officially reverted to its former name of Chambarak. Just to add to the confusion there is a third Martuni in Nagorno Karabagh.

Beyond Martuni the road swings east. After about another 20km it crosses the short channel which links the hydro tunnel bringing the water from the Arpa river to Lake Sevan and immediately afterwards the village of **Artsvanist** lies to the south of the road. In a gorge on the southern side of the village is the secluded and appealing monastery of Vanevank. The main church, dedicated to St Gregory and on the left-hand side, was built in 903 by Prince Shapuh Bagratuni together with his sister Miriam, the same Miriam who was also responsible for other churches in the district already mentioned. It was restored at the end of the 10th century by King Gagik I Bagratuni when the surrounding wall was built, parts of which can still be seen, notably on the hillside above and behind the monastery. The rather plain church building is itself basalt but the octagonal tambour is of contrasting red tuff. The right-hand church is of similar style, though, with only a single-nave and without a dome. It has a somewhat elongated appearance and is also built of basalt but has contrasting red tuff at the top of the gable ends. The gavit between the two churches was added at a later date.

Makenis and Ayrk

Makenis is reached by continuing east from Artsvanist for about 6km and then turning right to head south for another 5km. Picturesquely situated at the edge of the village overlooking the Karchaghbur river is Makenyats monastery. Quite apart from the monastery, Makenis is an evocative village: one woman winnowing grain in the street, another washing clothes in an irrigation channel, others making lavash. Few tourists reach it and the elderly caretaker of the monastery is determined to make the most of those who do: it is not possible to avoid the hospitality and unmarried young women should further note that at the time of writing she is looking for a suitable match for her grandson. According to 13th-century chroniclers, the monastery was founded by Prince Gregory Supan in 851. This seems slightly early and a date later in the 9th century seems more plausible. It is a three-apse, cross-dome church built of basalt with a circular tambour and surrounded by a substantial wall. There are large chapels on both sides of the altar dais with carved doorways and through the northern one water runs. At the west end there are large high corner rooms. Carvings of horses decorate the base of the southern pillar and the inside of the lintel of the main door. At the west gable is a small belfry. There is also a baptismal font. The gavit is now ruined but there is a small chapel to the southwest. The river must have changed its course slightly since the monastery was built as the conspicuous latrine in the perimeter wall is now a few metres from it. There is a good collection of khachkars, some of which have been incorporated into garden walls and one of which has been removed to act as a bridge over a modern drainage channel.

Vardenis is the principal town in the eastern part of Gegharkunik and looks as though it experienced better days before it became almost a dead-end following the closure of the border with Azerbaijan. From it a poor road runs southeast to **Ayrk** which has two small medieval churches. Ayrk itself is pleasantly set in rolling countryside but looks poor and even more rundown than Vardenis with many empty houses, probably deserted by fleeing Azeris and, with little potential employment to attract Armenians fleeing in the opposite direction, they have remained unoccupied. The two churches are about 150m apart. Both have barrel-vaulted roofs and good collections of khachkars. The northernmost church, dedicated to the Mother of God, dates from 1181 and the southernmost, St George's, is slightly later.

To the north of Lake Sevan

Although Vardenis is virtually a dead-end so far as Armenians are concerned, this is not necessarily the case for tourists who can either continue the circumnavigation of the lake or else continue across the difficult northern route to Nagorno Karabagh. Few tourists do either. The area at the extreme eastern end of the lake used to be an important wintering ground for wading birds but the reduction in lake level has destroyed the habitat. In autumn, however, greater flamingos can still be seen around the southeastern part of the lake. The northern side of the lake has few specific tourist attractions although there are some pleasant beaches. A railway parallels the road: it was built to serve the gold mines at Sodk but there are no longer passenger services beyond Hrazdan except in summer when the service is extended to Shorzha.

The beautiful Getik valley, quite different from the Sevan basin, can be reached by heading north from Shorzha over the Chambarak Pass (2,176m) although the road may be closed in winter by snow. The valley itself is very pleasant, particularly further west, although it lacks any specific sites of interest. Two which are sometimes mentioned are both near the village of **Martuni**, not to be confused with Martuni on the south shore of the lake. The so-called fortress of Aghjkaghala, built in the 10th century, can be seen on the top of a hill high above the north side of the road just west of Martuni. Those who make the climb, probably under an extremely hot sun from which there is no respite, will be rewarded with an unimpressive tiny rectangle of stone walls which might have been a signal station but could never have held a significant garrison. Inside the small rectangle formed by the walls are phenomenal numbers of flies which, given the unusual location, might prove to be an undescribed species of interest to *Diptera* enthusiasts though not to others. There are pleasant views from the site but nothing particularly special by Armenia's high standards.

The other site, also just to the west of Martuni but south of the road along a bad dirt track, comprises the remains of Getik monastery: in reality there are just a couple of courses of stonework to be seen along with a few remains of walls and pillars and some fallen stones. The site is historically important since it was the destruction of this monastery in an earthquake in the late 12th century which led Mkhitar Gosh to leave Getik and found Nor Getik ('New Getik'), now called Goshavank. (See the section on Tavush province for more information.)

Travelling north from Sevan to Dilijan should shortly become easier as a new road tunnel is due to open in October 2003 avoiding the Sevan Pass (2,114m). Unfortunately some of the earthworks on the improved road seem to have been carried out with scant regard for the stability of the hillside and frequent landslips are predictable.

KOTAYK

A half-day excursion from Yerevan to Garni temple and Geghard monastery is probably Armenia's most popular trip for visitors and is well worth making. About halfway from Yerevan it is worth stopping at the memorial arch to the writer Eghishe Charents (see page 40) as it offers splendid views across the valley to Ararat. The provincial capital of Hrazdan is a very rundown post-industrial town with pot-holes spectacular even by Armenia's deep standards. Elsewhere in Kotayk the village of Tsaghkadzor is Armenia's principal ski resort and also offers pleasant walking in the surrounding wooded countryside.

Accommodation is available at Tsaghkadzor ('Valley of Flowers') in various guesthouses including the House of Creativity of Writers (tel: 281081, 282101; fax:

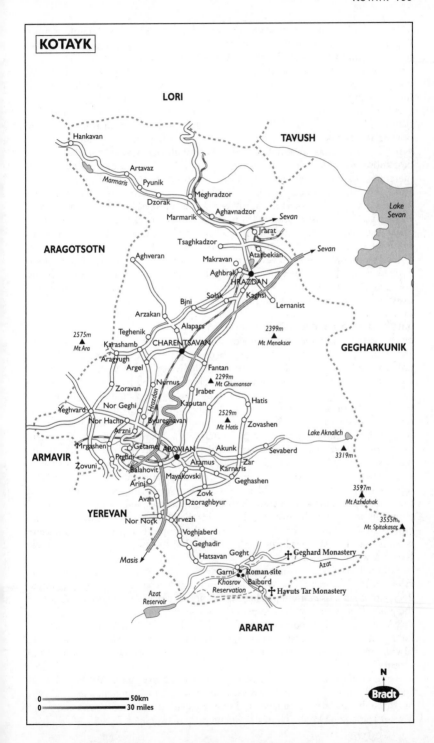

62160; email: writers@hrazdan.am; web: www.hrazdan.am/writers). Singles US$26 and doubles US$32. Set in pleasant grounds and very clean, this is possibly the most comfortable guesthouse in Armenia. To stay here was until recently a pure Soviet experience and it remains largely stuck in a time warp. The staff uniforms were evidently designed around 1948, the women wearing dresses with full skirts and starched frilly headgear. However, each room is no longer allocated a table in the dining-room laid out with the correct number of pieces of bread or cake and at the fixed meal times the waitresses no longer push round a trolley bearing the choice of dishes. Instead there is a buffet but it still includes such wonders for breakfast as semolina, boiled beef or chicken ravioli. For some reason best known to the staff there are never enough sachets of Nescafé laid out (though there are ample tea bags) but they will be unsmilingly supplied on request. The atmosphere in the dining-room is typified by the waitress who, spotting me walking past the dining-room (on my way to the adjacent bar) 20 minutes before service was due to begin glowered at me and pointedly locked the door. The place really does give an insight into the Soviet past. Anybody wanting wine or beer with the meal should go and buy it in the bar beforehand and then take it into the dining-room. The bar, however, must be the only one in Armenia where Armenian brandy is, at the time of writing at least, not on sale. The guesthouse can also hire out equipment for skiing on the nearby slopes. The statue in front of the guesthouse is of the writer Eghishe Charents.

Yeghvard and Kaputan

These two villages in southern Kotayk have churches very similar in style although built of contrasting stone: warm pink in the case of Yeghvard but a rather forbidding grey at Kaputan. Both are dedicated to the Mother of God and are small in floor area but disproportionately tall, having two storeys and being topped not by a tambour with cupola but by a belfry supported by columns. The lower storey of each is more or less square and at Yeghvard the entrance is actually down steps from the present ground level. The upper storey is a cross-shaped church and is highly decorated externally at Yeghvard but not at Kaputan, probably because of the use of basalt which is difficult to carve. Access to the upper storey was by an external cantilevered staircase of which the top steps were stone while the lower were wooden and have now vanished. The only way now into the upper storey is by ladder. The belfry at Yeghvard has 16 columns but there are only eight at Kaputan. Both belfries have a conical cupola. Yeghvard church is in the middle of the village while Kaputan is on a hilltop above the village. At Yeghvard the bell has now been rehung in the upper church but there is no bell at Kaputan. Yeghvard is the earlier church and dates from 1301 while Kaputan was built in 1349.

Although Yeghvard is in Kotayk province it is probably more conveniently visited from Ashtarak to the west. Taking the main Ashtarak road the turning to Yeghvard is signposted right just before Ashtarak is reached. It is about 10km from the junction to Yeghvard. The upper church is particularly notable for its very fine carved animals: a lion and a bull on the west façade, an ibex on the north, a leopard killing an ibex on the east, and an eagle with a lamb in its talons on the south. Elsewhere in the village are the remains of a basilica church of the 5th or 6th century.

To reach Kaputan leave the main Yerevan to Sevan road at the Abovian turn-off and take the Kotayk road. At Kotayk take the left fork for Kaputan. The road goes on through this treeless upland to circumnavigate the eroded volcanic cone of Mount Hatis (2,529m).

North from Yerevan

The main road from Yerevan to Sevan bisects the province from south to north. Leaving Yerevan it is notable for the number of casinos since they were banished from the city and also for the number of sheep herded into pens for sale. To the right of the road, on top of a hill, can be seen the large, architecturally gaudy walled mansion of the owner of the Kotayk brewery while a short distance away on the same hill is the small church which he has contrastingly had built in traditional style.

The first point of interest is the ruinous church of **Ptghni** which can be seen from the road on the left-hand side in the middle of the village. To reach it take the exit for Ptghni shortly after crossing the railway: in practice this apparently requires doing a U-turn and then turning right. The church is a large basilica of the 6th century whose cupola and roof have collapsed. The north façade of the church and much of the west end are still standing and were stabilised in 1939–40. Further restoration was undertaken in 1964 which included demolishing a 19th-century church that had been built adjacent. The size of the building is impressive as is the massiveness of the one surviving arch of the four which once supported the cupola. Over the windows carvings depict angels, hunting scenes, saints, plants and fruits.

Continuing north on the main road the next turn-off to the left leads to **Arzni** which has a tiny 7th-century octagonal church built on a square base. Its red-painted metal roof is anachronistic. Arzni's main claim to fame is that it was developed from 1925 onwards as the Soviet Union's first purpose-built spa. Beyond the old village the road descends into the Hrazdan gorge which is lined here with huge guesthouses, nowadays all apparently disused and spoiling what must once have been an attractive setting. The sheer number of people who could have been treated here simultaneously with the water from the mineral springs is truly amazing.

The main road north now climbs steeply upwards to reach the plateau. Shortly before the summit, more conspicuous when travelling southbound, Lenin's name is clearly legible spelled out in trees on the hillside. Up on the plateau the industrial town of Charentsavan can be seen to the left. Most of the industry is now closed. Leave the road by the Charentsavan exit just north of the town and head west bypassing it to Arzakan. At Arzakan turn right for **Bjni** which has a fortress and two interesting churches. The fortress was built in the 9th or 10th century by the Pahlavuni family. Parts of the northern and western walls remain but there are only traces of other buildings in what is a fairly large area. The entrance to the secret passage down to the village can be seen but it is blocked after 40m. The main church in the village, dedicated to the Mother of God, dates from 1031. It has a disproportionately large circular tambour and umbrella cupola as well as some fine khachkars from the 13th to 15th centuries. The small belfry was added in 1275 and the fortified wall in the 17th century. Used as a byre in the Stalinist era, it was restored in 1956 with assistance from the Gulbenkian Foundation. The small church at Bjni on top of a hill is dedicated to St Sargis and dates from the 7th century. It has an octagonal tambour and retains a roof of tuff tiles.

It is possible to continue from Bjni direct to Hrazdan town along the scenic Hrazdan river. The number of often grandiose holiday homes shows that this is a place where the well-heeled of Yerevan come to get away from the city. Hrazdan itself has no appeal although in the suburb of Makravan is the monastery of Makravank whose 13th-century church dedicated to the Mother of God has a circular tambour and a conical cupola.

Tsaghkadzor and Kecharis monastery

Tsaghkadzor is Armenia's principal ski resort and the number of guesthouses reflects this. It is also an excellent centre for walking and the scope for doing so is extended by using the chairlift which operates all year though only at weekends at quiet times.

Kecharis monastery is situated in the village of Tsaghkadzor, Kecharis being an earlier name for the village. The main church, dedicated to St Gregory, was erected in 1003 by Grigor Pahlavuni (990–1059). Given his age, his personal involvement must have been slight. Son of the Lord of Bjni, he was to become a distinguished theologian and writer acquiring the title Grigor Magistros from the Byzantine rulers after their takeover of the kingdom of Ani from Gagik II in 1045. The circular tambour and conical cupola were damaged by an earthquake in 1927 but were restored between 1997 and 2000. To the south of St Gregory's lies the small Holy Cross chapel which was probably erected shortly after it also in the early 11th century. It too has a conical cupola but its circular tambour is decorated with six arcatures. After the construction of these buildings the Seljuk conquest put paid to any further work, the region remaining under their rule until their defeat by the Georgians with Armenian support in 1196. Work immediately restarted and by 1206 St Gregory's had acquired its large gavit whose roof is supported by four free-standing columns. The final church, the so-called cathedral, lies to the south of Holy Cross and was built immediately after the gavit by Prince Vasak Prosh, being completed in 1214. As in other churches of the period, the corner rooms at the west end have two storeys with the upper storey being accessed by cantilevered stairs. It too has a conical cupola, the circular tambour having 12 arcatures. The Mongol invasions in the late 1230s saw Kecharis badly damaged but it was restored by 1248. Presumably it was at this restoration that the tympanum of the doorway leading from the gavit into St Gregory's acquired its Georgian-style frescos. About 100m from the main group of buildings is the small chapel of the Holy Resurrection with its high circular tambour and another conical cupola. It dates from 1220 and was probably used as the family burial vault for the founders of the cathedral.

East from Yerevan
Garni temple

Garni temple, as it is called, is Armenia's only Graeco-Roman-style building. Although usually said to be a 1st-century-AD pagan temple, probably devoted to Mithra, more recently some historians have suggested that it is more likely to be the tomb built for a Romanised ruler, probably Sohaemus, in which case the construction would have been in CAD175. It is the best-known building on what is an extensive archaeological site, a triangle of readily defensible land jutting out into a bend of the Azat river far below. Archaeologists have discovered the remains of: a Neolithic encampment; an inscription in cuneiform from the early 8th century BC on a *vishap* stone recording the capture of Garni fortress by the Urartian King Argrishti I (*vishap* is the Armenian for dragon; *vishap* stones are large carved stones from the first two millennia BC generally found near watercourses and probably of some religious significance); a Greek inscription on a huge basalt block recording the construction of a later fortress here by King Trdat I; a 3rd-century royal palace and bath house; churches from the 5th and 7th centuries; and the 9th-century palace of the Katholikos. Plainly the site has had a long and important history.

The 'temple' itself was destroyed in the great earthquake of 1679 but well restored between 1969 and 1975. It is easy to see which stones are the surviving

Previous page Spitakavor Monastery
Above Valley of the Sisian, near Tasik
Right Fortress of Smbataberd
Below Medieval bridge over the Urut, Lori Berd

originals and which are the modern replacements. It is one of the few historical monuments in Armenia for which an admission charge is made. The building looks rather like a miniature Parthenon and has 24 columns supporting the roof with Ionic capitals and Attic bases. The frieze depicts a variety of leaves and fruits while the cornice shows the heads of lions exhibiting a variety of expressions. Nine steep steps lead up to the interior in which you'll find a reconstructed and probably inauthentic altar and sacrificial pit. The building differs from most other Graeco-Roman buildings in being constructed of basalt; the use of such a material probably required the employment of Armenian craftsmen skilled in the technique of carving so hard a rock.

Close to the temple are the remains of other buildings. The circular building next to the temple on the west side was a 7th-century church with four apses while northwest of the church was a palace and beyond it a bath house. The bath house has a mosaic floor underneath a modern shelter. The mosaic depicts sea gods framed by fish and nereids together with the ambiguous words 'We worked but did not get anything'. Recently some further reconstruction has been started and the walls of the church and palace have been built up slightly. This does give an idea of the original layout but work on the church in particular has been most insensitively carried out using black and bright red stones which look garish and out of place. There have been understandable protests at the desecration so it may be suspended.

Other sights in Garni

Garni has several other sights, notably the churches of the Mother of God and St Mashtots as well as the monastery of Havuts Tar. The Mother of God church in the centre of the town is a 12th-century basilica with a small porch incorporating a belfry. The more elaborate church of St Mashtots is in the eastern part of the town. It is a small square single-aisle church with a 12-sided tambour. The pink cupola and roofs contrast attractively with the grey stonework of the walls and tambour. The tambour is surprisingly elaborate with much geometric carving and windows in four of the sides. Havuts Tar monastery is accessed from Garni gorge up a track which can be exceedingly muddy. Allow an hour for the walk. The monastery is slightly east of Garni on the edge of the plateau almost opposite the village of Goght and a visit can be combined with a walk along the gorge from Garni to Geghard. Although dating from the 11th to 13th centuries it was very badly damaged in the 1679 earthquake and much of what is now seen supposedly dates from its rebuilding in the early 18th century. It must be wondered how much rebuilding actually took place as the appearance of the site is such as to give the impression that Havuts Tar was effectively abandoned in 1679. The buildings are divided into two groups. The west group is dominated by a cross-dome church whose walls are constructed in a chessboard pattern using alternately red and dark grey tuff blocks. This is probably the Holy Saviour church founded in 1013 by Grigor Pahlavuni (c990–1058), founder also of Kecharis, although some sources state that Holy Saviour is the church in the east group. On the south side of this church is a small vaulted chapel built at a later date. The eastern group of buildings is surrounded by a fortified wall. The main church of the east group once had a gavit of which few traces remain. On its north side work commenced in 1772 on the construction of a new church but it was never finished.

Geghard

One of the great sights of Armenia and on the UNESCO World Heritage List since 2000, Geghard ('Spear') monastery in its gorge setting should ideally be seen when several of the country's less extraordinary churches have been visited.

It is then easier to appreciate what makes this one different. Its unusual feature is that it is partly an ordinary surface structure and partly is cut into the cliff. The name dates from the 13th century and reflects the bringing here of a spear said to have been the one which pierced the side of Christ at Calvary. This spear, a shaft with a diamond-shaped head into which a Cross has been cut, can now be seen in the treasury at Ejmiatsin. It is inside a gilded silver case made for it in 1687. Visiting Geghard on Sunday morning is an enthralling experience with beautiful singing of the choir and the beautifully groomed animals brought for sacrifice after the service.

The first monastery at this site was called Ayrivank ('Cave monastery'). It was founded as early as the 4th century but was burned down and plundered in 923 by Nasr, a subordinate of Yusuf, the caliph's governor of Azerbaijan. Yusuf had just spent five years in prison for rebelling against the caliph. Nasr continued the rebellion, seeking to extend his own power and to enforce the conversion of the Christian population to Islam.

Thereafter the monastery declined until the revival of monastery building in the late 12th century. The earliest surviving part, the chapel of the Mother of God, dates from before 1164 and is situated above the road just before the gateway to the main monastery complex. It is partly a surface structure and partly hewn into the rock, rectangular in plan but with a semicircular apse. Adjoining it are other passages and small rooms in the rock.

In total surrounding the main site are more than 20 other rock-hewn chapels and service premises, many of which have carvings. Also outside the gate are small ledges on to which visitors try to throw stones. If a stone remains on the ledge then the thrower's wish is supposed to come true.

The main buildings of the monastery are surrounded by walls on three sides and a cliff face on the other. Construction was started by the Zakarian family who came into possession of it after they had commanded Armenian forces which joined with the Georgians to defeat the Seljuks. The main cathedral was built in 1215 and is of the cross-dome type, the circular tambour being decorated with graceful arcature and narrow windows and topped by a conical cupola. Between the spans of arcature and on the portals and cornices are depicted a variety of birds and animals as well as floral and geometric patterns. The southern façade is particularly interesting. Above the doorway with two doves facing each other is a lion attacking an ox, the emblem of the Zakarian family. The gavit at the west side which is attached to the rock face was completed by 1225. It is much plainer than the main church though the tympanum has an attractive floral design within an ogee arch.

The Zakarians sold the monastery to the Prosh family who constructed the subterranean part carved out of rock. In the first cave church, on the northwest side, is a spring. It bears the architect's name, Galdzag, and incorporates some fine khachkars as well as stalactite decoration around the roof opening. The Prosh family mausoleum and the second cave church at the northeast were probably by the same architect and completed by 1283. On the north wall of the mausoleum above the archways is a relief carving of a goat with a ring in its mouth to which is attached a rope whose two ends are round the necks of two lions which are looking outwards. The ends of the tails of the lions are dragons looking upwards. Below all this an eagle with spreading wings grasps a lamb in its talons. Both here and in the rock cut churches there is much elaborate carving of crosses, geometrical shapes and khachkars. Rather surprisingly to the right of the entrance to the mausoleum are carved two sirens, mythical creatures with the crowned head of a woman and the body of a bird. These creatures who lived on rocky islets off the coast of Sicily lured men to their death, either by enchanting them with their singing so that they

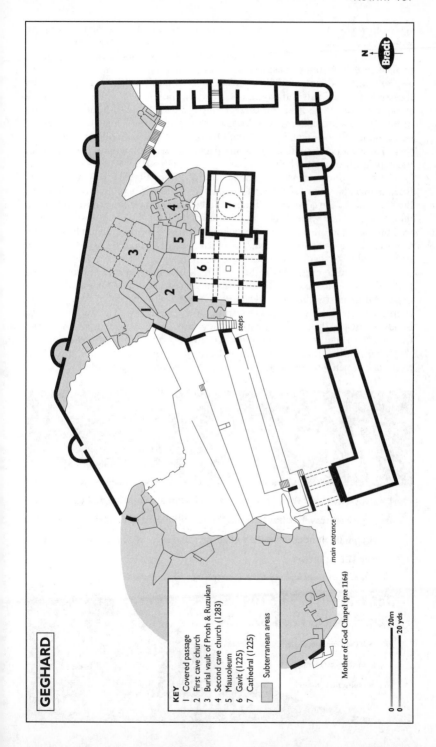

GEGHARD

KEY
1 Covered passage
2 First cave church
3 Burial vault of Prosh & Ruzukan
4 Second cave church (1283)
5 Mausoleum
6 Gavit (1225)
7 Cathedral (1225)

Subterranean areas

steps

main entrance

Mother of God Chapel (pre 1164)

0 ——— 20m
0 ——— 20 yds

were shipwrecked on the rocks or, in some versions, by lulling the men to sleep with their singing so that the sirens could murder them while they slept.

The second cave church, dedicated to the Mother of God, leads off from the mausoleum. Some of the khachkars show human figures including one who holds a spear pointing down while he blows an uplifted horn. To the right at the stairs leading to the altar dais is the figure of a goat. At the left side on the altar dais is a stone seat with a lion's head forming the end of the top of the back and to the right of the dais is a khachkar of two doves each side of a cross. The church, despite being underground, retains the same cross-shape with tambour and cupola as other Armenian churches. There is an opening to the outside world at the top of the cupola which admits light.

The gavit which formed the burial vault of Prince Papak Prosh and his wife Ruzukan was hewn in 1288. It is at a higher level and to reach it go up the steps at the west end of the complex and then follow the narrow subterranean passage to the right decorated with khachkars carved into the rock. The roof is supported by four pillars and in the floor is a hole looking down into the mausoleum below. The acoustics in this gavit are amazing. Anyone standing here and singing, particularly by the northeast pillar, sounds like an entire choir.

Another feature of interest is the small rock-hewn chapel adjacent to the steps leading up to the gavit. Over the door is a carving of a figure wearing what appears to be a Mithraic-style hat. The *orhnakar* is in front of this chapel but the *mataghatun* is outside the small eastern gateway. Around the boundary wall are various service buildings; that at the northeast corner is a bakery complete with *tonir*. Most date from the 17th century but those at the southwest corner only from 1968–71.

After so much culture it is worth, on leaving Geghard, buying some fruit *lavash* from the women who sell it near the entrance. The plum is particularly good.

The Northern Provinces

The three northern provinces of Shirak, Lori and Tavush are very different from each other. Shirak is mostly a high plateau while Lori is characterised by its deep gorges. Tavush retains extensive forest cover. Visitors who combine a visit to Armenia with one to Georgia cross Lori between Yerevan and the Georgian border, seeing some of the monasteries of the Debed valley en route. Others go to the one-time resort town of Dilijan in Tavush with its attractive wooden buildings. The monasteries of Sanahin, Haghpat and Haghartsin are all much visited, and others such as Goshavank and Odzun receive a fair number, though such gems as Makaravank and Hnevank see only a few and the immensely worthwhile Khuchap and Khorakert hardly any.

SHIRAK

Shirak province is bounded to the west by Turkey and to the north by Georgia. Mostly a high plateau, it becomes increasingly hilly nearer the Georgian border and to the east where it borders Lori province. Shirak is off the main tourist routes and even such fine monasteries as Marmashen and Harichavank are seen by few tourists. Those interested in churches should also visit Anipemza whose church, although roofless, is one of the oldest in Armenia and built in a quite different architectural style. The only **hotels** are in Gyumri: the Gästehaus Berlin, 25 Haghtanaki Avenue (tel: 23148 and 37659; email: drk@shirak.am) was opened by the German Red Cross after the earthquake – hence the name – and is attached to a clinic although being ill is not a requisite of staying here. It has ten rooms; doubles from US$50. The newer Hotel Isuz, 1/5 Garegin Njdeh Avenue (tel: 25151, 33399; fax: 39993; email: isuz@shirak.am; web: www.isuz.am) lies to the north of the centre and has 12 rooms each with a kitchenette. Very pleasant and well equipped internally, the façade preserves that of a former factory which was destroyed in the earthquake. Doubles from US$70. Gyumri also boasts one of Armenia's pleasantest restaurants, the Kamar ('Arch'), 14 Gai Street (tel: 23095). It is in a basement with the entrance down some steps below street level.

Gyumri

Gyumri is the principal city of northwest Armenia and the administrative centre of Shirak. At 11.41 on Wednesday, December 7 1988 – when most adults were at work and most children at school – around 60% of the buildings were destroyed by an earthquake. The epicentre of the earthquake, which measured 6.9 on the Richter scale, was 30km east of Gyumri in Lori province near the small town of Spitak (population then about 25,000) where every building was destroyed. In all, around 25,000 people were killed and 500,000 made homeless in Gyumri and the

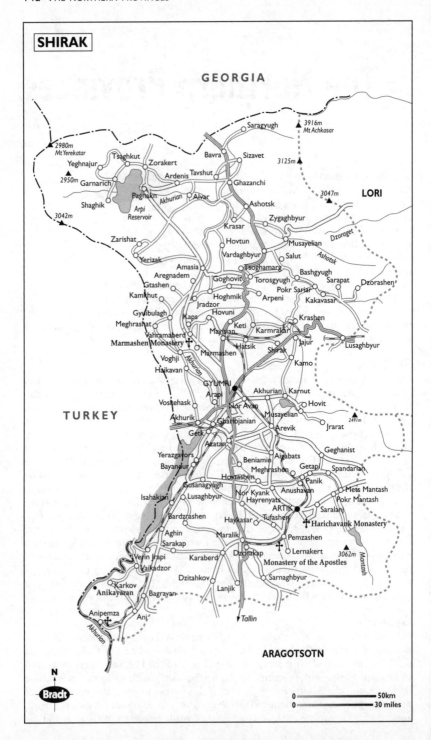

SHIRAK

GEORGIA

2980m
Mt Yerekatar

Saragyugh

3916m
Mt Achkasar

Yeghnajur   Tsaghkut   Zorakert   Bavra   Sizavet

3125m

2950m Garnarich   Ardenis   Tavshut   Ghazanchi

3047m   LORI

Paghakn   Akhurian   Alvar   Ashotsk

Shaghik   Arpi   Zygaghbyur

3042m   Reservoir   Krasar   Musayelian   Dzoroget

Zarishat   Hovtun   Ashotsk

Yerizak   Vardaghbyur   Salut

Amasia   Tsoghamarg   Bashgyugh   Sarapat   Dzorashen

Aregnadem   Goghovit   Torosgyugh   Pokr Sariar

Gtashen   Hoghmik   Arpeni   Kakavasar

Kamkhut   Jradzor   Hovuni

Gyulibulagh   Kaps   Keti   Krashen

Meghrashat   Mayisian   Karmrakar   Lusaghbyur

Vahramaberd   Hatsik   Jajur

Marmashen Monastery   Marmashen   Shirak

Voghji   Kamo

Haikavan   Akhurian

GYUMRI   Karnut

Arapi   Akhurian

Vosketask   Nor Avan   Hovit

Akhurik   Musayelian   2491m

Gharibjanian   Arevik   Jrarat

Getk   Azatan

Yerazgavors   Aigabats   Geghanist

Bayandur   Beniamin   Getap   Spandarian

Meghrashen   Panik   Mets Mantash

Hovtashen   Anushavan   Pokr Mantash

Gusanagyugh   Nor Kyank   ARTIK   Saralanj

Isahakian   Lusaghbyur   Hayrenyats   Harichavank Monastery

Bardzrashen   Haykasar   Tufashen

Aghin   Maralik   Pemzashen   3062m

Sarakap   Lernakert   Mantash

Verin Irapi   Karaberd   Dzhrakap   Monastery of the Apostles

Vaikadzor   Dzitahkov   Lanjik   Sarnaghbyur

Karkov
Anikayaran   Bagrayan

Anipemza   Ani   Tallin

Akhurian

TURKEY

N

Bradt

ARAGOTSOTN

0   50km
0   30 miles

surrounding region. (See boxed text for more information.) The problems Armenia has had in dealing with the aftermath of the earthquake have long made any visit to Gyumri a salutary experience. However, not to go there means missing an important aspect of modern Armenian history. Apart from the direct impact of the earthquake, an indirect consequence was the shutting of Metsamor nuclear power station because of its vulnerability to any further earthquake. It was the closure of Metsamor, by far Armenia's biggest source of electricity, coupled with the blockade by Azerbaijan and Turkey as a result of the war over Nagorno Karabagh, which led to most Armenians having no electricity and hence no heat during the winters of 1992/93, 1993/94, and 1994/95.

Gyumri was called Leninakan at the time of the earthquake and there is a certain irony in that Lenin's entire system of government was to collapse so soon after a city which had been named in his honour. Immediately after the earthquake, Gorbachev promised the inhabitants that the city would be rebuilt within two years. That timetable was unachievable in the last days of the Soviet Union and, after the Armenian vote for independence in 1991, the Armenians ceased work on the partly completed buildings since they had not been designed with adequate earthquake protection. Nowadays, approaching the city from many directions, visitors see unfinished blocks of flats with derelict tower cranes alongside. In most Western countries the local scrap merchants would have removed the cranes long ago and the fact that these abandoned cranes have lasted so long evidently reflects either the honesty of the Armenians or the lack of demand for scrap.

Some of the blocks were almost finished. In others merely the foundations had been dug. They were being built on good agricultural land and here and there small fields have been recreated amongst redundant foundations or between skeletal blocks. Elsewhere, further out from the city, large areas of land have been used for dumping rubble from the many buildings which collapsed in 1988.

Nearer the centre of the city, the present-day homes of the residents are encountered. As recently as 2001 around 40% of the population were still living in old railway containers into which windows had been cut. It was not really until 2002 that the air of depression started to lift and it was possible to imagine that eventually sufficient new housing might be built for those who had so far spent almost 15 years in these metal boxes. There are also notices here and there around the town stating that, thanks to USAID, houses have been provided for those inhabitants who meanwhile had been living in a particular school or museum building. However, it must be uncertain how many residents really want to stay in a place which suffered two earthquakes in the 20th century: 300 had been killed in a smaller one in 1926.

The city itself is an ancient settlement, and was caught up in the long struggles for supremacy between the Persian and Ottoman empires. However, the older surviving buildings, mostly in the centre, date from the period after Russia gained control of the region following the Russo–Turkish war of 1828–29. A fortress was quickly built to defend the new border and in 1837, when Tsar Nicholas I visited Gyumri, the town was renamed Alexandropol after Nicholas' wife, Tsaritsa Alexandra Fedorovna. That name lasted until 1924 when it was again renamed, this time in honour of the recently deceased Lenin. The survival of the older buildings indicates that under Tsarist rule construction was to higher standards than in the Soviet era.

There are probably more surviving Tsarist-era buildings here than in any other Armenian city and the older central streets offer an insight into 19th-century Russian provincial architecture. On the main square, two 19th-century churches face each other, Mother of God on the north side and Holy Redeemer on the

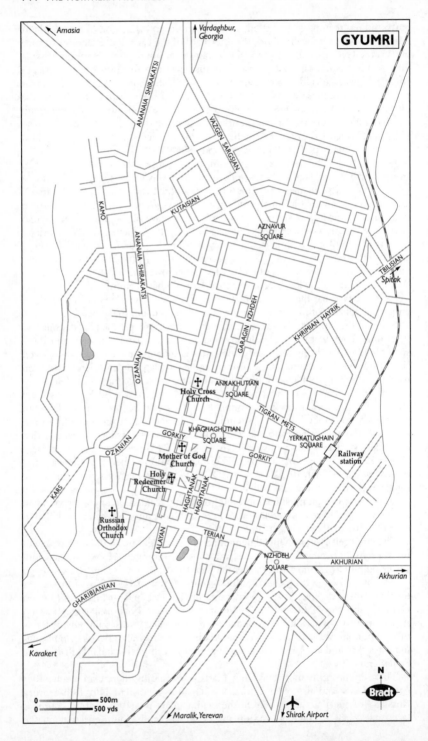

south. Both were damaged by the earthquake, the latter suffering considerably when its large central cupola collapsed. Money for rebuilding churches is apparently readily available and Mother of God is functioning again while Holy Redeemer is currently under restoration. By contrast, Gyumri's largest and most impressive 19th-century church, Holy Cross, which is situated to the north of the centre on Shahumian street, escaped lightly although it too is currently under renovation. The small Russian Orthodox church, in typical Orthodox style with a silver-coloured onion dome, appears to have suffered little damage but is now closed. None of these churches need detain the visitor long but they do combine with the older residential streets to provide one of the few extant pictures of the Tsarist era in Armenia.

Plans even exist to attract tourists by turning the centre of Gyumri into a sort of Tsarist-era theme park (they were outlined at a conference in November 2001)

> where rows of craftsmen, small and medium-sized hotels, restaurants, cafes, studios, workshops, art salons, museums, concert and theatre halls will be accommodated on an area of 200 hectares, on which no less than 1,115 historic buildings are preserved. All this will be in the atmosphere and surrounding of the 19th century, with horse-drawn carriages going round in the old town. The cafés and restaurants will serve dishes, sweets and beer based on 100-year-old Gyumri recipes.

It must remain conjectural just how many tourists would be attracted by such a venture and what would happen to local businesses with the streets full of phaetons and diligences.

The **Local History and Craft Museum** (47 Haghtanaki Street) is one of the few such museums still functioning in Armenia and merits a visit. The museum is located in a restored 1872 town house, the façade of which comprises black and orange-red tuff blocks together with a wrought-iron balcony. Inside are paintings by local artists and rooms furnished as they would have been in Tsarist days. It is particularly conspicuous that virtually all items in the rooms for the wealthier inhabitants came from western Europe and little from Russia, eastern Europe or Asia. This presumably reflects the aspirations of prosperous Armenians under Tsarist rule. The museum is open from 11.00 to 17.00 daily except Mondays.

Southeast of the city is Shirak airport which still has a few flights including a weekly one from Moscow. Anyone landing here should note that there are no taxis at the airport and there are no phones to summon one. The airport was reportedly designed to look like an airport in provincial Turkey so that, in the event of a hijacking, a plane could be diverted here and the hijackers then deceived into thinking that they had made it to the West. Apparently the normal airport signs could be rapidly changed to (apparently) Turkish ones, there were stocks of Turkish uniforms for the staff, and suitable photographs of such people as the Turkish president.

Marmashen

The monastery of Marmashen is one of Armenia's most interesting and is beautifully situated. It is, however, not on a main tourist route and is consequently little visited. To reach it take the main north road out of Gyumri and then fork left at the edge of the town. Continue along this dreadful pot-holed dirt road past the village of Marmashen as far as the village of Vahramaberd (about 8km from the left fork). At Vahramaberd turn left between fields where rubble has been dumped and after about 2km the road starts to descend into the valley of the Akhurian river. The monastery can be seen below the road, picturesquely situated by the river and surrounded by fruit trees. The road eventually zigzags down to it.

1988 EARTHQUAKE

The first shock, of magnitude 6.9, was at 11.41. It lasted for 47 seconds. Four minutes later there was a second shock of magnitude 5.4 and within the first fortnight there were 1,500 tremors. Unfortunately most of the hospitals and schools were of modern Soviet construction and so collapsed immediately: urgent medical care for the survivors was difficult, not just because of the collapse of the hospitals but because over half of Gyumri's doctors died in the ruins. All 60 expectant mothers in the maternity hospital died along with the new-born and their mothers. In one area of nine-storey flats only five or six of the original 49 blocks remained. (Flats similar in design to these are common even today throughout earthquake-prone Armenia.) Out in the villages the older peasant houses sometimes survived but the children had usually been in modern schools and hence died.

The wounded had to be evacuated by helicopter to hospitals in Yerevan and emergency supplies (including large numbers of coffins) had to be flown in. As well as useful items, numerous bureaucrats also arrived with no ability to organise anything but with a feeling that Soviet bureaucrats are important people and therefore should be there. Gorbachev himself cut short a trip to the USA to visit the scene. Help came from abroad as well as other parts of the Soviet Union – even from Azerbaijan despite the growing tension over Nagorno Karabagh. However, Armenian television was able to show Muslim demonstrators on the streets of Baku with placards: 'Allah be praised, He has punished the infidel'; 'Hurrah for the earthquake'; 'God is just, He knows whom to punish'.

Electricity, telephone and water supplies all failed. The absence of electricity and telephone, coupled with the perpetual shortage of batteries (to power radios) in the Soviet Union, meant that people, especially in the villages, had no sources of information and there were many who believed for days that the entire world had been affected. As well as being bereaved, many survivors had lost most of their possessions and were financially ruined. Looting and pillaging soon broke out and as a result cars leaving the region were searched by soldiers and the forces of the Ministry of the Interior.

Could the earthquake have been predicted? Probably not, at least so far as the exact date and location were concerned, although after the event some shepherds said that they had noticed changes in the preceding days: specifically that the water in the artesian wells had become several degrees warmer.

There are three separate buildings. The main church was built between 986 and 1029 in red tuff and is in the style of those at Ani, the former capital. It is particularly elegant with decorative arcatures on each façade and columns supporting the corners of the umbrella cupola. Inside, the front of the altar has been restored using the original carved stones where possible but supplemented where necessary with other stones found on the site. Much restoration has been expertly carried out, funded by an Italian–Armenian couple who went to the length of having experiments carried out in Italy to find an ideal mortar to repair the stonework. Apart from the other two churches on the site, one of which is rather like a smaller version of the main church, archaeologists have uncovered the foundations of a fourth, much earlier, church. There is also a good array of khachkars: those marking the graves of men in front of the church with those of women to the sides and back. Close by the monastery complex there is a waterfall on a minor tributary of the Akhurian.

Jrapi and Anipemza

Heading southwest from Gyumri and parallel to the Turkish border, the road crosses the only rail link between Armenia and Turkey at a level crossing. This rail link was opened in 1898 to provide a connection between Tiflis (present-day Tbilisi, Georgia) and Kars (in present-day Turkey) at a time when both cities were in the Russian empire. By the latter days of the Soviet Union there was only one train each week across the border but even this has been suspended because the border is officially closed. Continuing southwest and very close to the border the nests of white storks can be seen on top of telegraph poles: the storks have only a limited distribution in Armenia but there are several pairs here. The military significance of the area, the frontier between the former Warsaw Pact and NATO, can be judged from the continued presence of Russian soldiers and by the markings on one stretch of road which enabled it to be used as an emergency runway. (Any aircraft attempting to land nowadays would crash into one of the pot-holes.)

After about 38km the ruins of 10th–11th-century **Jrapi caravanserai** can be seen on the left. There is also a small 7th-century church and another building which might have been another church. The road continues through pleasant hilly country and as it starts to descend again to the plain there is a small picnic spot with a natural spring on the east side. An early summer lunch break here might be enlivened by nesting crag martins, Isabelline wheatears and blackheaded buntings.

Continuing south past the town of Bagravan a road branches off right to **Anipemza** whose Yereruyk church, though roofless, is one of the most architecturally important in Armenia and often features in collections of photographs of the country. Its significance rests with its early date (5th–6th century) and the idea it gives of early Armenian church architecture which was modelled on the style of churches in the eastern provinces of the Roman empire. The basilica-style building is erected on a large plinth approached by steps. The porches are framed by elaborately carved pediments of Graeco-Roman style, contrasting with the different style of the carved window arches and the plain pilasters. Even the name Anipemza has particular significance for Armenians since it reminds them of their inaccessible capital Ani; the pemza part of the name refers to pumice which is mined locally.

The Turkish border is only a few hundred metres from the church and, on a clear day, both Mount Aragats, the highest peak in present-day Armenia, and Mount Ararat, the highest peak in historic Armenia, can be seen. Heading back towards Gyumri, a road heads off west towards the village of Anikayaran and beyond that to a specially constructed viewpoint over the abandoned capital of Ani which is immediately over the border in Turkey. However, advance permission to go into this sensitive area has to be obtained from the Foreign Ministry in Yerevan and a small fee paid. It is quite easy to secure the permission but several days' notice is required. For Western visitors it may be more satisfactory to visit Ani itself via the Turkish city of Kars. Even then it is necessary to seek police permission in Kars. That the Armenians are cut off from their historic capital is a consequence of the Soviet–Turkish treaty of 1921 which ceded to Turkey areas including Kars and Ani even though they had been under Russian control since 1877 and had even been awarded to Armenia under the Treaty of Sèvres in 1920. (See the *History* section on page 13 for a discussion of this issue.) The possible return of Ani to

Armenia in exchange for two Kurdish villages further north was raised in inter-governmental talks as recently as 1968 but nothing resulted.

To the Artik district

The easiest way to get there (in that the road has the best surface) is to head south from Gyumri towards Yerevan. Some 15km south from Gyumri there is a crossroads. Anyone wishing to see an 11th-century church, disused since Soviet days (and guarded by hostile geese on the occasion of my visit), plus two surviving fragments of wall from a medieval castle at the heart of a (decidedly) unspoilt village, should turn right for Gusanagyugh. However, the detour does not really justify the time spent.

About 25km south of Gyumri the road reaches Maralik. Turn left towards Artik just before the railway bridge. On the right, opposite the road junction, there is a gigantic example of Soviet central planning: an enormous cotton-spinning factory, now operating at a fraction of its original capacity. It was typical of Soviet economic policy to site a large cotton-spinning factory far from the sources of cotton (in Uzbekistan and Tajikistan), far from the markets for cloth (mostly in the western USSR), requiring a dedicated railway line to be built to transport materials in and out, and not even near significant sources of power.

Several interesting monasteries lie close to this road. The first, which can be seen across the fields to the right, is the **Monastery of the Apostles**. Built of red tuff it can be approached to within a few hundred metres by dirt road and a quiet walk after leaving the vehicle might be rewarded by the sight of European sousliks (a burrow-dwelling member of the squirrel family) between the road and the monastery. The dome of the 11th-century monastery has collapsed but it is still possible to get a good idea of how the building must have looked. Notwithstanding its roofless state, it is still used and there are the remains of recently burnt candles and of the cloths and handkerchiefs which believers leave when a special wish is expressed.

Turn right in Artik to cross the railway line by an improbably large flyover and then turn right and right again. Part way up the hill southwest of the town is **Lmbatavank**. This small 7th-century monastery whose single-aisle church is dedicated to St Stephen is also built of red tuff and, with its high dome, is very well preserved being particularly notable for its frescos. There are good views to the north from the hillside location. Scattered around the church are old hollowed-out coffins, also made of tuff. The practice was apparently to place the corpse in the coffin and then pile earth on top.

Returning to the main road and continuing into the town of Artik is quite a shock. Artik has a few older buildings but most of the town obviously dates from the post-1945 Soviet period. It was developed as a centre of tuff mining and the recent upsurge in construction work means that unemployment has fallen slightly although many bored-looking listless men still hang around street corners in the middle of the day, obviously with no jobs and no money. The down-at-heel air is exacerbated by the layer of grey dust from the tuff quarries which covers everything.

Harichavank

To reach the large and important monastery of Harichavank turn left in Artik after crossing the railway and then turn right up the hill. Just before the prison turn right for the village of Harich: the monastery of Harichavank is at the far end of the main street. It is situated on the edge of a small ravine.

The monastery was founded by the 7th century and expanded during the 13th. Most of the ancillary buildings were added after 1850 when the Katholikos moved his summer residence here. The original 7th-century church, St Gregory's, has a round dome. Its belltower, resting on large columns, is a 19th-century addition as are the small chapels which adjoin it. The much larger Mother of God church of 1201 has an unusual 16-sided umbrella dome and much elaborate decoration around the tambour. In between the two churches is a very large gavit whose porch is particularly finely decorated with small twisted columns and inlaid, carved red and black stones which show a striking oriental influence. On the east façade of the Mother of God church is a relief showing the founders of the church and also one of a lion. An unusual feature is the small chapel perched on top of a high pillar of rock in the gorge; it owes its present inaccessible location to an earthquake.

LORI

Lori, Armenia's largest province in terms of land area, is very beautiful. Largely a high plateau with small mountain ranges, its outstanding features are the deep gorges which fissure the landscape. Apart from these river valleys, Lori is sparsely populated. The principal rivers are the Debed and the Dzoraget. The Debed rises in the southwest of the province where it is called the Pambak, flows east and then turns north towards the Georgian border. It ultimately joins the Kura whose delta is on the Caspian Sea south of Baku, Azerbaijan. The Debed valley on the Georgian border is the lowest-lying part of Armenia with an altitude of 400m above sea level. The Dzoraget rises to the west in Shirak province and then flows east past Stepanavan to join the Debed halfway between Vanadzor and Alaverdi. The spectacular gorges of these rivers are excellent places to find eagles, vultures and also interesting smaller birds such as rock nuthatches. In addition they are where Lori's most appealing sights, its ancient monasteries and fortresses, are to be found.

The biggest problem for visitors at present is the lack of good accommodation, especially in the areas where they are most likely to want to go. There is a good **hotel** in Vanadzor, the Argrishti, 1 Batoumi Street (tel: 051 42556, 42557) with 14 rooms and attractive marble floors and stairs. Doubles cost from US$50. The motel at Amrakits, about 4km south of Stepanavan on the Vanadzor road, is also acceptable (tel: 056 22005, 22124 and 32127). Doubles start at US$20. A former holiday guesthouse offers accommodation for US$8 just above Odzun (tel: 023 22518) and is certainly a better option than the Hotel Debed at Alaverdi which is a dump. The opening of a new 34-room Tufenkian Heritage Hotel at Dzoraget (roughly halfway between Vanadzor and Alaverdi) will improve matters considerably for those with money. As ever, homestays are the recommendation for budget travellers. One of Armenia's pleasantest restaurants is the Flora at Alaverdi (tel: 053 22474). It is reached by crossing the main bridge at Alaverdi (the one which is actually two separate bridges, one for each direction) and then turning immediately left. The restaurant is 1km along this road on the right. Armen, the proprietor, can also arrange homestays.

Vanadzor

Vanadzor, the provincial capital, is situated on the River Debed at 1,350m above sea level between the Pambak mountain range to the south and the Bazum range to the north; both ranges exceed 3,000m in height. Prior to 1935 Vanadzor was called Kharaklisa. In 1935 it was renamed Kirovakan after Sergei Kirov (1886–1934), the Head of the Communist Party in Leningrad, whom Stalin arranged to have assassinated because his popularity in the Party made him a potential rival. In 1993 the city acquired its present name from the local Vanadzor river. Formerly the third largest city in Armenia it was damaged by the 1988

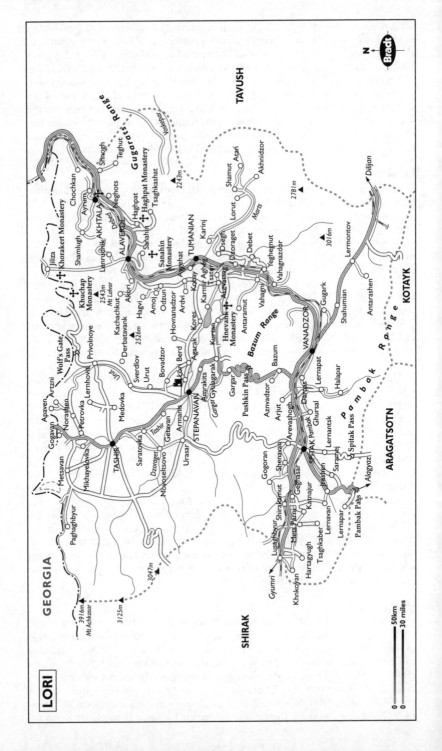

earthquake but not to anything like the same extent as Gyumri and Spitak and its central square with buildings of pink tuff and its main shopping street survived more or less intact. Since then Gyumri's falling population means that Vanadzor is now Armenia's second city. An important industrial centre in Soviet times, most of the former chemical plants making products as diverse as glue and nail-polish remover are now closed but the ammonia plant reopened in 2001. The continued closure of most of the huge factories means that the city no longer lives under a dense pall of acrid smoke and the atmosphere is now clean and pleasant. Although there is little to tempt visitors to stay except as a transit stop on the way to Georgia or the monasteries further north, Vanadzor could also provide a suitable base for hiking in the surrounding hills because such good accommodation is available.

Spitak
West from Vanadzor the main road and rail lines to Gyumri follow the Debed to pass by the town of Spitak in the district where many of Armenia's cabbages and carrots are grown. Spitak was close to the epicentre of the 1988 earthquake and was completely destroyed by it. Much rebuilding, including a new church, has been funded by the international community but the former factories still lie ruined and derelict. The immaculately kept graveyard is particularly poignant with many graves showing not only a picture of the deceased but also a clock face with the hands pointing to 11.41, the time the earthquake struck. Still remaining in the graveyard is the prefabricated metal church which served in the immediate aftermath of the earthquake and was erected within 40 days of the disaster. Opposite the graveyard is a hill whose summit is crowned by the official memorial to the victims of the earthquake. Visiting it is thought-provoking. Firstly it is reached by a long flight of concrete steps, over half of which have disintegrated and all of which are overgrown by tall thistles as well as a colourful range of weeds. At the top of the steps one reaches the rather grandiose memorial, now equally neglected with much of its marble cladding having fallen off and giving the appearance that total collapse may not be long delayed. The contrast with the well-kept graveyard is striking. Possibly the memorial's neglect reflects the residents' wish not to remember, to look, as far as possible, forward rather than back. Or is there an implied criticism of the shoddy Soviet building standards which contributed so much to increasing the death toll? It is readily apparent that local residents never go there and perhaps they even wish it to be removed. There is no inscription in any language.

The Pushkin Pass
There are two main roads north from Vanadzor, both of which continue to Georgia. The more westerly can be reached by heading west out of the city for about 6km along the main Gyumri road and then turning right. The present-day road avoids the Pushkin Pass (2,037m) by a 2km-long tunnel which has now been renovated and (dimly) lit. If driving, keep to the 40km/h speed limit in the tunnel: on the last two occasions I used it there were unlit obstructions blocking half the road. On one occasion a driver was changing a tyre of his lorry and the next time workmen were carrying out repairs.

The pass gets its name from Pushkin who, on a visit to the Caucasus, met there in 1829 a cart carrying the body of Alexander Griboyedov (1795–1829) who had been killed in Persia, an incident described in Pushkin's *Journey to Erzrurum*. Griboyedov, whom Pushkin knew well, was a satirical playwright whose best-known play, *Woe from Wit* (1824) was only performed and published posthumously (see page 38). Griboyedov was also a diplomat and instrumental in Russia's peace negotiations with Turkey following the war of 1828–29 when Russia gained control of much of Armenia. After that he was appointed Russia's ambassador to Persia. Russia's defeats of Turkey and Persia and its consequent territorial expansion was followed by a change of tack in Russia's foreign policy as it was now considered important to ensure that both Turkey and Persia nevertheless survived as significant powers. Russia feared that dissolution of either might lead to the possible appearance of other, stronger, powers on its borders. Both states accepted Russian control of the Caucasus but while Griboyedov was in Teheran negotiating with Persia an angry mob stormed the Russian embassy. His mangled body, barely recognisable, was being returned on the cart which Pushkin encountered.

Stepanavan and Lori Berd

After the tunnel the road descends a long series of zigzags to reach the town of Stepanavan. There is a dramatic change of scenery as one emerges from the tunnel: gone are the bare stony hillsides and in their place are lush wooded ones. In early summer the fields as one descends are an amazing sight of yellows and reds with masses of buttercups and poppies.

Stepanavan suffered damage in 1988 but has received little outside help and the scars are still evident. It very much gives the appearance of being seriously run-down. Stepanavan is named in honour of Stepan Shahumian (1878–1918), an Armenian who was instrumental in imposing Bolshevik rule in Baku, Azerbaijan. Faced with an uprising he fled but was captured and executed by local anti-Bolsheviks, with some British involvement.

Stepanavan itself has nothing of tourist interest to offer. However, just outside is **Lori Berd** ('Lori Fortress'), one of Armenia's most impressive medieval fortress sites. To reach it turn right and cross the large viaduct over the gorge of the Dzoraget ('Gorge River') at the north end of the town. At the far end of the viaduct, turn right again and continue for about 3km to the village of Lori Berd. When you reach the village bear right for about 1km along a road, whose surface deteriorates even further, for about 1km. There is a small car park just before the fortress where substantial remains of the defensive wall and towers survive as well as other buildings. A locked gate formerly prevented direct entry and it was necessary to climb over the ruined wall. However, the gate is now usually left open. As at other fortresses in Armenia, you may find that the local cattle and sheep are also visiting. The triangular site is spectacularly situated between two gorges: that of the Dzoraget and that of the Urut. The only side of the site not protected by these gorges, which are too steep-sided to scale easily, is the northern one and this was protected by a high stone wall with towers, at the foot of which there was a moat. As well as the area within the fortifications the town spread outside them and outlying districts also developed across the two gorges. Bridges were constructed to provide access from these outlying districts: that over the Urut survives and can be seen from the eastern part of the site. It can be reached by a steep path which winds down from just inside the gate and which is very slippery in wet weather.

The fortress was built by David Anghonin (ruled 989–1049), member of a junior branch of Ani's Bagratid dynasty, to be the new capital of the Tashir-Dzoraget kingdom: there were five Armenian kingdoms at the time. Though suffering heavy casualties the Seljuk Emir Kizil managed to capture Lori Berd in 1105 and it subsequently came under Georgian rule following the Seljuk defeat by Davit IV Agmashenebelis (David the Builder, ruled 1089–1121). Davit's great-granddaughter Queen Tamar transferred Lori to the ownership of the Armenian prince Sargis Zakarian for his assistance in inflicting further defeats on the Seljuks between 1195 and 1204. The town subsequently flourished under his rule and that of his son, but in 1228 Shah Jala-Edin of Khoremsk captured the outlying districts and in 1238 the fortress itself fell to the Mongol Khan Jagat, allegedly because the captains charged with organising the defence spent too much time drinking and too little praying – or so their brother-in-law wrote. The town was ransacked and for over 200 years it passed through various hands, only to fall to invaders again in 1430. Decline, however, continued and the last inhabitants left as recently as 1931, largely because of problems with the water supply.

Within the fortress can be seen a rectangular-roofed building comprising six square-domed bays with pillars supporting the arches dividing the bays. The building incorporates medieval tombstones and the doorway is flanked by two khachkars. The fortress remained under Muslim occupation until the 18th century and this building has a niche in the south wall facing Mecca, indicating that it dates from that period. It is home to a family of redstarts in the breeding season. Another ruined building may have been a kitchen (to judge from holes in the roof) and on the side of the Dzoraget gorge there is evidence of pipes suggesting a washroom or latrine.

Northwest from Stepanavan

To head north from Stepanavan one should turn left after crossing the viaduct. For some distance the road keeps east of the river at a distance of a few hundred metres. It is well worth stopping and walking across to look down into the immensely impressive gorge. The road passes through a series of Russian villages built by refugees who fled here to avoid religious persecution during the time of Catherine the Great. The houses typically have two storeys with living accommodation for the family being on the upper storey with its balcony and the lower storey being used for storage. About 15km from Stepanavan the road reaches the small town now called **Tashir**. Founded in 1844, it was originally named Vorontsovka after Prince Mikhail Vorontsov (1785–1856), Viceroy to Tsar Nicholas I, who had been brought up in Britain where his father was Russian ambassador. Vorontsov's role in the Caucasus was considerable. Appointed Governor General of New Russia with 'unlimited powers' during the reign of Tsar Alexander I he was so successful in integrating southern Ukraine into Russia that he was promoted to viceroy in 1845 and his mandate was extended to the newly acquired territories in the Caucasus. In 1935, Vorontsovka was renamed Kalinino after Mikhail Kalinin (1875–1946), the communist functionary who became titular head of the Soviet state.

At the far end of Tashir a road branches left from the main road to Tbilisi and heads northwest across marshy ground to the village of **Metsavan**. On the hillside at the far end of Metsavan is the small 10th-century monastery of St John. Church and graveyard are themselves surrounded by a wall made itself of gravestones. Retracing one's steps and then bearing left through the village the bad road becomes a worse track across grasslands before reaching, in about 4km, the exceptionally ruined church of St George. In no way does the surviving fragment of a wall justify the visit but the whole area on a fine sunny evening is magical. The lower grassy slopes give way to a stupendous natural rock garden on the higher ground with its wonderful carpets of alpine plants. There are views across the plain to the distant eastern mountains and a small river tumbles down from the Georgian border. However it wouldn't be worth going in the rain!

Northeast from Stepanavan

The road northeast from Stepanavan is in poor condition for the first part where it follows the fertile valley of the Urut and in dire condition later on when it crosses the pass. It should be attempted only in dry weather and preferably on a lorry.

Ten kilometres from Stepanavan the Urut is crossed at the village of **Sverdlov**, named after Yakov Sverdlov (1885–1919), a Bolshevik who was instrumental in overthrowing the elected Russian constitutional assembly in January 1918. He died from influenza the following year. The bridge is in a poor state with the central pier partly collapsed and a vehicle with high ground clearance is desirable. Beyond Sverdlov the monastery of Derbatavank can be seen across fields to the right. Dating from the 11th century it is a tall, single-nave structure with barrel vaulting. Although attractively situated it was insensitively restored using concrete blocks during the Soviet era.

Continuing up the narrowing valley the road passes Privolnoye, a village with a Russian church and Russian-style houses and the last point where food or drink can be bought. Turn right and then second left in the village. Four kilometres beyond the village a customs post can be seen straight ahead. Turn right before reaching it to climb up to the Wolf's Gate Pass (1,787m). The road is closed in winter and absolutely dreadful in summer with sections which resemble the bed of a river, deep pot-holes, deep mud and huge puddles. Eventually, 33km from Stepanavan one reaches the border post. It is possible to negotiate with the border guards to continue to Khuchap monastery, negotiation being necessary because of the need to cross a sliver of Georgian territory. Negotiations are easy as the border guards are only too happy to have visitors to relieve the monotony of their job in this isolated spot which doesn't even have telephone communication with the outside world. However, it is actually better to visit Khuchap via the village of Jiliza as Khuchap can then be combined with equally worthwhile Khorakert (see page 161). The border guards are likely to press the usual Armenian hospitality on visitors and will almost certainly send someone to act as a guide for anyone going to the monastery, partly because it is hard to find, partly for something different to do, and partly because they will have cleared with their Georgian opposite numbers permission to cross the bit of Georgia. It takes about an hour to walk to it in a side valley south of the river: it takes longer to return because visitors will have been spotted as they walk past a small isolated house on the way out and will be unable to refuse coffee and refreshments on the way back. The walk is very beautiful along the river and then through orchards into the forest. It involves crossing the river and wading may be required.

The Debed gorge

The other road north from Vanadzor, as well as the railway to Tbilisi, follow the scenic gorge of the Debed. The gorge is noteworthy for having five of Armenia's finest churches, all of them worth visiting, as well as two of Armenia's museums which can be more relied upon than most to be open. Of the churches two are very touristy, two see few tourists, and the other is somewhere in between. Leave Vanadzor by Tumanian Street, cross the river and continue straight on. (For anyone who is coming from Stepanavan and has transport it is much better to head east from there and visit Hnevank as well. See below.) There are several short tunnels on this road, some of them curving and all unlit. Drive very carefully indeed through these tunnels – the official speed limit is 35km/h – as they are used by pedestrians and have some memorable pot-holes.

After 20km a road goes off right across the river to follow the valley of a tributary for a few kilometres before turning abruptly left to wind up the side of the valley to the plateau. It reaches the village of **Dsegh** where is situated the house museum of the poet Hovhannes Tumanian (1869–1923; see page 40). Although tourists who do not speak Armenian are unlikely to have encountered his works, the museum itself gives an interesting insight into living conditions in Tsarist days, notably the two older rooms with their rock floors and chest-like bed. The monument outside the museum was erected after the collapse of the Soviet Union when Vano Siradeghian, minister of internal affairs, decided that the poet's heart should be buried here rather than kept in a jar in the anatomical museum of the medical university in Yerevan. Opposite the museum is a church, built in the 7th century and quite unlike most Armenian churches; it resembles a large village hall, very plain and with a flat wooden ceiling. Retracing one's steps to the main road it is worth stopping to admire the view over the valley. Golden eagles and lammergeiers, Europe's largest vultures, are quite common here and alpine swifts nest in crevices in the valley side.

Kobayr

Back at the main road turn right to head north again. At the village of Dzoraget the road from Stepanavan via Hnevank comes in on the left shortly before the site of the new Tufenkian Hotel (under construction at the time of writing). In about 5km the road passes the small industrial town of Tumanian, named after the poet and seriously marred by a huge abandoned brick factory. About 2km further north look out for a small railway station up above the road on the left. This is Kobayr, site of one of Armenia's most impressive ruins. About 400m south of the station a track goes off left, passing underneath the railway by a low bridge. Walk up here; don't attempt to drive and be sure to take a torch to see the frescos in the monastery chapel. The track becomes steps which wind back and forth between small houses with their gardens. The steps have now been extended most of the way up to the monastery replacing the former path which was difficult in wet weather. Keep making for the monastic-looking building straight ahead, bearing right at the spring and then left. The ten-minute climb is well worth it.

According to an inscription, the main church was built in 1171 by Mariam, daughter of Kyurik II. At this time the Turkish Seljuks ruled Armenia but delegated control to local princes. Following Georgian victories over the Seljuk Turks in 1195 and 1202 the monastery came under Georgian rule, passing into the control of the Zakarian family who adhered to the Georgian Orthodox Church rather than the Armenian Church. (The Georgian Church differed in having accepted the views of the Council of Chalcedon, which took place in 451, over the duality of Christ's nature. See page 28.) This explains the occurrence of Georgian features, notably the Georgian-style frescos and carved inscriptions. One of these inscriptions records the building of the belltower and mausoleum in the centre of the monastery in 1279, the mausoleum being to house the tombs of Shahnshah Mkhargryel and his wife Vaneni. Much of the south side of the complex has now descended into the gorge below but the roofless apse and parts of the other walls survive with Georgian-style frescos in the apse and chapel. They were well restored in 1971 but those in the apse are exposed to the elements. In the apse they comprise three rows: in the top row the Virgin Mary and archangels, in the middle row Jesus and the Last Supper, in the bottom row figures of saints. The frescos in the chapel are in a similar style with vivid portrayals of Jesus and the disciples. The belltower has also collapsed and only the foundations and the bases of pillars can be seen. The 13th-century refectory is on the northwestern side of the main church slightly up the hill. Surrounding the whole complex was a fortified wall, and the well-preserved gateway together with a further small church dated 1223 lie to the north of the main group of buildings. It is possible for those suitably shod to climb further up the hillside and look down on the site. The views from there are even more impressive and there is another excellent chance of seeing lammergeiers.

Odzun and Ardvi

Continuing north along the main road one reaches the left turn for Odzun in about 7km. Odzun itself is on the plateau and the road winds up the valley side to reach it. Odzun is worth visiting for its church constructed of pink felsite. It is a large building, dating from the 6th century, reconstructed in the 8th, and one of Armenia's finest basilicas with cupola. The two small belltowers at the eastern end were a much later addition in the late 19th century. On the north and south sides of the church were unusual arcaded cloisters though those on the north no longer exist. The west cloister has a blind wall with an arched entrance in the middle. Inside there are three naves, the two side naves very narrow. The roof is barrel vaulted and the rib-vaulted octagonal tambour is supported by four free-standing columns. There are two additional supporting columns at the western end of the church. The most notable feature of the exterior carving is on the east façade above the central window where Christ can be seen holding open the gospel of St John with angels below. At each side of the central window on the south side stands an angel with traces of another figure, probably Christ.

In the surrounding graveyard the clergy were buried near the church and were depicted on the gravestones holding staffs. Beside the church is a most unusual funerary monument, one of only two in this style in Armenia – the other is at Aghudi in Syunik province. It comprises a stepped platform supporting two slender obelisk-shaped carved stelae set between double arches. The carvings on the stelae are divided into panels depicting, on the east and west sides, biblical scenes together with the coming of Christianity to Armenia, and on the north and south sides, geometrical motifs and floral shapes. It has been suggested that the monument might commemorate Hovhannes Odznetsi, who was Katholikos from 717 until 728 and undertook rebuilding work at Odzun, but its style suggests an earlier date and erection in the 6th century seems more likely.

Continuing through Odzun across the plateau the road heads south and then west towards **Ardvi**. It is worth stopping on a fine day and going across to the ruined Horomigh church which is right on the edge of the gorge. It was built in the 7th century and rebuilt in the 13th using a darker stone which contrasts considerably and, having scarcely weathered, almost has the appearance of concrete. The view down into the gorge of the Debed is impressive. The tiny Holy Cross chapel can be seen below and in spring the plateau is covered by an amazing carpet of flowers. Continuing to Ardvi the 10th-century Holy Resurrection church is on the left as you enter the village, a small rectangular structure on a knoll. The roof of the barrel-vaulted nave has collapsed but that of the apse still stands. Two of the gravestones here depict a figure with a smaller figure within it, indicating the grave of a woman who had been pregnant when she died. Beyond the village is the small monastery of St John on a hillside. The 17th-century church and its separate belltower have very low doors, only a little over a metre high. The belltower incorporates an unusual khachkar of a person wearing a hat and shoes and carrying a round object and a square one. The cemetery, on an adjoining hillock, has a very fine collection of khachkars; graves here span the centuries from the 6th to the 19th.

Alaverdi and Sanahin

The two monasteries of Sanahin and Haghpat were, in 1996, Armenia's first sites to be added to UNESCO's World Heritage List. Returning through Odzun to the main road it is a short distance to the important copper-mining centre of Alaverdi ('Allah gave' in Turkish). This industrial city clings to the side of the gorge and is the commercial centre of the district. The famous monastery complex of Sanahin

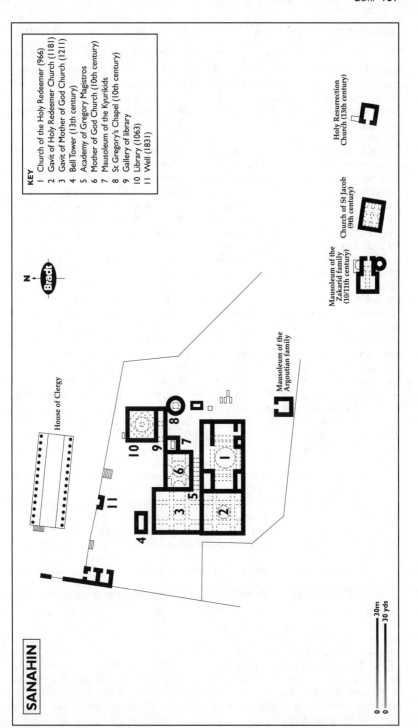

SANAHIN

House of Clergy

N

Bradt

KEY
1 Church of the Holy Redeemer (966)
2 Gavit of Holy Redeemer Church (1181)
3 Gavit of Mother of God Church (1211)
4 Bell Tower (13th century)
5 Academy of Gregory Magistros
6 Mother of God Church (10th century)
7 Mausoleum of the Kyurikids
8 St Gregory's Chapel (10th century)
9 Gallery of library
10 Library (1063)
11 Well (1831)

Holy Resurrection
Church (13th century)

Church of St Jacob
(9th century)

Mausoleum of the
Zakarid family
(10/11th century)

Mausoleum of the
Argoutian family

0 ———— 30m
0 ———— 30 yds

is just outside the city limits of Alaverdi. To reach it on foot continue up the river to the medieval bridge built in 1192: note the carved animals on top of the parapet. Cross this bridge and walk up the hill for about 500m. Another possibility is to go by cable car from close to the copper factory 500m north of the centre up to the plateau close to the Debed Hotel: the cable car had the steepest climb of any in the former Soviet Union. Alternatively, to get there by road cross the newer bridge further south and continue up the hill past the Debed Hotel before bearing right through an uninspiring area of Soviet-era buildings to reach the monastery. Nowadays one of Armenia's most frequently visited sights, it was established in 966 by Queen Khosrovanush, wife of King Ashot III Bagratuni, on the site of two existing churches, St Jacob which dates from the 9th century and the Mother of God which was built some time between 928 and 944. Sanahin became a centre of considerable cultural influence during the 10th and 11th centuries with its monastic school and important library where copyists worked to produce illuminated manuscripts. Sanahin's role declined as Armenia suffered waves of invaders although the local Argoutian family was exceptional in managing to retain its estates through to the 20th century.

The ensemble is very picturesque but does rather give the impression of having grown piecemeal. It is dominated by the church of the Holy Redeemer with its conical dome; construction probably began in 966. This church, built of basalt, has its eastern façade decorated with arcature and the main window is similarly decorated. The gable of this façade has a sculptural relief depicting Smbat and Gurgen Bagratuni, two of the three sons of the founder, with a model of a church, the first appearance of such a scene in Armenia. Smbat became King Smbat II of the Bagratid dynasty, rulers of Ani, and Gurgen was the father of David Anghonin who constructed Lori Berd. The church of the Holy Redeemer is separated from the smaller Mother of God church by a gallery covered by a barrel vault, the academy of Gregory Magistros, which is believed to have been used for teaching. Possibly the students sat in the niches between the monumental pillars.

On the west side of the churches are large gavits constructed in 1181 and 1211 and somewhat different from each other in style. The gavit of the church of the Holy Redeemer is the earlier. Its has four tall free-standing internal pillars supporting arches. The bases and capitals of the columns are decorated with carvings and reliefs depicting the heads of animals and fruits as well as geometric patterns. The gavit of the Mother of God church is a three-nave hall with much lower arches than the earlier gavit and with less elaborate bases and capitals for the columns. Externally the western façade of this gavit has six arches, two to each gable. Abutting the gavit at its northern end is the belltower, crowned by a small rotunda, which is also early 13th century and thought to be Armenia's earliest.

On the complex's north side is the library of 1063 which has an octagonal tent roof resting on diagonally arranged arches. At the eastern end of the library is the small, domed, round chapel of St Gregory the Illuminator built in the late 10th century. It is a two-storey structure with a pointed roof. To the southeast of the main complex are two mausoleums which date from the 10th and 11th centuries and beyond them are the 9th-century church of St Jacob (the nearer one) and the early 13th-century Holy Resurrection church which has two identical apses. Much of the floor of the gavit is covered by gravestones and there is also a wealth of khachkars, not all of them religious: one commemorates the building of the bridge at Alaverdi in 1192 and another the construction of an inn in 1205. By the boundary wall on the north side is the monastery's spring. It is covered by a structure which dates to 1831.

Sanahin's other claim to fame is as the birthplace of the brothers Anastas Mikoyan (1895–1978) and Artem Mikoyan (1905–70). A museum about them is located in a former school down the hill from the monastery. Anastas achieved the distinction of being the longest-serving member of the Soviet Politburo. He survived a series of political upheavals to remain a member from 1935 to 1966 and was involved in many important events In 1939 he was responsible for the discussions with Germany on trade prior to the signing of the Nazi–Soviet pact; in 1955 he was part of the delegation which sought to heal the rift with Tito in Yugoslavia; in 1962 he dealt with Cuba during the missile crisis (he spoke Spanish); in 1964 he was instrumental in ousting Khruschev. Artem Mikoyan by contrast played a leading role in the development of Soviet fighter aircraft. He was named head of a new design bureau in 1939. His bureau collaborated with that headed by Mikhail Gurevich and at first produced a number of relatively unsuccessful planes. Then the turbojet-powered MiG-15, which first flew in 1947, proved a world-beating design and was the forerunner of a series of light fighter aircraft which saw extensive deployment during the cold war era. MiG is actually an acronym for Mikoyan and Gurevich.

Haghpat

Haghpat monastery is contemporaneous with Sanahin and very similar in style. Pilgrims in the monasteries' heyday were inevitably driven to compare the two and from this comparison derive the present names: Haghpat means 'huge wall' because that was one of its striking features whereas Sanahin means 'older than the other'. Although Haghpat can be seen from Sanahin, to reach it requires a return to Alaverdi. Then head east along the main road for about 5km and turn right up the hill. A left fork leads to the monastery which can be seen high on the hillside. It is nowadays much more attractively situated than Sanahin, and consequently more pleasant to visit, as the approach is not through an area of rundown Soviet-era buildings. It is, however, also touristy. The main church with its huge dome is dedicated to the Holy Cross and was built between 976 and 991 at the behest of Queen Khosrovanush, also the founder of Sanahin. From the exterior it appears rectangular but internally is cross-shaped and, as at Sanahin, there is a relief of Smbat and Gurgen holding a model of a church on the east façade. Unlike Sanahin the buildings which were gradually added do not lead directly off each other. A smaller church, dedicated to St Gregory the Illuminator, was added in 1005 at the southwest side of the site and a domed Mother of God church was added on the northwest side in 1025. The St Gregory church lost its dome during rebuilding in 1211. A gavit was built in 1185 to the west of the cathedral and the cathedral itself gained a magnificent porch in 1201.

The three-storey belltower was built in 1245, a much more substantial structure than at Sanahin. Its ground floor has the plan of a cross-dome church and serves as a chapel. The second storey by contrast is rectangular with the corners cut off thus turning into an octagonal shape. The transition between the two shapes is ingenious. The third storey, the belfry, is, unusually, seven sided and supported by seven columns. Another gavit, called the Hamazasp building after its donor, was built to the north of the cathedral in 1257 and is unusual for a gavit in being free-standing. The library, originally built with a wooden roof in the 10th century, was rebuilt with a stone roof in 1262. One of Armenia's most famous and beautiful khachkars, the Holy Redeemer khachkar of 1273, is in the passage leading to the library. This amazing work shows Christ crucified surrounded by saints and apostles with angels looking down and God the Father raising his hand in blessing. Haghpat's library became a storeroom after invaders had taken the manuscripts and the floor now has

many storage jars sunk into it. The 13th-century refectory is an isolated building on the north side of the site. It is a long building whose tall roof is borne by intersecting arches supported by pairs of free-standing columns. The central section is crowned by octagonal domed vaults which admit light. This unusual structure adjoins the defensive wall of the monastery. Also notable to the west of the refectory is the spring. It is in a three-arched structure built in 1258. There are stone troughs along the back wall for watering cattle and a reservoir for general use.

Akhtala

Akhtala is further north towards the Georgian border and receives only a fraction of the visitors who go to Sanahin and Haghpat. It is built in a quite different style but its setting is equally dramatic, perched up on a cliff. Unfortunately the view is now marred by copper mining taking place on the opposite side of the valley. To reach it take the main road east from Alaverdi for about 15km until there is a bridge left over the Debed into an industrial area. Cross the bridge and turn right, crossing the railway at a level crossing. Follow the road as it bears left along a tributary gorge. When you come to a fork next to a bridge you can see the monastery high up on a promontory in front of you. Keep right. The road goes past the monastery but then bears left to approach it from the north side.

Akhtala is surrounded either by precipitous drops or by defensive walls. Entry is through the main gate in the defensive fortifications. Although this may be locked entry can easily be achieved as there is an inconspicuous wicket gate within the main gate. Take very great care on the site as the long grass conceals drops into subterranean rooms of the original fortress whose roofs have collapsed. The 10th-century fortifications, constructed of basalt, were built by the Kurikian branch of the

Bagratid dynasty: Kurikian was a vassal state of the king at Ani. The fortress is contemporary with that at Lori: Akhtala, like Lori, was a highly defensible site and one of the main strongholds of northern Armenia. Within the fortress stands the monastery and the remains of other buildings can be seen. The main existing church, dedicated to the Mother of God, was built between 1212 and 1250 at the behest of Prince Ivan Zakarian who belonged to the same dynasty as obtained control of Lori Berd and Kobayr monastery. It was therefore built as a Georgian Orthodox church but is on the site of an earlier Armenian one. It is of the domed basilica type but the dome collapsed in the eighteenth century and the existing small pyramidal roof was itself replaced in 1978. Built, like the fortress, of basalt the monastery is quite different in appearance from those at Sanahin and Haghpat, reflecting the Georgian influence on its design. In particular the interior is richly decorated with frescos: especially notable are the Virgin Mary enthroned in the apse, the Last Judgement in the west arm, and figures of saints on the pillars which divide the building into three naves. Large relief crosses on each façade together with smaller more intricate crosses on the elaborate arcaded porch also show Georgian influence. Gaining entry is possible by finding the caretaker who lives in the village.

To Jiliza, Khuchap and Khorakert

A visit to this remote corner of Armenia is very worthwhile. The village of Jiliza is only 1km from the Georgian border and is ideally situated in beautiful countryside for visiting the fascinating but rarely seen monasteries of Khuchap and Khorakert. The village is a 7km walk from Khuchap, 4km from Khorakert and the monasteries are 5km from each other. The very helpful mayor of this isolated village will help with accommodation. Until 1992 no road linked the district with the rest of Armenia but, following independence, a new road was constructed direct from Alaverdi: it has still not found its way on to most maps. Unfortunately poor drainage has made parts of it a sea of mud with some deep pools to be navigated. It can however be managed by a 4WD in dry weather although bus aficionados might like to try the local vehicle which is a 6WD (!) lorry chassis with a bus body mounted on top. For most of the year it operates from Alaverdi on Tuesdays and Fridays returning from Jiliza on Sundays and Thursdays. Note that as Jiliza receives its electricity from the Georgian system rather than the Armenian it is subject to all the vagaries of supply which that implies and electricity is usually available only for one to two hours daily.

To get to **Jiliza**, leave Alaverdi by the Madan road which climbs out of the valley behind the copper plant. At the far end of Madan there was formerly a customs post as the whole of this northern area has numerous minor crossing points to Georgia. However, the customs point was not functioning in April 2003. The road winds through increasingly forested country for 30km with many beautiful views. Jiliza itself has a post of border guards who are very helpful and probably glad of having someone different to talk to.

Khuchap monastery, at the foot of Mount Lalvar, is well worth the trouble of reaching. It is a beautiful building, delightfully situated and hidden away in its small wooded valley. It was abandoned in the 1940s when the last nuns left but the main church, which dates from the 13th century, is intact. Red felsite was used for construction of the outer walls and forms an unusual and pleasing contrast with the yellow felsite used for the window surrounds, large crosses on two of the gable ends, and to produce a banded effect on the tall tambour. The church is entered through the door in the west façade (close it again on leaving to keep out the cattle) which, like the south façade, sports a large carved cross as part of its decoration. Inside, the church is rectangular with a very high cupola and two supporting octagonal pillars. There are separate naves at the west end of the church and vestibules were added at the east end some time after the construction. Outside the decoration is amazingly varied with door and window surrounds being carved with a whole range of geometric patterns while carved figures of animals and projecting carved animal heads can be seen high up on the tambour. Every one of the 12 carved windows around the tambour has a different geometric pattern. On the west façade the remains of a cloister-like addition with four arches make a picturesque addition. North of the main church are the remains of other monastic buildings, much plainer and built of grey andesite.

To reach **Khorakert**, slightly nearer the village on the west side, involves fording the river and can be difficult at times of flood. Built in the late 12th and early 13th centuries, the really striking feature, unique in Armenia, is that the tambour (which has ten sides – very rare in Armenia) is not a solid construction but comprises in the upper part 30 separate six-sided columns. The effect of this open-sided tambour is to admit light into the church. The interior of the cupola is also most unusual: six intersecting arches form a six-pointed star in the centre of which is a hexagon which itself encloses another six-pointed star. The gavit of 1257 was also highly distinctive in that it was roofed by another set of intersecting arches but unfortunately this collapsed in an earthquake in 1965. The whole ensemble gives the impression that it would not survive another. Outside the church on the south side is a stone frog which has been placed on a plinth, another unexpected sight. It looks as if the frog could originally have been mounted on a roof and there is certainly an unidentified animal on top of the cupola of the church. Traces of the main gateway, chapels and various other buildings also survive as does the well with its secret passage down to the river.

From Stepanavan to the Debed

Rather than travelling via Vanadzor it is possible to travel via Hnevank, a very worthwhile route but lacking public transport and unsuitable for larger vehicles at the eastern end. From Stepanavan head back towards Vanadzor for 10km as far as the village of Gyulagarak. In the village turn left. The road then passes the derelict village church of 1874 on the left. Where the main road bears left continue straight on passing the extremely ruinous 6th-century Toromavank on the right. Ahead of you is DendroPark, an arboretum covering 35 hectares which was founded by a Pole in 1931 for the cultivation and acclimatisation of trees. Adjoining the arboretum is a sanatorium used by invalids with lung diseases. Apparently the clouds of pollen blowing from the conifers are regarded as therapeutic.

If you do not wish to visit DendroPark then keep left after the 1874 church. The road runs east through an area of strip farming with the Dzoraget river in its increasingly deep gorge on the right and (often snow-capped) peaks in the distance. Just before Kurtan village the road bears right to cross the river and shortly after this there are some immensely impressive views down into the gorge on the left. It is worth stopping and walking not just because of the views but because this is an excellent area for eagles. Both booted eagles and golden eagles can be seen along the gorge. The highlight comes in a few minutes when, during the descent of some hairpin bends, the extensive ruins of **Hnevank** monastery can be seen down in the gorge on a small hill close to the confluence of the Dzoraget and Gargar rivers. This spectacularly beautiful sight can be reached by scrambling down the hillside into the gorge and then clambering through waist-high vegetation. In early summer the sheer brilliance of colour is stunning. The monastery was founded in the 7th century but rebuilt in 1144. The gavit dates from the late 12th century and various other contemporaneous buildings remain here largely undisturbed. Eagles can again be seen in this magical spot.

Continuing east the unsurfaced road eventually leaves the plateau and descends countless zigzags to reach the Debed river at Dzoraget village, a short distance south of the confluence of the Dzoraget and the Debed.

TAVUSH

Armenia's heavily wooded and most northeasterly province is bounded to the north by Georgia and to the east by Azerbaijan. Land captured from Azerbaijan in 1994 has in effect (even if not in law) since been incorporated into Tavush: in particular the road from the provincial capital of Ijevan north to Noyemberian and on to Lori and the Georgian border crosses an area which was formerly in Azerbaijan but has since 1994 effectively been Armenian. The aftermath of the war is evident in other ways in Tavush: some sites close to the border, notably Khoranashat monastery, are inaccessible because of the risk from Azeri snipers and also the former main road and rail routes from Yerevan to Georgia and the rest of the former Soviet Union are closed at the border with Azerbaijan since they crossed Azeri territory to reach Tbilisi. The rail route is actually completely closed north of Dilijan and the overhead catenary has been dismantled: abandoned locomotives and wagons can be seen at various places. Freight trains do still operate from Yerevan as far as Dilijan, passing under the Arjanots range by the 8,311m-long Margahovit tunnel, but passenger services have been withdrawn. Tavush's two largest towns, Ijevan and Dilijan, are sited on the Aghtsev river whose valley broadens out as it flows northwards towards Azerbaijan. It rises in the southeast of Lori province in the Gugarats range and, as is the case with other north-flowing Armenian rivers, its waters join the Kura river ultimately to reach the Caspian Sea south of Baku.

Ijevan

The name of Ijevan, meaning 'inn' recalls the scarcely imaginable days when silk-route traders passed through these forests. Ijevan is nowadays a pleasant though unremarkable town with good accommodation and there are many excellent walking possibilities in the hilly forests. Its appearance is enhanced by the extensive use of white felsite for building. The local dry red and white wines, made from grapes more usually associated with Georgia, are among Armenia's best. The province's more improbable visitors have included the English composer Benjamin Britten (1913–76) and his friend the tenor Peter Pears (1910–86) who spent their summer holiday in Dilijan in August 1965 as guests of the Armenian Composers' Union along with the cellist Mstislav Rostropovich and his wife the soprano Galina Vishnevskaya. Both Peter Pears and Galina Vishnevskaya have left accounts of the experience: while everybody seems to have enjoyed their visit the English visitors had to listen to performances of the latest compositions of the Armenian composers while headaches for the hosts included having to deal with Benjamin Britten wanting to buy a pair of shoes when his existing ones gave out – shoes were virtually unobtainable in the Soviet Union at the time.

The best accommodation in the province, a good alternative to homestays, is the **Spitak Lich** ('White Lake') **Motel** (tel: 35344) on the southern edge of Ijevan by the reservoir. The food here is unusually good.

Northeast from Ijevan

The former main rail and road routes to Azerbaijan follow the gradually broadening valley of the Aghtsev. The first turn right after leaving Ijevan leads to the village of **Lusahovit** where the Tsrviz or Moro-Dzor monastery is located. Established in

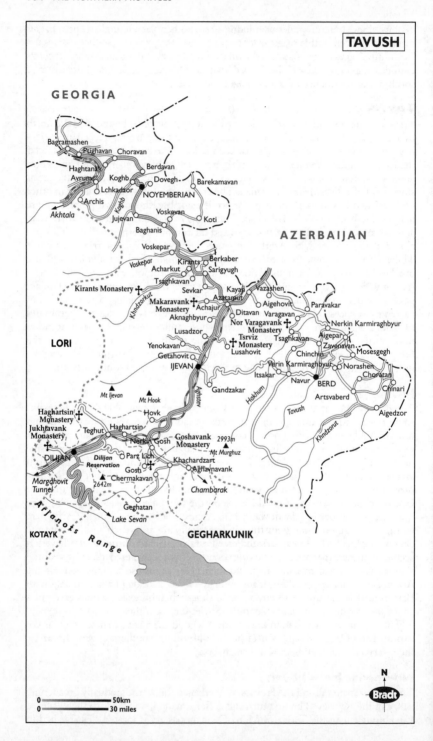

TAVUSH

GEORGIA

Bagramashen
Ptighavan Choravan
Haghtanak   Berdavan
Avrum   Koghb   Dovegh
Lchkadzor   NOYEMBERIAN   Barekamavan
Archis
Akhtala   Jujevan   Voskevan   Koti
Baghanis
Voskepar   AZERBAIJAN
Voskepar   Kirants   Berkaber
Acharkut   Sarigyugh
Tsaghkavan   Sevkar   Kayan   Vazashen
Kirants Monastery   Makaravank   Achajur   Aigehovit   Paravakar
Monastery   Ditavan   Varagavan
Aknaghbyur   Nor Varagavank   Nerkin Karmiraghbyur
Lusadzor   Monastery   Tsaghkavan   Aigepar
Yenokavan   Tsrviz   Zavonavan   Mosesgegh
Getahovit   Monastery   Chinchin   Norashen
IJEVAN   Lusahovit   Verin Karmiraghbyur   Choratan
Itsakar   Navur   BERD   Chinari
Gandzakar   Aigedzor
Mt Ijevan   Mt Hook   Artsvaberd
LORI   Hovk   Tavush
Haghartsin   2993m   Khndzorut
Monastery   Haghartsin   Goshavank
Jukhtavank   Teghut   Nerkin Gosh   Monastery
Monastery   Mt Murghuz
DILIJAN   Parz Lich   Khachardzart
Dilijan   Gosh   Aghavnavank
Reservation   Chermakavan
Margdhovit   2642m   Chambarak
Tunnel
Geghatan
Lake Sevan   GEGHARKUNIK
KOTAYK   Range
Aflanots

0   50km
0   30 miles

N
Bradt

the 5th century the main Mother of God church was rebuilt in the 12th and 13th and has been restored fairly recently. It has a curious appearance, rather like a small dome surrounded by even smaller ones. After 32km the main road reaches the border and is obstructed by an improvised barrier to prevent further progress. Turn right just before the barrier and continue along this bad road as it winds up and over a pass with numerous hairpin bends as far as the village of **Varagavank**. Turn right on to the main street of the village and continue through it: the monastery can be seen high on the opposite hillside. The road winds up through attractive forest where both green and black woodpeckers can be found. After around 3km there is a picnic table on the left. Fork left by the table and the road eventually reaches the monastery in another 500m. The monastery of Nor Varagavank is very important historically but in a sadly ruined state. It was founded by David Bagratuni, son of King Vasak I under the name Anapat. The oldest part of the complex is the church of the Holy Cross built in 1198 at the southwest side. A two-storey burial vault was added at the north side in 1200. The monastery's importance however increased considerably in 1213 when it was chosen as the site for a relic, a piece of the True Cross brought to Armenia by Sts Hripsime and Gayane, which had been removed from the monastery of Varagavank, near Van in present-day Turkey, when that monastery was threatened by Mongol invaders. Hence the name Anapat was changed to Nor (New) Varagavank. (The relic, by then back at the original Varagavank, was destroyed along with the monastery during fighting in 1915.) The Mother of God church was built between 1224 and 1237 by David Bagratuni's son King Vasak II. There are unusual door portals, fine carving, and interesting khachkars at this attractive site overlooking the forest.

Makaravank

Makaravank on the slopes of Mount Paytatar is beautifully situated with fine views over the Aghtsev valley and into Azerbaijan, is well restored, has probably Armenia's finest carvings, is accessible by car, and yet is scarcely visited by tourists. To reach it from Ijevan take the main road towards the Azerbaijani border as far as the junction with the road to Noyemberian. At this junction, just after a barracks on the left built following the precepts of the Disneyland school of architecture, turn left on to a dirt road heading for the village of Achajur. In Achajur keep left and then continue for 6km keeping a lookout on the right for the domes of the monastery peeping out of a clump of trees.

The monastery is approached through a gate in the wall. The oldest church, whose dedicatee is unknown, was probably built in the 10th century. Inside it has beautifully carved window surrounds and an equally beautiful front to the altar dais with floral and linear designs. However, even this fine carving is wholly overshadowed by the amazing carving of the main church, built in 1205 by Vardan, son of Prince Bazaz. The dedicatee of this church is also obscure. The carving here is wonderful. In particular the front of this altar dais is covered with eight-pointed stars separated by octagons in each of which is a different elaborate design: a man in a boat, sphinxes, sirens, birds, floral arrangements and other unusual designs. Outside there is more fine carving; the south façade has a sundial above the main window and a bird below it while the smaller round windows each have a different intricate design. The gavit was added by Prince Vache Vachutian early in the 13th century. Plain outside except for a bull and lion fighting to the left of the door and a winged sphinx with a crown on its head to the right, it is a riot of carving inside. Adjoining the original church on the north side is a bakery for the making of communion loaves. Behind the complex is an unusual church built in 1198 and dedicated to the Mother of God. It has an octagonal base but a round tambour.

Northward towards Lori

Taking the Noyemberian road from the surreal Disneyland barracks the village of Kirants is reached after 10km. To go to **Kirants** monastery turn left here and continue through the village of Acharkut for about 4km until the road ends at a gate. It is possible to get the gate opened but the track is so bad beyond here that walking is preferable. To reach the monastery it is necessary always to keep close to the Khndzorkut river but to remain on the north side without crossing it. After about 1km the track passes the ruins of a caravanserai demonstrating again just how much trade passed through this region in late medieval times. A few yards beyond the caravanserai a track goes right uphill to the ruins of **Arakelots Vank** (Apostles monastery). From the caravanserai ruins to Kirants monastery is about another 9km. It is in a small clearing above and to the right of the track. Although the ruins themselves are in a sorry state the fortified surrounding wall is impressive and there are some fine khachkars. The monastery is very unusual in that it is constructed of fired tuff bricks decorated with glazed tiles. The main church dates from the 13th century and has a tall octagonal tambour with an octagonal dome. The monastery was built as a Georgian Orthodox foundation and Georgian influence can be seen in the interior frescos.

Immediately after the Kirants turn-off the Noyemberian road crosses territory which until 1994 was part of Azerbaijan. The road passes through several ruined villages in some of which just one wall of each building has been left standing. A weird sight on a hillside right of the road is the completely restored 7th-century **Voskepar** church surrounded by ruined and abandoned houses. The road re-enters Armenia proper and 41km from the junction with the former main road to Azerbaijan it reaches the town of Noyemberian, damaged by an earthquake in July 1997. Beyond the town it crosses the Koghb river before reaching Lori province and joining the main road north from Alaverdi south of the Georgian border.

Dilijan

Dilijan, a major holiday and health resort in Soviet days, lies 36km southwest of Ijevan and is one of the country's most attractive towns though most of the hotels and guesthouses are now closed and much further renovation is needed. Many of the surviving 19th-century buildings are built in a distinctive style, unique in Armenia: they have wooden balconies with carved handrails which are often supported by wooden struts. Efforts are being made to attract visitors again and some newer buildings are reverting to this older style in contrast to Soviet-era dreariness. Some 23,400 hectares of the surrounding forest has been designated as a nature reserve since 1958 and, as at Ijevan, there is considerable scope for walking over the forested hills or in the valley of the Aghstev river on which Dilijan lies. There are also three monasteries nearby each of which is in good walking country. Lack of accommodation is still a problem however at the time of writing. Close to the main road in Dilijan is a striking Soviet-era monument erected to mark the 50th anniversary of Soviet power in the Caucasus: its design was intended symbolically to represent the eternal union of Armenia, Georgia and Azerbaijan under Soviet rule. That it is still standing perhaps shows that the Armenians have a well-developed sense of irony. Dilijan also has a well-known spring to the west of the town and the mineral water bottled there is a familiar sight.

Haghartsin

Haghartsin lies in forest and is one of Armenia's most-visited monasteries. To reach it head east towards Ijevan for 7km and then turn left under a railway bridge and continue up the winding road for 9km. On the way through the forest can be seen the remains of a never-completed chairlift intended to take visitors directly to the monastery: the thought of a chairlift to a monastery sounds unlikely but in Soviet days Haghartsin was regarded as a museum rather than as a working church and a chairlift to a museum is at any rate marginally less odd. There are also several picnic tables, barbecue sites and springs by the roadside but, amazingly enough, the numerous free-range pigs seem to prefer a natural diet and show no interest in what people are eating – quite possibly one of their relatives given the Armenian liking for barbecued pork.

The well-preserved monastery is both evocative in itself and beautifully situated. As at so many monasteries the original small church had additional buildings added over the centuries and is now rather dwarfed by its less-ancient neighbours. The oldest part is the St Gregory church, probably dating from the 10th century and with an octagonal tambour although the original building was damaged by Seljuk invaders and had to be reconstructed after the Georgian victories over them. This reconstruction was followed by a large increase in the monastery's size and an important school of church music became established here which developed a new system of notation for the Armenian liturgy. The original church acquired a gavit at a lower level reached by steps, St Stephen's church was built in 1244, the large refectory in 1248 and bigger Mother of God church with a high 16-sided tambour, and also with gavit, was added in 1281. A relief of the donors with a dove (symbolising the Holy Spirit) above them can be seen on the east façade pointing to a model of the church. Among the other buildings which can be seen are the monastic bakery complete with oven.

HAGHARTSIN

0 ———— 10m
0 ———— 10 yds

N

Bradt

KEY
1 Mother of God Church (1281)
2 St Stephen's Church (1244)
3 Chapel (13th century)
4 St Gregory Church (10th century)
5 Mausoleum of Bagratid family (12th century)
6 Gavit of St Gregory Church (12th century)
7 Service buildings including bakery (13th century)
8 Refectory (1248)

Contemporaneous with this spate of building is the large walnut tree at the southeast corner of the Mother of God church: it is estimated to be around 700 years old and was probably planted as a source of food. Walnut trees are often found at the sites of monasteries. To the south of the gavit of St Gregory's are the the remains of royal tombs of the Bagratid dynasty. By the roadside east of the site (a good photographic vantage point) are some small chapels and both here and at the monastery are particularly fine khachkars. The interesting refectory, divided into two parts by arches, has stone benches along the sides. In recent years a rather incongruous modern floor has been installed and tables and chairs fashioned from logs also have been put there. Whether or not they bear any resemblance to 13th-century monastic furniture seems uncertain.

Goshavank

To reach the village of Gosh it is necessary to continue along the Ijevan road for another 8km beyond the turn-off for Haghartsin and then turn right towards Chambarak. The road to Gosh branches right off this road after about 2km. To reach Goshavank continue uphill into the centre of the village. Goshavank is unusual among Armenian monasteries in that an explanatory leaflet in English, prepared by US Peace Corps volunteers in 2002, is available inside. Unfortunately it is not always correct, saying for example that a chapel dedicated to St Gregory is actually dedicated to St Gevorg (St George), and the plan marks the gavit as if it were the church. The naming of chapels here is indeed confusing since two separate chapels are both dedicated to St Gregory. The leaflet also states that the mortar used in construction was made from milk, eggs, sand and clay with many kilometres of clay pipes being laid to transport the milk to the building site from the summer pastures above the village. Eggs were certainly a normal ingredient but milk seems less likely and clay pipes to transport it more unlikely still.

Goshavank was established in the late 12th century by the cleric Mkhitar Gosh (1130–1213) with the support of Prince Ivan Zakarian to replace the monastery of Getik, about 20km further east, where he had previously worked but which had been destroyed in an earthquake. Originally called Nor ('New') Getik, it was renamed in honour of its founder immediately after his death. The earliest part of the complex, the Mother of God church, dates from 1191; its gavit was completed in 1197 followed by the two St Gregory chapels, the free-standing one with its particularly fine carving in 1208 and the one attached to the gavit in 1237. The library with its belltower was completed in 1291, at its peak holding 1,600 volumes until Mongol invaders set fire to it in 1375. It was at Nor Getik that Mkhitar Gosh first formally codified Armenian law (partly as a defence against the imposition of Islamic shariah law) and also wrote his fables which make moral points using birds as the protagonists. Another feature of the monastery is the particularly fine khachkar by the door which dates from 1291. Poghos, its sculptor, carved two identical khachkars for his parents' graves and the other is in the History Museum in Yerevan. The two small rooms to the south of the gavit were used as studies by religious students. There is again a walnut tree, at the north of the site, and of similar age to the monastery.

Mkhitar Gosh spent the last years of his life as an ascetic in a retreat at some distance from Nor Getik. Although it was normal for founders to be buried at the monastery they had established he requested that this should not be done and a mausoleum was built away from the site.

In the grounds of the monastery is a small museum which the caretaker will open for you on request. By far the most interesting items there are large pottery bell-shaped objects which were hung from the dome with the open end downward

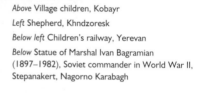

Above Village children, Kobayr

Left Shepherd, Khndzoresk

Below left Children's railway, Yerevan

Below Statue of Marshal Ivan Bagramian
(1897–1982), Soviet commander in World War II,
Stepanakert, Nagorno Karabagh

Right Looking north over the Tartar River to the Mrav range, Nagorno Karabagh

Below left Dadivank, Nagorno Karabagh

Below right Monument symbolising mothers' grief, war cemetery of the 1989–94 war, Stepanakert, Nagorno Karabagh

to try to improve the acoustic by reflecting sound back downward into the church. The solution to the problems of some more recent concert halls such as the Albert Hall, London was clearly anticipated at Goshavank!

A very pleasant walk is to continue along the path beyond the chapel opposite the monastery for about 45 minutes to reach the small lake of Goshalich which lies deep in the forest. The trees offer welcome shade in the summer heat and the setting of the lake is very beautiful with trees rising on the hillside behind. Goshalich is audibly a Mecca for some of Armenia's noisiest frogs.

Jukhtakvank

Head west from Dilijan for 3km along the main Vanadzor road and then turn right to pass under a high railway viaduct whose girders are painted in red ochre. Drive up this road for about 2km until a sign points right along a dirt track to Jukhtakvank. Do not attempt to drive any further as the track has been washed away. It is about ten minutes' walk to the monastery. Compared with the architectural glories of Haghartsin and Goshavank this monastery is modest indeed with its two small churches. The nearer one, dedicated to St Gregory, has lost its dome although it retains some very elaborate carving inside and a frieze round the walls. The further church, probably the older one, is dedicated to the Mother of God and bears an inscription indicating that it was built in 1201. This peaceful site in the wooded valley makes a visit here very pleasant, the only other visitor when my wife and I went being a calf which had escaped the summer heat by lying down in front of the altar inside the Mother of God church.

The Southern Provinces

Southern Armenia is the least visited part of the country. That is a pity and is largely the consequence of visitors giving themselves inadequate time. There is much here to interest.

VAYOTS DZOR

Many visitors come to Vayots Dzor ('Gorge of Woes') on a day trip from Yerevan – principally to see the monastery of Noravank – but it is not really possible to see much else in this province except by staying for a few days. Vayots Dzor is crowded with interesting historic sights, all attractively situated, and a few days here are well justified. There is a rundown hotel in the provincial capital, Yeghegnadzor, but the best **accommodation** is in the motel at Arpi which is on the main road from Yerevan about 10km north of Yeghegnadzor. The motel (tel: 081 2550) has rooms from US$20 per night and is situated about 300m north of the cluster of roadside stalls next to the Hotel Noy. Try to get a room at the back to minimise the noise from the Iranian lorries which come and go 24 hours a day and to enjoy the view of the river.

At present all but a tiny handful of visitors coming to Vayots Dzor travel down the main road from Yerevan, entering the province at the Tukh Manuk Pass (1,795m). This route has been completely rebuilt and is in good condition throughout. It carries heavy lorry traffic, mainly Iranian vehicles travelling between Teheran and Yerevan. The only other road from the north crosses the Selim Pass (2,410m) and is open only in summer. Four-wheel drive is at present advisable for those travelling via the Selim Pass although reconstruction of that route too may happen within the next few years.

For the most part, Vayots Dzor certainly lives up to the Dzor ('gorge') part of its name. Visitors travelling from Yerevan cross the pass and then descend to the Arpa river whose gorge is at times narrow and spectacular, notably between Areni and Arpi and even more so beyond Gndevank. Even in autumn after a long dry summer, the river is surprisingly full, presumably because of water management at the hydro-electric power station, and despite the abstraction of the water which is being diverted in an attempt to raise the level of Lake Sevan (see page 126). The Arpa rises in the northeast of the province between Mount Sartsali (3,433m) and Mount Chaghat (3,333m), flows south through Jermuk before assuming a more westerly course until it enters Nakhichevan after which it joins the Arax. There are many other gorges in the province, the more wooded ones being good places to see golden orioles in the breeding season, flocks of rose-coloured starlings, and also offering the occasional view of a Levant sparrowhawk.

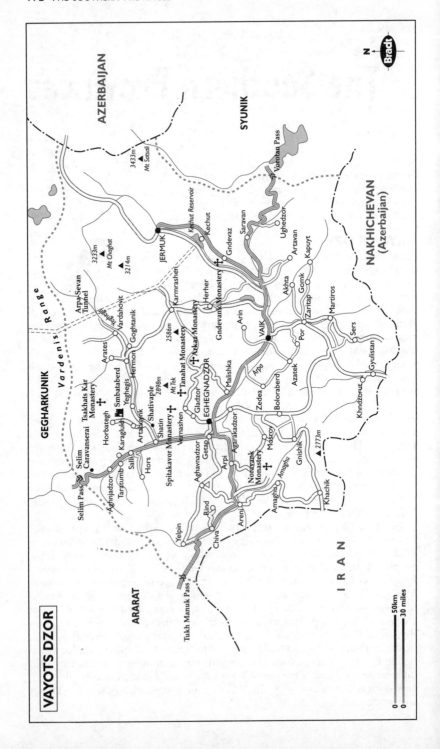

Areni

Heading south from the provincial border the road descends a side valley to join the gorge of the Arpa at the village of Areni, a centre of Armenia's wine industry. It is possible to visit the winery on the east side of the main road in the village where the visitor centre has recently been considerably extended. It is also possible to visit the one at Getap, just east of Arpi, which is signposted to the south of the main road although it is sometimes unexpectedly closed. Areni village gives its name to an indigenous grape variety used for making dry red table wines as well as a range of semi-sweet wines.

In Areni village, but on the opposite bank of the Arpa, can be seen in the distance from the main road a red cross-dome church dedicated to the Mother of God and built in 1321. It was restored in 1997. The church's most remarkable feature is the tympanum of the west door which is a wonderfully carved effigy of the Virgin Mary created by Momik, one of Armenia's greatest stonecarvers and also a great illustrator of manuscripts; he worked in this region in the late 13th and early 14th century. High on the west façade, the representation of a head gazing down is said to be that of a Mongolian, a reminder that at the time the church was constructed Armenia was under Mongol rule and that persecution of non-Muslims was increasing. Inside the church in the pendentives below the tambour are more fine carvings, again by Momik, of the symbols of the four evangelists. The graveyard too has some exceptional carving with tombstones apparently demonstrating Areni's long wine-making history as they show a figure with a wine flask or wine glass. Another tombstone shows a horse and also a person playing a *saz*, a musical instrument rather like a lute and the ancestor of the Greek bouzouki. Close by there is a row of five modern graves belonging to young men killed in 1992 in the war with Azerbaijan, a reminder that the frontier is only 5km away.

Noravank

Just south of Areni a road goes off west across a bridge and enters the narrow gorge of the Amaghu. It leads after 6km to one of Armenia's best-known and most worthwhile tourist sights: Noravank ('New Monastery'). About 1km from the junction a gigantic boulder which has fallen from the cliff bridges the Amaghu and now forms the backdrop to many a photograph. Another 2km further on carpets can be seen hanging across the entrance to a cavern. There is no sign and, while it would be reasonable to suppose that the cavern is the premises of a carpet vendor, that would be wholly incorrect as it is actually a pleasantly situated café. There is no sign indicating that it is a café since the proprietor believes one to be unnecessary as 'Everyone knows it is a café'. Shortly beyond the café, Noravank can be seen high on the cliff face to the left. Its construction in red stone set against the similarly coloured rock of the mountainside is particularly evocative in the early morning or late evening light. If at all possible avoid coming here in the middle of the day as that is when the place is thronged with tourist buses from Yerevan and it is also stiflingly hot in the valley in summer. Nowadays however the monastery does boast a café where it is possible to recover from the heat if one is obliged to visit in the middle of the day.

According to Bishop Stepanos Orbelian, who was writing almost 200 years after the events he described, Noravank was founded by Hovhannes, Bishop of Vahanavank (in Syunik province). Hovhannes reportedly went to the Seljuk Sultan Mahmud and came back with a *firman* giving him possession. He then moved here in 1105 and built the original church dedicated to John the Baptist (though present-day historians date this now-ruined church rather earlier), establishing a firm rule which barred all women and lewd persons. Meanwhile, however, the emir of nearby Hrashkaberd plotted to kill him and destroy the monastery. Hovhannes then went to Isfahan (in present-day Iran), where he cured the sultan's sick son and was rewarded with the title deeds to Hrashkaberd as well as other nearby estates. In consequence of this Hovhannes took a band of armed followers who captured the emir and his family and pushed them off a cliff. Bishop Hovhannes thereafter reportedly led a holy life and worked numerous miracles, such as catching in his hands unharmed a woman and infant who fell off a cliff, though presumably not near the monastery from which the mother would of course have been barred.

Approaching the monastery today one reaches first a striking building that is actually a mausoleum and the newest part of the establishment. The larger complex of buildings beyond is older; the oldest part of all, the 9th- or 10th-century church of John the Baptist is the ruin at the southeast corner.

The site was developed mainly in the 13th century by the Orbelian princes. They were a branch of the Mamikonian family which had settled in Georgia in the 9th century and members of which had held the position of commander-in-chief of the Georgian forces in the 10th and 11th centuries. The Georgian army, which included many Armenians, defeated the sultan in 1204 and many families from Georgia moved into Armenia including the Orbelians who settled in Syunik. The Orbelians built several churches to act as a burial place for the family and the see of the bishopric of Syunik was moved here to Noravank. The oldest intact church is the one in the centre of the further complex of buildings. Erected in 1221–27, it is also, like the ruined church, dedicated to John the Baptist and is of the cross-dome type with two-storey corner rooms. To judge from a fragment of the church model which has survived it originally had an octagonal tambour with an umbrella cupola but this collapsed during an earthquake in 1840 and has been replaced by a circular tambour and conical cupola. The more modest church of St Gregory was added on the north side in 1275 as the burial place of the Orbelians. In the floor are gravestones including one dated 1300 for Elikum, son of Prince Tarsayich Orbelian, who is represented by a lion figure resting its head on one paw. There are two carved doves by the altar dais which is flanked by khachkars and the remains of frescos can be seen. The window is set slanting in the east wall, probably so that on some particular day of the year the rays of the dawning sun will illuminate the grave of Prince Smbat who is also buried here.

The original gavit of the John the Baptist church was built on the west side in 1261 by Prince Smbat Orbelian but it was completely rebuilt in 1321 following earthquake damage. Both the gavit and the Mother of God church nearer the car park are the work of Momik who was also responsible for the fine carving at Areni (see above). The two tympana (one above the other separated by a window opening) of the doorway are in every way remarkable. The carved relief of the upper, pointed one shows God, with his almond-shaped eyes looking straight ahead while a dove is entangled in his beard. He is raising his right hand in blessing while holding a head in his left. Whose head must remain a matter of speculation: possibly that of John the Baptist to whom the church is dedicated and who was decapitated, or perhaps it is the head of the Son or perhaps that of Adam. Above the head is a dove symbolising the Holy Spirit. To the right there is the winged head of a child, the medieval symbol of a seraph, while to the left the scene of crucifixion. The lower tympanum is semicircular and depicts Mary, wearing a dress whose folds are accurately depicted, sitting with Jesus in her arms on a patterned rug which is adorned with tassels. She is surrounded by a tracery of shoots, leaves and flowers. Inside the gavit there is further carving but nothing to rival the tympana.

The two-storey church nearer the entrance also has very fine carving. Built by Prince Burtel Orbelian, it is dedicated to the Mother of God and was completed in 1339, proving to be Momik's last work. Considerable damage was caused by the 1840 earthquake and the church lost its tambour and cupola which were not restored until 1997 using fallen fragments as a pattern. The appearance of this church is very unusual: the lower storey is rectangular but the upper is of cross-dome form. The lower storey can be accessed by descending six steps at the west end and comprises the burial vault of the donor and his family. Over the doorway the tympanum depicts Mary with Jesus in her arms, but sitting on a throne this time, flanked by the archangels Gabriel and Michael. Inside the vault can be seen the figures of the evangelists. The church, in the upper storey, is accessed by narrow steps cantilevered up the outside face of the upper façade. Only those who are happy on narrow ledges should climb them. The tympanum over the upper doorway depicts a half-length Christ flanked by the apostles Peter and Paul. From the ceiling of the corner room to the right of the altar the head of a lion looks down.

The reinstated conical cupola is, unusually, not supported by a tambour but by 12 columns. On three of the columns at the western end can just be seen (binoculars help) carved figures of Mary with Jesus and of two donors of the church, one of whom is holding a model of it. There are still some very fine khachkars here although the finest of all have been moved to Ejmiatsin. One good and very intricate one which remains was carved by Momik in 1308.

Descending into the gorge again but then turning left along the river before following a track up to the left leads to the small chapel of St Pokas, in which is a 4th-century khachkar, oval with a simple cross, and a spring whose water is covered by a film of oil, supposedly oil from the saint's burial ground. According to Stepanos Orbelian writing in the late 13th century, surprising miracles formerly occurred here: all manner of pains, whose cure by men was impossible, such as leprosy and long-infected and gangrenous wounds, were cured when people came here, bathed in the water and were anointed with the oil. However in cases where the diseases were incurable, the people died immediately upon drinking the water!

The Yeghegis valley

After Areni the main road turns east to follow the Arpa. About 15km beyond Areni the road crosses the Yeghegis river, a tributary of the Arpa. Turn left immediately after the bridge to see a number of interesting and attractively located sights although some walking is required to reach most of them and for the one which is close to the road, Selim Caravanserai, 4WD is recommended pending an upgrade of the road. This route along the Yeghegis is marked on maps as a main road of national importance linking the east end of Lake Sevan with southern Armenia. Do not, however, be deceived into imagining that a tourist bus could at present get over the pass nor even cars if there has been recent rain.

For 10km from its junction with the main road, the Selim road follows the Yeghegis river north but the river then turns east into the village of Shatin. Go into Shatin and near the far end of the village fork right down to the river which you cross on a bridge. About 150m beyond the bridge fork right and then 500m beyond that left up a hill to the village cemetery. In a 4WD it is just about possible to drive beyond here to the monastery of **Shativank** but it is a pleasant 7km walk along the track with fine views down into the valley on each side from the crest of the ridge. (Note that there is an alternative direct path up from the gorge. It is shorter but much steeper, frequently muddy, and there are no views.) From the village cemetery the track to the monastery goes up between the graves and then bears left.

After a few kilometres it is possible to see Shativank in the distance and the track winds down to it. Shativank was founded in 929 but was destroyed in the 14th century and then rebuilt. Like other Armenian churches in the late medieval period it was provided with massive fortified walls which are here well preserved and the substantial remains of three round defensive towers can also be seen on the south side. The Zion church itself, rebuilt again in 1665, is a three-aisle basilica built of basalt and of limited interest apart from its evocative site. The remains of other monastic buildings and khachkars can be seen.

Tsakhats Kar and Smbataberd

The next two sights along the Yeghegis, the monastery of Tsakhats Kar and the fortress of Smbataberd, can be combined to give a pleasant walk. Continuing east from Shatin village take the left fork towards Artabuynk. About 1km beyond Artabuynk a track angles steeply down on the right-hand side fording an irrigation channel as it descends. At the bottom of the hill the track formerly crossed the Yeghegis by a bridge but this is no longer safe for vehicles although it can be used by pedestrians. Vehicles must now ford the river and, while this is possible for a lorry with high ground clearance it is risky for others unless the river is exceptionally low. It is therefore better to park here and walk. Tsakhats Kar should be visited first as this makes the navigation easier and gets the greater part of the climbing accomplished earlier in the day. A moderately fit person should allow 90 minutes to walk from the river up to Tsakhats Kar, then 45 minutes from Tsakhats Kar to Smbataberd, and 30 minutes back from Smbataberd to the river plus some time at each site and to admire the views. Follow the main track up from the far side of the ford. In about 500m there is a spring on the right where water bottles can be filled although there is another spring at Tsakhats Kar itself.

Continue up the main track always keeping left if in doubt. The monastery can be seen high up on the mountainside to the left long before reaching it but in practice it is hard to detect, so similar is the colour of its basalt stone to the colour of the mountainside. The ruined monastery is reached after about 5km of continuous ascent and is astonishingly large for so isolated a place. The easternmost of the two churches, Holy Cross, dates from the 11th century and appears to have been a mausoleum. A square entrance area, above which is what looks as if it could have been a second storey, leads through to a lower chapel. A large stone structure has been built across the original entrance for the full width of the building and on it stand large khachkars.

The westernmost of the two churches, St John the Baptist, was built in 1041 but it is less ruinous and the circular tambour and cupola are fairly intact. Outside on the north wall can be seen a carving of a lion tearing a lamb, possibly the coat of arms of the Orbelian family who built the church. The doorway is elaborately decorated with geometric designs and inscriptions and the remaining slabs of the altar dais show carved jugs which may once have formed a design across the whole. Outside there are many khachkars including two very large ones near the entrance as well as a stone depicting an eagle clutching a lamb in its talons.

The main part of the monastery was at a distance from these churches on the west side. Extensive remains of buildings can be seen, most of them presumably the service buildings of the monastery although including further churches dedicated to the Mother of God and, at the southern end, to St John. The latter bears an inscription dated to 999. There are what appear to be the remains of cloisters and all these buildings on the western side were once surrounded by a defensive wall of which only the eastern part with its gateway survives. An inscription at the gateway records its restoration in 1221. The sheer scale of these remains which stretch for over 200m indicates clearly the former importance of this now forgotten place. From the site the view is over alpine meadows and apple trees down into the valley below but a mountain ridge stretches away to the south on the furthest summit of which can be seen with binoculars the fortress of **Smbataberd**. It is fairly easy to work out a route, the key point being to determine how far to retrace the route up from the river before branching off left along the side of the ridge.

The walk again provides magnificent views down into the valley on each side and is mostly downhill apart from the final slope up into the fortress. The easiest way to get inside the walls is to continue on the path beyond the entrance gateway until roughly on the same level as the gateway and then to double back; this is preferable to trying to scramble up the steep bank. Smbataberd (Fortress of Smbat, prince of Syunik) was probably founded in the 5th century but considerably strengthened in the 10th and is perhaps Armenia's most impressive fortress. Few visitors can fail to be impressed by the gigantic ramparts built on the precipitous cliff face, especially those on the eastern side. (Those without a head for heights should avoid climbing on to the eastern wall.) Smbataberd is in a magnificent defensive position, crowning the southern end of the ridge and guarded by steep cliffs on three sides. Even on those sides, walls with frequent towers were built wherever the drop was less than precipitous and much of this survives. Inside the walls relatively little remains although the outline of buildings can be discerned around the walls as well as the fortress's keep at the highest point of the site. According to local legend, Smbataberd fell to the Seljuk Turks when they employed a thirsty horse to sniff out the water supply: it came in an underground pipe from Tsakhats Kar. This would indicate an 11th-century date. However other reports suggest that the castle was defended until the 13th century which would imply that it was eventually captured by the Mongols rather than the Seljuks.

Yeghegis

Looking far down into the valley from the eastern rampart of Smbataberd can be seen the ruins of the town of Yeghegis by the Yeghegis river. The town had two separate periods of prosperity: firstly during the Syunik princedom (10th–11th century) at the end of which it was destroyed, possibly by an earthquake; and then under the Orbelians from the 13th century to the 15th. At present Yeghegis is no more than a village and can be seen to the northeast. A visit there is worthwhile but can seem rather a let-down after a morning spent up on the ridge. It is possible for those highly experienced in hill walking to scramble down the steep side of the valley but it is much easier simply to walk back to the car, retrace the route as far as the junction with the Yeghegis road, and then return up the parallel valley.

Yeghegis is a pleasant unspoiled village with three churches and an old Jewish cemetery. The three-aisled basilica church with a grass-covered roof in the centre of the village was built in 1708 and is dedicated to the Mother of God. Four massive pillars support the roof of this basalt structure. A curious feature, apart from the absence of a cupola, is that it is built into the hillside so that the roof at the back is almost at ground level. At the east end of the village the 13th-century church of John the Baptist does have a cupola and has a surprisingly small interior for its height. However, the village's most notable church is the Zorats ('Army') church dedicated to St Stephen. It is highly unusual, not only by Armenian standards, in that the congregation stood in the open air facing the altar. The roof was only built to cover the east end of the church and covers just the altar in the centre with a sacristy on each side. The name Zorats, and possibly the reason why it was an open-air structure, came from its use as the place where arms and horses were consecrated before battle. Obviously it would have been more convenient not to have the horses inside a building! The church was constructed in 1303 by a grandson of Prince Tarsayich Orbelian, governor of the province of Syunik. In season the walnut tree planted below the church still yields excellent fruit!

The Jewish cemetery here was rediscovered in 1996 by the Bishop of Syunik. It is one of the oldest-known in the world and has been excavated since 2000 by a team from the Jewish university of Jerusalem under Professor Michael Stone. It is reached by a rickety footbridge over the Yeghegis river built in the 1930s whose supports themselves contain a number of gravestones removed from the cemetery. The bridge is likely to be replaced and the gravestones reinstated. So far more than 60 gravestones have been identified including those used for the foundations of the footbridge and others used in the foundations of a mill. At the cemetery, some of the stones are positioned on open graves while others are on sealed graves. A number of the stones have magnificent ornamentation. Some of the symbols on the Jewish gravestones – like a spiral wheel – were also in use on Armenian Christian stonecrafts around the same time. It is most interesting that the same decorative motifs were shared by Jews and Christians. While some of the inscriptions have been worn down over the centuries, a lot of them are decipherable. One stone dated the 18th of Tishrei of AD1266 is of 'the virgin maiden, the affianced Esther, daughter of Michael. May her portion be with our matriarch Sarah'. The opposite side quotes 'Grace is a lie and beauty is vanity' (Proverbs 31:20) and continues with a statement that Esther was 'God-fearing'. Another gravestone contains an emotional statement from a father mourning his son's passing in which the father claims that the soul is eternal and cites passages from the book of the prophet Isaiah that relate to the resurrection of the dead.

Comparing the style of the Jewish stones with those in Christian cemeteries of the period it seems likely that they were carved by the same craftsmen who served both communities. The evidence suggests that Jews were important members of the society at Yeghegis, probably engaged in flour milling since the remains of three watermills have been uncovered in the Jewish district. On the evidence of the graves discovered Jews probably arrived here in the 13th century during the period of Mongol rule, remained throughout the era of Turkmen control but left in the 15th, possibly around the time of Ottoman takeover.

Selim caravanserai

Selim caravanserai is the best-preserved in Armenia and one of the best-preserved in the world; its remote site high on the Selim Pass has evidently prevented its being quarried for building materials. To reach it, retrace the route as far as Shatin and then turn right on to the main road. The good surface gives way after a while to bad dirt as the road starts to wind up the mountainside by numerous hairpin bends. (Note that the temporary diversion put in place after the main route was blocked by a landslide in 2000 has now been abandoned as the original route has been cleared.) The caravanserai is situated just below the summit of the pass (2,410m) and affords wonderful views down along the valley. Its remarkable state of preservation and its remote location on a once important trade route make it an enthralling place to visit.

Constructed of basalt and with a roof of flat tiles, it is a long building with a single entrance at one end; having only one entrance made the building more readily defensible against thieves. To the left of the doorway of the entrance vestibule is a griffin while to the right there is a lion. Above it is an inscription written in Persian using Arabic letters, while inside the vestibule to the right there is one in Armenian, recording that the caravanserai was built in 1332 by Chesar

Orbelian during the reign of Khan Abu Said II. The main hall of the caravanserai is divided into three naves by means of seven pairs of pillars. The two narrower side naves were used for the merchants and their wares while the animals were kept in the central one. Stone troughs provided foodstuffs for the animals and there is a basalt trough in one corner to supply them with water. Light and ventilation were provided by small openings in the roof but the interior is dark and a torch is useful although not essential. Looking at all these arrangements it is possible to capture an image of the life of the 14th-century merchants who passed this way to an extent which can rarely be experienced anywhere in Europe. The restoration carried out in 1956–59 did nothing to mar the atmosphere and it is only to be hoped that the promised (threatened?) reconstruction of the road will leave it similarly unscathed.

Yeghegnadzor

The centre of the provincial capital lies to the north of the main road. Yeghegnadzor ('Valley of the reeds') has a couple of museums but is not in itself otherwise of any interest except as a place to shop or change money. There are, however, a number of interesting sights outside the town. Just visible in the distance from the main road immediately east of its junction with the Selim road is a 13th-century bridge over the Arpa. The bridge can be reached by taking the track which heads across the fields towards the river from just north of the main road's junction with the Selim road. The bridge, once upon a time on the main road to Julfa, consists of a single arch of 16m span. The bridge is unlike other medieval Armenian bridges in being a lancet arch: in other words it is an acutely pointed arch having two separate centres of equal radii. This gives it a pointed appearance with a high clearance over the river in the centre. The bridge is very picturesquely situated away from any main road and makes an ideal place for a picnic.

Spitakavor

From the centre of Yeghegnadzor a road leads up the hill through residential areas. The museum of Gladzor university is at the top of the town on the left in the suburb of Vernashen. The museum is housed in a former basilica church. Park by the museum and take the track to the left immediately beyond it to visit the monastery of Spitakavor ('White-ish'); the determined can also visit the fortress of Proshaberd although there isn't much to see. It is possible to drive to the sights in a 4WD but the track is in poor condition and the walk of about 6km is very pleasant if rather steep at times. The first short section is through the village after which the stream is crossed. The main track turns left but walkers should ignore the sign in Armenian instructing vehicular traffic for Spitakavor to turn left and should carry straight on while keeping the stream and a small dam on the right. The rocky path then ascends up the side of the ever narrowing and dramatic gorge until it angles left and emerges into an alpine meadow as the gorge widens out. There are caves on the hillside in which presumably the bears live whose droppings can be seen along the path. The next section of the path is through a summer village where farmers from the villages below come to pasture their stock during the warmer months. The only way any visitor will ever be allowed to pass through here without accepting hospitality is by promising to stop on the way back. Beyond the summer village keep right and you will soon see Spitakavor high above you. In places the path has been washed away but it is fairly easy to follow the stream which flows down the steep mountainside from the monastery. There is a very welcome spring at the top. Watch out for interesting reptiles on the way such as the nose-horned viper and Caucasian green lizard.

The church, dedicated to the Mother of God, dates from 1321 and was built by Prince Prosh of the Proshian family on the site of a 5th-century basilica. The belltower was added in 1330 and there is a semi-ruined gavit with, unusually, four doors. The church itself is a cross-dome church with cylindrical tambour and conical cupola. It has apses on the north and south sides but just arches on the east and west. The tympanum is richly carved in a style similar to Areni and Noravank: stalactite decoration arches over a beautiful Madonna and Child.

Outside the church the modern grave is that of Garegin Nzhdeh. He was born Garegin Ter-Harutyunian in 1886, the son of a village priest in Nakhichevan. Later he led an Armenian band fighting alongside the Bulgarians in 1912 as Bulgaria battled for independence from the Ottoman empire. During World War I he fought alongside the Russian troops against Turkey. By 1921 his guerilla band was holding off both Bolshevik and Turkish forces in Syunik and Zangezur (southern Armenia) and he declared an independent Republic of Mountainous Armenia at Tatev monastery in May 1921. This he used as a bargaining tool with Lenin to ensure that Syunik and Zangezur were incorporated into Armenia rather than into Azerbaijan as the Bolshevik government had at first agreed in its bid to achieve good relations with Turkey. After agreement with Lenin was reached, the tiny state capitulated in July 1921 and Nzhdeh went into exile via Persia. He later negotiated fruitlessly with Nazi Germany in a bid to recover the lost territories of western Armenia and in 1945 he was arrested in Bulgaria by Soviet troops. He was executed in 1955 for 'anti-Soviet activities'. He is regarded as the person who saved southern Armenia for the nation and, in the light of more recent events, he may almost be regarded as the saviour of Armenia since it is doubtful whether Armenia could have survived the early 1990s without the lifeline to Iran which those territories provided. His remains were secretly brought to Armenia in 1983 and reburied here at Spitakavor after independence.

The track behind the monastery continues uphill. Passing another summer village on the right-hand side, it bears left and on the hilltop to the right can be seen the remains of the small fortress of Proshaberd, also built by Prince Prosh. A rectangle of walls survives with a tower at each corner and a deep pit inside. Only the very determined should bother making the ascent.

Gladzor monastery

Returning to the museum of Gladzor university, it is possible to visit the museum before going on to the site. The museum is worth a quick look if passing but does not rank among Armenia's must-sees. The caretaker lives next door and opens the museum on request. The former church in which it is housed has been well restored apart from the incongruous shiny reddish floor tiles and the seven unattractive modern khachkars outside representing the seven subjects of medieval learning: the trivium or lower part comprised grammar, rhetoric and logic while the quadrivium or higher part comprised arithmetic, geometry, astronomy and music. The museum has photographs of the various monasteries to which the university moved (it moved from place to place according to the wishes of the principal of the day), illustrations of illuminated manuscripts produced at the university, and maps showing places where former students went to establish schools. In all 350 *vardapets* graduated between 1282 when the university was established by Momik (see under Noravank, page 173) and 1338 when it ceased to function. Throughout its working life the monastery was concerned with maintaining the independence of the Armenian Church and the rejection of papal authority.

Tanahat monastery, where Gladzor university was probably first established, is 7km beyond the museum on the same road. A monastery was first established here in 753 but the present buildings date from 1273–79. Approaching it on a late summer day, its dark basalt is a striking and beautiful contrast to the arid hills with only the occasional tree presenting any contrasting green colour. The lavishly laid-out car parks and remains of other facilities were provided for celebrations which marked the 700th anniversary of the university's founding in 1982. The main church is a cross-dome structure with 12-sided tambour and umbrella cupola. Rather plain inside, there is much elaborate carving outside with a heavy preponderance of ones depicting animals and birds. Above the sundial on the south façade, two doves drink from a common cup. The crest of the Orbelian family (a lion and a bull) is high on the tambour; that of the Proshians (an eagle holding a lamb in its talons) is on the side over the door. Another eagle has a smaller bird in its claws and round the top of the tambour can be seen a whole range of animal heads. To the north of St Stephen's church is the small 14th-century church of the Holy Cross. There are more animals here – the tympanum depicts a mounted horseman attacking a lion. The reason for so much animal carving is not clear – it is certainly atypical – and the suggestion has been made that it was wishful thinking on the monks' part since the monastic diet at Tanahat monastery consisted largely of soup. The foundations of numerous other buildings can be clearly seen, indicating that the monastery was once large and important.

About 3km beyond Tanahat monastery along the same road is the monastery of **Arkaz**, dedicated to the Holy Cross. Rebuilding in 1870–71 has deprived it of interest although it is a significant pilgrimage site in early October as under the walls is said to be a piece of the True Cross, given by the Byzantine emperor Heraclius (ruled 610–641) to the wife of Burtel, prince of Syunik. After the Persians were defeated by Heraclius they retreated from Egypt to their country. On their way back they passed through Jerusalem, a Persian prince entered the church of the Cross which had been built by the Empress Helena, mother of the Roman emperor Constantine, to house the Cross which she had discovered in 326. In the church he saw a bright light shining from a piece of wood. He reached for it and it burst forth with fire which burnt his fingers. The Christians in the church told him that this was the base of the Holy Cross and that no-one was able to touch it except a Christian. The Persian deceived the two deacons who were standing guard over it and bribed them to carry this piece back with him to Persia. When Emperor Heraclius heard this, he went with his army to Persia and travelled about searching for this piece of the Holy Cross. However, the Persian prince had ordered the two deacons to bury the box containing the Holy Cross in his garden after which he killed them. One of the captives of the Persian prince, the daughter of one of the priests, was looking out of the window by chance and saw what happened. She told Heraclius what she had seen so that Heraclius was able to recover it and take it in state to Constantinople in AD628. It is a portion of this relic which is supposedly buried here in Arkaz.

From the church there are some fine views of Mount Ararat towering high over Tanahat. Bear droppings can be seen in the vicinity; the bears are partial to the bunches of ripe grapes in the autumn vineyards.

Vaik and Martiros

The main road south passes through Vaik, at the north end of which is the new St Trdat III church, consecrated in 2000 and very much in the American Armenian style with pews, and a balcony for the choir as well as several modern paintings and a chandelier. The floor is of marble and the whole is lit by far more windows than are normal in Armenia. Despite all this modernity and obvious diaspora influence, it manages much more successfully than the cathedral at Yerevan to embody the spirit of Armenian tradition.

Shortly beyond Vaik a road goes off right across a bridge over the river. It leads to Martiros whose church, if not especially beautiful, is at least decidedly curious. In the first village, Zaritap – a centre of tobacco growing – keep right at the fork and continue with the river on the left. On reaching Martiros keep left until the military barracks is in front of you. Turn left in front of it and then left again. After 2km the road turns sharp left but instead take the rough track which turns right, runs along the base of a hill and then goes left towards a lone khachkar. Keep on the track as it winds around until you reach a picnic table. Park here, descend the steps to the river, cross the river, and scramble a few metres up the other bank until you reach a faint path parallel to the river. Turn left and walk down the path keeping at roughly the same height. In a couple of hundred metres there is a door in the hillside on your right outside which is a picnic table, a tree with handkerchiefs tied to it and a few broken khachkars. The door belongs to an entirely subterranean church, dedicated to the Mother of God, and built here by the Proshian family in 1286. It comprises the main church together with a small separate chapel. There is a little light inside from windows high up in the hillside but a torch is useful. The most bizarre feature of this extraordinary excavation is that the form of the church is exactly that of a typical cross-dome church. Standing inside, the shape one sees is the same as if one were in the interior of any normal Armenian church.

Eastern Vayots Dzor

About 6.5km beyond Vaik there is a left turn for Herher. The road skirts a hydro-electric dam before reaching the village which has a tiny 7th-century Zion monastery, which is more like a hermitage and to which it is necessary to walk, as well as a more modern, basilica-type church.

On the main road slightly beyond the Herher junction the Arpa river changes direction. It is well worth leaving the main road to explore its valley between here and Jermuk. There is a road each side of the river. The new road is up on the plateau on the east side of the river, does offer some splendid views down into the gorge, and is accessible to tourist buses. The old road follows the west bank of the river down in the gorge and is far more spectacular than the new road, but beyond the monastery of **Gndevank** it is accessible only to a 4WD and even then only in good weather when there have been no recent rock falls. Gndevank is just off this old road across a bridge about 15km from the junction with the main road south.

To reach Gndevank from the new road, leave it at Gndevaz village (from which splendid views of Gndevank can be obtained looking down on it in the ravine) and then walk down the path from the end of the village: it takes about 45 minutes though the walk back may take longer depending on your degree of fitness.

Gndevank was founded in 936 by Princess Sophia of Syunik who claimed that 'Vayots Dzor was a ring without a jewel; but I built this monastery as the jewel for the ring'. The main church, dedicated to St Stephen, is of the cross-dome type with circular tambour and conical cupola. A large gavit was added in 999 and encircling fortified walls were added later. On the southern and western parts of the site are other buildings formerly used by the monks. The complex was restored between 1965 and 1969 following earthquake damage. There are some particularly fine gravestones here: one shows ibex being hunted alongside falconry while another depicts a boar hunt. There are picnic tables at the monastery which is an exceedingly pleasant place to visit.

The real gem of the district is, however, the old road on from here to Kechut reservoir on the Arpa. It hugs the side of the narrow gorge underneath beetling cliffs with breathtaking views of the river and the ravine. However there is ample evidence of numerous rockfalls and it would be unwise to use the road at times of high avalanche risk. The route is strongly recommended and even those without a 4WD should consider walking down the valley; there is hardly any traffic to mar the experience. Those wishing to access the road from the north end can do so by crossing the Kechut dam over which a road has been built. This dam, although originally constructed for hydro-electric purposes, is now also the starting point for the tunnel which carries water from the Arpa river under the Vardenis range to help maintain the level of Lake Sevan (see page 126).

Beyond the reservoir the roads continue to **Jermuk** whose name is one which every visitor to Armenia is likely to learn since it is the source of much of the country's mineral water. The town was a very large and popular Soviet spa resort but today it has many fewer visitors, most of the hotels and sanatoria are no longer functioning, and the whole place has rather a rundown air. Although Jermuk would be a good centre for walking, the unattractive concrete buildings of the town itself lack character. In the centre of the town is a row of urns each of which has water of a different temperature pouring from a tap. Down by the river is a waterfall near a café which has been built under a natural land bridge.

SYUNIK

Armenia's southernmost province has two well-known sites and one which, although much less well known, ranks as one of the most interesting in the country. The far south along the Iranian border is, not surprisingly, the warmest part of Armenia and a centre of fruit growing. The original road to the far south crossed Nakhichevan and the closure of the border has required a difficult hill road to be considerably upgraded to take the heavy lorry traffic to and from Iran. **Accommodation** in the provincial capital of Kapan the Hotel Darist, 1A Aram Manukian Street (tel: 085 62662, 64322) has been refurbished and has singles for US$25 and doubles for US$30. The cooking is excellent though only a selection of items from the extensive menu is actually available. In Sisian there is a choice. The Hotel Dina, Sisakan Street (tel: 0830 3333) is probably the cleanest and most comfortable of the old Soviet-era provincial hotels in Armenia though only the two 'luxe' rooms have private facilities (at US$18 for the room) and some of the other toilets are of the squat variety. The staff are extremely friendly and the cooking is good. More extensively modernised is the Hotel Basen, Aram Manukian Street (tel: 0830 5370 and 5264) which has separate cottages with private facilities mostly shared between two bedrooms. From US$25 per person. Sisian even has a **restaurant**, the Armenian Kitchen on the road out to the north, which advertises turkey on the signboard. Although it's a pleasant spot with tables by the river don't expect the turkey actually to be available unless you order in advance for a group large enough to eat it.

Most visitors enter Syunik along the main road from Yerevan. The border with Vayots Dzor at the Vorotan Pass (2,344m) is marked by a large concrete structure on each side of the road: the symbolic Gates of Syunik. The road then descends past Spandarian and Shaghat reservoirs running parallel to the Vorotan river which lies some distance to the south. The right turn into the town of Sisian is just beyond a permanent police checkpoint.

Mount Mets Ishkhanasar

Mount Mets Ishkhanasar (3,548m) lies to the left of the road but visitors wishing to see the immensely worthwhile and fascinating petroglyphs at Ughtasar will need a local guide and, probably, transport since the track is too rough for even a Niva 4WD. The very helpful manager of the Hotel Dina in the centre of Sisian can

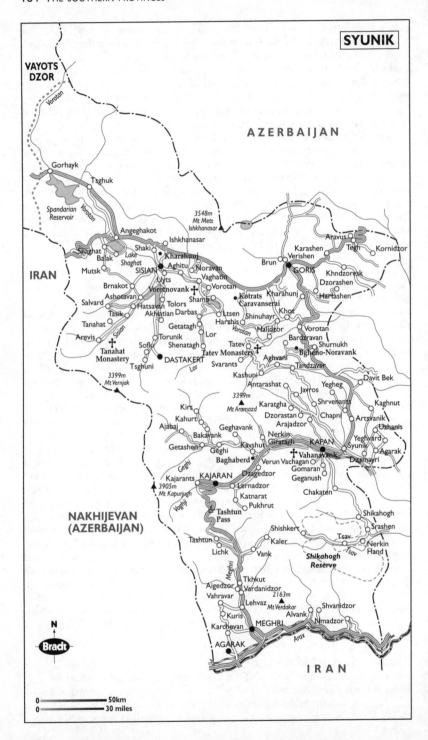

SYUNIK

VAYOTS DZOR

AZERBAIJAN

Voroton

Gorhayk

Tsghuk

Spandarian Reservoir

Voroton

Aravus

Angeghakot

Ishkhanasar

3548m Mt Mets Ishkhanasar

Karashen Verishen

Tegh

Kornidzor

Shaghat

Balak

Shaki

Lake Shoghat

Kharahunj

Brun

GORIS

IRAN

Mutsk

Aghitu

Noravan

Khndzoresk

Brnakot

SISIAN

Vaghatin

Vorotan

Dzorashen

Salvard

Ashotavan

Uyts

Vorotnovank

Shamb

Kotrats Caravanserai

Kharahunj

Hartashen

Tasik

Hatsavan

Tolors

Darbas

Ltsen

Khot

Tanahat

Akhlatian

Shinuhayr

Sision

Getatagh

Harzhis

Vorotan

Halidzor

Vorotan

Arevis

Soflu

Torunik

Shenatagh

Lor

Voroton

Tatev

Bardzravan

Shurnukh

Tanahat Monastery

Tsghuni

DASTAKERT

Lor

Tatev Monastery

Svarants

Aghvani

Bgheno-Noravank

3399m Mt Vernjak

Kashupi

Antarashat

Tandzaver

Davit Bek

3399m Mt Aramazd

Javros

Yegheg

Shrvenants

Kaghnut

Kirs

Karatgha

Dzorastan

Chapni

Artsvanik

Kahurt

Ajabaj

Geghavank

Arajadzor

Uzhanis

Bakavank

Nerkin Giraragh

KAPAN

Yeghvard Syunik

Agarak

Getashen

Geghi

Kavshut

Vahanavank

Ditsmayri

Geghi

Baghaberd

Verun Vachagan

Gomaran

3905m Mt Kapurjugh

Kajarants

KAJARAN

Dzagedzor

Lernadzor

Geganush

Chakaten

Vogtji

Katnarat

Pukhrut

Shikahogh

NAKHIJEVAN (AZERBAIJAN)

Tashtun Pass

Shishkert

Srashen

Tsav

Nerkin Hand

Tashtun

Kaler

Tsov

Lichk

Vank

Shikahogh Reserve

Meghri

Tkhkut

Aigedzor

Vardanidzor

Vahravar

Lehvaz

2163m Mt Verdakar

Shvanidzor

Kuris

Alvank

Nmadzor

Karchevan

MEGHRI

AGARAK

Arax

IRAN

N

Bradt

0 ——— 50km
0 ——— 30 miles

organise a guide and transport but she doesn't speak any English so it might be better to fix something up in advance through a Yerevan agent. The going rate on the spot is US$40 including transport and guide or horses can be hired for US$25 each. It takes about 90 minutes to drive to the site from Sisian although the last 500m has to be walked as the vehicle cannot make the steep ascent when fully laden. The petroglyphs are only accessible from mid-July to late September because of snow and it can be bitterly cold at the high site even in summer. To anyone who has seen rock carvings in museums the petroglyphs here are an absolute revelation with numerous designs scattered on boulders over a large area. The site is beautiful in itself with the volcano towering above and a small lake. It is also the haunt of bears and wolves as is attested by the droppings and footprints.

Petroglyphs, called 'goat letters' in Armenian, are found in several parts of Armenia but these at Ughtasar are the most accessible. The site itself is at 3,300m and over 2,000 individual petroglyphs have been found here scattered over tens of square kilometres. Some of the carvings depict animals, mostly the wild animals of the region but also domestic ones. Deer and wild goats are especially common as are aurochs, ancestors of domestic cattle. There are carvings of hunting scenes and ones showing the impedimenta of hunting. Birds, however, are rarely depicted although snakes feature frequently. People also feature in scenes depicting dancers, either two dancers together or communal dancing. Some rocks have just a single design but others have a whole collection of carvings, as many as 50 in extreme cases. The preponderance of hunting scenes and cattle has led to speculation that the people who carved the stones lived partly by cattle breeding, presumably pasturing their cattle here in summer, and partly by hunting. They must have been at least semi-nomadic since it would not be possible to survive here in winter. The age of the carvings is difficult to ascertain but estimates have varied between 10,000BC and 2000BC.

Sisian and Karahunj

Much better known than the petroglyphs is another, slightly more recent site. Karahunj, sometimes called Armenia's Stonehenge although the appellation is misleading since the two look very different, comprises 204 rough-hewn stones. They are arranged in an elaborate layout and almost certainly formed an ancient astronomical observatory dating from some time prior to 2000BC. The stones are basalt and the largest, 3m tall, weigh 10 tonnes. Of the stones, 76 have apertures near the top. The configuration is of 39 stones laid in an oval formation with its main axis running east–west for a distance of 43m. Within this oval are some contemporary graves. Bisecting the oval is an arc comprising a further 20 stones. Three arms of stones lie off this central shape running to the north, south and southeast. The north and south arms are much longer than the southeast arm and bend west towards their tips. Stones with apertures occur only in the arms but not all stones in the arms have apertures.

There has been much theorising on how the monument was used. It certainly seems clear that the apertures must be significant but they are too large (at least 5cm in diameter) to look through a single one in a precise direction and they don't seem to be lined up with each other for looking through pairs of apertures. Had this been possible it would have facilitated more precise observation. Conceivably the stones could have been used for observing the moon but observation of stars seems difficult to imagine. Anyone looking at the sun would have suffered severe damage to their central vision. Karahunj, on its rock-strewn site, is impressive but the lack of any convincing explanation makes a visit somewhat frustrating.

Some sizeable lizards (40cm in length) of rather prehistoric appearance clamber about on the stones. They are Caucasian agama (*Laudakia caucasius*), a species despite its name with a range from northeast Turkey to Pakistan.

Some material excavated from Kharahunj is now in the Historical Museum in the centre of Sisian. In front of the museum, readily visible from the street, is a collection of gravestones in the form of sheep brought from various churches in the province. The museum staff formerly demanded a fee of US$50 per photograph from anyone snapping them even though they are totally visible to passers-by. Now they say that photography is forbidden because tourists might claim that they found the stones themselves in some country other than Armenia. Such a combination of avarice and stupidity on the part of the Sisian Historical Museum staff is probably unique in Armenia where almost everyone else tries hard to be reasonable and helpful.

Visitors will be much more welcome at Sisavank, the fine early church dedicated to St John which overlooks the town. Similar in style to the church of Saint Hripsime at Ejmiatsin, this was built of basalt by Prince Kohazat and Bishop Hovsep I between 670 and 689. Of cross-dome style, it has a conical cupola supported by a circular tambour decorated with 12 graceful arcatures: there is a window in the arcature positioned directly over each of the four apses. The interior of the church is decorated by a sort of frieze depicting vineleaves and grapes which runs round most of it, presumably a reference to Jesus being the true vine since this is not a district traditionally associated with wine-making.

Around Sisian

Taking the road southeast from Sisian, after about 5km the first village is **Aghitu** where there is an unusual 6th- or 7th-century funerary monument, unlike anything else in the country apart from the monument at Odzun church in Lori province. It is mounted on an arched base. Above that two rectangular columns support a two-tier structure. The lower tier has a circular central column with decorated capitals while the smaller upper tier has two carved round columns, again with decorated capitals. For whom such an elaborate monument was created is unknown and it is paradoxical that the efforts to ensure that he would be remembered have come to nought.

The road continues beyond Aghitu. Keep the Vorotan river on your right until, about 9km from Sisian you encounter the monastery of **Vorotnavank** above the river. The oldest church, dedicated to St Stephen, was built in 1000 by Queen Shahandukht. It is barrel vaulted and has a much lower gavit on the west side. (Beware the extremely deep hole at the west end of the gavit.) In 1007 the queen's son Sevada built a second church dedicated to John the Baptist. It is a cross-dome construction and lies to the southeast of the first church. Both churches have arcaded cloisters, uncommon in Armenia, but of different styles and presumably of different dates. A further, smaller church, various service buildings and a fortified wall complete the complex. There was severe damage here in the 1931 earthquake but it has mostly been repaired. What makes a visit so worthwhile is the plethora of gravestones which have rich figure carving. Some of them have at some time (since restoration after the earthquake?) been incorporated into the buildings. The carvings depict both human beings, often in domestic scenes, and domesticated animals such as horses and cattle. Just why such decoration was considered appropriate for gravestones is not apparent.

Southwest from Sisian town a road follows the Sisian river. To reach it cross the bridge in the town and turn left at the T-junction, then right, then left and finally right again just after the large electricity substation. The ride along the valley is extremely beautiful and worth experiencing for its own sake. Just after a road branches off right for Tanahat village the remains of **Tanahat monastery** can be seen on an outcrop on the valley side across the river. Unlike its namesake, Tanahat monastery in Vayots Dzor, this monastery is very ruinous but reaching it involves a pleasant walk with many flowers in early summer. There are two footbridges across the river, one just after the road branches off to Tanahat and the other some way past the monastery. The latter has partly collapsed but it is still possible to cross. At times it may be possible to ford the river in a vehicle but this is impossible when the river is in spate. Some work was evidently planned at the site but no restoration of the pink 5th-century single-nave church has been undertaken. There is some surviving decoration which looks rather like tulips – highly appropriate since wild white tulips are one of the earliest flowers to appear here after the snow has melted. An unusual feature of the cemetery at the west side is that some of the graves look very like the chambered tombs of northwest Europe, the burial vault being covered by up to three large slabs. One 11th-century khachkar found here reused a stone with an earlier cuneiform inscription and is now in the museum at Erebuni.

South from Sisian
The main road to the south actually heads east as far as Goris. About 20km after the Sisian turn-off a road branches right for the village of Harzhis. About 2.5km along this road a track branches off right and after 500m reaches the remains of the smallish Kotrats caravanserai built in 1319 by the Orbelian family. It is still possible to see the interior layout although most of the roof has collapsed. There is an inscription in Persian and Armenian over the doorway. In the area are several standing stones with a hole (sometimes broken) near the top. According to local people there used to be many more of them and they were signposts indicating the location of the caravanserai; the hole was to enable the stones to be hauled into position using animals. It does not at any rate seem likely that their function was really as signposts since there is one right next to the caravanserai.

Tatev
Syunik's best-known site, Tatev monastery, is reached by continuing down the main road beyond the Sisian turn-off for a further 25km and then turning right. The road to Tatev first passes Shinuhayr whose 17th-century church dedicated to St Stephen is on the valley side a long way below the village. The first part of the path offers good views into the broad valley of the Vorotan with its striking rock formations but it then winds down through orchards and after one zigzag becomes the bed of a stream in which it is difficult to find a dry route. The three-aisled basilica church is ruinous as are the ancillary buildings formerly used by the monks. Many of these ancillary buildings have been adapted by the local residents for growing vegetables: one monk's cell now supports a good crop of runner beans while another houses potatoes. The climb back up to the village is long and hot.

There is a legend about Tatev monastery. It is said that the architect couldn't get down when he finished the cupola of the main church. He cried out: '*Togh astvats indz ta-tev*', which means 'May God give me wings'. And so the monastery got its name. The first sight is in some ways more impressive than seeing it close up. An excellent distant view can be had from the left of the road where there is is a small gazebo-type structure. The gazebo is variously stated to mark the signalling point from which the monastery could be warned of the approach of possibly unwelcome visitors, or alternatively the spot from which a young lady threw herself into the gorge rather than submit to an unwelcome marriage with

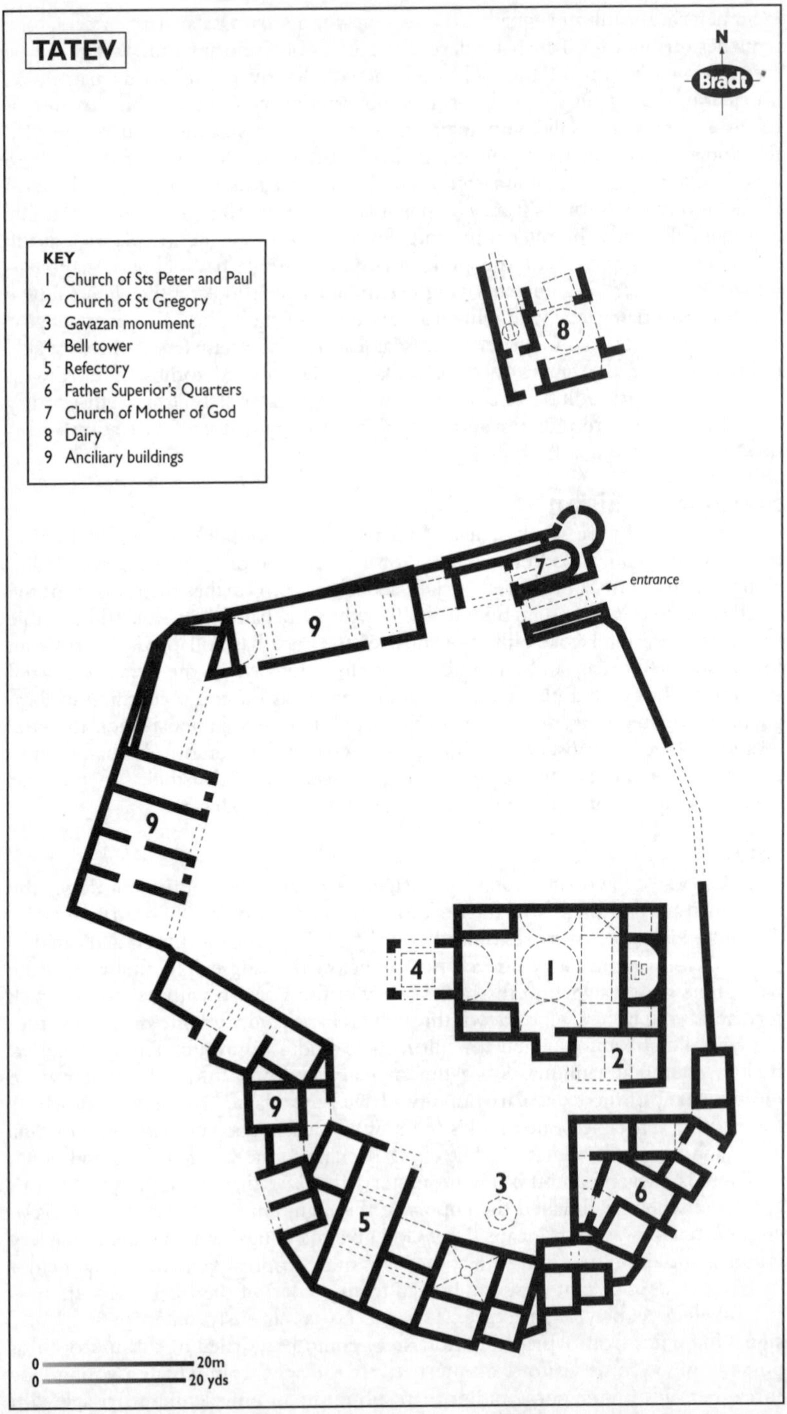

TATEV

KEY
1 Church of Sts Peter and Paul
2 Church of St Gregory
3 Gavazan monument
4 Bell tower
5 Refectory
6 Father Superior's Quarters
7 Church of Mother of God
8 Dairy
9 Anciliary buildings

N

Bradt

entrance

0 ———— 20m
0 ———— 20 yds

a local Muslim ruler. After the gazebo the road winds down to the Vorotan and crosses it adjacent to the so-called Satan's bridge, a natural bridge over the swift-flowing river. It then winds up the far side of the valley to the monastery. There is a café adjacent.

The date of the now-vanished first church at the site is unknown but in 844 Bishop Davit persuaded the princes of Syunik to grant lands which would support the founding of a monastery worthy to house the relics which the church in Syunik possessed. It was his successor, Bishop Ter-Hovhannes who built the main church, dedicated to Sts Paul and Peter between 895 and 906. It was badly damaged by the earthquake in 1931 during which the cupola collapsed but the whole has now been restored except for the belltower which formerly had three storeys. It is planned to complete the restoration of the belltower in due course which is why the large crane has been left *in situ* for several years disfiguring many visitors' photographs. Tatev's reconstruction has not always been sensitively carried out: installing a marble floor rather than stone flags in the church and library rather jars, for example, although its removal is now promised. However the restoration does give an excellent idea of how the monastery must have looked when it was a thriving centre of learning and 1,000 people lived here; its greatest importance was in the 14th and 15th centuries under Hovnan Vorotnetsi (1315–88) and Grigor Tatevatsi (1346–1411). Tatevatsi was both a philosopher and a painter and is portrayed surrounded by his students in one of the few portraits in Armenian manuscript illustration. This is in the 1449 *Interpretation of the Psalms of David* and is presumably the work of one of his former pupils.

The complex is surrounded by a large fortified wall on which it is possible to walk. The church is somewhat intermediate in style between the earlier domed basilica churches and the later cross-dome churches. The umbrella cupola is supported by an unusually tall decorated circular tambour. On the east façade long snakes are looking at two heads while on the north façade two shorter snakes are looking at a person: Armenians supposedly regarded snakes as protectors of their homes. On the north façade are also representations of the founders of the church – Prince Ashot, his wife Shushan, Grigor Supan, the ruler of Gegharkunik, and Prince Dzagik. In 930 the walls of the church were decorated with frescos but these have almost totally vanished except for some scant remnants in the apse and the interior is now rather plain. Grigor Tatevatsi is buried inside the small chapel on the south side of the main church. His tomb is the highly decorated structure which abuts the church.

Outside the church on the south side is a monument erected in 904 called the *gavazan*. It is an octagonal pillar built of small stones with an elaborate cornice and a small khachkar on top. The pillar formerly detected earth tremors by rocking on the horizontal course of masonry on which it is constructed. It does not appear to have worked, however, for some years and the lower part is bound up by rusting iron bands.

The modest St Gregory church adjoins the main church also on the south side. Dating from 1295 it replaced an earlier 9th-century building. To the west of the St Gregory church there is a vaulted gallery with arched openings on the southern side and, to the west of Sts Paul and Peter church, the belltower built in the 17th century on the site of a gavit which had been destroyed in an earlier earthquake. Built over the main entrance to the complex and the adjoining chapel is the unusual 11th-century Mother of God church. It is a small cross-dome church with an octagonal tambour and umbrella cupola. The chambers of the clergy, the refectory with a kitchen and storerooms, the dwelling and service premises form a rectangle around these structures within the fortified wall. They date from the

17th and 18th centuries. Outside the walls can be seen the ruins of various buildings including a creamery and the school.

To Southern Syunik
Goris
Goris, situated on the Goris river, is the most attractive town in southern Armenia with many two-storey houses built of grey stone and an absence of tall blocks of flats. The houses whose design was apparently influenced by a German architect who came to live here, have doors opening directly on to the street and some have balconies. The 17th- or 18th-century church has sheep gravestones outside which, unlike those at Sisian, can be freely photographed. On the south façade can be seen the trajectory of an artillery shell which narrowly missed the building while the town was being bombarded during the conflict with Azerbaijan. The setting of Goris is very pleasant and from the café some strikingly jagged rock formations can be seen on the hillside.

Khndzoresk
To reach the cave village of Khndzoresk take the Stepanakert road from Goris for about 6km until the road to the village goes off right underneath a metal gateway which bears the legend *Welcome to Khndzoresk* in Russian and Armenian. At the far end of the village turn right down the hill to Old Khndzoresk. Most visitors give themselves half an hour here but half a day is needed to do justice to the place. The old village comprised cave dwellings hewn into the soft rock amidst the spectacular limestone karst rock formations. The caves ceased to be used for housing people in the 19th century though some are still used even today for storage and for livestock (and some were temporarily reoccupied during the Karabagh war while Goris was being shelled). As the villagers left the caves they built surface buildings nearby but the village was devastated by the 1931 earthquake and a decision was made to relocate to the higher location of the modern village.

The caves are spread out over a surprisingly large area indicating that a sizeable population lived here. Some of them are very simple and some quite elaborate with windows and niches cut into the hillsides. The two churches both date from the 17th century and survived better than most of the other surface buildings. The lower one, St Hripsime, was in the centre of the village and dates from 1663. Across the stream at the bottom of the gorge and slightly further south is the 17th-century hermitage where Mkhitar Sparapet is buried along with his wife and followers. He succeeded David Bek as leader of the rebellion against Ottoman rule. In 1730 he was murdered by the villagers of Khndzoresk because of Turkish threats that they would be attacked if they harboured him. Apparently the Turkish pasha in Tabriz to whom they presented his head had the murderers beheaded for what he regarded as their treachery.

South to Kapan
South from Goris the road follows the narrow gorge of the Goris river. In Soviet days the road more or less marked the boundary between Armenia and Azerbaijan and was actually on the Azerbaijan side of the border at times. Since 1994, however, the de facto border is further east, between Armenia and the enlarged Nagorno Karabagh. After leaving the gorge the road descends a long series of hairpin bends in to the much deeper gorge of the Vorotan which is eventually bridged close to a hydro-electric station. The ascent up the other side is even longer with innumerable hairpins and some fantastic views. The right turn signposted to Bardzravan leads after 3km to the remains of the monastery

of **Bgheno-Noravank** in thick forest. The monastery is invisible from the road: look for a small turning on the right. The only surviving part is a small reconstructed basalt church of 1062 which incorporates several stones carved with human figures. There is also much geometric carving including swastika designs around the doorway and on the pillars. The monastery is evidently popular for picnics.

Kapan

Yet another watershed is crossed before the descent into the gorge of the Voghji. Kapan is a complete contrast to Goris. Formerly an industrial city whose workers lived in high-rise flats, the industry has now closed and the flats look as if they won't survive the next earth tremor. Kapan is bisected by the Voghji river. The statue of a horseman by the bridge in the centre is of David Bek. Otherwise Kapan has little to attract the visitor but a visit to the railway station offers an unusual experience. In 1932 a branch line was opened to Kapan from Mindzhevan in Azerbaijan and it was operated by the Azerbaijan division of Soviet railways. The Nagorno Karabagh war meant that the line became isolated from both the Armenian and Azeri rail networks. As a consequence a dozen Azeri diesel locomotives were marooned here along with an assortment of goods wagons and passenger coaches. In place of passengers bustling to and fro, cattle browse in leisurely fashion along the grass-grown tracks. Work has eventually started on cutting up the derelict rolling stock: even though the diesel locomotives were of modern Soviet design (Class 2TE10M – built at Lugansk, Ukraine from 1981 onwards) either no further use could be envisaged for them or else it was too difficult to move them anywhere.

To the east of the city is **Shikahogh Reservation** which it is necessary to obtain a permit to visit by contacting the director of the park in Kapan. Bears are found in the forest although they are difficult to see without guidance. The rivers have some large freshwater crabs. The most unusual feature is an avenue of catalpa trees some of whose bases are as much as 5m in circumference. Catalpa trees are not native to Armenia and it is speculated that merchants on the silk route stuck their staffs into the ground and then forgot them: catalpa is readily propagated in this fashion as it sprouts easily.

South to Meghri

About 6km from Kapan a road goes off left to the monastery of **Vahanavank**. It was founded in 911 by Vahan, son of Prince Gagik of Kapan, who sought to become a monk in order to rid himself of the demons which possessed him. He is buried at the site and in the 11th century Queen Shahandukht of Syunik built the Mother of God church here. The site, in woodland, is pleasant but the monastery itself has been ruined by the grossly insensitive restoration which began in 1978. It has now evidently ceased. All the surviving material from the old buildings has been piled up and completely new stones of a garish pale colour have been used for the reconstruction. Building anew a monastery in medieval style might have some merit but it needn't have been done here, destroying the integrity of what remained. Considering just how much appropriate and sympathetic reconstruction has been carried out in Armenia it is sad to see such philistinism at Vahanavank. The monastery is famous for the large arches of one of its buildings. These can still be seen.

After the turn to Vahanavank there is a statue of a bear by the river with a ring in its mouth. There should be a key hanging from the ring as that is the arms of Syunik. However, the key has disappeared. About 15km from Kapan the Geghi river flows south into the Voghji and just beyond is the fortress of **Baghaberd**. It is difficult to see the main part of the fortress when heading south (although much easier heading north) but a small fortification adjacent to the road on the right is conspicuous. A path leads up from the village just beyond to the site. It is extremely steep and also difficult because of the loose scree. Baghaberd was briefly capital of the Syunik kingdom in the 12th century before it was sacked by the Seljuks in 1170. It was reoccupied by David Bek in the 18th century and has significant remains of the boundary wall but little else.

Continuing south, the road follows the river as far as the molybdenum-mining town of Kajaran which was relocated here in the 1960s after earthquake damage on its former site further up the hill. In the town turn left over the bridge and then head up the hill. The road climbs up over Tashtun Pass (2,480m according to the map but 2,535m according to a sign by the road) and then descends to the Iranian border.

Meghri

The principal town in the most southerly region of the country, Meghri, has some attractive houses of the 18th and 19th centuries and is pleasantly situated amidst an arid mountainous landscape, the well tended and watered gardens making a stark contrast with the surrounding barrenness. The Mother of God church in the centre of the town was built in the 15th century and rebuilt in the 17th. It has the singular distinction of housing the first piano brought to Armenia. The pale-coloured stonework of the church contrasts with the 12-sided pink tambour and cupola. The plain exterior in no way prepares visitors for the interior which is covered with 19th-century murals and unlike any other church interior in Armenia as a result. Those on the arches and cupola are mainly abstract or floral in design but the walls and pillars depict saints or Bible stories. In the baptism of Jesus he is shown standing on a snake while Hell looks suitably Brueghelish in the Last Judgement. The church was used as a store in the Soviet era and the murals were apparently painted over so it is pleasing to see how well they have survived.

Overlooking the narrow lanes of the town are the remains of a small fortress, originally built in the 10th century but rebuilt in the 18th by David Bek. It is an excellent viewpoint although not particularly interesting in itself. South from Meghri the road continues another 5km to the Iranian border. Another abandoned railway follows the border: the former main line from Yerevan to Baku.

Nagorno Karabagh

INTRODUCTION

Known by the name Artsakh to its inhabitants and to Armenians, the alternative name Nagorno Karabagh dates from the khanate of Karabagh's formal entry to the Russian empire in 1813, *Nagorno* being Russian for 'Mountainous'. (*Karabagh* is Turkish for 'black garden'.) Nagorno Karabagh is very predominantly inhabited by ethnic Armenians, the language in the streets of its towns is Armenian, and the banknotes are Armenian. However, it is not part of Armenia: it has its own government with its own foreign ministry, its own flag, its own stamps and its own national anthem. Despite all this, its existence as a state is unrecognised by any other country and no Western government can provide consular services there. It can be entered only from Armenia. Why go? One answer is that it has some magnificent scenery. It isn't called Nagorno for nothing: even within the pre-1994 boundaries the land rose to 2,725m at Mount Kirs but the incorporation of the territory which formerly separated Nagorno Karabagh from Armenia means that the highest point is now the 3,584m summit of Mount Tsghuk. Other reasons for going are that it has some very fine monasteries, and some thought-provoking damaged streets from which the ethnic Azeri population has fled. There are differences from Armenia. Inevitably, the military presence is more conspicuous. Additionally, Christian repression was greater here in Soviet days and all Nagorno Karabagh's churches were closed by the 1930s. Since 1991 nineteen have so far reopened. A more mundane difference is that the groups of men in the street are often playing cards rather than backgammon which is the norm in Armenia.

Nagorno Karabagh has some interesting sights although they do tend to be rather spread out and the profusion of historic places which is so typical of Armenia doesn't really exist here. Certain of the best sights are inaccessible because of their proximity to the ceasefire line and the risk from snipers. Hiking would be superb but should not be attempted without a local guide because of the continued existence of minefields. Some of these are being cleared but local knowledge is vital before leaving obviously used routes. Some visitors consider the abandoned Azeri villages with their ruined houses to be of interest though they are hardly very appealing. Burnt-out military hardware can be seen in many places. The territory is under martial law: problems can arise with roads being closed for military manoeuvres.

HISTORY

Nagorno Karabagh was under Persian rule in 1805 when, along with other areas in eastern Transcaucasia, it was annexed to the 'everlasting rule' of the Russian empire. The Gulistan (1813) treaty signed by Russia and Persia ratified this. (Russian expansion into other parts of historic Armenia continued after this date. Persia did

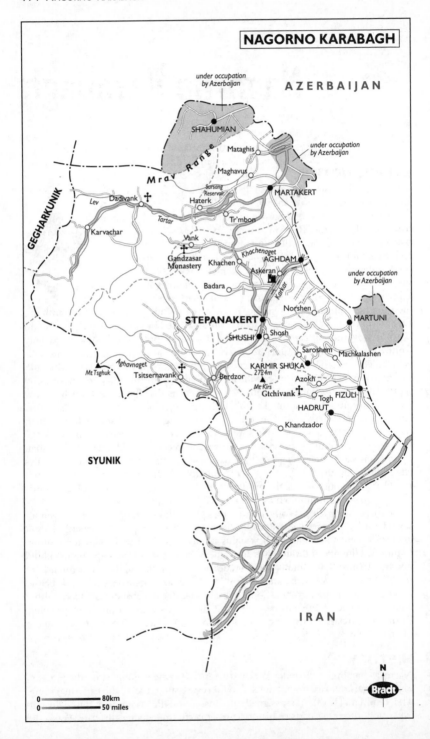

NAGORNO KARABAGH

AZERBAIJAN

under occupation
by Azerbaijan

SHAHUMIAN

under occupation
by Azerbaijan

Mataghis

Mra   Range

Maghavus

MARTAKERT

Lev   Dadivank ✝

Sarsang
Reservoir

Haterk

GEGHARKUNIK

Tartar

Tr'mbon

Karvachar

Vank

Khochenaget

Gandzasar
Monastery

Khachen

AGHDAM

Askeran

under occupation
by Azerbaijan

Badara

Karkar

MARTUNI

Norshen

STEPANAKERT

SHUSHI   Shosh

Saroshem   Machkalashen

Aghavnaget

KARMIR SHUKA
2724m

Mt Tsghuk   Tsitsernavank ✝   Berdzor

Azokh

Mt Kirs
Gtchivank ✝   Togh   FIZULI

HADRUT

Khandzador

SYUNIK

IRAN

N

Bradt

0 ———— 80km
0 ———— 50 miles

not withdraw entirely from Armenia until 1828 and after that Russia continued to make further territorial gains at Turkey's expense until 1878.) The collapse of the Russian empire in 1917 resulted in a changed arrangement of states in the Caucasus. The newly formed Republic of Armenia and the equally new Azerbaijan Democratic Republic both sought control over Nagorno Karabagh between 1918 and 1920. From the outset the Azerbaijan Democratic Republic made territorial demands for large areas of historic Armenia even though the Tsarist census of the whole Karabagh region showed in 1917 a population which was 72% Armenian. Taking advantage of the confused state of affairs resulting from World War I, the collapse of the Russian empire, and continuing persecution of Armenians by Turks, Turkish forces along with Azeri military units destroyed hundreds of ethnically Armenian villages. (It was a feature of the whole region that all villages were dominated by one ethnic group: some Armenian, some Azeri, and elsewhere some Georgian and some Turkish.) Organised massacres of Armenians took place in Baku and Elizavetpol (present day Gyandzha). Only in Nagorno Karabagh did the Armenian population succeed in repelling the attacks. In July 1918 the First Armenian Assembly of Nagorno Karabagh declared the region to be self-governing and created the Karabagh National Council. In August 1919 this National Council entered into a provisional treaty arrangement with the Azerbaijan government to try to halt the military conflict. This, however, did not prevent Azerbaijan's violation of the treaty, culminating on March 28 1920 with the massacre of Armenians, accompanied by burning and plundering, in Shushi, the then capital. As a result the Karabagh Assembly nullified the treaty and declared union with Armenia.

The First League of Nations had its inaugural meeting in late 1920. Applications for membership were considered by the 5th committee, chaired by Chile, which recommended that Azerbaijan should not be admitted (mainly because of its Bolshevik government) while consideration of Armenia's admission should be postponed (because it was occupied). However, the League of Nations, before final resolution of the issue, recognised Nagorno Karabagh as a disputed territory since it had not in practice been ruled by any outside power since the Russian collapse in 1917. That only changed when Bolshevik forces occupied Nagorno Karabagh in 1920. Immediately following the establishment of the Soviet regime in Armenia, the Azerbaijan Revolutionary Committee on November 30 1920 formally recognised Nagorno Karabagh, as well as Zangezur (southern Armenia) and Nakhichevan, to be parts of Armenia and in June 1921 Armenia itself declared Nagorno Karabagh to be part of Armenia.

Meanwhile the Bolshevik leaders in Russia were having visions of an imminent international communist revolution and believed that the new Turkish government under Ataturk was a believer in their cause. This resulted in a change of attitude regarding Turkey's ethnically close relations with Azerbaijan and the question of the disputed territories including Nagorno Karabagh. Stalin, Commissar of Nationalities in the Council of People's Commissars in Moscow, therefore persuaded the Caucasian Bureau of the Russian Communist Party to adopt, on July 5 1921, a policy of annexing Nagorno Karabagh to Azerbaijan rather than Armenia. This was despite the fact that both Armenia and Azerbaijan were still independent, albeit communist controlled, countries: the Soviet Union into which they would be incorporated along with Russia was not formed until December 1922 and it was no business of the Russian Communist Party to decide on the wishes of the Karabagh population. This Russian decision was put into effect but with the proviso that Nagorno Karabagh would be granted the status of an autonomous region.

On July 7 1923 the Soviet Azerbaijan Revolutionary Committee resolved to dismember Nagorno Karabagh and to create on only part of its territory amounting to 4,400km² the promised autonomous region. A large part of the remainder, comprising the present-day districts of Lachin and Kelbajar, became the Kurdistan Autonomous Soviet Socialist Republic. Thus Armenia and Nagorno Karabagh were now separated by the territory of Kurdistan. In 1929 Kurdistan was abolished and the territory fully incorporated into Azerbaijan, so that from 1929 onwards Armenia was separated from Nagorno Karabagh by Azerbaijan proper.

In 1935 there were protests in the region against Nagorno Karabagh remaining within Azerbaijan and these became an almost annual feature after 1960 following the Khrushchev thaw. Gorbachev's policy of openness, established after he came to power in 1985, merely served to bring matters further into the open. The year 1988 became a turning point in the history of Nagorno Karabagh. Mass demonstrations started there on February 11 1988 demanding union with Armenia. On February 20 in an extraordinary session of the Nagorno Karabagh Autonomous Republic Council the People's Deputies voted to secede from Azerbaijan and join Armenia and appealed to the Supreme Soviet of the USSR to recognise this decision. This was matched by massive demonstrations in Yerevan, accompanied by a petition signed by 75,000 Armenians, demanding the annexation of Nagorno Karabagh. A pogrom on February 28 at Sumgait, Azerbaijan which was directed against ethnic Armenians resulted in around 30 deaths. This was followed by even bigger mass protests in Armenia itself when almost a million people are estimated to have participated. The inaction by Moscow produced massive unrest with an estimated 200,000 Azeris fleeing Armenia and 260,000 Armenians fleeing Azerbaijan. In July the Nagorno Karabagh Supreme Soviet, Nagorno Karabagh's supreme governing body, took the decision to secede from Azerbaijan and adopted measures to become part of Armenia.

The members of the Karabagh Committee, the group leading the fight for union with Armenia, were arrested in December 1988 and held in Moscow without trial whilst on January 12 1989 direct rule of Nagorno Karabagh from Moscow was imposed. International protests eventually led to the Karabagh Committee members being freed on May 31. Showing how little control of events Moscow had by now (the Soviet empire in central and eastern Europe was fast disintegrating at the time) Azerbaijan started partially blockading Armenia in September. With a breathtaking disregard for the likely consequences Moscow abandoned direct rule of Nagorno Karabagh on November 28 and handed control to Azerbaijan.

Armenia's response was swift and on December 1 the Armenian Supreme Soviet voted for unification with Nagorno Karabagh. The vote was declared illegal by the Supreme Soviet of the USSR to which Yerevan's response was to pass a new law giving it the right of veto over laws passed in Moscow. As from January 10 1990 residents of Nagorno Karabagh were allowed to vote in Armenian elections. The year 1990 was to be a year of conflict between Armenians and central Soviet forces with massive protests over the Karabagh issue and often brutal police and military repression: six Armenians were killed by troops in a confrontation on May 24. Eventually, after two changes of leadership, the appointment of Levon Ter-Petrossian as Chairman of the Supreme Soviet of Armenia on August 4 led to Armenia declaring independence within the USSR on August 23.

The next year was to see momentous change. The failed coup against Gorbachev on August 19 led to the inevitable breakup of the Soviet Union at the end of the year. More immediately Azerbaijan's response on August 27 was to annul Nagorno Karabagh's status as an Autonomous Region which then led on September 2 to the declaration of the independent Republic of Nagorno Karabagh – the goal had changed and union with Armenia had ceased to be the objective. A plebiscite in Nagorno Karabagh on December 10 resulted in an overwhelming vote for independence. Azerbaijan began a blockade of the territory (which of course it completely encircled) and launched military attacks using the equipment of the USSR 4th army stationed in Azerbaijan. Meanwhile newly emergent Russia saw Armenia as a key ally – notably because of its long border with Turkey, a member of NATO. Accordingly Russia signed a treaty of friendship and co-operation with Armenia on December 29, two days before the demise of the USSR. This was to be followed, much more crucially for Nagorno Karabagh, by a collective security pact signed by Russia and Armenia along with Kazakhstan, Kyrgyzstan, Tajikistan and Uzbekistan on May 15 1992.

Azeri military attacks made initial territorial gains but by May 8 1992 they had been driven back from Martakert and Shushi while on May 18 the Armenian army was able to force a corridor through the Azeri lines at Lachin and break the blockade of Nagorno Karabagh. This however was to be followed by a renewed Azeri offensive which resulted in considerable further Azeri gains so that by the end of July they had taken the whole of the Shahumian region, a great portion of the Martakert region, and portions of Martuni, Askeran and Hadrut, controlling about 60% of the entire territory. These Azeri victories had several effects: there were demonstrations against Ter-Petrossian, by now the Armenian President, and he survived an assassination attempt on August 17; the US Congress adopted a resolution condemning the actions of Azerbaijan and prohibited US government economic assistance; and Ter-Petrossian on August 9 invoked the less than three-month-old security pact asking for Russian help.

Russian support arrived in the form of supplies and equipment. By March 1993 the Armenian army was able once more to go on the offensive and over the next few months it not only recouped its losses but gained almost all of Nagorno Karabagh together with the former Kurdistan and a considerable swathe of Azeri territory bordering Iran. Finally on May 5 1994 a ceasefire brokered by Russia, Kyrgyzstan and the CIS inter-parliamentary council was signed which took effect on May 12. By this time Azerbaijan had lost 10% of its territory. Since then Nagorno Karabagh has incorporated into its administrative districts even the occupied areas of Azerbaijan which were not in the former autonomous region, considerably increasing its size in the process.

The job of finding a solution to the conflict is in the hands of the Minsk group of the Organisation for Security and Cooperation in Europe which was set up in 1992. It looks as far away as ever. Azerbaijan might be willing to hand over Nagorno Karabagh to Armenia in exchange for southern Armenia but that is unacceptable to Armenia since Armenia would lose its important direct link to Iran. Armenia wants a resolution of the problem which it believes would help economic growth but Armenians feel that they cannot desert their kith and kin. Meanwhile the ceasefire holds, despite occasional sniper fire across the ceasefire line with no war and no peace either.

VISITING NAGORNO KARABAGH

Visitors require visas which are normally valid for seven days and cost US$25 plus a consular fee of AMD1,000. They can be obtained from the Republic of Nagorno Karabagh permanent representation in Yerevan at 11 Moscovian Street (tel: 526428, 505637; fax: 151778, 587191; email: ankr@arminco.com). It normally takes around two hours to obtain a visa. There are also permanent representations in Beirut, Moscow, Sydney and Washington DC but they cannot issue visas. If there is any possibility of travelling in future to Azerbaijan then it is essential to obtain the visa on a separate piece of paper in which case a photograph is required. A Nagorno Karabagh visa entered in a passport means that entry to Azerbaijan will be refused.

After arrival in Stepanakert passports must be taken to register with the consular department of the Foreign Ministry at 28 Azatamartikneri Street. You will be asked to state the places you want to visit which, provided they are in safe areas, will be written on a form which you keep and which serves as a travel permit, though nobody usually asks to see it. The staff speak only Armenian and Russian and if you want to go somewhere off the beaten track you will have to show them on the map where it is.

There are two buses daily from Yerevan to Stepanakert, the capital, which leave at 08.00 and 09.00, taking around eight hours for a fare of AMD7,000. There are also more frequent minibus services. The helicopter from Yerevan's Erebuni airport was discontinued in 2002. For those travelling by car it is possible to use the good main road from Goris to Stepanakert in which case the driver must stop at the checkpoint at Lachin on entering and leaving so as to register the vehicle. There are also more northerly routes from the east side of Lake Sevan: 4WD strongly recommended on these routes.

Public holidays

January 1–2	New Year
February 20	Day of Artsakh's Revival
March 8	International Women's Day
April 7	Day of Motherhood and Beauty
May 9	Victory Day, Day of the Nagorno Karabagh Republic's Defence Troops, Day of Liberation of Shushi
September 2	Day of Declaration of the Nagorno Karabagh Republic's Independence
December 7	Memorial Day for Victims of the Earthquake

GOVERNMENT

Nagorno Karabagh is a de facto independent state with the necessary organs of government (though not a central bank which issues currency). The president, who is eligible to stand for no more than two five-year terms, and the 33 members of the chamber of deputies are directly elected by the population of around 140,000. Nagorno Karabagh has its own police, court system, education system and so on. The national flag of the Nagorno Karabagh is basically the Armenian one but with a white five-toothed stepped arrow pattern on the right-hand side. The government has given assistance to the estimated 40,000 people who have settled in Nagorno Karabagh since 1991 (mostly ethnic Armenian refugees fleeing Azerbaijan) in the form of allocating housing, providing livestock and charging half the Armenian price for electricity.

ACCOMMODATION

As in Armenia, it is best either to book into one of the modern hotels, concentrated in Stepanakert and nearby Shushi, or else to opt for a homestay. The older rundown Soviet-era hotels which have not been refurbished can rarely be recommended. Homestays in different parts of Nagorno Karabagh can be booked via a Yerevan travel agent before leaving as can the hotels.

Hotels
Stepanakert
Lotos 85 Vagarshian St; tel: 43882, 41620; email: lotus@nk.infostack.net. This 25-room hotel opened in 1998 and is 15 minutes' walk from the centre. Very clean and with a good restaurant. Extremely pleasant but note that there are a lot of stairs and there is no lift. Singles from US$42 and doubles from US$55.
Nairi 14a Hekimian St; tel: (07) 171503; email: nairi@arminco.nk.am; web: www.nairi.nk.am. Modern hotel north of the centre with 26 rooms all of which have refrigerators. Singles from US$35 and doubles from US$50.

Shushi
Shoushi 3 Amirian St; tel: (07) 731357; email: reservation@shoushihotel.com; web: www.shoushihotel.com. Opened in 2001 with 12 rooms in the centre of town close to the cathedral. About 20 minutes' drive down the hill into Stepanakert. Double from US$35.

Food and drink
This is basically the same as in Armenia but a local speciality is herb bread, a classic flatbread into which are incorporated seven fresh herbs. One of the seven is obligatory but the other six vary seasonally and with the preference of the baker. It's absolutely delicious though beware of some inferior imitations. Local wine, vodka and brandy tend to be inferior to Armenian products.

GETTING THERE
The main road from Goris has been largely reconstructed (except at the Armenian end). The road crosses the so-called Lachin corridor through what had been since 1929 part of Azerbaijan proper. (Somewhat confusingly the town of Lachin has now been renamed Berdzor.) The road descends to the valley of the Aghnavnaget and immediately after crossing there is a police checkpoint at which it is necessary to stop. Visitors are nowadays usually asked for their passports here. The foreign ministry staff in the capital, Stepanakert, state that to avoid problems it is best to obtain visas before leaving Yerevan although they can issue them in Stepanakert. The road continues and enters Nagorno Karabagh's pre-1994 boundaries just before the town of **Berdzor**. This is the last sizeable place before Shushi 43km further on and has over 50% of its houses damaged and unoccupied. The remaining ones have been largely occupied by refugees. The road then climbs up and after the summit runs through sparsely populated country to bypass Shushi and descend rapidly into Stepanakert.

There are two other roads into Nagorno Karabagh from Armenia. That from Norabak (Armenia) to Karvachar (Nagorno Karabagh) is in dire condition and should not be attempted in any normal vehicle. That from Zod (Armenia) over the Zod Pass (2,400m) is passable in summer though 4WD is recommended. After the pass the road follows the beautiful valley of the Lev, at times with toweringly high cliffs on each side until its confluence with the Tartar where the road meets another coming along the Tartar valley. Turn left at the junction and follow the Tartar until Nagorno Karabagh's pre-1994 borders are entered just past the monastery of Dadivank on the left. The road is extremely scenic all the way along the valley to Sarsang reservoir.

WHAT TO SEE
Stepanakert
Formerly Khankendi, the capital of Nagorno Karabagh (population 40,000) was renamed Stepanakert in 1923 in honour of the Armenian Bolshevik Stepan Shahumian (1878–1918) after whom Stepanavan is also named. The town suffered considerable damage in the war but this has now been repaired. Apart from the market (where it is possible to see the herb bread being made) there are a few other places of interest. The **museum**, at 4 Sassounti David Street, is just up the hill from the market. It gives an interesting portrayal of Nagorno Karabagh from prehistoric times to the present day. The Soviet era is not totally ducked as sometimes happens but, World War II apart, the focus is on the positive side (industrialisation) rather than the negative (the purges). The two sides in the days of the First Armenian Republic, the Bolsheviks and the Dashnaks, are given complementary displays opposite each other.

On the north side of Stepanakert is a statue reproduced in a thousand Karabagh souvenirs. The creation of the sculptor Sargis Baghdasarian in Soviet times, it is called 'We are our mountains'. Looking like an elderly couple with peaked skulls, the statue is intended to symbolise the unity of the Karabagh people with their mountains. It is universally referred to as *Mamik yel Babik* (Granny and Grandad). On the way to the statue the former railway station can be seen on the right. It was the terminus of a branch line from Mingechaur in Azerbaijan but was inevitably closed by the war. All track has been lifted and the formation breached in places though a few items of rolling stock survive including a TEM2-class diesel loco. This was a design built at Bryansk, Russia for shunting duties between 1967 and 1987. It is unlikely ever to pull a train again.

Northeast from Stepanakert

Some 15km from Stepanakert just before the town of **Askeran** the main road passes right through the fortress known variously as Mayraberd ('Head Fortress') or Zoraberd ('Powerful Fortress'). It was reinforced in 1788–89 by the Persians because of the increasing Russian threat and most of what can be seen today dates from then. The fortress is on both sides of the Tartar river and locals say that originally the two parts were connected by a continuous rampart 1.5km long. That seems improbable given the difficulty of constructing adequate foundations in the boggy land by the river and in the absence of any obvious traces of this central section today. What survives is a triangle of walls breached by the road on the northern side plus a smaller fortification together with several towers and a length of wall with the remains of a walkway on top on the southern side.

Beyond Askeran the road continues another 5km to the ruins of **Aghdam**. Aghdam was a sizeable town, formerly inhabited by Azeris, but it was destroyed by the Karabagh army after they captured it to prevent it falling back into Azeri hands. To go there is either weird or depressing depending on perspective but many visitors do so.

North from Stepanakert

One part of the new north–south road which has been completed reduces journey times considerably. After passing *Mamik yel Babik* turn left and then right at the roundabout to access the new road. About 40km from Stepanakert the road descends a hill into the valley of the Khachenaget river which it bridges. After the bridge it is back to the old roads.

Gandzasar monastery

Gandzasar ('Treasure Mountain') monastery, dedicated to John the Baptist, is on a hilltop outside Vank ('Monastery') village, Askeran district. The name derives from the presence of silver deposits in the district. To reach it turn left after crossing the bridge over the Khachenaget and continue 14km to Vank following the river valley. Gandzasar has been fully restored since 1991 and is now a working monastery. It is particularly notable for its exquisite carved detail. Surrounded by walls, outside which are graves, it is a cross-dome church with a 16-sided tambour topped by an umbrella cupola. Owing to its inaccessibility, Nagorno Karabagh partly avoided the large-scale Seljuk invasion in the 11th and 12th centuries, as well as the Mongolian invasions in the 13th century. Consequently some of the finest Armenian architecture of the period is found here. The monastery was founded in 1216, the church being built between 1232 and 1238, while the gavit was added in 1261. The founders were Melik Jalal-Dolan, ruler of Khachen, the most important of the principalities of the region, together with his wife Mamkan and son Atabeg. The monastery was to serve as the burial place of the Khachen rulers and, until the 19th century, as the seat of the Katholikos of Agvank (eastern Armenia).

The tambour is an outstanding work of art, decorated with numerous sculptured images. On the western side two bearded figures with long moustaches are sitting in an oriental posture with their feet tucked under them. On the south side are kneeling figures facing each other with arms outstretched and halos round their heads while angels spread their wings over them in blessing. One side shows the Virgin and Child, there are two bulls' heads and an eagle with spreading wings. The gavit obscures another sculptural composition – a crucifix under the gable of the west façade with seraphs hovering over Jesus and Mary and John the Baptist kneeling in prayer with outstretched hands. The north façade shows a bird in the west and the south façade shows galloping horses. The west and east façades have large relief crosses. The gavit has an immense door portal which shows two birds as well as much varied abstract design. It is surmounted by a belfry supported by six columns. The interior is also pleasing with the finely carved front of the altar dais, the pattern of each triangle or square being different. There are further carvings of bulls as well as abstract designs.

Dadivank

Dadivank, one of the largest monastery complexes of medieval Armenia, is on the northern route to Armenia from Nagorno Karabagh. The road to Dadivank leaves the Gandzasar road just after the Khachenaget bridge. In this case keep straight on up the hill after crossing the bridge. The road climbs up a thickly wooded hillside. After about 12km a river is crossed and immediately beyond the bridge turn left. After crossing the river another couple of times the road continues north until eventually Sarsang reservoir can be seen with the village of Trmbon in the foreground and the Mrav range forming a backdrop. Descending to the reservoir, turn left and follow the Tartar river as far as the monastery. It is an extremely beautiful journey along the gorge by the fast-flowing river.

It is possible to drive up to the monastery in a 4WD, the road winding round two slag heaps which look none too stable. Dadivank is traditionally believed to be on the site of the grave of St Thaddeus who was martyred in the 1st century for preaching Christianity, Dadi being a phonetic translation of his name. Although there was probably a church here by the 4th century, the oldest surviving remains date from the 9th century. The church was pillaged in 1145–46 by the Persians but reconstruction started in the 1170s. The monastery went into decline in the 18th century and the monastery estates were only half occupied when the khan of Shushi invited Kurds to move on to them from Yerevan. The late 18th century saw further Persian military action and plague and famine in 1798 saw the final abandonment of the site. Restoration is under way.

The layout is exceedingly complex and there are buildings on two levels. The 9th-century church of St Thaddeus, built over his grave, is at the north side of the complex. To its west lies a chapel built in 1224 and there are further contemporary buildings to the west of that within the wall. Southeast of St Thaddeus is the main cathedral which dates from 1214. The 16-sided tambour has graceful arcatures and the cupola is conical. In front of it is a 14th-century arcaded structure which extends as far as the belltower of 1283. To the south there is a small square church with circular tambour and a tiled dome; its date is uncertain. On the lower level are the kitchen, refectory, wine press, as well as accommodation but the building with four round pillars on square bases is, according to an inscription of 1211, the temple.

DADIVANK

KEY
1 Cathedral (1214)
2 Columnar Hall (14th century)
3 St Thaddeus Church (9th century)
4 Chapel (1224)
5 Small domed church
6 Temple (1211)
7 Refectory
8 Winery; princely quarters on upper floor
9 Pilgrims' House; Father Superior's quarters on upper floor

N

Bradt

0 ——————— 20m
0 ——————— 20 yds

Shushi

The former capital of Shushi is about 15 minutes up the hill from Stepanakert and lies to the left just off the main Goris road. Prior to 1988 the town had a mixed Armenian and Azeri population notwithstanding the destruction of many Armenian homes during fighting in 1920. Now the Azeri population has gone while the Armenians remain. Half the blocks of flats are occupied, the other half are burnt-out shells. What the town's inhabitants think as they walk each day past these scorched roofless reminders is difficult to say. In one way the place is more striking than the completely abandoned towns and villages because here life goes on around the destruction. The town itself, set on a precipice overlooking the impressive gorge of the Karkar has several other points of interest. Part of the town wall remains and two 19th-century churches have been restored, both striking with their very pale stone. The massive almost white Ghazanchetsots cathedral (Ghazan refers to some very large vessels which were gifted to the church) was built between 1868 and 1887. Like all Karabagh churches it was closed during the Soviet period and saw service variously as a granary, a garage and for storing munitions. Inside it is plain apart from some modern paintings. Oddly enough the belltower decorated with figures of angels playing musical instruments which stands beside it was built earlier, in 1858. The other church is the so-called green church. It has a silver metallic cupola and was completed in 1847. Elsewhere in the town mosques survive: religious buildings were not destroyed after the war.

Southeast from Stepanakert

Take the main Goris road as far as the city boundary but then turn left down the hill. The road heads out through Shosh where there are many plantations of mulberry trees as silk was made here in Soviet days. There is a possibility that the industry might be revived but meanwhile the mulberries are used for producing mulberry vodka. The ruined 12th–13th-century Pirumashen church, a single-aisle basilica, is passed before the village of Sarushen and the road continues to the large village of Karmir Shuka. Continue through the village and out the far end following the river which is on the right. In a few kilometres there is a right turn over a new bridge to another completed section of the new north–south highway. Turn right over the bridge and continue to the far end of the new road where it is back to pot-holes. A scramble up the hillside from the end of the new road is **Azokh cave**. The eight linked caves have a total length of 600m and an area of 8,000m^2 with the largest chamber being 3,000m^2. The caves are equally famous for their stalactites and stalagmites and for the prehistoric finds which have been made there. These include the 1–1.5m-year-old remains of Palaeolithic and Mesolithic man together with more than 2,000 bones from 45 species of animal, some of them now extinct.

Continuing beyond Azokh across the river and then turning right leads to the village of Togh. At the far end of the village bear right on a dirt road and continue until another dirt road goes off right in about 2km. Take this right turn and continue until the summit is reached and there is a small parking place on the right. Unless the cloud is low it is possible to see the tambour and cupola of the monastery of **Gtchivank** breaking the skyline on the hill to the right. From the top of the parking area a path (faint in places) leads up the hillside and then across left to the monastery. (There is also a track up from the other side, possibly accessible by a 4WD in good weather but impossibly muddy when I was there.) It is a very beautiful walk up the flower covered hillside with wonderful views over hilly countryside of southern Karabagh. The approach to the monastery is one of the finest imaginable but the monastery itself is an incredibly sad place. Where so many lived and worked to the glory of God vandals have spray-painted with graffiti every square inch inside and out, even climbing up to the most inaccessible parts of the cupola to cause as much desecration as possible. The graffiti comprise mostly people's names, written in Russian letters, and often dated. The earliest date noticed was 1970 and the latest 2000 so the latter at least could not have been carried out by disgruntled Azeris. The monastery was the seat of the archbishopric as early as the 5th century. The inscription records that the existing main cross- dome church was built between 1241 and 1248 by the brothers Sargis and Vrtanes, bishops at Amaras. It was a time of much trouble with the Mongols, who conquered Armenia between 1236 and 1244 and imposed severe taxes leading to an attempted rebellion in 1248–49. The gavit survives together with another very ruinous building and some fine khachkars. All are covered in graffiti. This is not a place where one wishes to linger.

Tsitsernavank

This monastery is very close to the Armenian border. From Stepanakert take the main Goris road until the border post in the Lachin corridor. Go through the border post and then turn immediately right and then left. Keeping the Aghnavnaget river on your left continue for 15km (4WD essential) until the monastery can be seen on an outcrop between the Aghnavnaget and its tributary the Khovnavar. The narrow, tall three-aisle basilica was built in the 4th century but renovated in the 5th and again in the 7th. The small medieval belfry looks a rather incongruous addition. Inside there is some decoration on the square pillars and outside one of the gravestones in particular shows very fine figure carving. The remains of the later fortified wall can also be seen.

Appendix 1

LANGUAGE

Armenian is an Indo-European language but a significant number of words have been borrowed from the country's various occupiers, mostly Persian and Turkish. There are differences in grammar, vocabulary and pronunciation between eastern Armenian (as spoken in Armenia) and western Armenian (as formerly spoken in Anatolia and still spoken by the diaspora) although the two are mutually intelligible. An older form of the language called Grabar is still used by the Church.

Some of the grammatical rules of eastern Armenian:

There is no gender and the same word is used for he, she and it. There are, however, separate masculine and feminine nouns where there is a clear difference, eg: man/woman; ram/ewe; male saint/female saint.

The definite article appears as a suffix to the noun (as in a few other Indo-European languages such as Swedish and Norwegian). There is no indefinite article: a noun without the definite article suffix is assumed to be indefinite. (This is different in western Armenian where the indefinite article appears as a separate word after the noun.)

Stress is always on the last syllable of a word but the definite article suffix is not regarded as a syllable for this purpose and is never stressed.

There is no interrogative form. Questions are indicated only by tone of voice in speech, and in writing by a special mark (´) over the stressed vowel of the word about which the question is being asked. For example in the question 'You have an apple?' the question mark in Armenian would be placed either over the word 'you' or over the stressed vowel of 'apple' depending on precisely what the questioner wanted to know.

Nouns decline (as in Latin, Russian, German). There are seven cases. One grammar book lists 11 declensions as well as the irregular nouns.

Pronouns also decline. Infinitives can act as nouns and then they similarly decline.

Adjectives are placed before the noun and are invariable. They do not change to agree with the case or number of the noun.

Most prepositions follow the noun rather than precede it (and are therefore sometimes called postpositions) and they govern the case which the noun takes.

There are two main conjugations of verbs plus irregular verbs.

Some Armenian words are never heard in spoken Armenian, the Russian equivalent being used instead.

The second person singular is used when addressing close family members, close friends and also God in prayer.

The Armenian alphabet

Ա	ա	Pronounced like the 'a' in father
Բ	բ	Pronounced like the 'b' in book
Գ	գ	Pronounced like the 'g' in go

Դ	դ	Pronounced like the 'd' in dog
Ե	ե	Pronounced like the 'ye' in yes at the beginning of a word; like the 'e' in pen within a word
Զ	զ	Pronounced like the 'z' in zoo
Է	է	Pronounced like the 'e' in elf
Ը	ը	Pronounced like the 'u' in but
Թ	թ	Pronounced like the 't' in today
Ժ	ժ	Pronounced like the 's' in treasure
Ի	ի	Pronounced like the 'ea' in meat
Լ	լ	Pronounced like the 'l' in lip
Խ	խ	Pronounced like the 'ch' in Scottish loch
Ծ	ծ	Pronounced like the 'tz' in Ritz
Կ	կ	Pronounced like the 'ck' in tricky
Հ	հ	Pronounced like the 'h' in healthy
Ձ	ձ	Pronounced like the 'ds' in lids
Ղ	ղ	Pronounced like a French 'r'
Ճ	ճ	Pronounced like the 'j' in job
Մ	մ	Pronounced like the 'm' in moon
Յ	յ	Pronounced like the 'y' in year
Ն	ն	Pronounced like the 'n' in nought
Շ	շ	Pronounced like the 'sh' in shoe
Ո	ո	Pronounced like 'vo' in vocal at the beginning of a word; like the 'o' in no within a word
Չ	չ	Pronounced like the 'ch' in children
Պ	պ	Pronounced like the 'p' in piece
Ջ	ջ	Pronounced like the 'j' juice
Ռ	ռ	Pronounced like the rolled Scottish 'r'
Ս	ս	Pronounced like the 's' in soft
Վ	վ	Pronounced like the 'v' in voice
Տ	տ	Pronounced like the clipped 't' in but
Ր	ր	Pronounced like an English 'r'
Ց	ց	Pronounced like the 'ts' in lots
Ու	ու	Pronounced like the 'oo' in fool
Փ	փ	Pronounced like the 'p' in pink
Ք	ք	Pronounced like the 'k' in key
Օ	o	Pronounced like the 'o' in stone
Ֆ	ֆ	Pronounced like the 'f' in fool
	և	(Lower case only) Pronounced 'yev'; it also has the meaning *and*.

Words and phrases
General expressions

Hello	Բարև ձեզ	*Barev dzez*
Good morning	Բարի լույս	*Bari luys*
Good evening	Բարի երեկո	*Bari yereko*
Goodnight	Բարի գիշեր	*Bari gisher*
Goodbye	Ցտեսություն	*Tstesootyoon*
Cheerio	Առայժմ	*Arayzhm*
How are you?	Ո՞նց եք	*Vonts ek?*
I'm fine	Լավ եմ	*Lav em*
Yes	Այո	*Ayo*
No	Ոչ	*Voch*
Please	Խնդրում եմ	*Khndroom em*

Thank you (except that most people use the French word *merci* for the sake of brevity)	Շնորհակալություն	*Shnorhakalatyoon*
Excuse me, Sorry	Ներողություն	*Nerorootyoon*
I don't speak Armenian	Հայերեն չեմ խոսում	*Hayeren chem khosoom*
Where are you from?	Որտեղի՞ց եք	*Vortereets ek?*
Australia	Ավստրալիա	*Avstralia*
Britain	Բրիտանիա	*Breetania*
Canada	Կանադա	*Canada*
England	Անգլիա	*Anglia*
Ireland	Իռլանդիա	*Eerlandia*
New Zealand	Նոր Զելանդիա	*Nor Zeelandia*
Scotland	Շոտլանդիա	*Shotlandia*
USA	Ամերիկա	*America*
Wales	Ուելս	*Ooeels*
Open	Բաց է	*Bats e*
Closed	Փակ է	*Pak e*
Right	Աջ	*Aj*
Left	Ձախ	*Dzakh*
Straight on	Ուղիղ	*Ooreer*
Where is…?	Որտե՞ղ է…	*Vorter e…?*
Church	Եկեղեցի	*Yekeretsee*
Monastery	Վանք	*Vank*
Castle	Բերդ/Ամրոց	*Berd/Amrots*
Museum	Թանգարան	*Tangaran*
Post office	Փոստ	*Post*
Bank	Բանկ	*Bank*
Hotel	Հյուրանոց	*Hyooranots*
Toilet	Զուգարան	*Zoogaran*
Market	Շուկա	*Shooka*
Bus station	Ավտոկայան	*Avtokayan*

Travel

Ticket	Տոմս	*Toms*

What time is the bus to…?
Ժամը քանիսի՞ է մեկնում ավտոբուսը…
Zhamu kaneeseen e meknoom avtoboosu…?

Which is the bus to…?
Ո՞ր ավտոբուսն է մեկնում…
Vor avtoboos ne meknoom…?

Is this the bus to…?
Սա…մեկնող ավտոբուսն է
Sa…meknor avtoboos ne?

Eating and drinking

How many of you? (always asked on going into a restaurant).
Քանի՞ հոգի եք
Kanee hokee ek?

Restaurant	Ռեսդորան	*Restoran*
Breakfast	Նախաճաշ	*Nakhajash*
Lunch	Ճաշ	*Jash*
Dinner	Ընթրիք	*Untreek*
Bread	Հաց	*Hats*
Lavash	Լավաշ	*Lavash*
Cheese	Պանիր	*Paneer*
Butter	Կարագ	*Karag*
Honey	Մեղր	*Meghr*
Salt	Աղ	*Agh*
Beef	Տավարի միս	*Tavaree mees*
Pork	Խոզի միս	*Khozee mees*
Lamb	Ոչխարի միս	*Vochkhari mees*
Chicken	Հավ	*Hav*
Barbecued	Խորոված	*Khorovats*
Soup	Ապուր	*Apoor*
Potato	Կարտոֆիլ	*Kartofeel*
Rice	Բրինձ	*Brindz*
Salad	Սալաթ	*Salat*
Tomato	Լոլիկ	*Loleek*
Cucumber	Վարունգ	*Varoong*
Ice cream	Պաղպաղակ	*Parparak*
White ice cream	Սպիտակ պաղպաղակ	*Spitak parparak*
Chocolate	Շոկոլադ	*Shocolad*
Water	Ջուր	*Joor*
Mineral water	Հանքային ջուր	*Hankayeen joor*
Wine	Գինի	*Gini*
Beer	Գարեջուր	*Garedshoor*
Brandy	Կոնյակ	*Konyak*
Coffee	Սուրճ	*Soorj*
Tea	Թեյ	*Tay*
Milk	Կաթ	*Kat*

Days of the week

Today	Այսօր	*Eyesore*
Tomorrow	Վաղը	*Varu*
Yesterday	Երեկ	*Yerek*
Monday	Երկուշաբթի	*Yerkooshabtee*
Tuesday	Երեքշաբթի	*Yerekshabtee*
Wednesday	Չորեքշաբթի	*Chorekshabtee*
Thursday	Հինգշաբթի	*Heengshabtee*
Friday	Ուրբաթ	*Yoorbat*
Saturday	Շաբաթ	*Shabat*
Sunday	Կիրակի	*Kiraki*

Numbers

1	*mek*	11	*tasnmek*	30	*yeresoon*
2	*yerkoo*	12	*tasnerku*	40	*karasoon*
3	*yerek*	13	*tasnerek*	50	*hisoon*
4	*chors*	14	*tasnchors*	60	*vatsun*
5	*hing*	15	*tasnhing*	70	*yotanasoon*
6	*vets*	16	*tasnvets*	80	*ootsun*

7	*yot*	17	*tasnyot*	90	*innusoon*
8	*oot*	18	*tasnoot*	100	*haryoor*
9	*innu*	19	*tasninnu*	1,000	*hazar*
10	*tas*	20	*ksan*		

Place names

In block capitals (as displayed on buses, signs, etc)

ԵՐԵՎԱՆ	YEREVAN
ԳՅՈՒՄՐԻ	GYUMRI
ՎԱՆԱՁՈՐ	VANADZOR
ՍՏԵՓԱՆԱՎԱՆ	STEPANAVAN
ԱԼԱՎԵՐԴԻ	ALAVERDI
ԴԻԼԻՋԱՆ	DILIJAN
ԻՋԵՎԱՆ	IJEVAN
ՍԵՎԱՆ	SEVAN
ԾԱՂԿԱՁՈՐ	TSAGHKADZOR
ԷՋՄԻԱԾԻՆ	EJMIATSIN
ԵՂԵԳՆԱՁՈՐ	YEGHEGNADZOR
ՋԵՐՄՈՒԿ	JERMUK
ՍԻՍԻԱՆ	SISIAN
ԳՈՐԻՍ	GORIS
ԿԱՊԱՆ	KAPAN
ՄԵՂՐԻ	MEGHRI

Appendix

FURTHER READING

Thanks largely to the diaspora, the literature on Armenia is vast. At the time of writing Amazon's UK website listed 480 books on the country but even this total was dwarfed by their US website which had 863. The specialist Armenian Bookstore claims 750: to find its complete list sensibly arranged and with helpful reviews go to www.cilicia.com and click on 'Books'. Add to these totals the out-of-print titles and it is clear that nobody could read more than a small fraction. The following represents no more than some of the books which the author has found interesting or useful.

History

Architectural Monuments in the Soviet Republic of Armenia Aurora Art Publishers, Leningrad, nd. Slightly more text than the following entry and covering a wider range of buildings, it is also a book of black-and-white photographs but they are less well reproduced.

Armenian Churches – Holy See of Echmiadzin Calouste Gulbenkian Foundation, 1970. Largely a book of black-and-white photographs with limited text, it is interesting to compare some of the 1960s photographs with the same church today and see the extent of reconstruction. Also covers a few churches in present-day Turkey.

Hasratian, Murad *Early Christian Architecture of Armenia* Inkombook, Moscow, 2000. Covers churches intact and ruined, large and small, well known and desperately obscure. Does not include churches from the later medieval period so some of the most famous are excluded.

Hovannisian, Richard G *The Republic of Armenia* (4 volumes) University of California Press, 1996. An exhaustive and scholarly but readable account of Armenia in the crucial years from 1918 to 1921.

Karapetian, Samvel *Armenian Cultural Monuments in the Region of Karabakh* Gitutian Publishing House of NAS RAA, Yerevan, 2001. An interesting up-to-date account of what is to be found there. It includes territories occupied since 1994 but regrettably does not include all districts so that Nagorno Karabagh's best-known sight – Gandzasar monastery – is omitted.

Khalpakhchian, O *Architectural Ensembles of Armenia* Iskusstvo, Moscow, 1980. This thorough survey would have been more useful if only it had been better translated. It desperately needed review by a native English speaker. Standing with it in hand at the place being described it is, however, usually possible to work out what the author probably means. Only covers 19 sites but quite thorough.

Nassibian, Akaby *Britain and the Armenian Question 1915–1923* Croom Helm, 1984. A good account of the British government's failure to help the Armenian people. Despite the title it includes the background to the events from the 1870s onwards.

Nersessian, Vrej *Treasures from the Ark* The British Library, 2001. The catalogue of the wonderful exhibition of Armenian art held in London that year, it is probably the best illustrated book of Armenian art treasures available.

Redgate, A E *The Armenians* Blackwell, 1998. A strongly recommended history of the Armenian people although rather sketchy on the period after 1100.

Rost, Yuri *Armenian Tragedy* Weidenfeld & Nicolson, 1990. A journalist's eye-witness accounts of the early stages of the conflict between Armenia and Azerbaijan and the devastating earthquake of 1988.

Natural history

Adamian, Martin S, and Daniel Klem Jr *A Field Guide to the Birds of Armenia* American University of Armenia, 1997. An invaluable, well-illustrated field guide.

MacDonald, David, and Priscilla Barrett *Collins Field Guide to the Mammals of Britain and Europe* HarperCollins, 1993. Omits a few species such as leopard but useful.

Maitland, Peter S *Hamlyn Guide to the Freshwater Fish of Britain and Europe* Octopus Books, 2000. Does not include all Armenian species but quite useful.

Szczerbak, N N *Guide to the Reptiles of the Eastern Palearctic* Krieger, 2003. Given how often one sees reptiles when walking in the Armenian countryside this new guide should prove useful.

Tuzov, V K (ed) *Guide to the Butterflies of Russia and Adjacent Territories* 1997 and 2000 (2 volumes) Pensoft, Sofia. A thorough guide illustrated with photographs of specimens and covering the whole of the former USSR but unfortunately not very portable.

Travel

Hepworth, Revd George H *Through Armenia on Horseback* Isbister, 1898. One of the best accounts of life among the Armenians of Anatolia shortly before the genocide, the evidently unbiased author gives an account of their hardships and oppression.

Kiesling, Brady, and Raffi Kojian *Rediscovering Armenia* Tigran Mets, 2001. A gazetteer which lists most of Armenia's villages and monuments and tells you how to find them. Not really a guidebook itself but it was often useful to the author of this one in indicating what exists.

Nansen, Fridtjof *Armenia and the Near East* George Allen & Unwin, 1928. The great Polar explorer was appointed League of Nations Commissioner for Refugees and in that capacity visited Soviet Armenia in its early days accompanied by Vidkun Quisling (later to become Norway's prime minister during the Nazi occupation and was consequently executed for treason) who acted as his secretary. He was favourably impressed by the plans to use the water from Lake Sevan to irrigate the Ararat valley.

PP (ie: Peter Pears) *Armenian Holiday August 1965* privately published, 1965. The English tenor's account of his visit with Britten, Rostropovich and Galina Vishnevskaya. The Russian soprano, Rostropovich's wife, also gives an account in her autobiography *Galina – A Russian Story* (Hodder & Stoughton, 1985).

Shaginyan, Marietta *Journey through Soviet Armenia* Foreign Languages Publishing House, Moscow, 1954. A wonderful period piece of Stalin-era writing – the Russian original was published in 1952 before his death. Unfortunately out of print but eminently worth seeking a copy for anyone with a taste for the bizarre.

Literature

Pushkin, Alexander *A Journey to Arzrum* (ie: Erzurum) 1835, English translation by Birgitta Ingemanson, published by Ardis, 1974. An excellent translation with extremely useful notes explaining matters unlikely to be familiar to modern Western readers.

Saroyan, William *The Human Comedy* (1943) and *Boys and Girls Together* (1963). Two works suggested as an introduction to this Armenian American author, both are readily available in paperback in the USA. From the UK can either be ordered direct from Amazon in the USA or else via the Amazon UK website.

Language

Andonian, Hagop *Beginners' Armenian* Hippocrene, 1999. While at least modern enough to include trains (though not cars) has an inappropriate title since the only beginners it might be suitable for are expert linguists with a good knowledge of language structure. Otherwise it is a reference book for those who already have knowledge of the language. It teaches western rather than eastern Armenian.

Aroutunian, Diana and Susanna *Armenian–English/English–Armenian Concise Dictionary* Hippocrene, 1993. This small dictionary is the only eastern Armenian dictionary available. For some unimaginable reason the Armenian–English section takes 152 pages while English–Armenian occupies 216 pages.

Gevorkian, A V *East Armenian Course* Yerevan, 2000. The best book available on the language but apparently unobtainable outside Armenia.

Gulian, Kevork H *Elementary Modern Armenian Grammar* Hippocrene, 1990. A strong contender for the most inappropriately named book on Armenia. Its modernity extends to no form of transport being mentioned more recent than a horse and carriage while the section on clothing includes frock coat, stays, tooth powder and pomatum. Also it teaches western rather than eastern Armenian.

Index